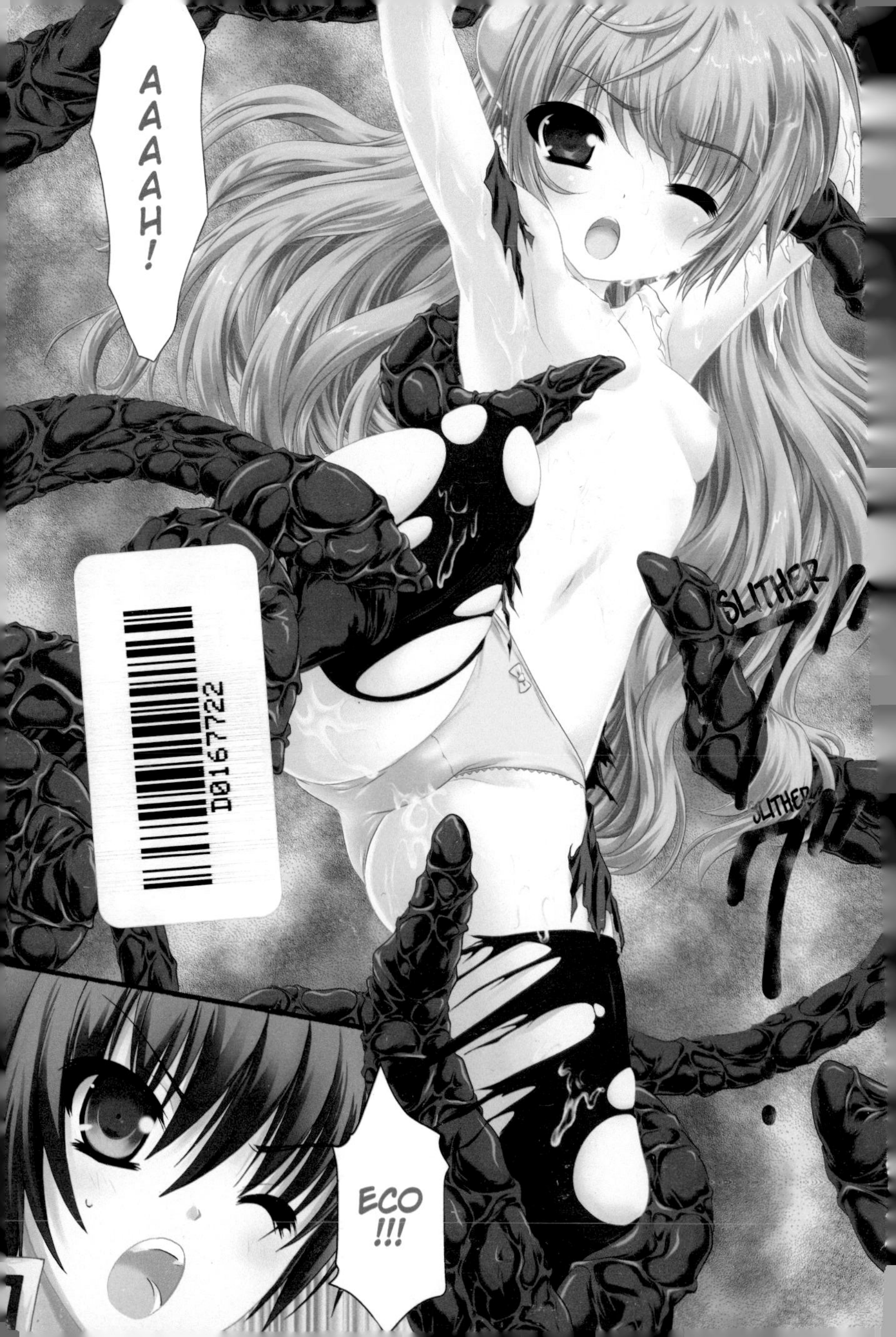
AAAAAH!
SLITHER
SLITHER
ECO !!!

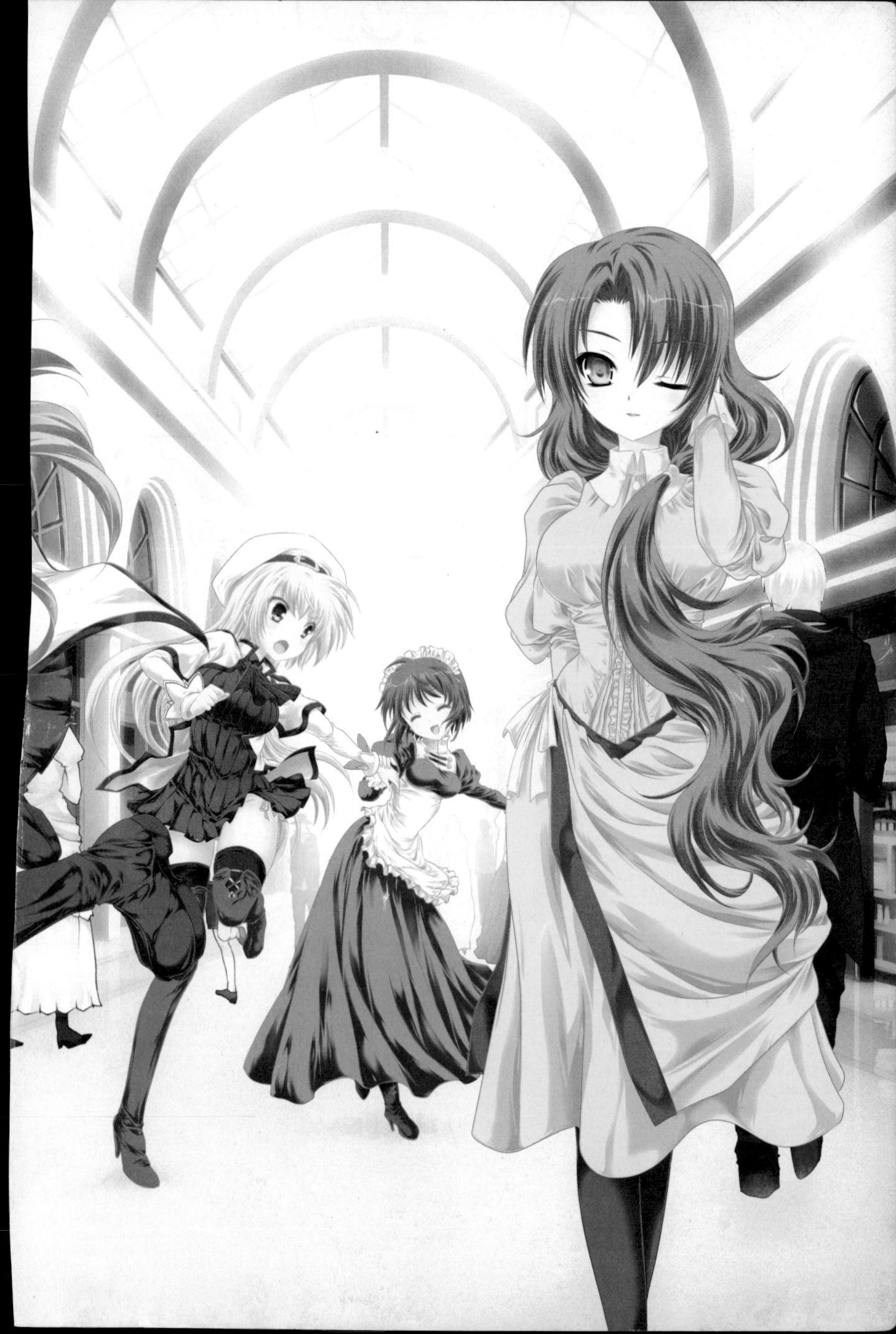

## Chapter VI
# Attack of the Necromancia

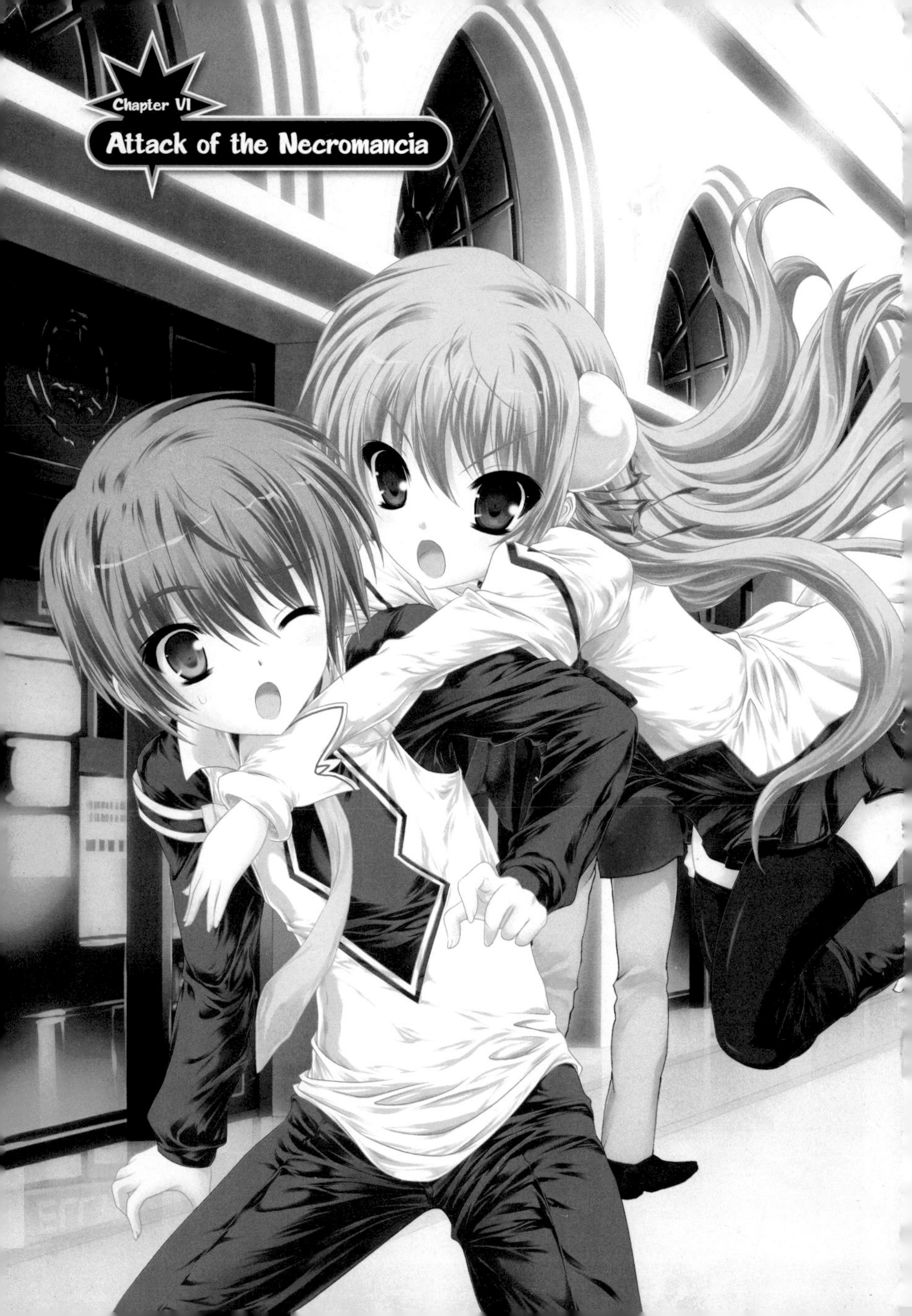

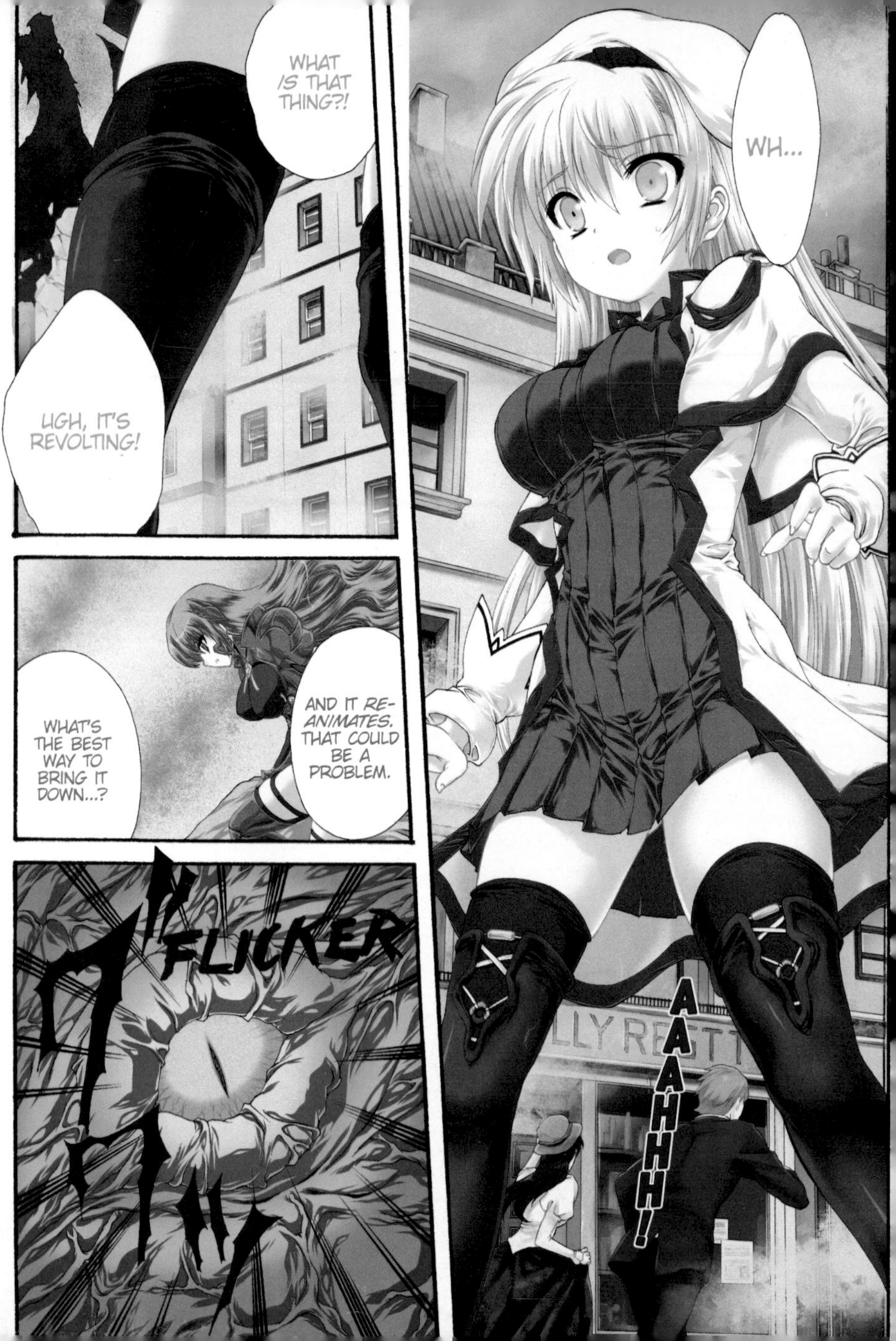
WH...
AAAAHHHH!
WHAT *IS* THAT THING?!
UGH, IT'S REVOLTING!
AND IT *RE-ANIMATES.* THAT COULD BE A PROBLEM.
WHAT'S THE BEST WAY TO BRING IT DOWN...?
FLICKER

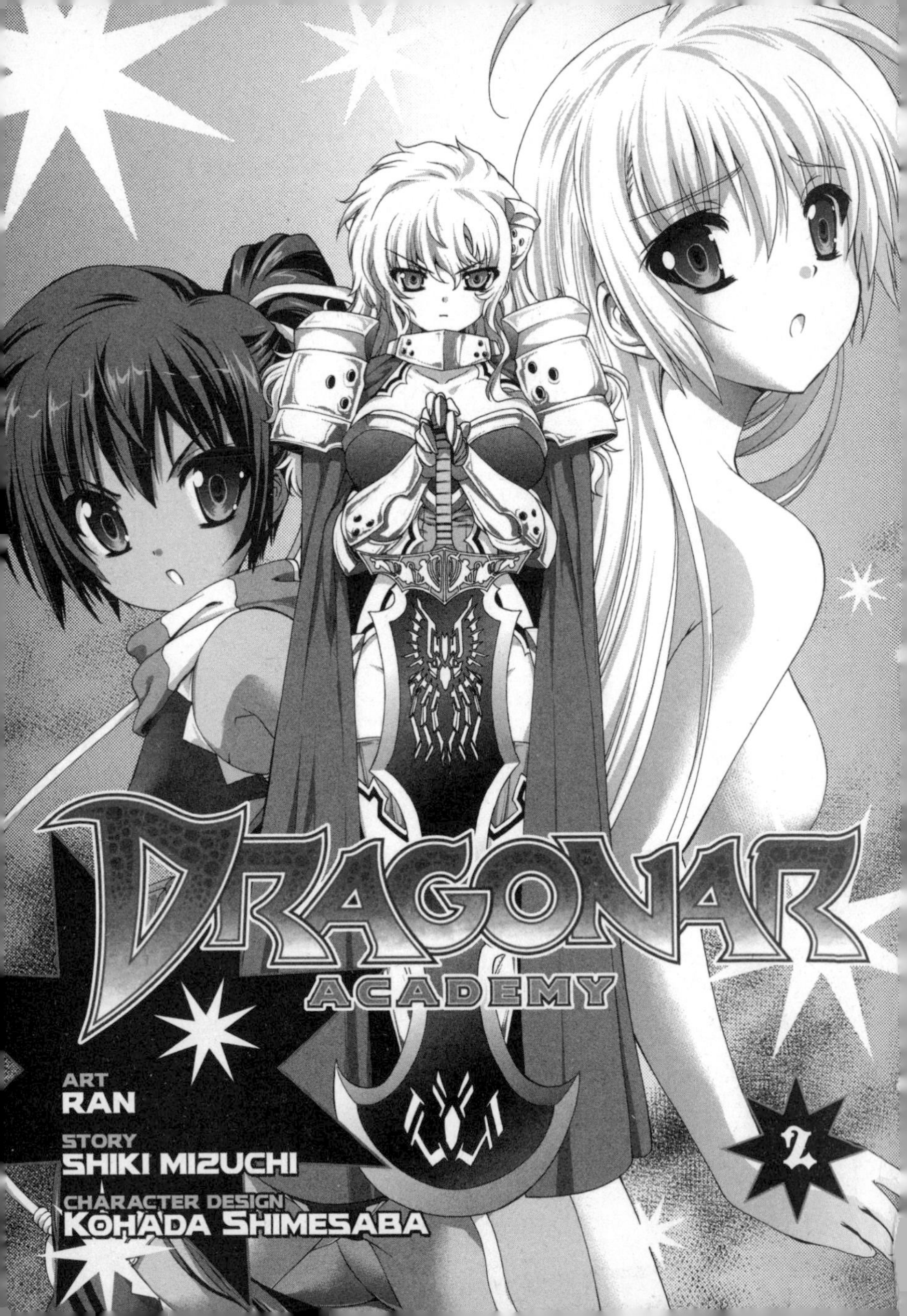
DRAGONAR
ACADEMY
ART
RAN
STORY
SHIKI MIZUCHI
CHARACTER DESIGN
KOHADA SHIMESABA
2

# SEVEN SEAS ENTERTAINMENT PRESENTS

# DRAGONAR ACADEMY
## VOLUME 2

art by **RAN** / story by **SHIKI MIZUCHI** / Character Design by **KOHADA SHIMESABA**

TRANSLATION
**Nan Rymer**

ADAPTATION
**Libby Mitchell**

LETTERING AND LAYOUT
**Paweł Szczęszek**

COVER DESIGN
**Phil Balsman**
**Nicky Lim**

PROOFREADER
**Lee Otter**
**Conner Crooks**

MANAGING EDITOR
**Adam Arnold**

PUBLISHER
**Jason DeAngelis**

DRAGONAR ACADEMY VOL. 2
© Ran 2012, © Shiki Mizuchi 2012
Edited by MEDIA FACTORY.
First published in Japan in 2012 by KADOKAWA CORPORATION, Tokyo.
English translation rights reserved by Seven Seas Entertainment, LLC.
under the license from KADOKAWA CORPORATION, Tokyo.

Seven Seas books may be purchased in bulk for educational, business, or
promotional use. For information on bulk purchases, please contact Macmillan
Corporate & Premium Sales Department at 1-800-221-7945 (ext 5442)
or write specialmarkets@macmillan.com.

Seven Seas and the Seven Seas logo are trademarks of
Seven Seas Entertainment, LLC. All rights reserved.

ISBN: 978-1-626920-16-3

Printed in Canada

First Printing: May 2014

10 9 8 7 6 5 4 3 2 1

FOLLOW US ONLINE: *www.gomanga.com*

# READING DIRECTIONS

This book reads from *right to left*, Japanese style.
If this is your first time reading manga, you start
reading from the top right panel on each page and
take it from there. If you get lost, just follow the
numbered diagram here. It may seem backwards at
first, but you'll get the hang of it! Have fun!!

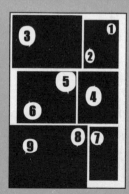

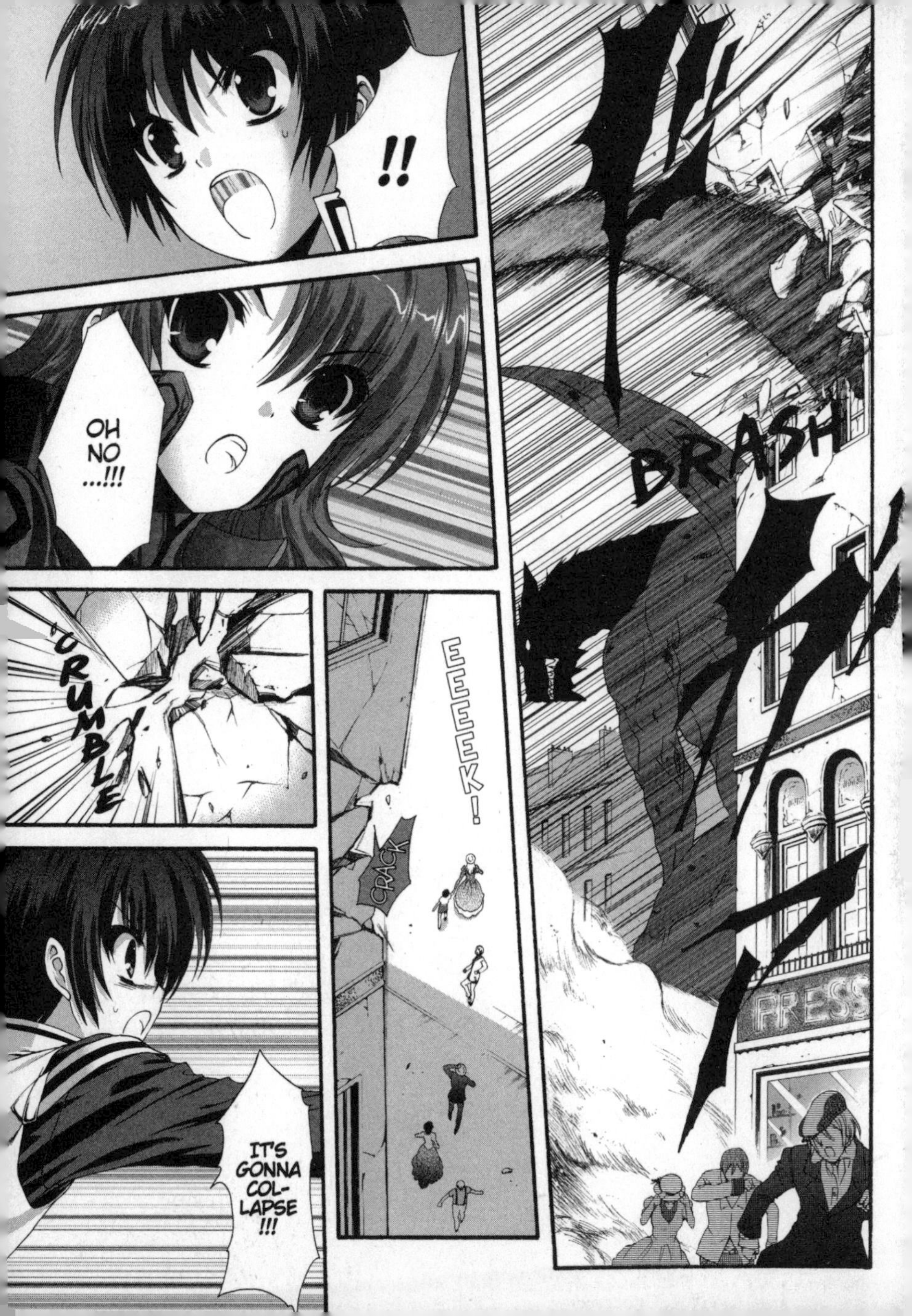

BRASH
PRESS
!!
OH NO ...!!!
EEEEEK!
CRACK
CRUMBLE
IT'S GONNA COL-LAPSE !!!

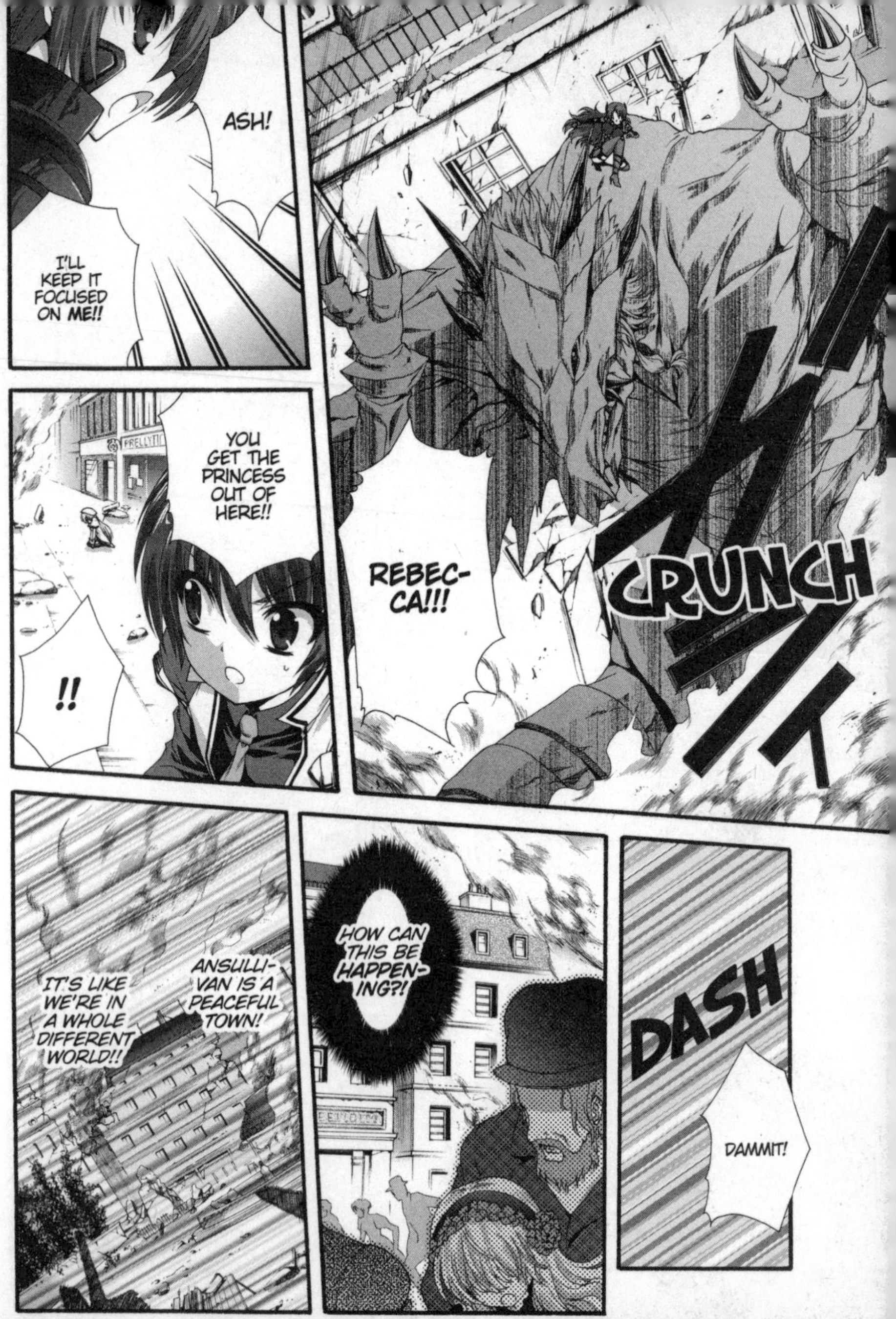
CRUNCH
REBEC-CA!!!
ASH!
I'LL KEEP IT FOCUSED ON ME!!
YOU GET THE PRINCESS OUT OF HERE!!
!!
DASH
DAMMIT!
HOW CAN THIS BE HAPPEN-ING?!
ANSULLI-VAN IS A PEACEFUL TOWN!
IT'S LIKE WE'RE IN A WHOLE DIFFERENT WORLD!!

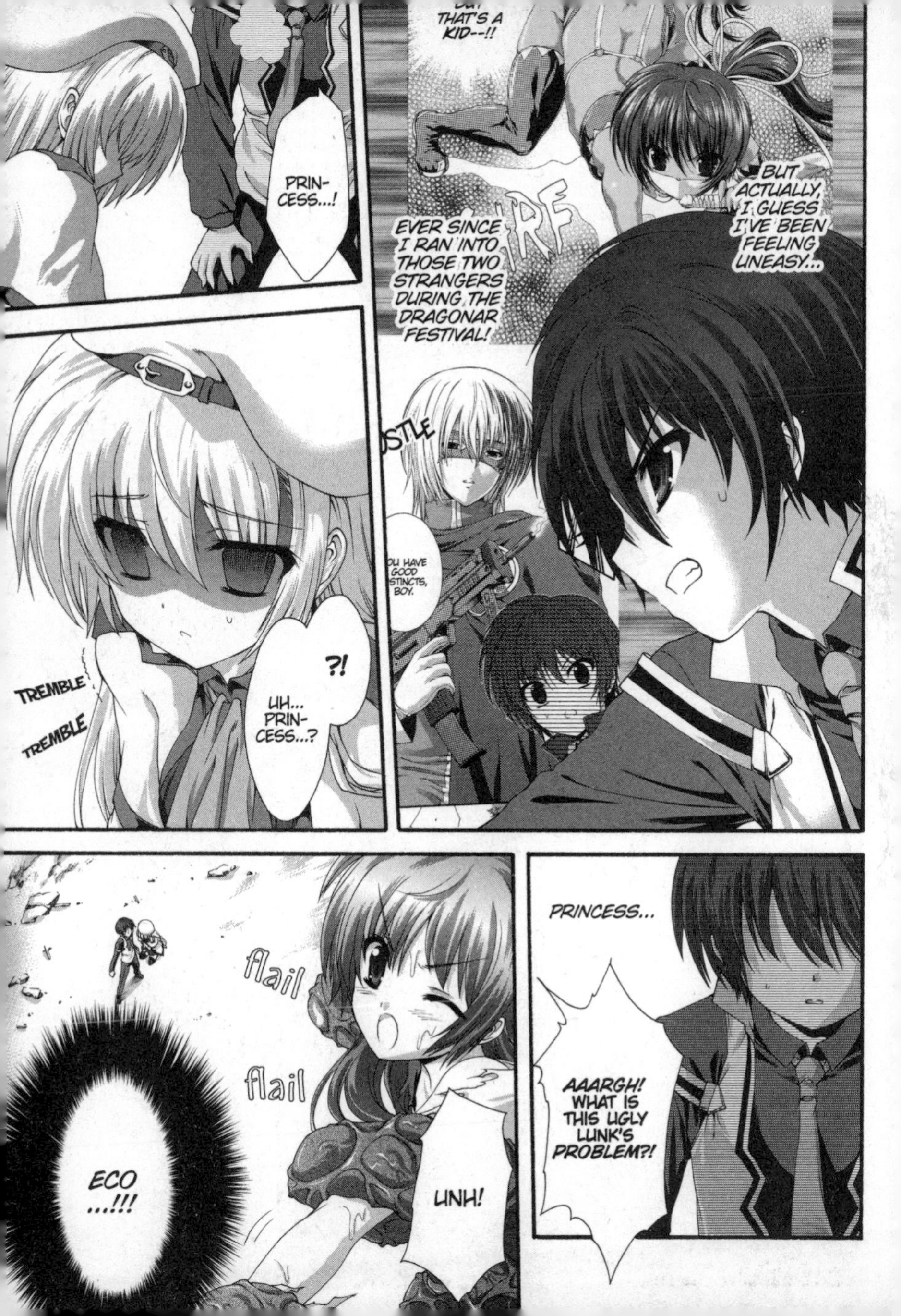
THAT'S A KID--!!
BUT ACTUALLY, I GUESS I'VE BEEN FEELING UNEASY...
EVER SINCE I RAN INTO THOSE TWO STRANGERS DURING THE DRAGONAR FESTIVAL!
RF
USTLE
OU HAVE GOOD STINCTS, BOY.
PRIN-CESS...!
?!
UH... PRIN-CESS...?
TREMBLE
TREMBLE
PRINCESS...
AAARGH! WHAT IS THIS UGLY LUNK'S PROBLEM?!
flail
flail
UNH!
ECO ...!!!

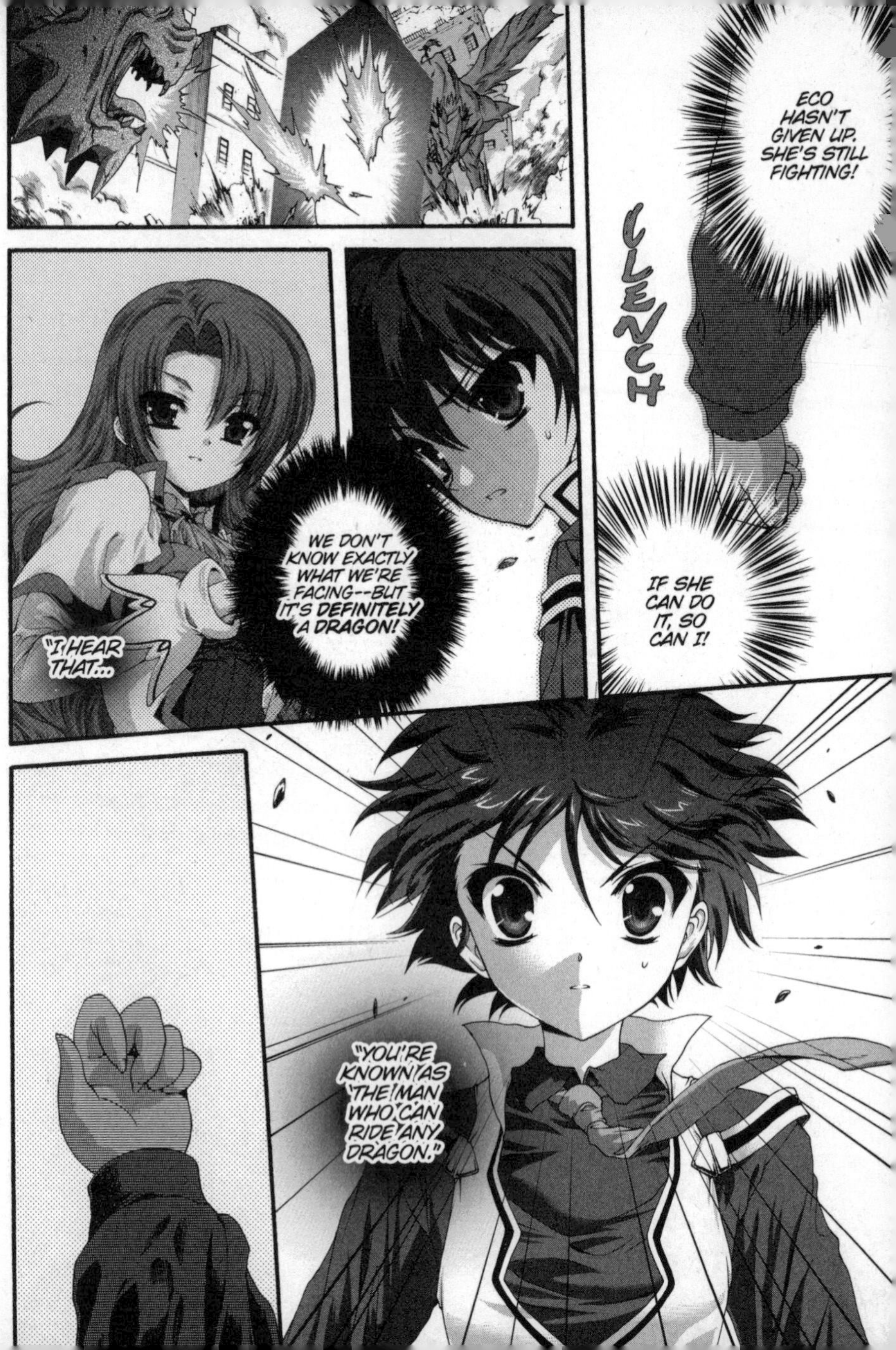
ECO HASN'T GIVEN UP. SHE'S STILL FIGHTING!
CLENCH
IF SHE CAN DO IT, SO CAN I!
WE DON'T KNOW EXACTLY WHAT WE'RE FACING--BUT IT'S DEFINITELY A DRAGON!
"I HEAR THAT...
"YOU'RE KNOWN AS 'THE MAN WHO CAN RIDE ANY DRAGON.'"

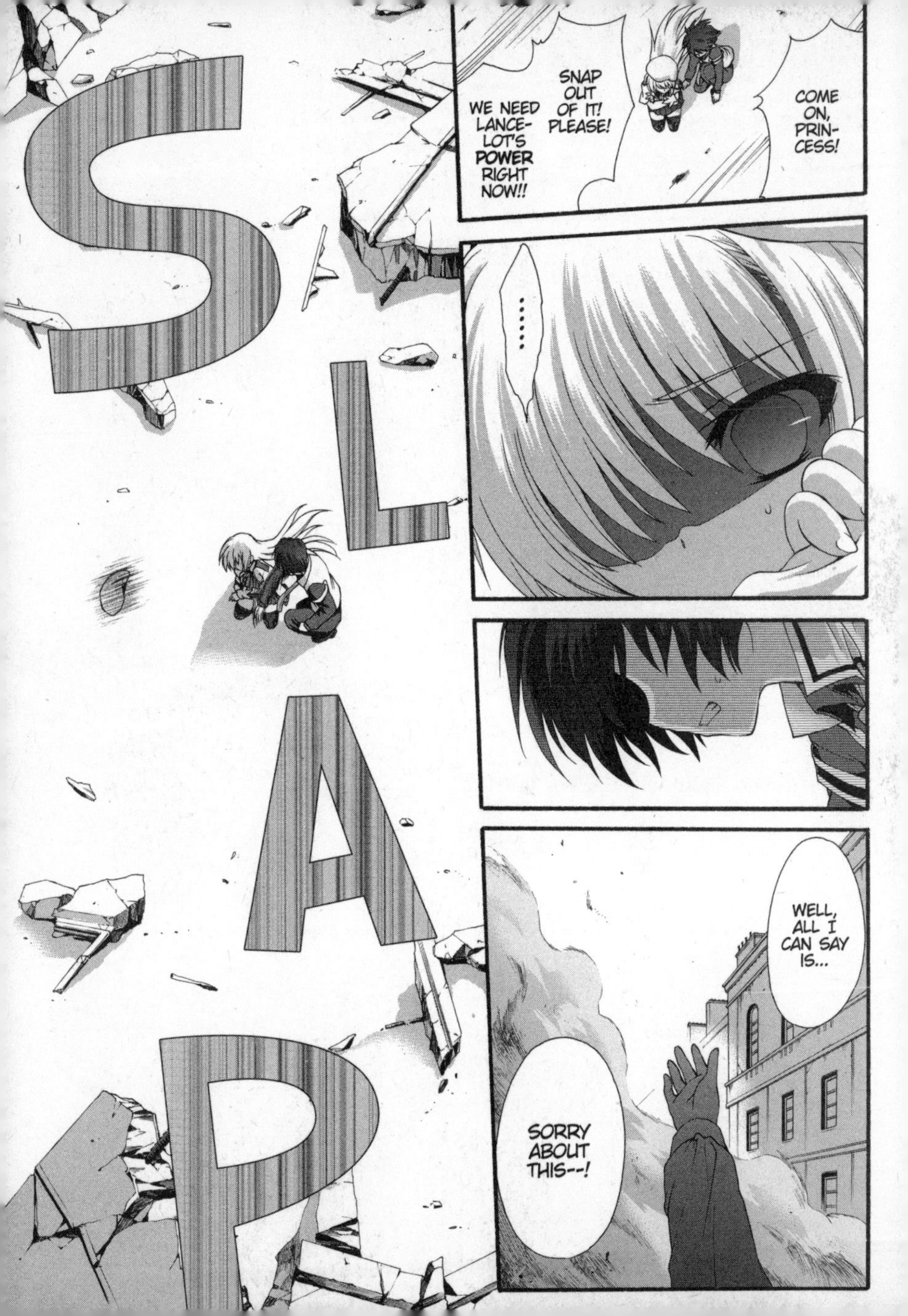
COME ON, PRINCESS!
SNAP OUT OF IT! PLEASE!
WE NEED LANCELOT'S POWER RIGHT NOW!!
......
WELL, ALL I CAN SAY IS...
SORRY ABOUT THIS--!
SLAP

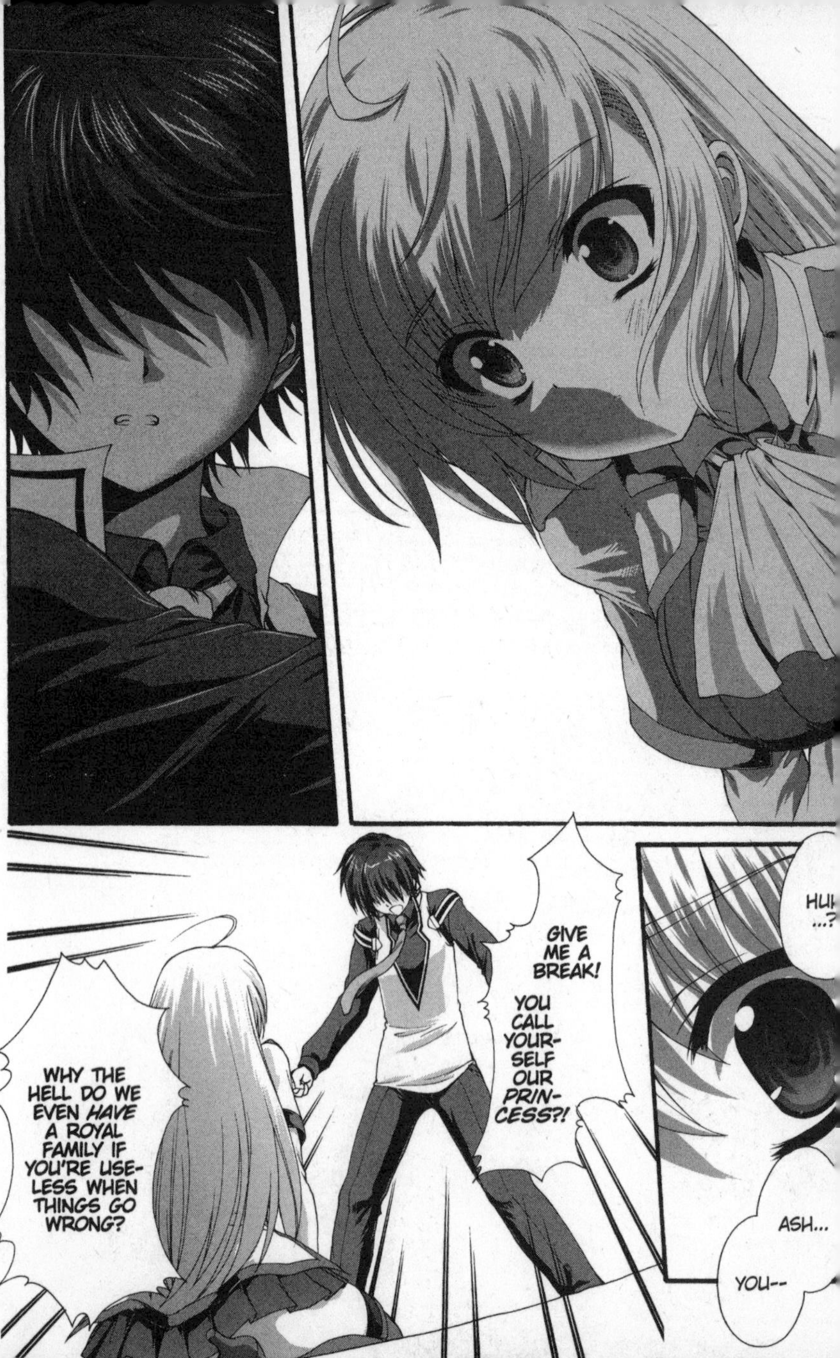
...?
ASH...
YOU--
GIVE ME A BREAK!
YOU CALL YOURSELF OUR PRINCESS?!
WHY THE HELL DO WE EVEN *HAVE* A ROYAL FAMILY IF YOU'RE USELESS WHEN THINGS GO WRONG?

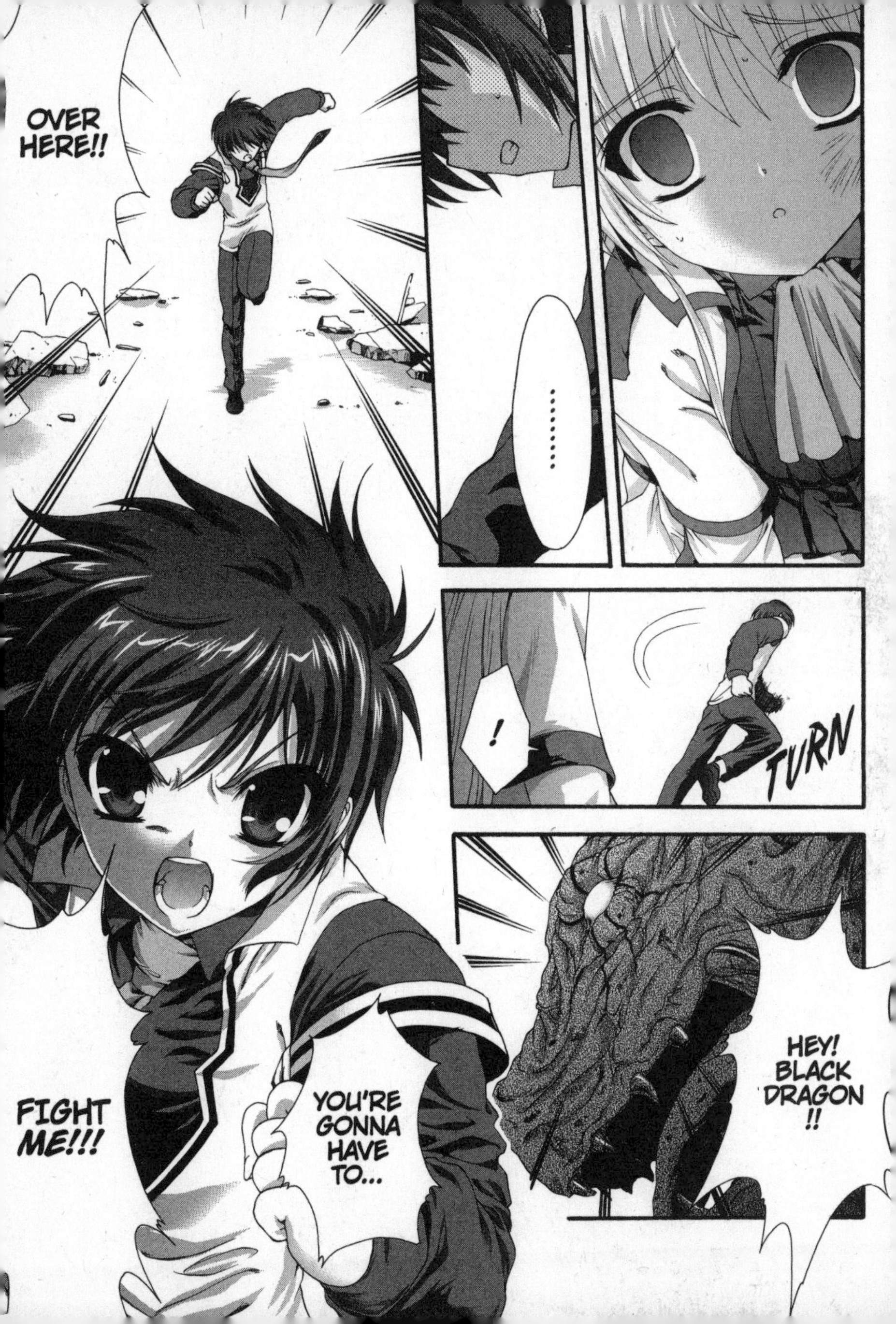
......
!
TURN
HEY! BLACK DRAGON !!
OVER HERE!!
YOU'RE GONNA HAVE TO...
FIGHT ME!!!

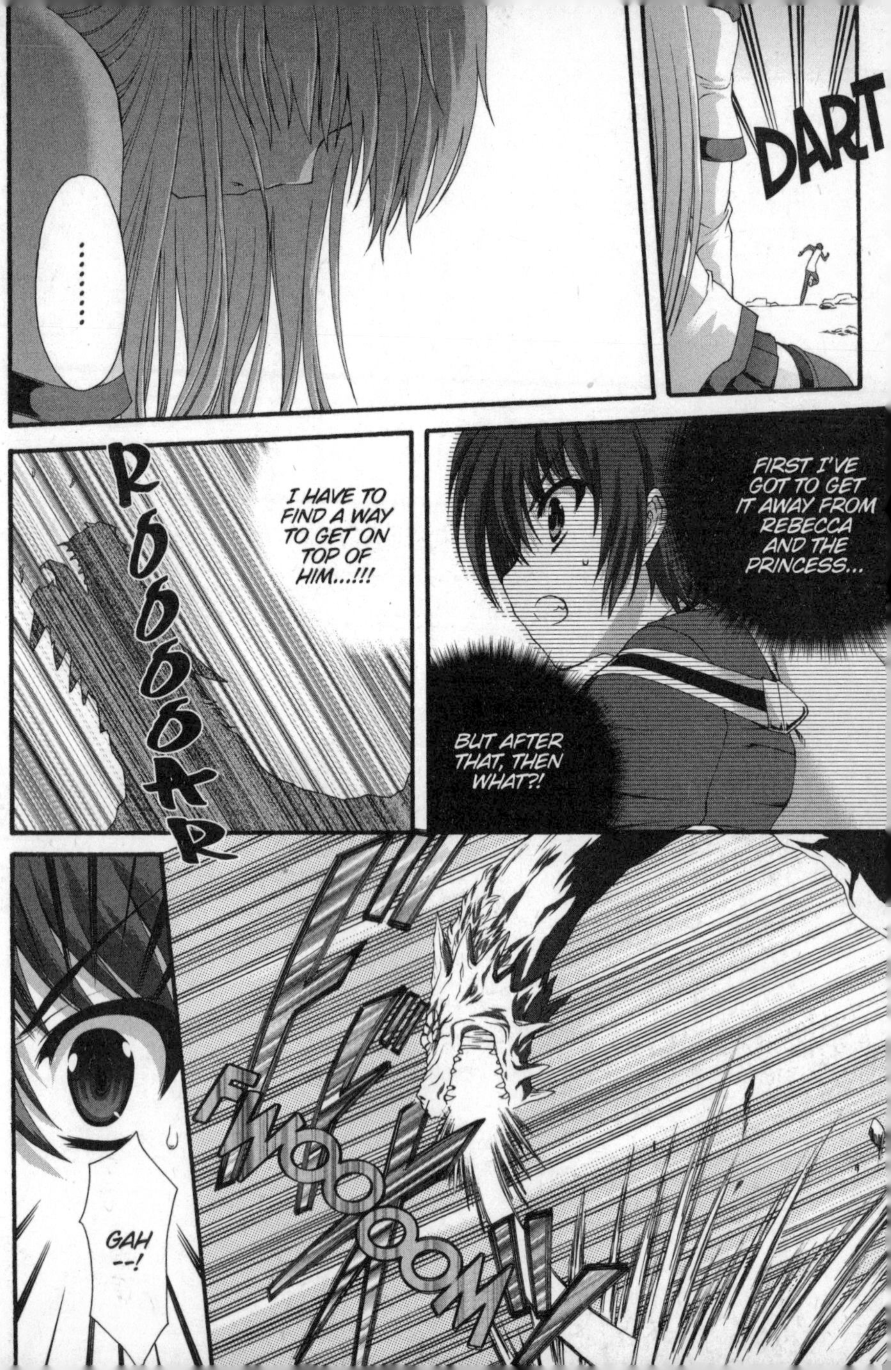
DART
......
FIRST I'VE GOT TO GET IT AWAY FROM REBECCA AND THE PRINCESS...
BUT AFTER THAT, THEN WHAT?!
I HAVE TO FIND A WAY TO GET ON TOP OF HIM...!!!
ROOOOAR
WHOOOOM!
GAH --!

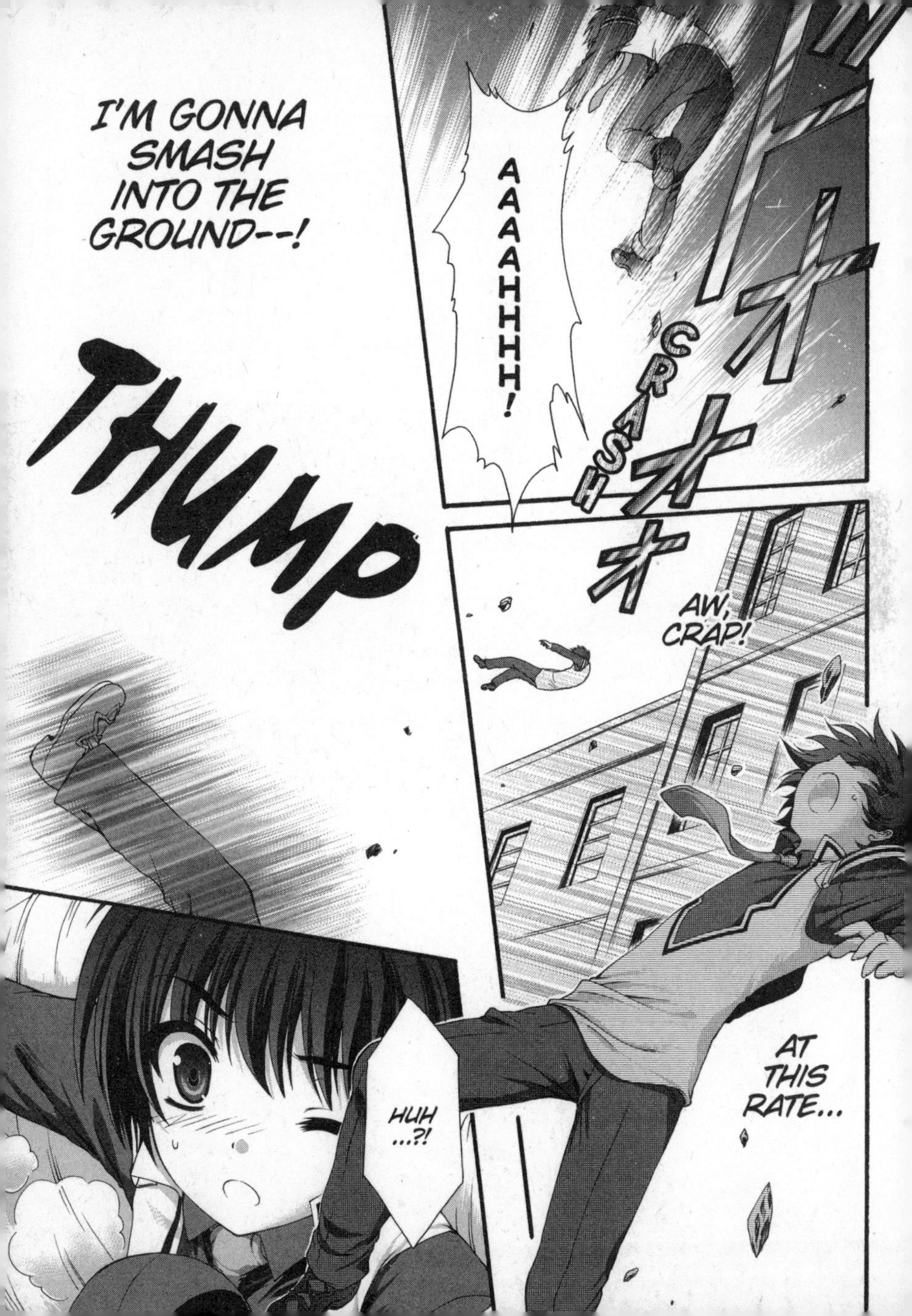
CRASH
AAAAHHHH!
I'M GONNA SMASH INTO THE GROUND--!
AW, CRAP!
THUMP
AT THIS RATE...
HUH ...?!

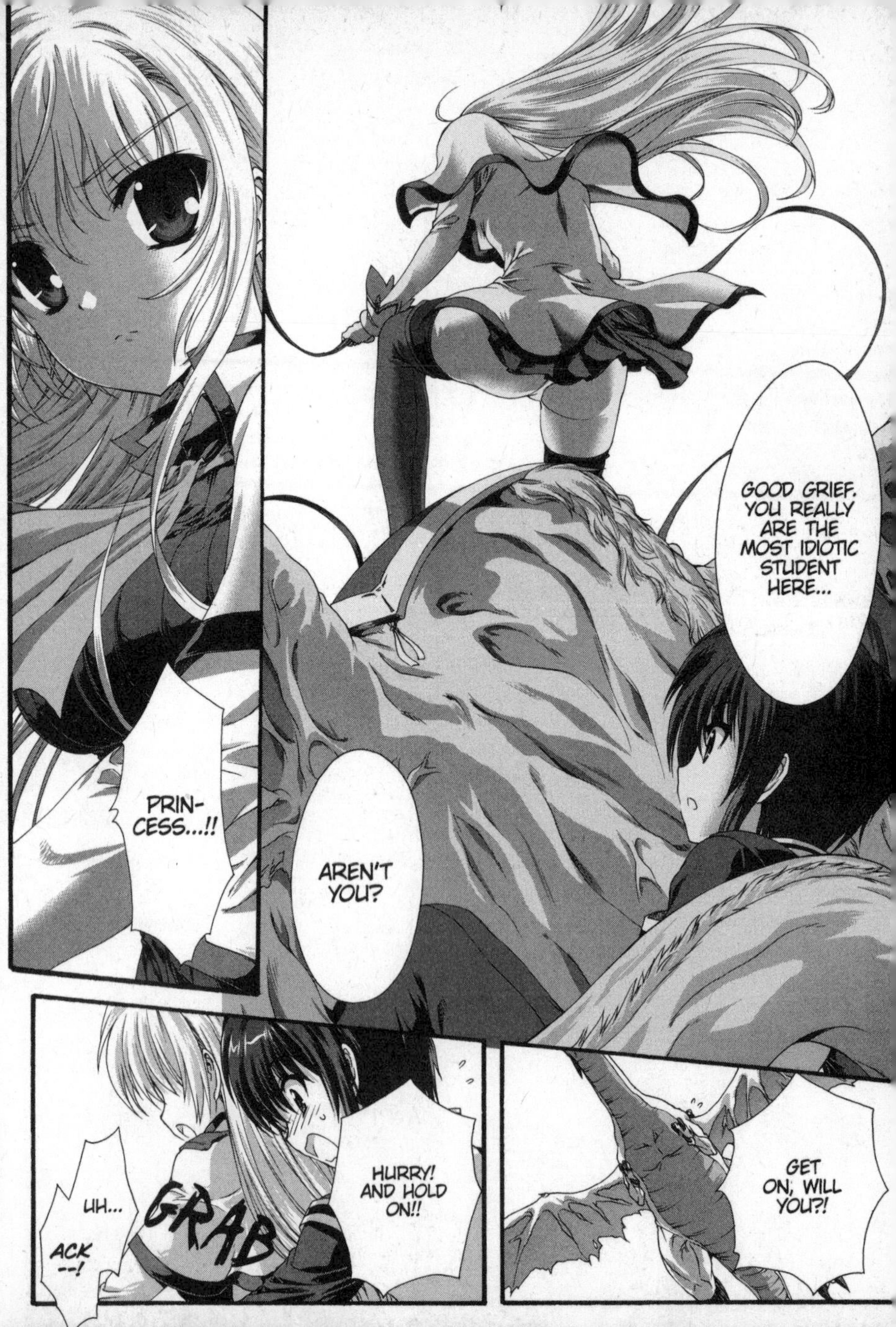
GOOD GRIEF. YOU REALLY ARE THE MOST IDIOTIC STUDENT HERE...
AREN'T YOU?
PRIN-CESS...!!
GET ON, WILL YOU?!
HURRY! AND HOLD ON!!
GRAB
UH...
ACK --!

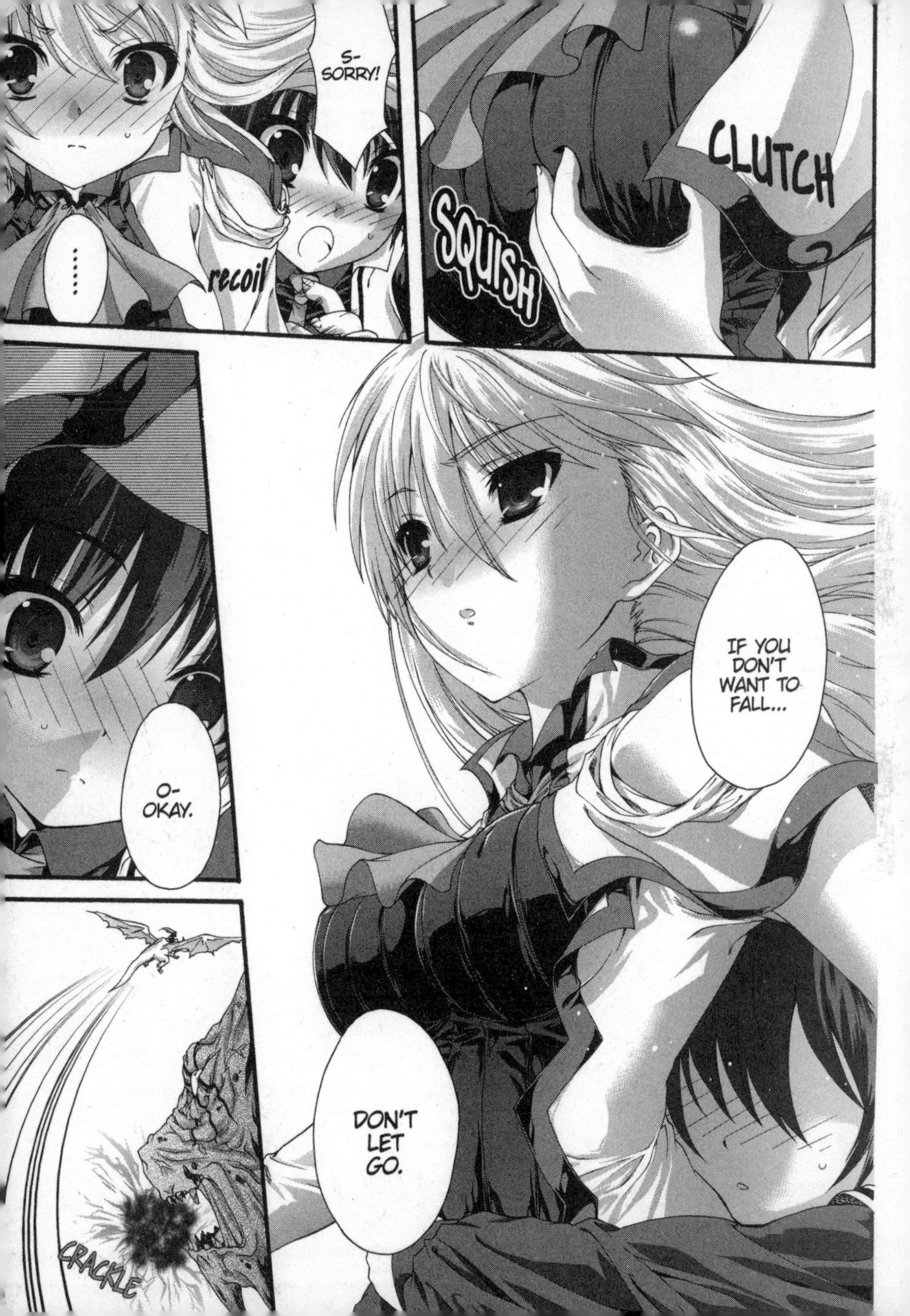
CLUTCH
SQUISH
S-SORRY!
......
recoil
IF YOU DON'T WANT TO FALL...
DON'T LET GO.
O-OKAY.
CRACKLE

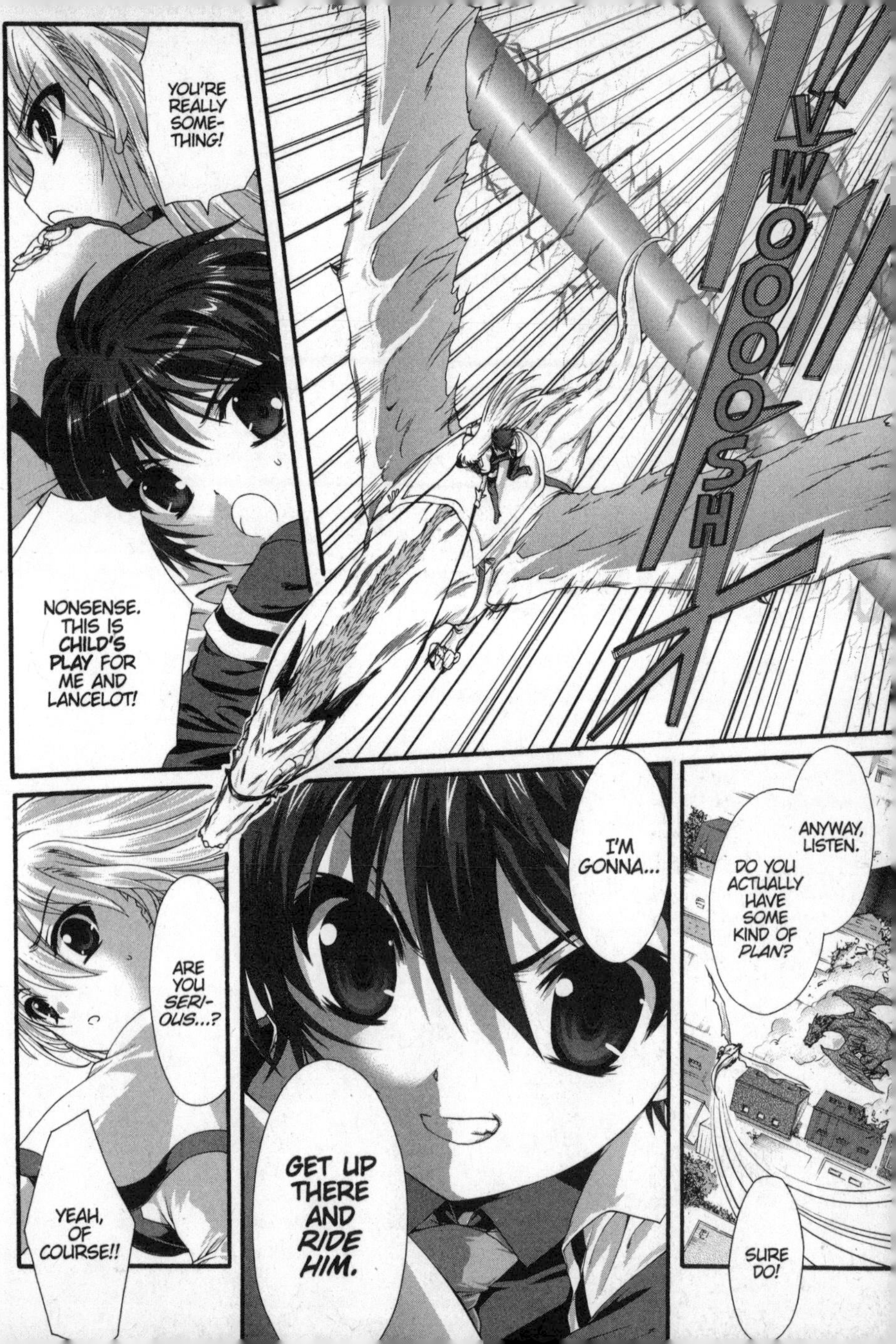
VWOOOOSH
YOU'RE REALLY SOME-THING!
NONSENSE. THIS IS **CHILD'S PLAY** FOR ME AND LANCELOT!
ANYWAY, LISTEN.
DO YOU ACTUALLY HAVE SOME KIND OF *PLAN*?
SURE DO!
I'M GONNA...
**GET UP THERE AND *RIDE* HIM.**
ARE YOU SERI-OUS...?
YEAH, OF COURSE!!

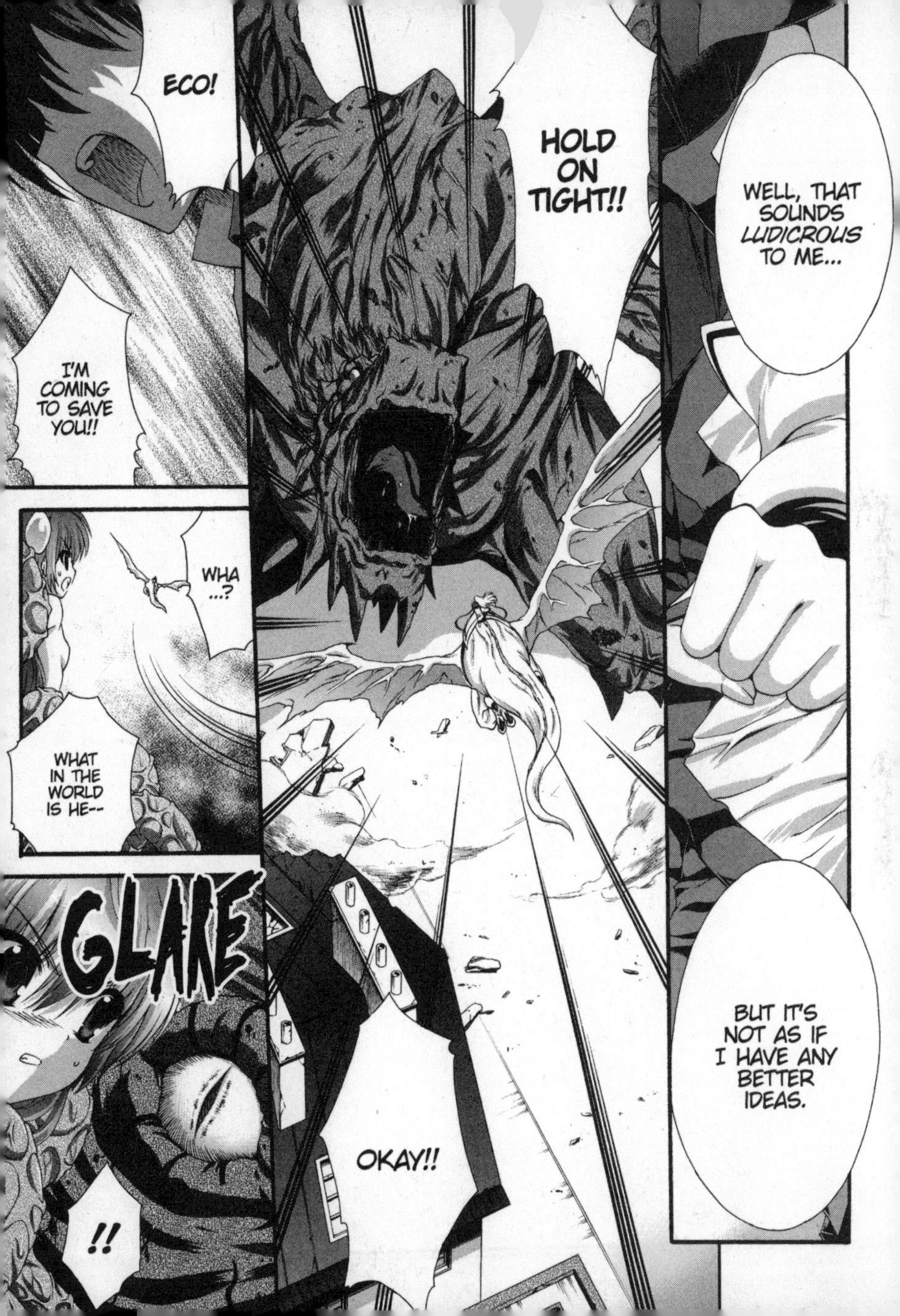
WELL, THAT SOUNDS LUDICROUS TO ME...
BUT IT'S NOT AS IF I HAVE ANY BETTER IDEAS.
HOLD ON TIGHT!!
OKAY!!
ECO!
I'M COMING TO SAVE YOU!!
WHA ...?
WHAT IN THE WORLD IS HE--
GLARE
!!

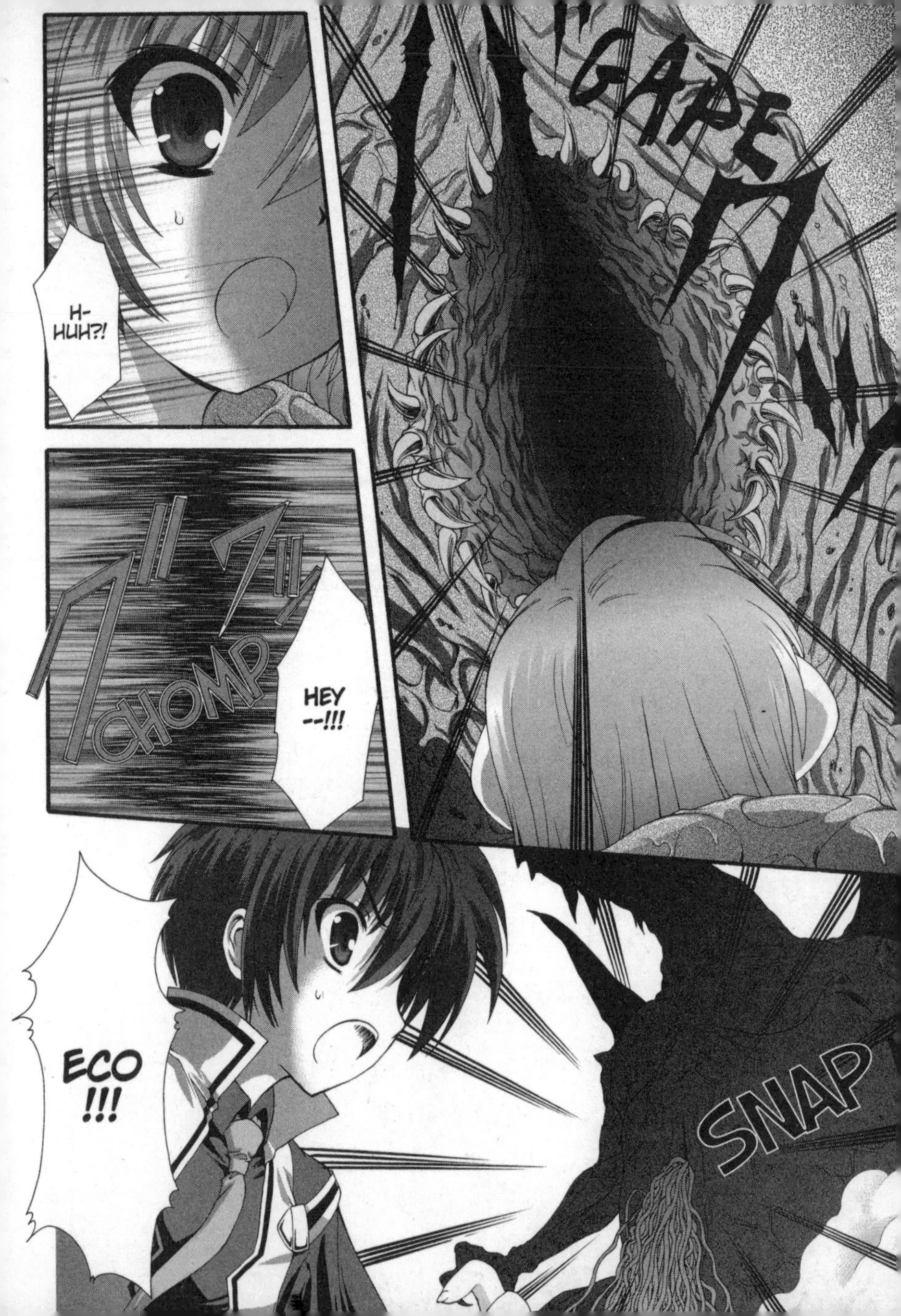
GAPE
H-HUH?!
HEY --!!!
CHOMP
SNAP
ECO !!!

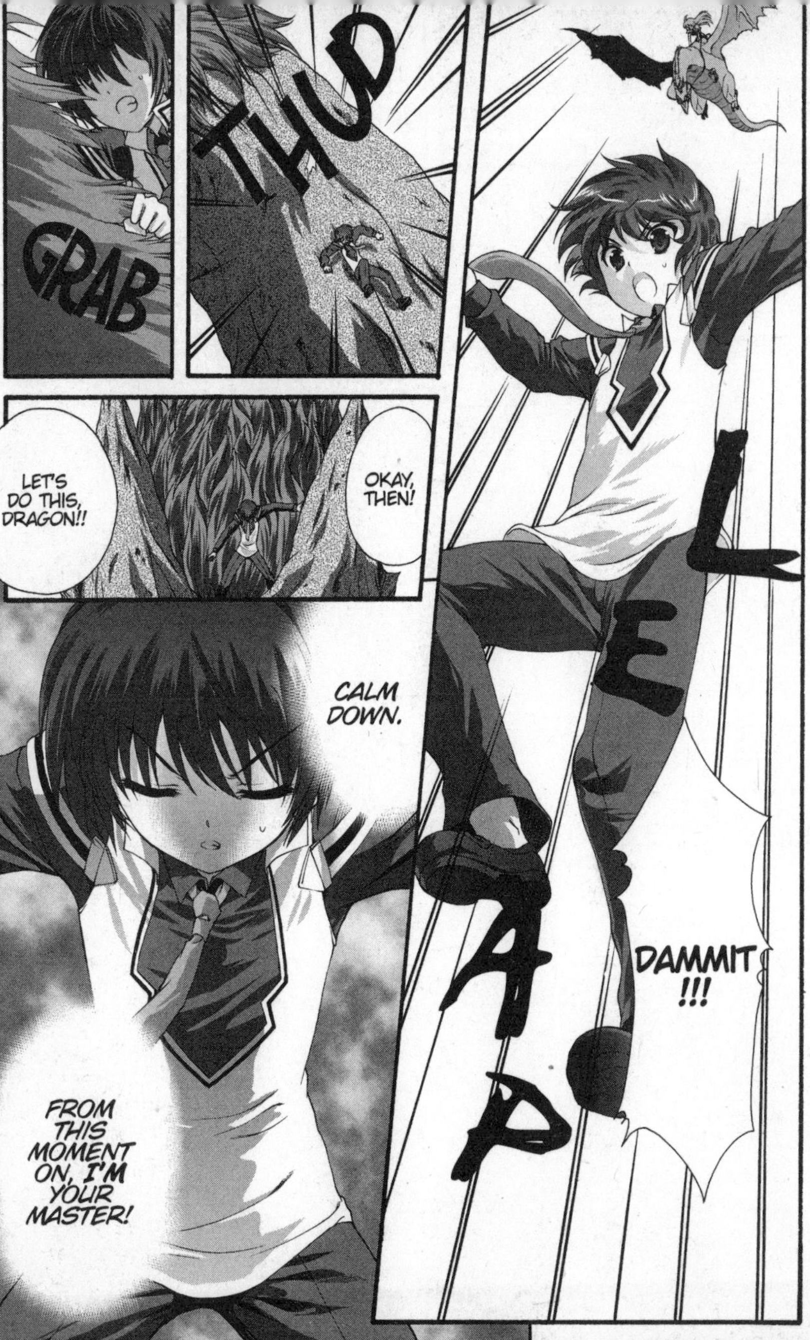
LEAP
DAMMIT!!!
THUD
GRAB
OKAY, THEN!
LET'S DO THIS, DRAGON!!
CALM DOWN.
FROM THIS MOMENT ON, I'M YOUR MASTER!

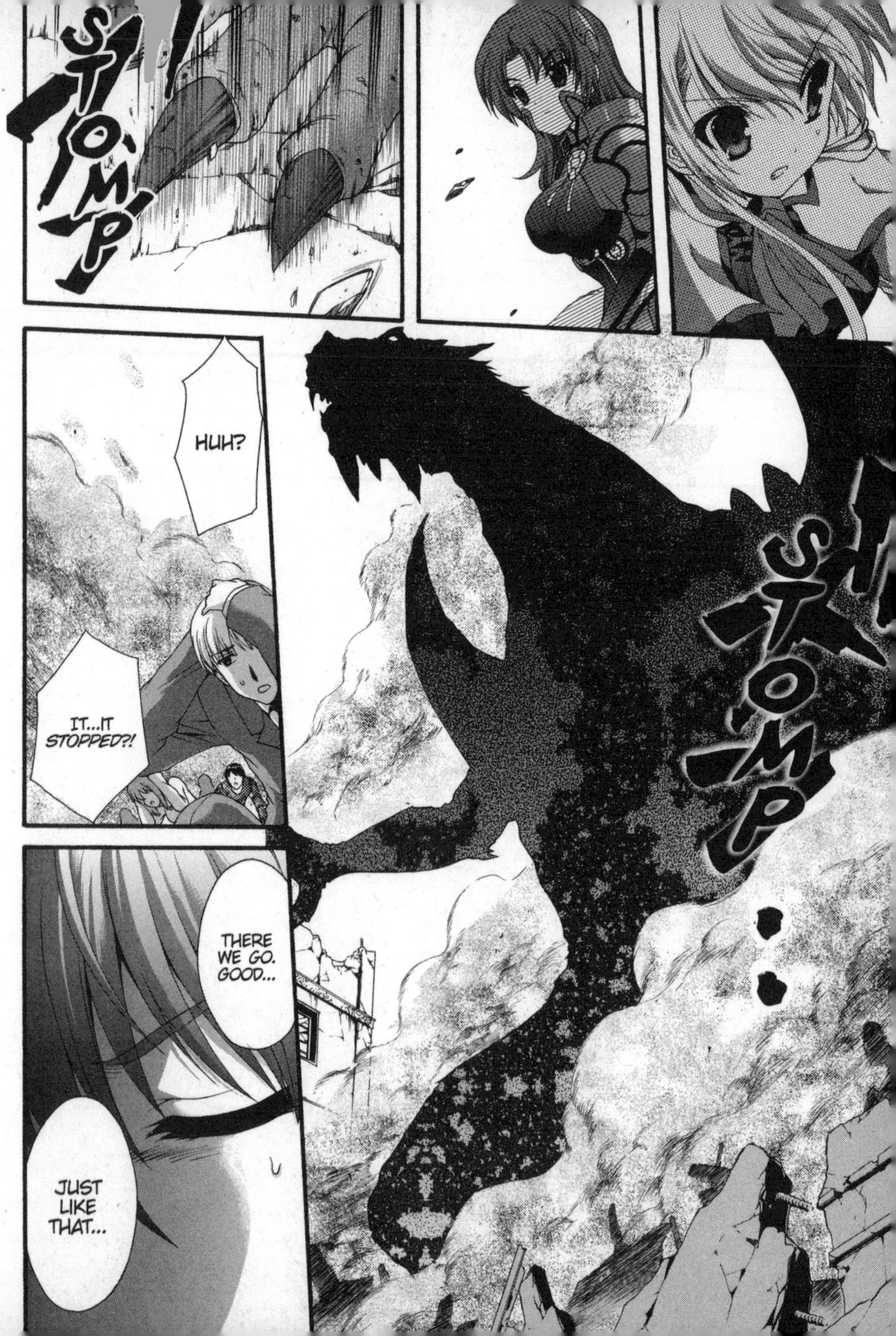
STOMP
STOMP
HUH?
IT...IT STOPPED?!
THERE WE GO. GOOD...
JUST LIKE THAT...

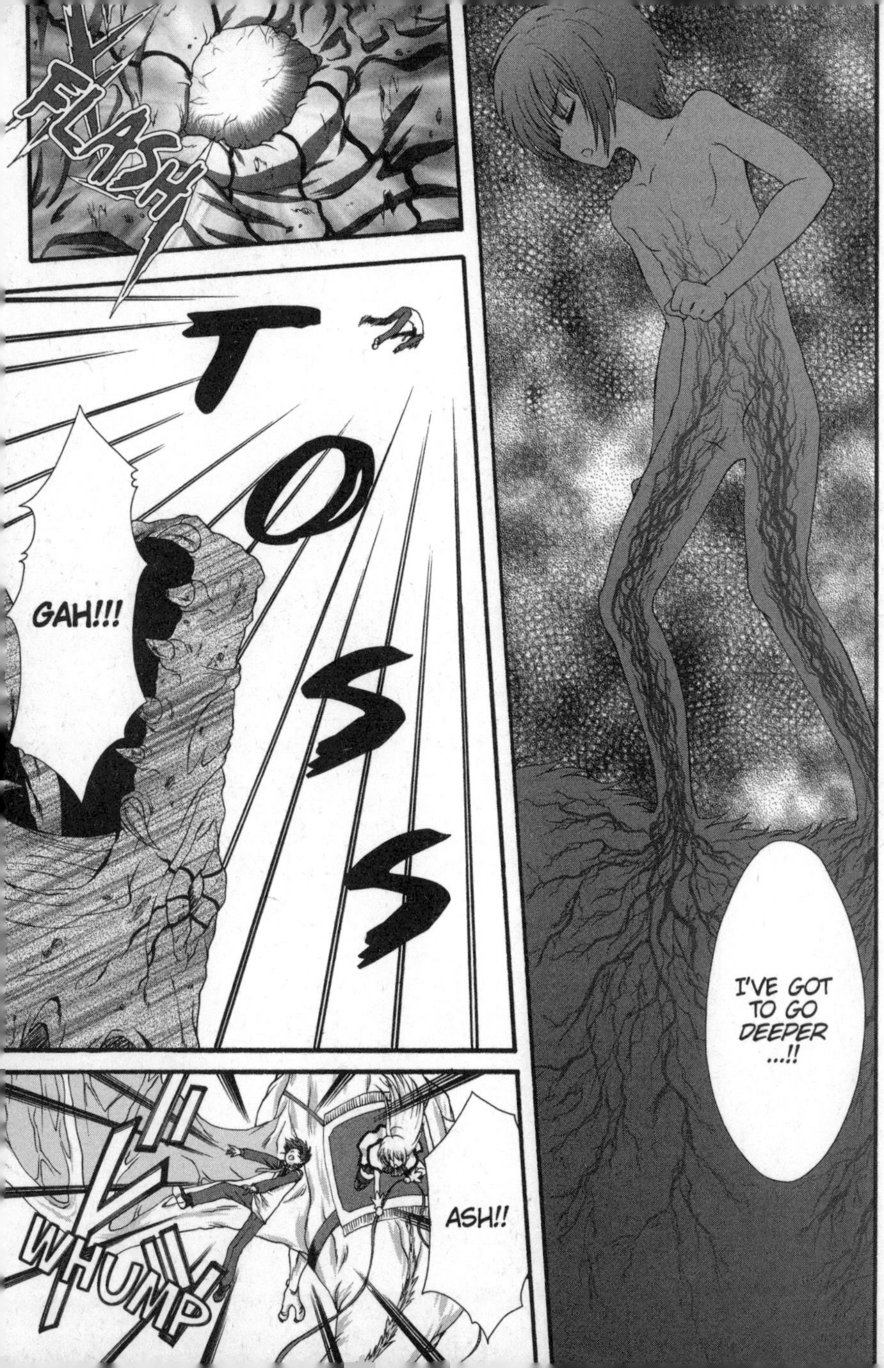
I'VE GOT TO GO DEEPER ...!!
FLASH
TOSS
GAH!!!
ASH!!
WHUMP

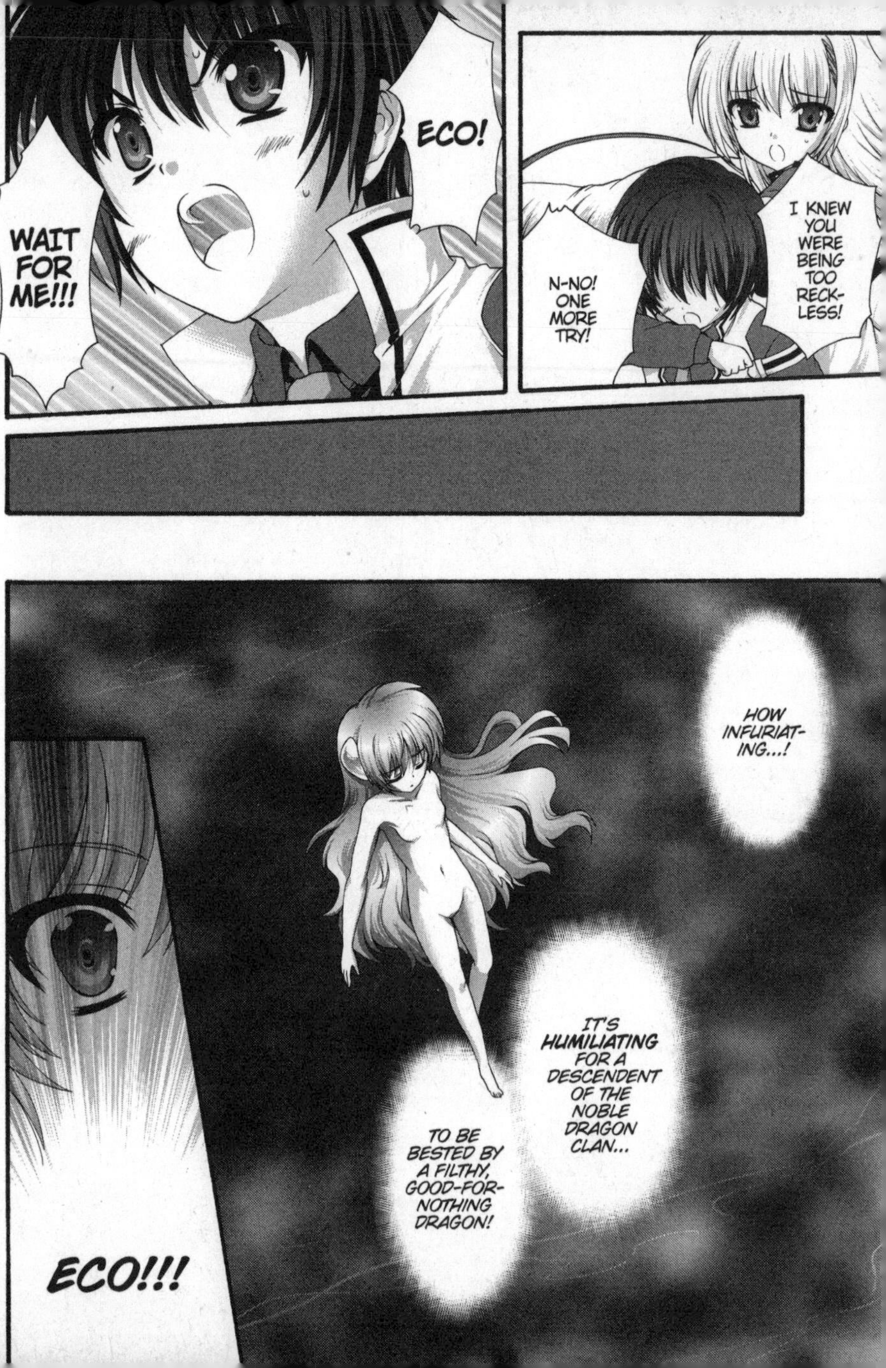
I KNEW YOU WERE BEING TOO RECK-LESS!
N-NO! ONE MORE TRY!
ECO!
WAIT FOR ME!!!
HOW INFURIAT-ING...!
IT'S HUMILIATING FOR A DESCENDENT OF THE NOBLE DRAGON CLAN...
TO BE BESTED BY A FILTHY, GOOD-FOR-NOTHING DRAGON!
ECO!!!

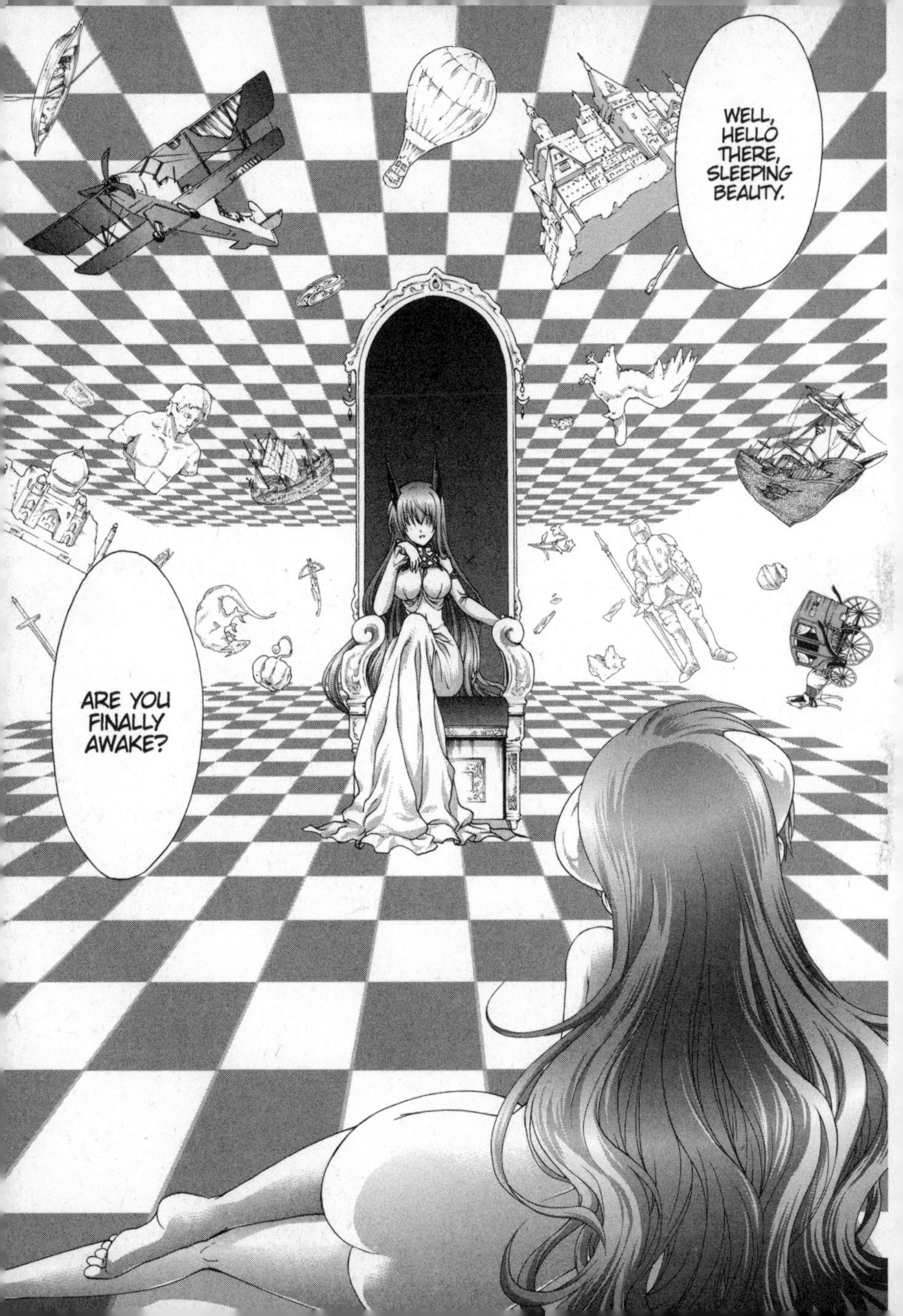
WELL, HELLO THERE, SLEEPING BEAUTY.
ARE YOU FINALLY AWAKE?

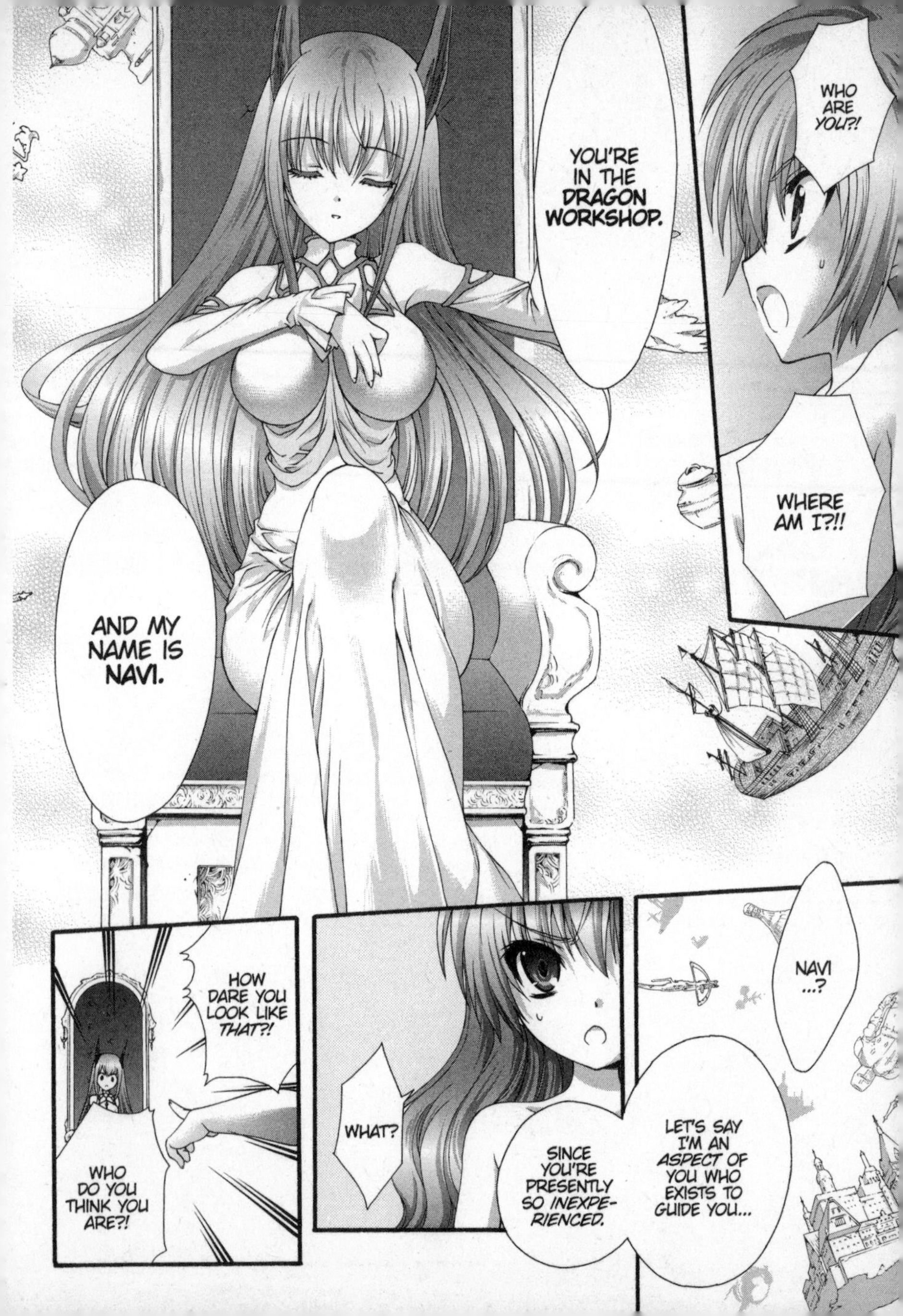
WHO ARE YOU?!
WHERE AM I?!!
YOU'RE IN THE DRAGON WORKSHOP.
AND MY NAME IS NAVI.
NAVI ...?
LET'S SAY I'M AN *ASPECT* OF YOU WHO EXISTS TO GUIDE YOU...
SINCE YOU'RE PRESENTLY SO *INEXPERIENCED.*
WHAT?
HOW DARE YOU LOOK LIKE *THAT?!*
WHO DO YOU THINK YOU ARE?!

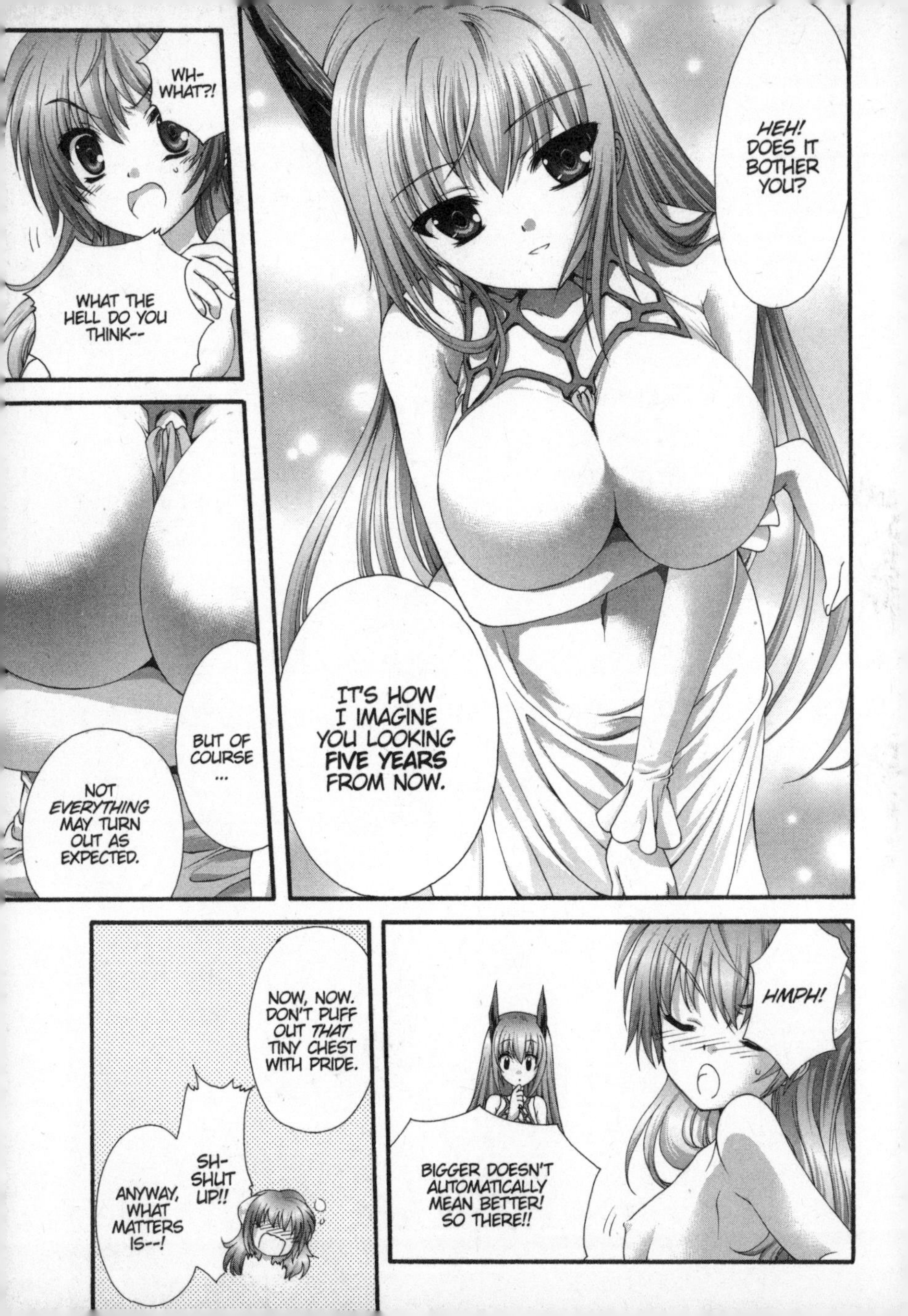
HEH! DOES IT BOTHER YOU?
IT'S HOW I IMAGINE YOU LOOKING **FIVE YEARS** FROM NOW.
WH-WHAT?!
WHAT THE HELL DO YOU THINK--
BUT OF COURSE ...
NOT *EVERYTHING* MAY TURN OUT AS EXPECTED.
*HMPH!*
BIGGER DOESN'T AUTOMATICALLY MEAN BETTER! SO THERE!!
NOW, NOW. DON'T PUFF OUT *THAT* TINY CHEST WITH PRIDE.
SH-SHUT UP!!
ANYWAY, WHAT MATTERS IS--!

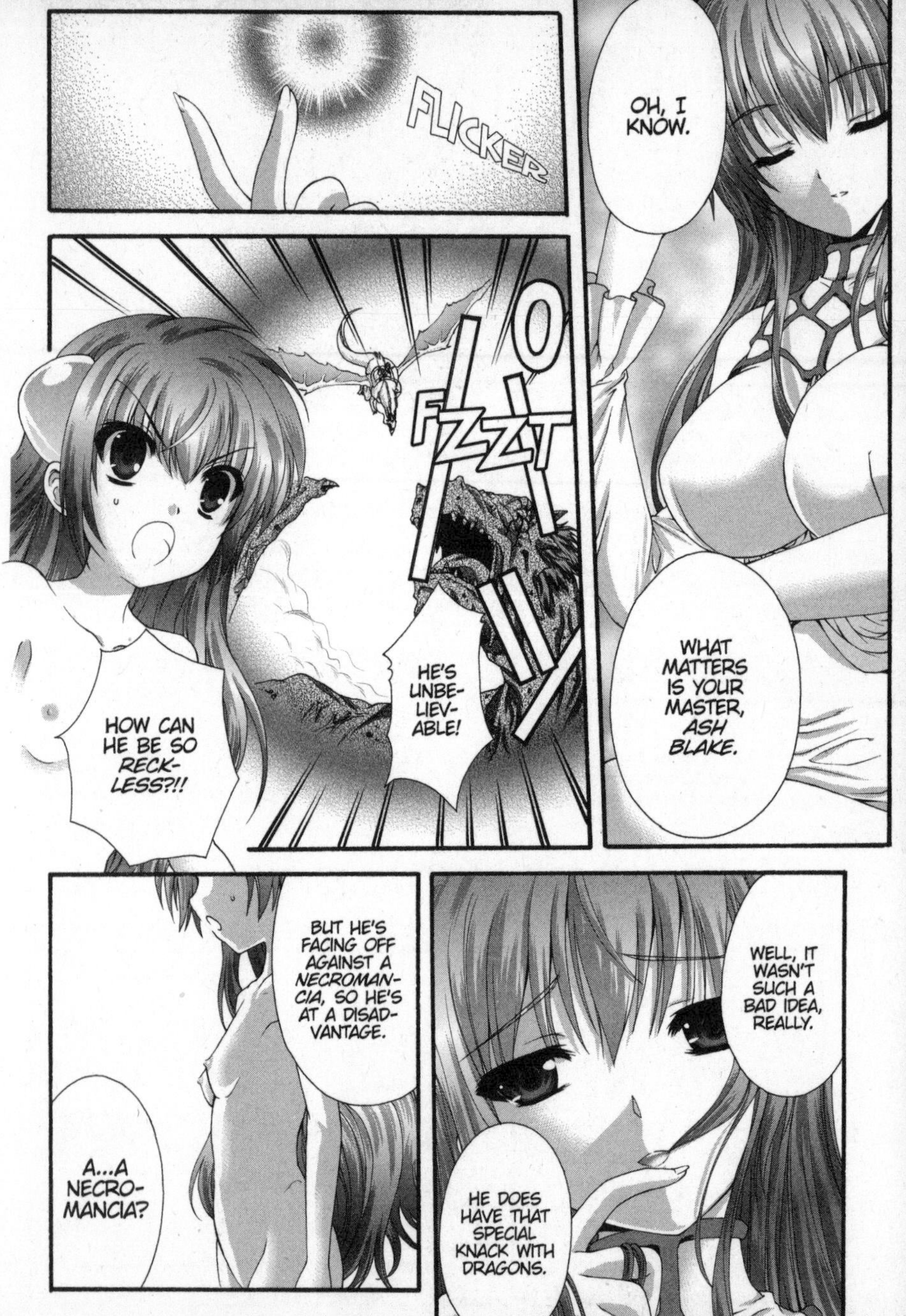
OH, I KNOW.
WHAT MATTERS IS YOUR MASTER, *ASH BLAKE.*
FLICKER
FZZZT
HE'S UNBE-LIEV-ABLE!
HOW CAN HE BE SO *RECK-LESS?!!*
WELL, IT WASN'T SUCH A BAD IDEA, REALLY.
HE DOES HAVE THAT SPECIAL KNACK WITH DRAGONS.
BUT HE'S FACING OFF AGAINST A *NECROMAN-CIA,* SO HE'S AT A DISAD-VANTAGE.
A...A NECRO-MANCIA?

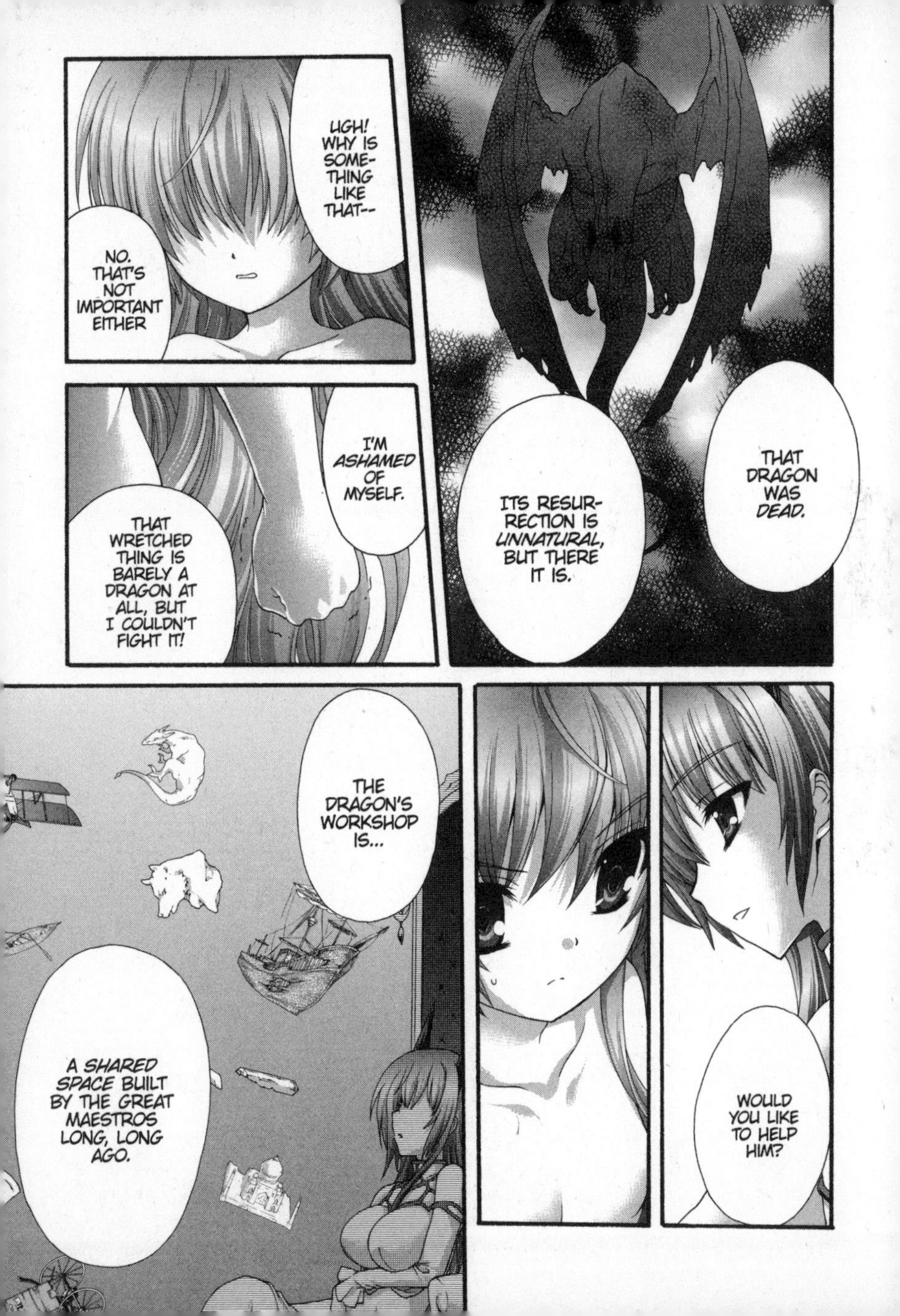
THAT DRAGON WAS *DEAD.*
ITS RESURRECTION IS *UNNATURAL,* BUT THERE IT IS.
UGH! WHY IS SOMETHING LIKE THAT--
NO. THAT'S NOT IMPORTANT EITHER
I'M *ASHAMED* OF MYSELF.
THAT WRETCHED THING IS BARELY A DRAGON AT ALL, BUT I COULDN'T FIGHT IT!
WOULD YOU LIKE TO HELP HIM?
THE DRAGON'S WORKSHOP IS...
A *SHARED SPACE* BUILT BY THE GREAT MAESTROS LONG, LONG AGO.

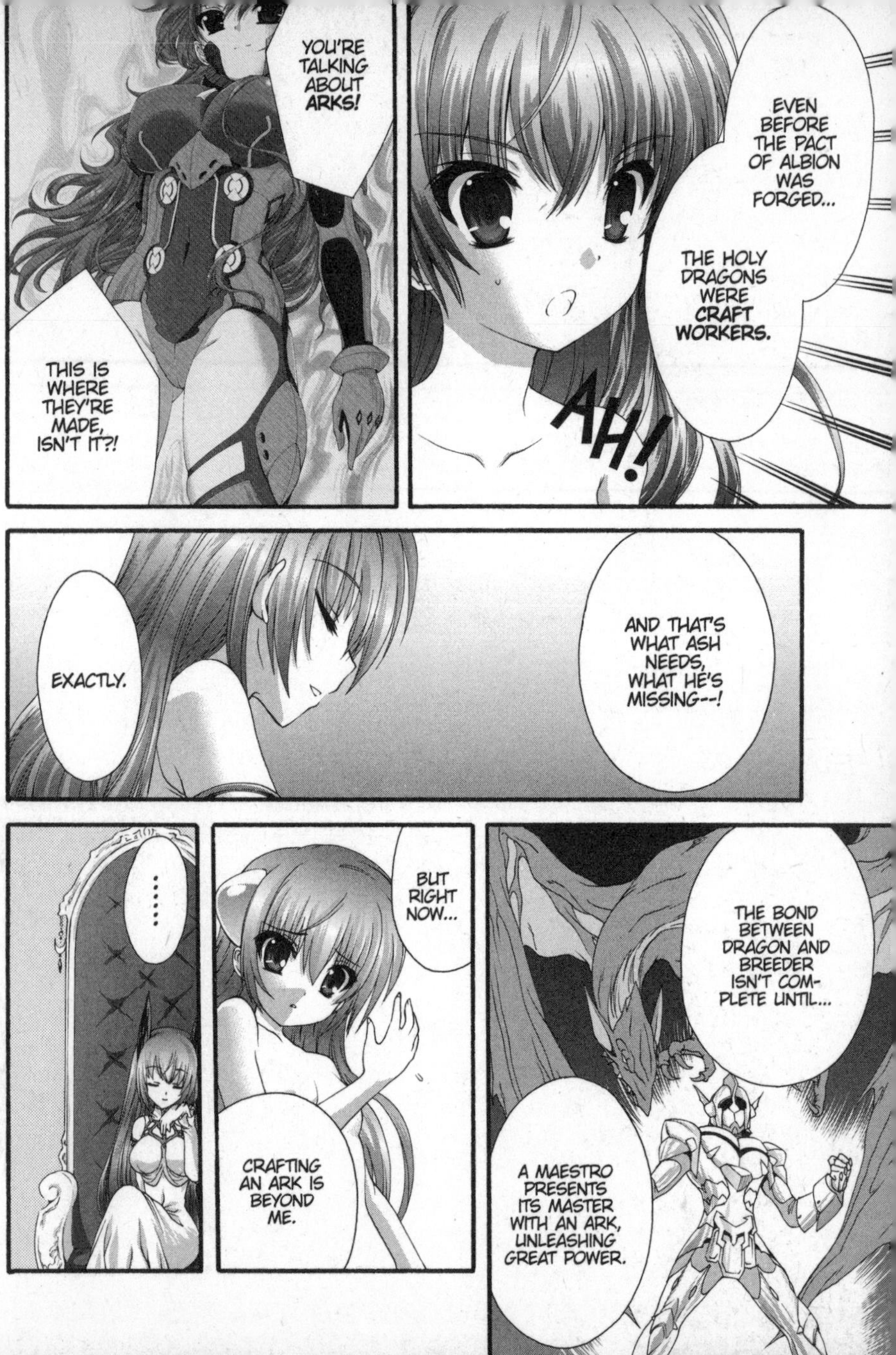
EVEN BEFORE THE PACT OF ALBION WAS FORGED...
THE HOLY DRAGONS WERE CRAFT WORKERS.
AH!
YOU'RE TALKING ABOUT ARKS!
THIS IS WHERE THEY'RE MADE, ISN'T IT?!
AND THAT'S WHAT ASH NEEDS, WHAT HE'S MISSING--!
EXACTLY.
THE BOND BETWEEN DRAGON AND BREEDER ISN'T COM-PLETE UNTIL...
A MAESTRO PRESENTS ITS MASTER WITH AN ARK, UNLEASHING GREAT POWER.
BUT RIGHT NOW...
CRAFTING AN ARK IS BEYOND ME.
......

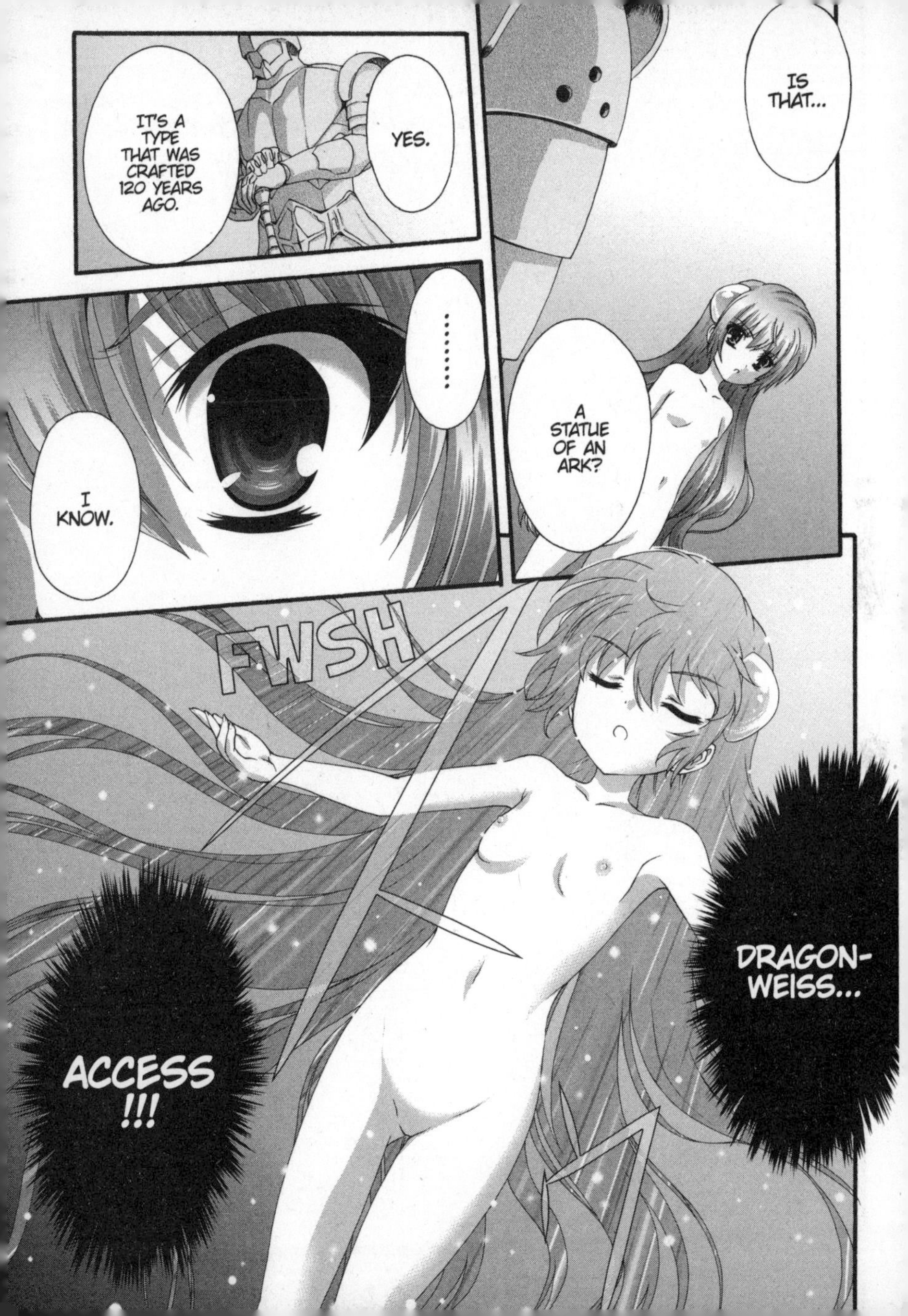
IS THAT...
A STATUE OF AN ARK?
YES.
IT'S A TYPE THAT WAS CRAFTED 120 YEARS AGO.
.........
I KNOW.
FWSH
DRAGON-WEISS...
ACCESS !!!

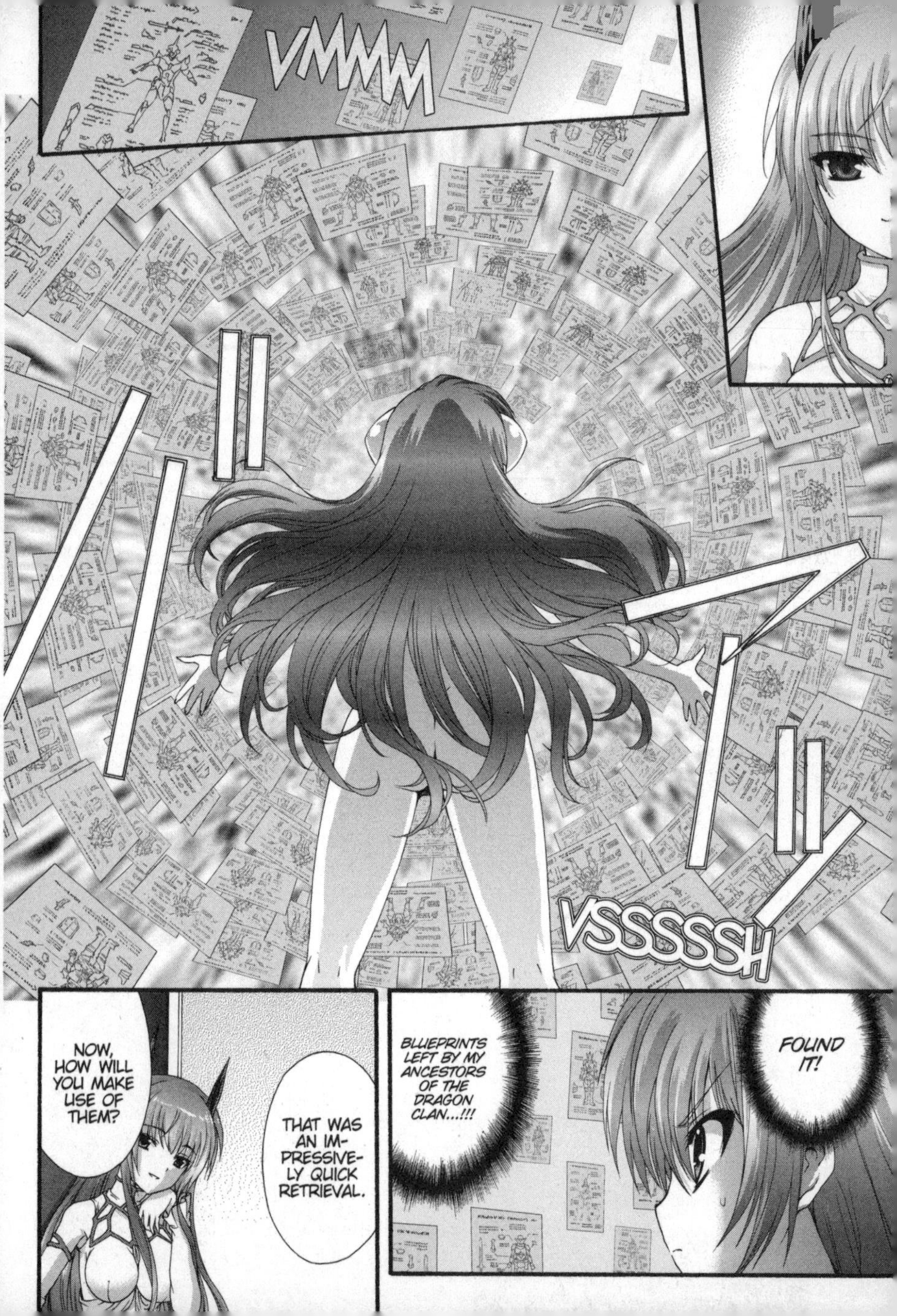
VMMMM
VSSSSSH
FOUND IT!
BLUEPRINTS LEFT BY MY ANCESTORS OF THE DRAGON CLAN...!!!
THAT WAS AN IM-PRESSIVE-LY QUICK RETRIEVAL.
NOW, HOW WILL YOU MAKE USE OF THEM?

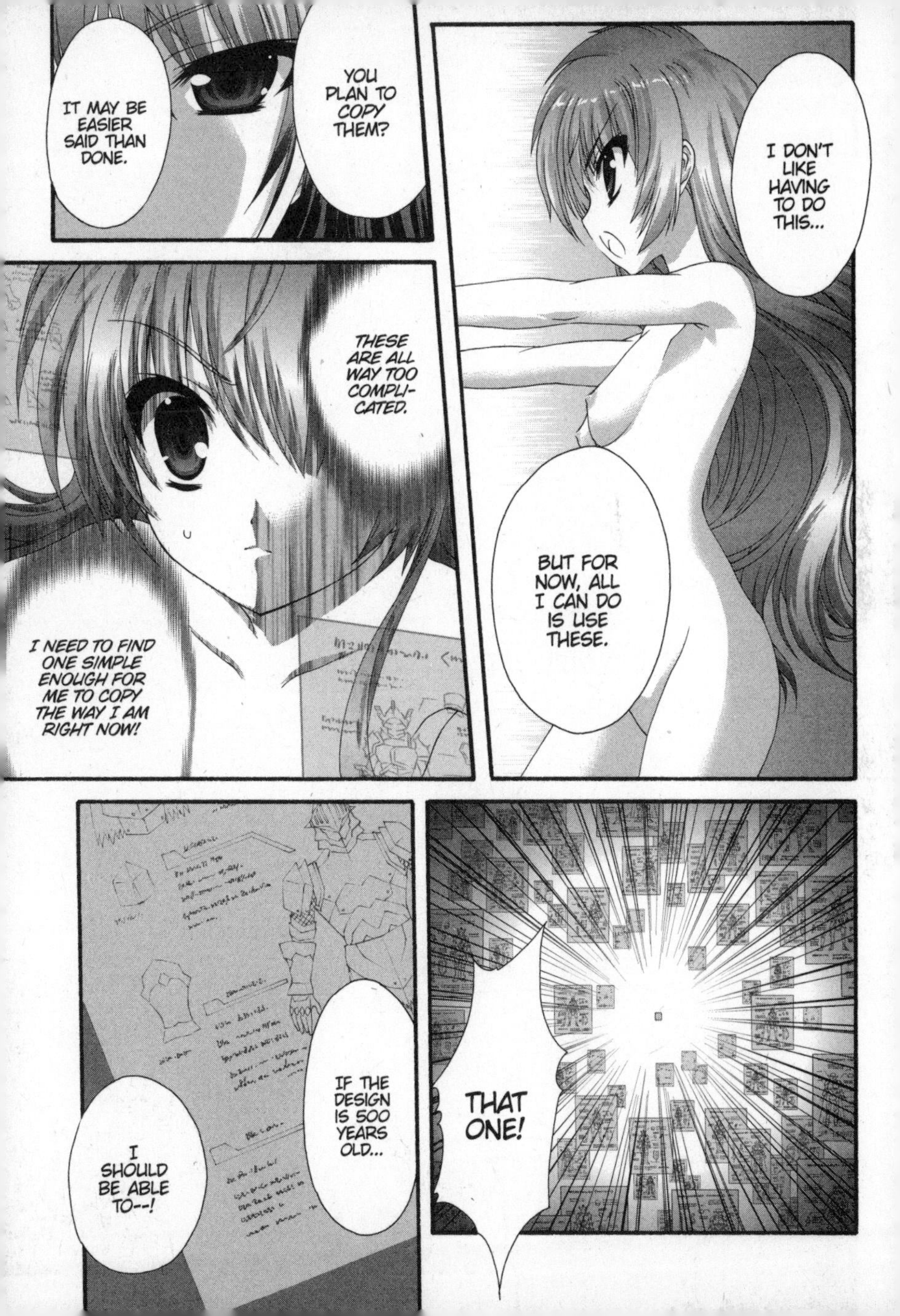
I DON'T LIKE HAVING TO DO THIS...
BUT FOR NOW, ALL I CAN DO IS USE THESE.
YOU PLAN TO COPY THEM?
IT MAY BE EASIER SAID THAN DONE.
THESE ARE ALL WAY TOO COMPLICATED.
I NEED TO FIND ONE SIMPLE ENOUGH FOR ME TO COPY THE WAY I AM RIGHT NOW!
THAT ONE!
IF THE DESIGN IS 500 YEARS OLD...
I SHOULD BE ABLE TO--!

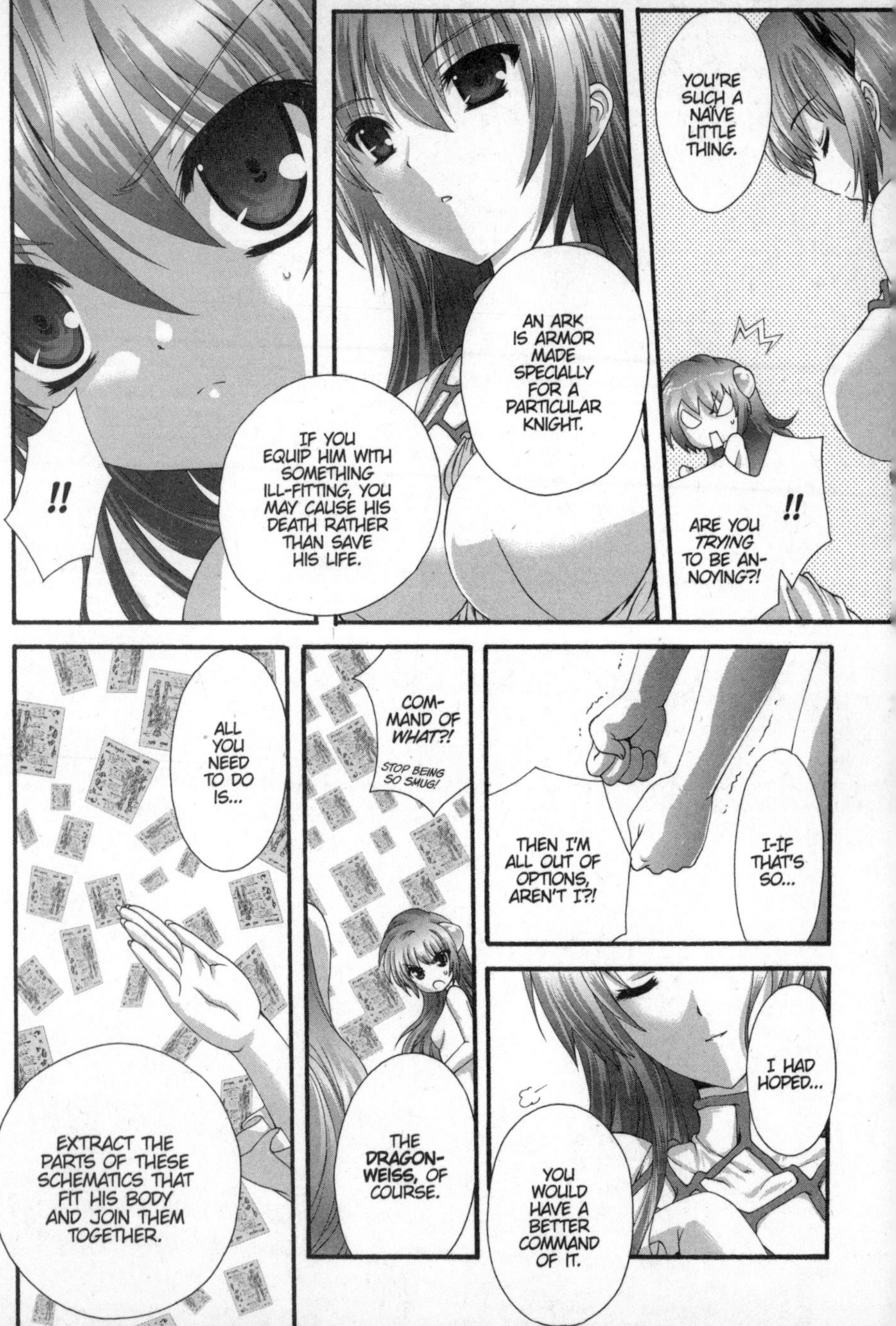
YOU'RE SUCH A NAÏVE LITTLE THING.
!!
ARE YOU *TRYING* TO BE AN-NOYING?!
AN ARK IS ARMOR MADE SPECIALLY FOR A PARTICULAR KNIGHT.
IF YOU EQUIP HIM WITH SOMETHING ILL-FITTING, YOU MAY CAUSE HIS DEATH RATHER THAN SAVE HIS LIFE.
!!
I-IF THAT'S SO...
THEN I'M ALL OUT OF OPTIONS, AREN'T I?!
I HAD HOPED...
YOU WOULD HAVE A BETTER COMMAND OF IT.
COM-MAND OF *WHAT?!*
STOP BEING SO SMUG!
THE DRAGON-WEISS, OF COURSE.
ALL YOU NEED TO DO IS...
EXTRACT THE PARTS OF THESE SCHEMATICS THAT FIT HIS BODY AND JOIN THEM TOGETHER.

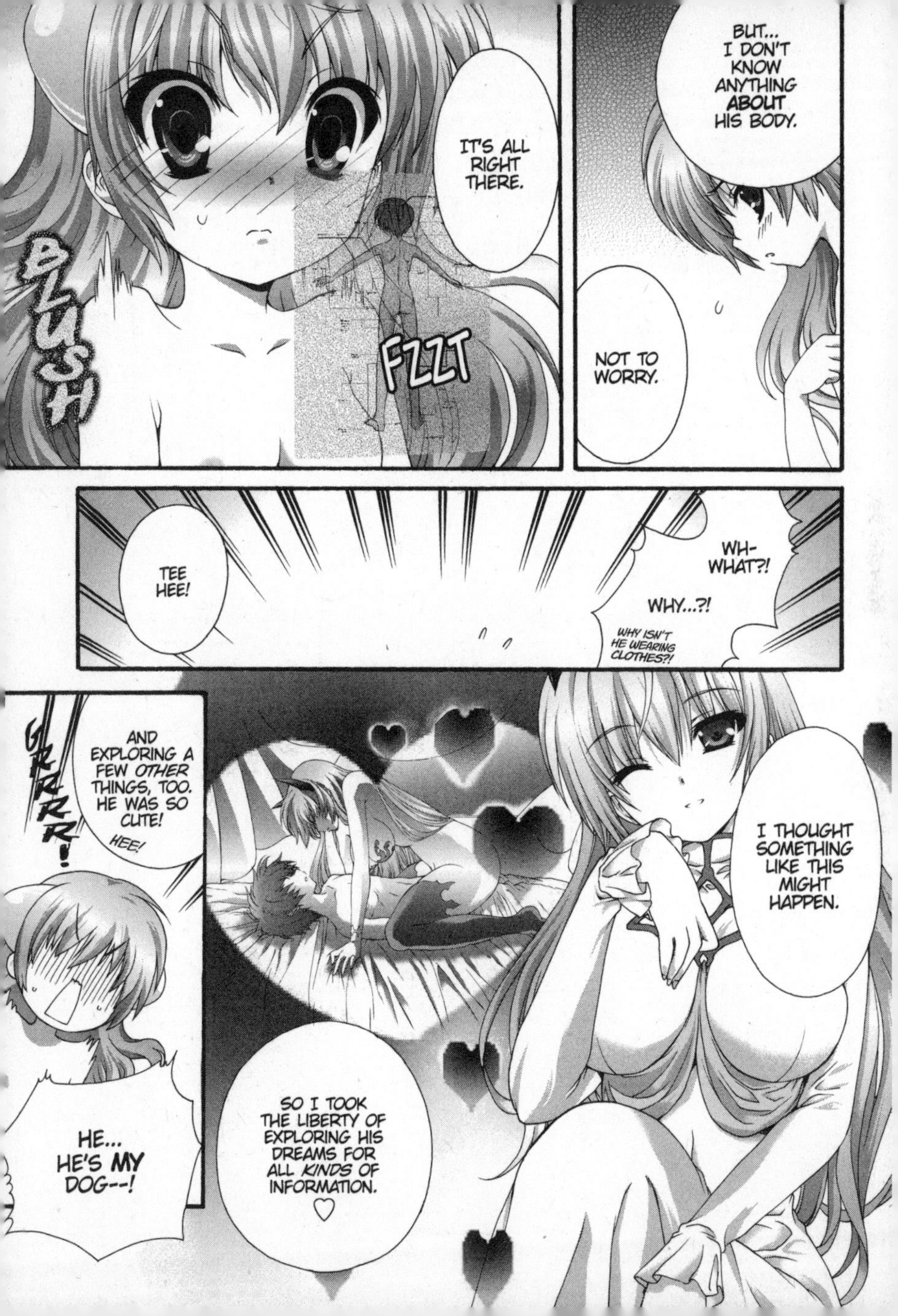
BUT... I DON'T KNOW ANYTHING ABOUT HIS BODY.
NOT TO WORRY.
IT'S ALL RIGHT THERE.
FZZT
BLUSH
WH- WHAT?!
WHY...?!
WHY ISN'T HE WEARING CLOTHES?!
TEE HEE!
I THOUGHT SOMETHING LIKE THIS MIGHT HAPPEN.
SO I TOOK THE LIBERTY OF EXPLORING HIS DREAMS FOR ALL KINDS OF INFORMATION. ♡
AND EXPLORING A FEW OTHER THINGS, TOO. HE WAS SO CUTE!
HEE!
GRRRRR!
HE... HE'S MY DOG--!

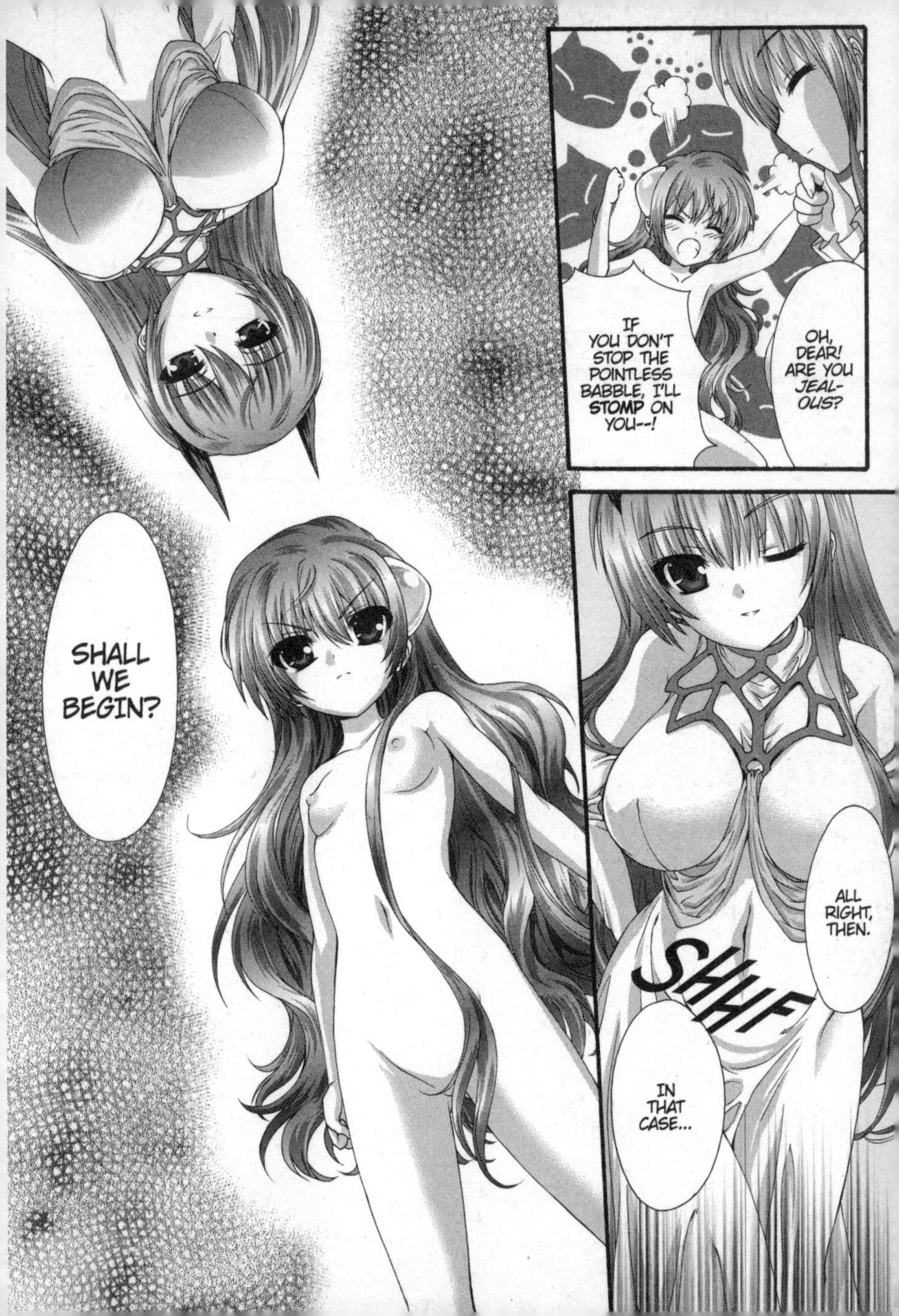
OH, DEAR! ARE YOU JEAL-OUS?
IF YOU DON'T STOP THE POINTLESS BABBLE, I'LL STOMP ON YOU--!
ALL RIGHT, THEN.
SHHF
IN THAT CASE...
SHALL WE BEGIN?

ASH!!!
WHAM
SORRY, PRINCESS.
COUGH!
THAT WAS MY FIFTH TRY.
IF I CAN'T DO THIS, ECO WILL--!
DON'T GIVE UP!!!
DON'T FORGET SHE'S A DRAGON!
HAVE FAITH IN HER, THE WAY I DO IN LANCELOT!!
PRIN-CESS...

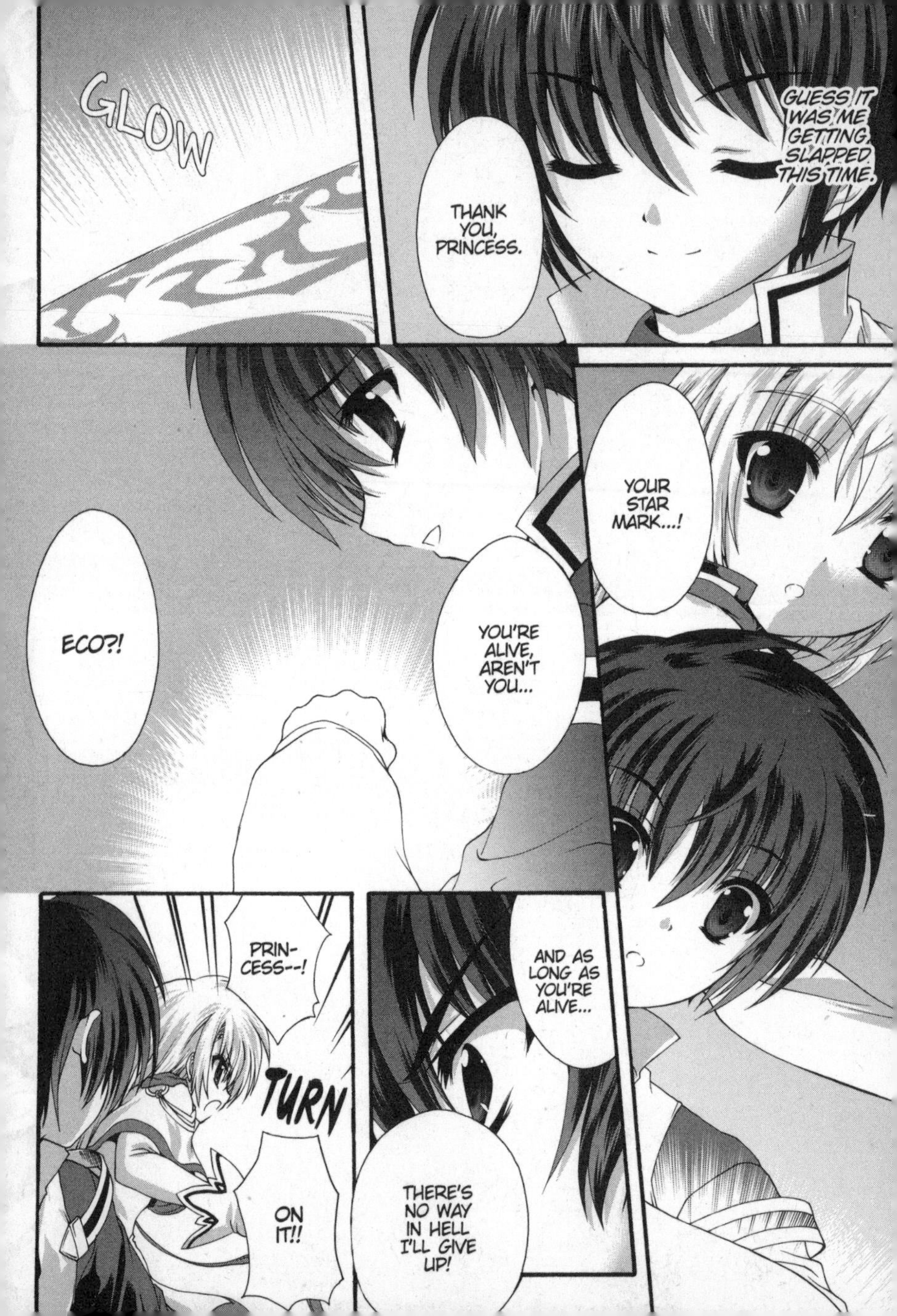
GUESS IT WAS ME GETTING SLAPPED THIS TIME.
THANK YOU, PRINCESS.
GLOW
YOUR STAR MARK...!
YOU'RE ALIVE, AREN'T YOU...
ECO?!
AND AS LONG AS YOU'RE ALIVE...
THERE'S NO WAY IN HELL I'LL GIVE UP!
PRIN-CESS--!
TURN
ON IT!!

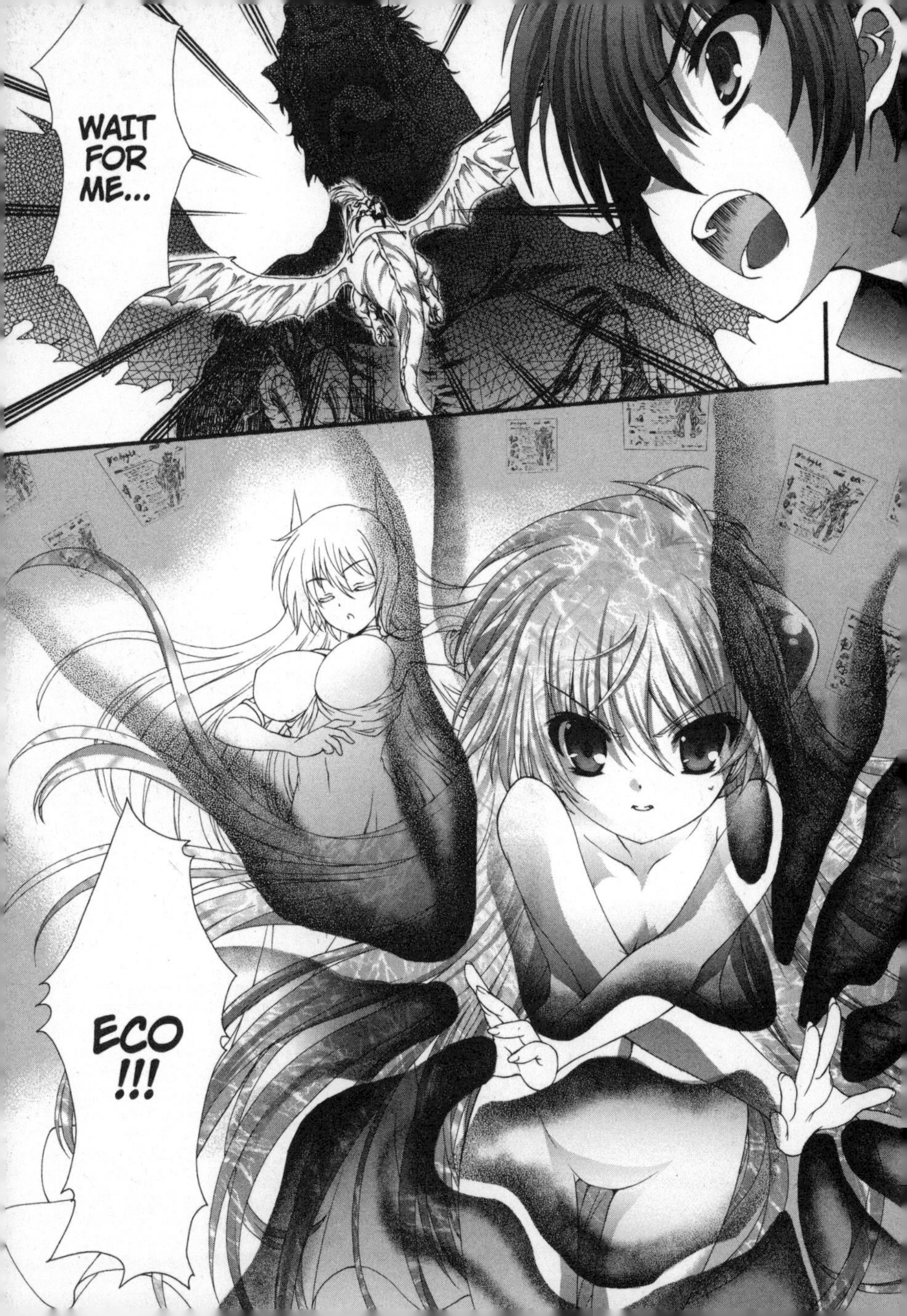
WAIT FOR ME...
ECO !!!

星刻の竜騎士

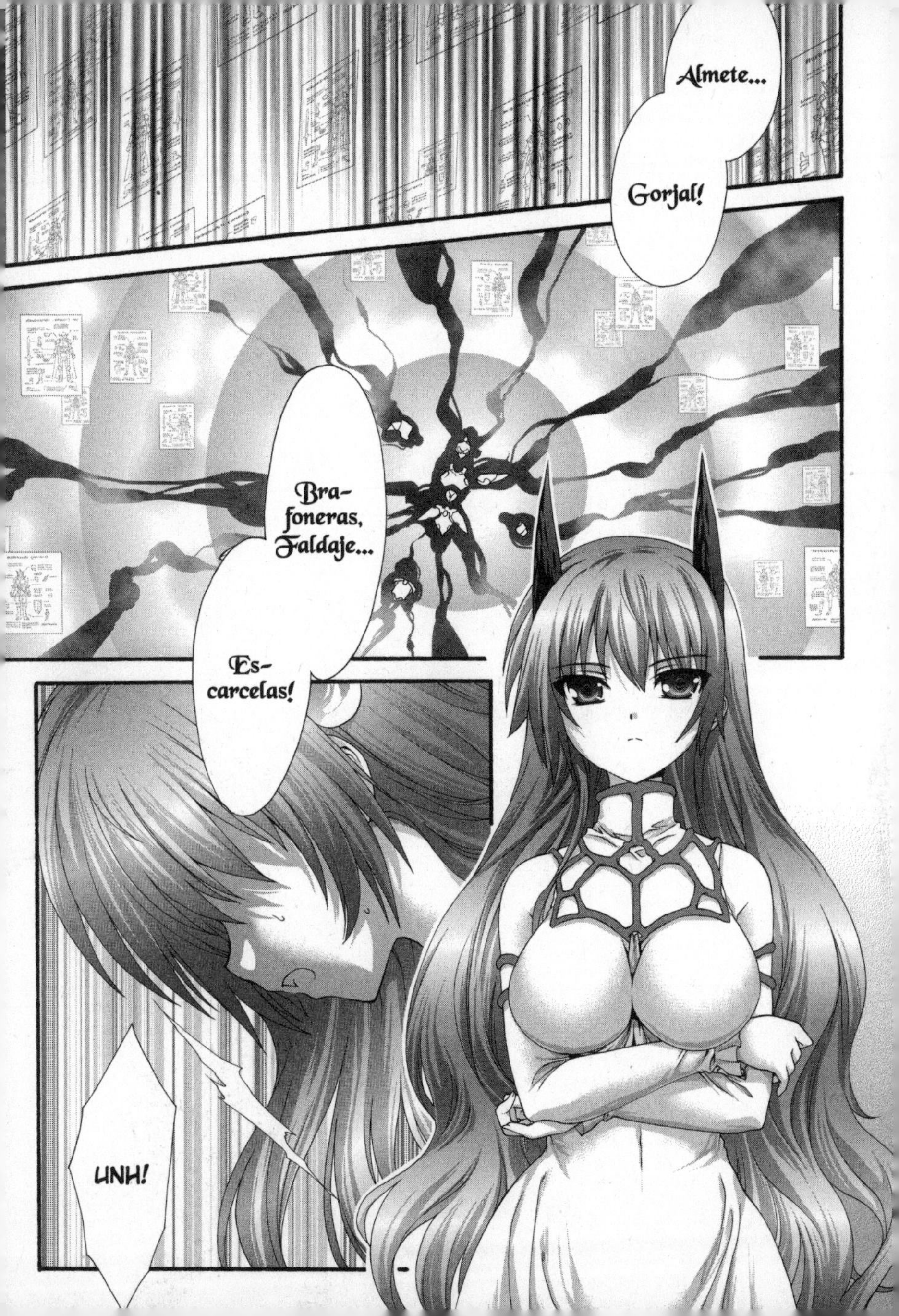
Almete...
Gorjal!
Bra-foneras, Faldaje...
Es-carcelas!
UNH!

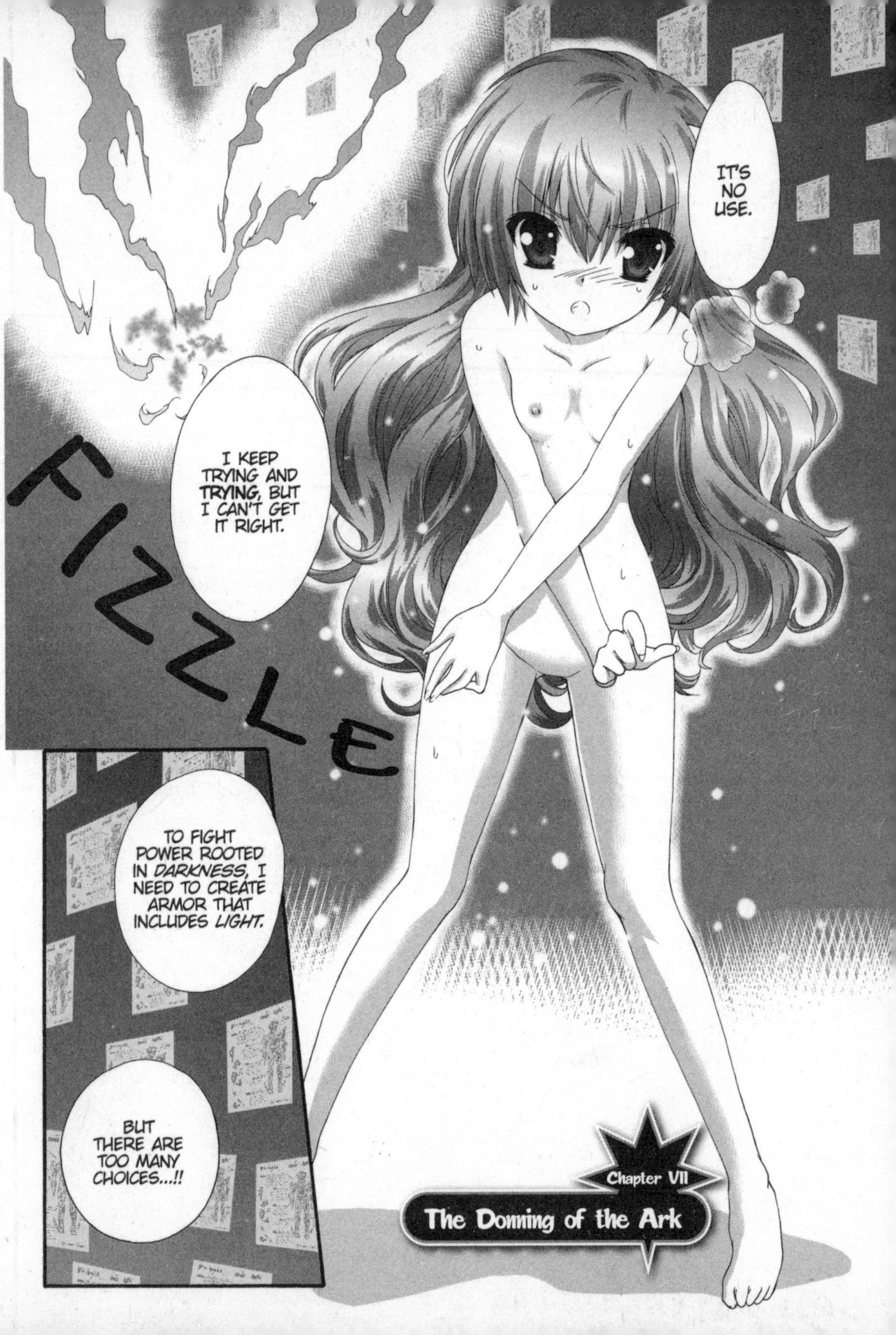
IT'S NO USE.
I KEEP TRYING AND TRYING, BUT I CAN'T GET IT RIGHT.
FIZZLE
TO FIGHT POWER ROOTED IN *DARKNESS*, I NEED TO CREATE ARMOR THAT INCLUDES *LIGHT*.
BUT THERE ARE TOO MANY CHOICES...!!
Chapter VII
The Donning of the Ark

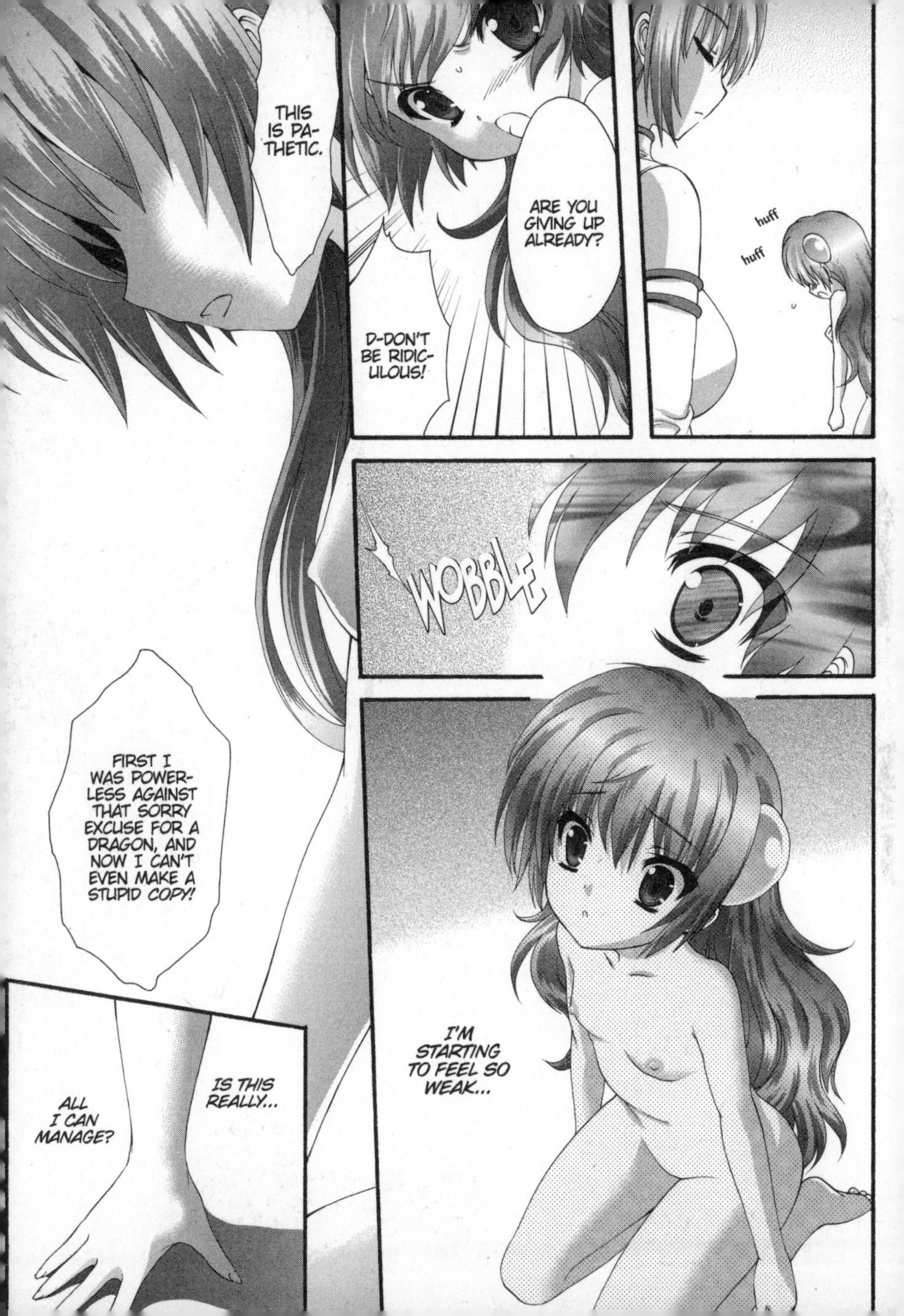
huff
huff
ARE YOU GIVING UP ALREADY?
D-DON'T BE RIDIC-ULOUS!
WOBBLE
I'M STARTING TO FEEL SO WEAK...
THIS IS PA-THETIC.
FIRST I WAS POWER-LESS AGAINST THAT SORRY EXCUSE FOR A DRAGON, AND NOW I CAN'T EVEN MAKE A STUPID COPY!
IS THIS REALLY...
ALL I CAN MANAGE?

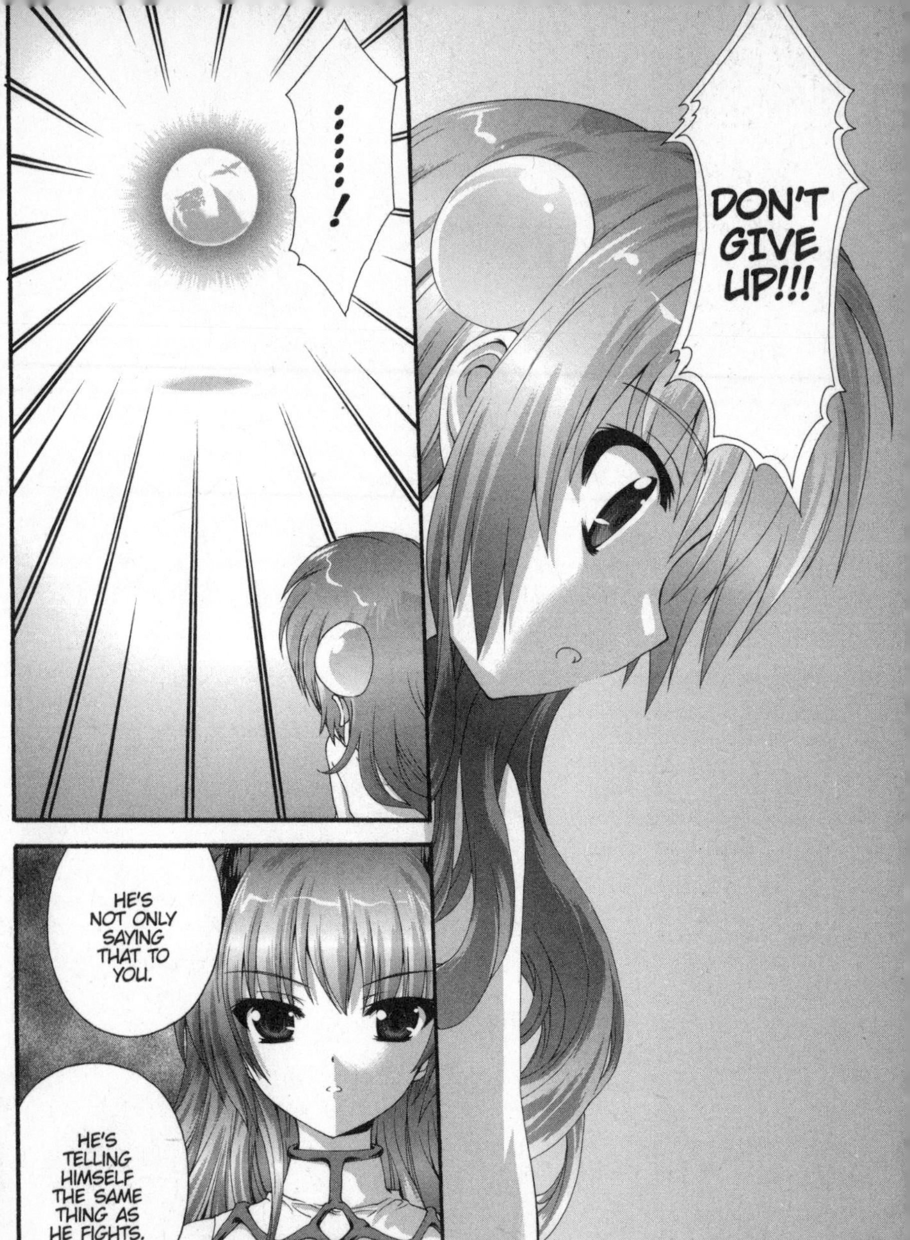
DON'T GIVE UP!!!
......!
HE'S NOT ONLY SAYING THAT TO YOU.
HE'S TELLING HIMSELF THE SAME THING AS HE FIGHTS.

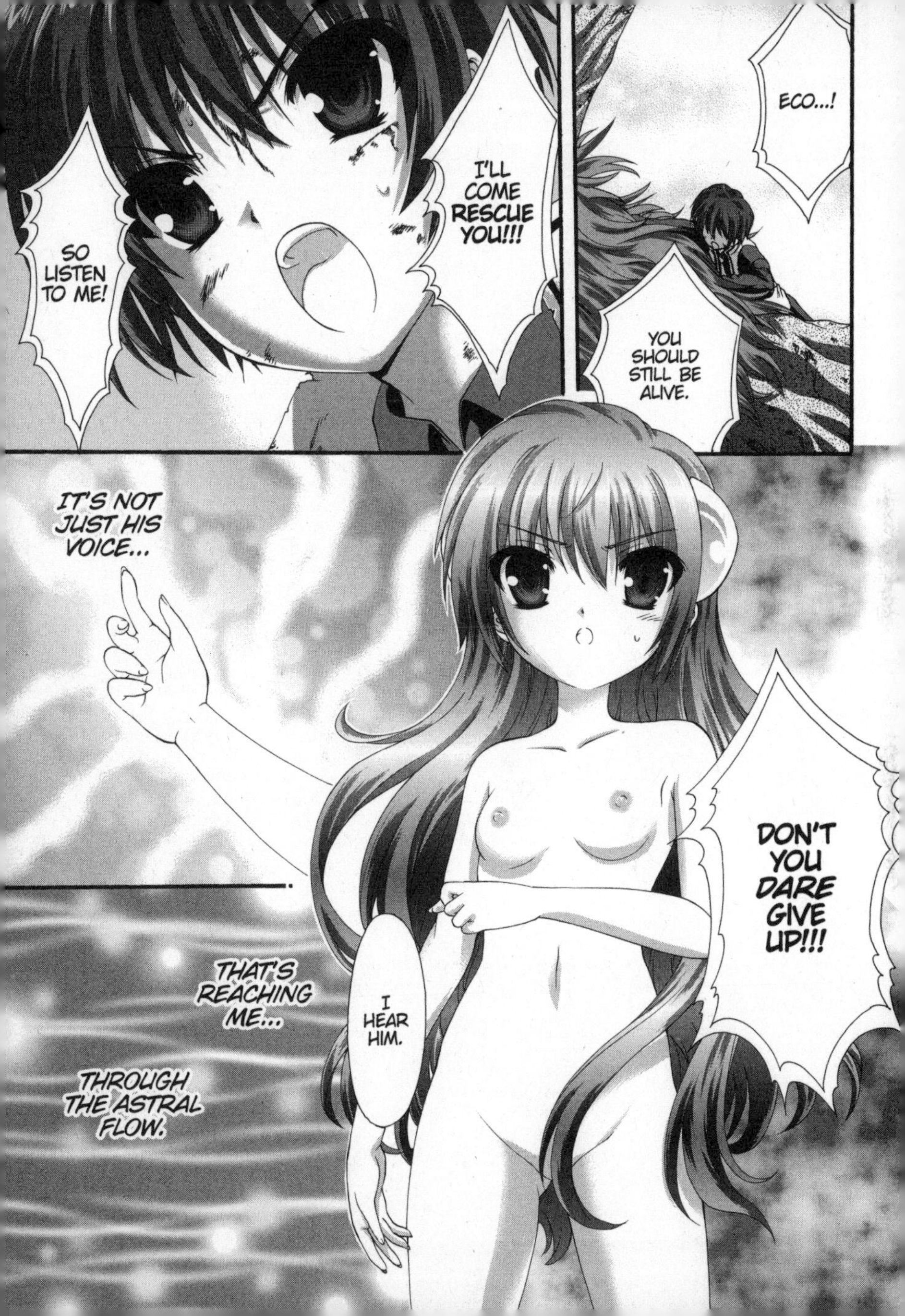
ECO...!
YOU SHOULD STILL BE ALIVE.
I'LL COME RESCUE YOU!!!
SO LISTEN TO ME!
DON'T YOU DARE GIVE UP!!!
I HEAR HIM.
IT'S NOT JUST HIS VOICE...
THAT'S REACHING ME...
THROUGH THE ASTRAL FLOW.

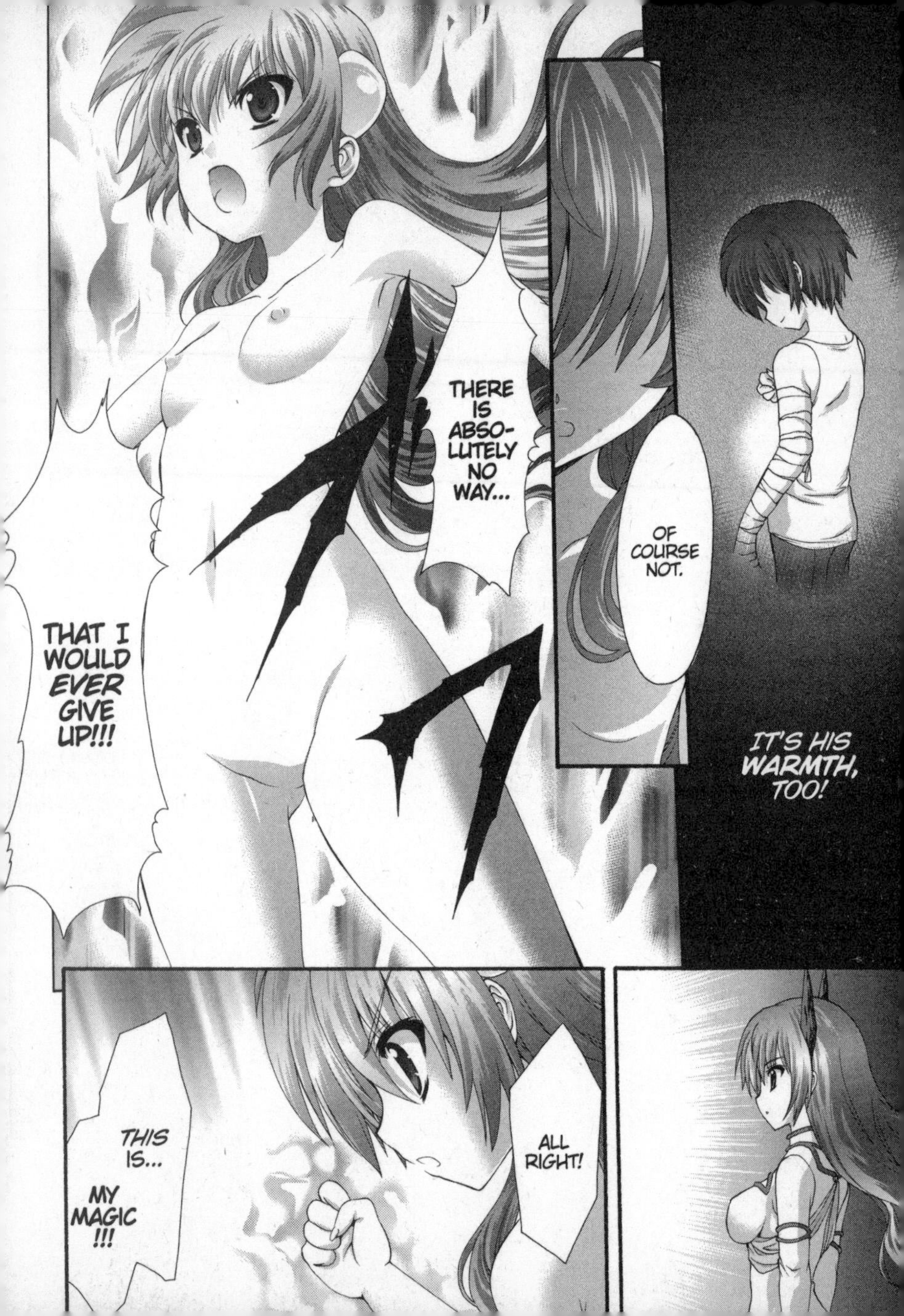
IT'S HIS WARMTH, TOO!
OF COURSE NOT.
THERE IS ABSOLUTELY NO WAY...
THAT I WOULD EVER GIVE UP!!!
ALL RIGHT!
THIS IS... MY MAGIC!!!

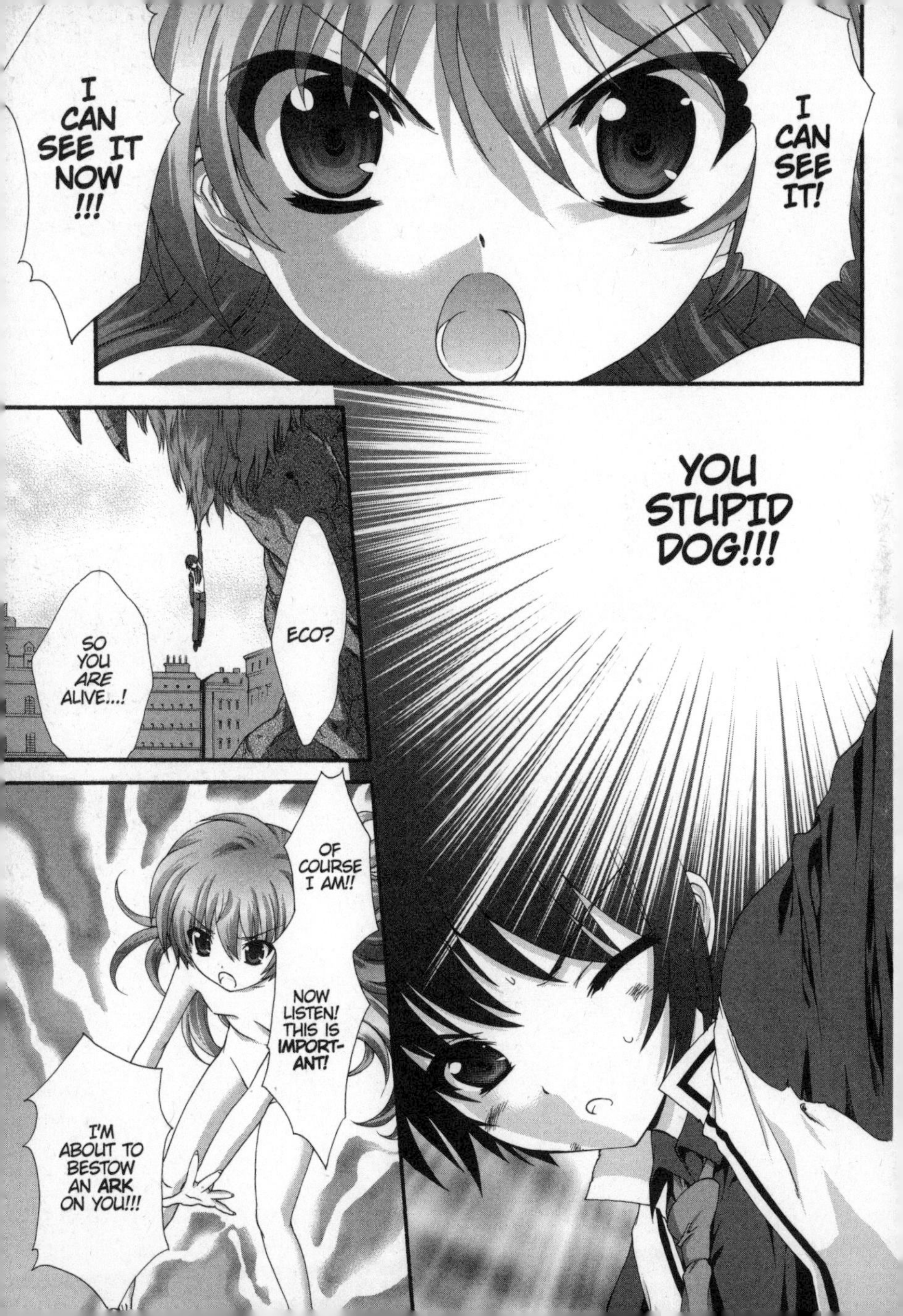
I CAN SEE IT!
I CAN SEE IT NOW!!!
YOU STUPID DOG!!!
ECO?
SO YOU ARE ALIVE...!
OF COURSE I AM!!
NOW LISTEN! THIS IS IMPORT-ANT!
I'M ABOUT TO BESTOW AN ARK ON YOU!!!

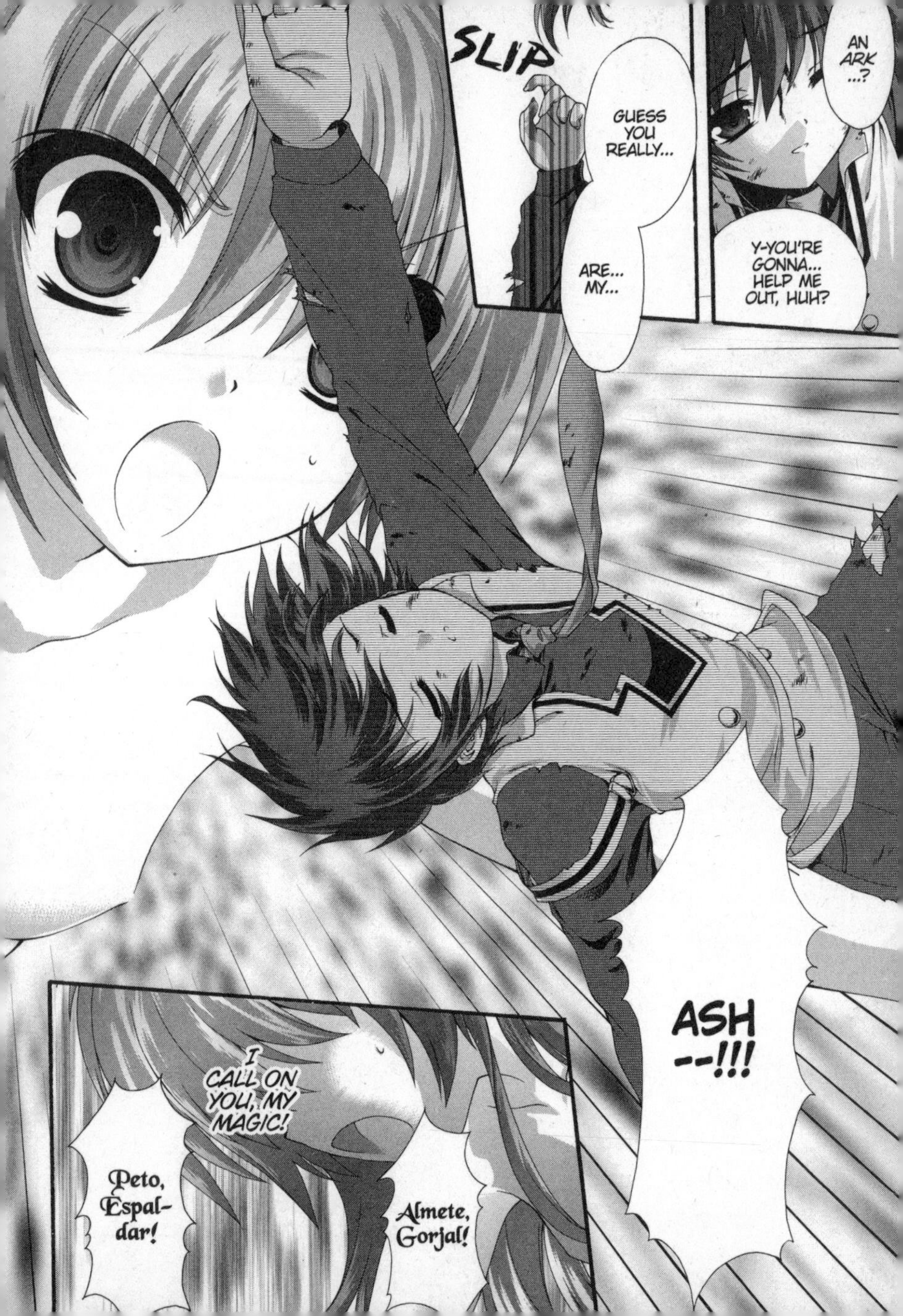
AN ARK ...?
Y-YOU'RE GONNA... HELP ME OUT, HUH?
SLIP
GUESS YOU REALLY...
ARE... MY...
ASH --!!!
I CALL ON YOU, MY MAGIC!
Almete, Gorjal!
Peto, Espal-dar!

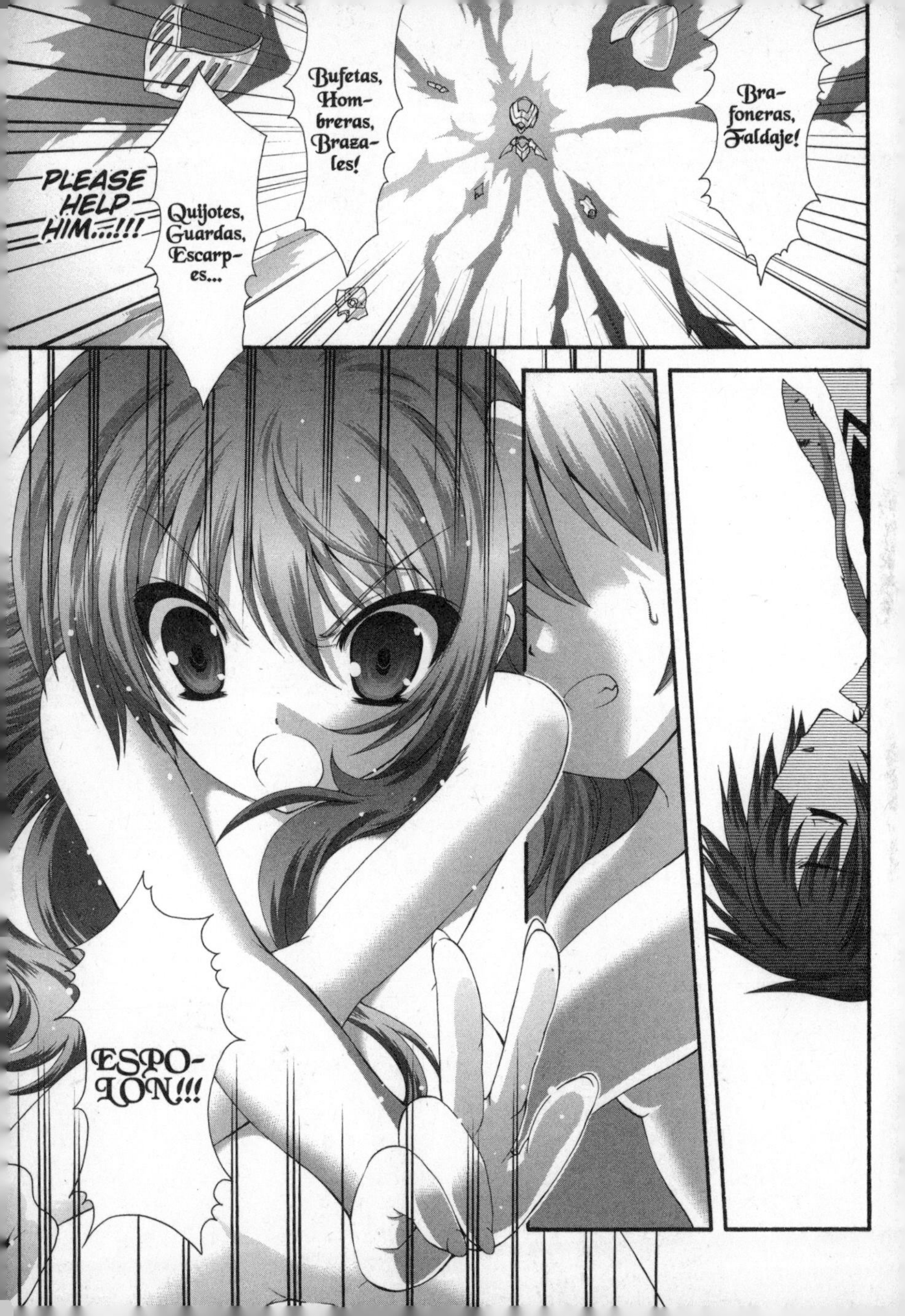
Bra-foneras, Faldaje!
Bufetas, Hombreras, Brazales!
Quijotes, Guardas, Escarpes...
PLEASE HELP HIM...!!!
ESPOLON!!!

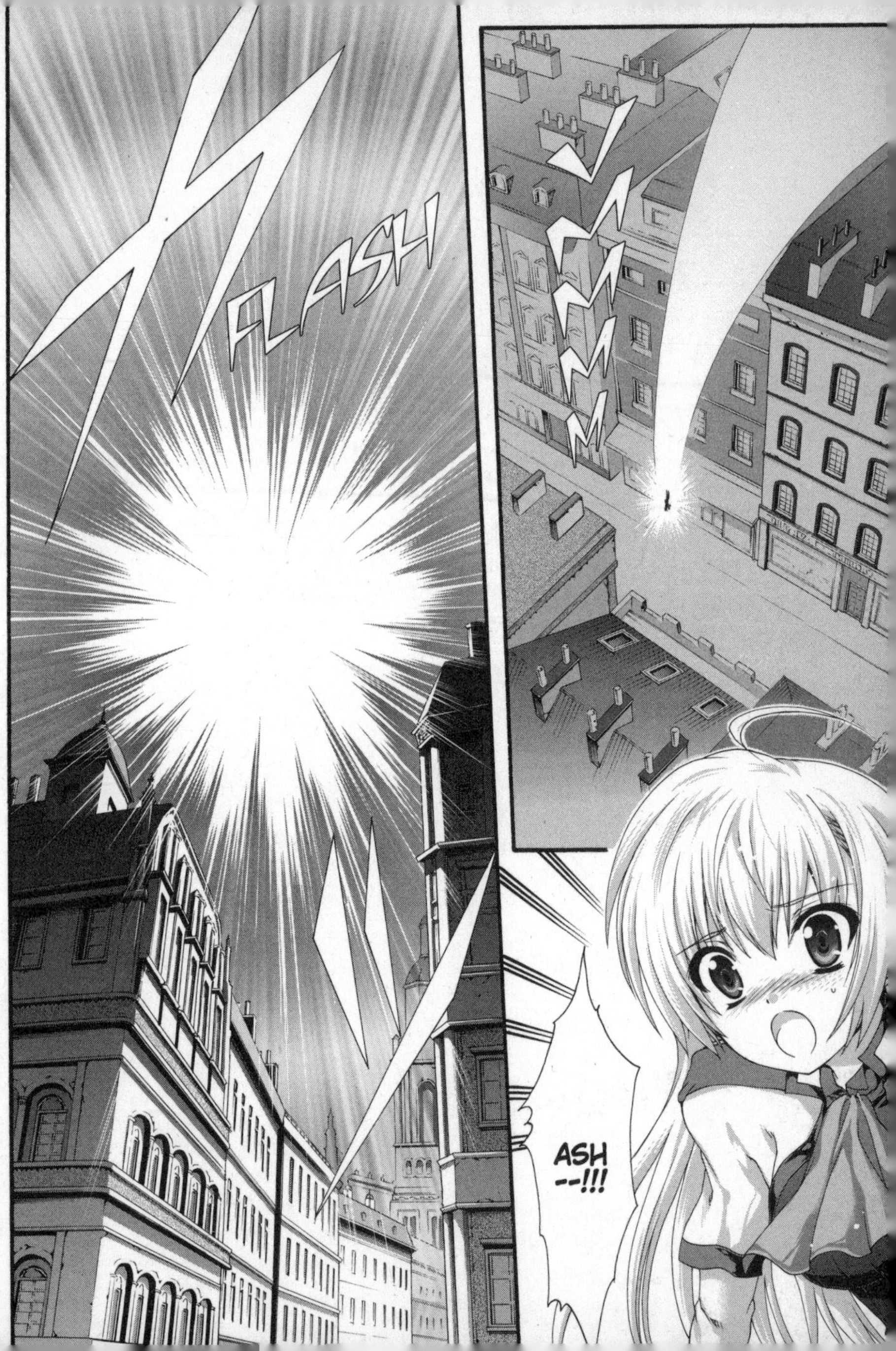
ASH
--!!!
FLASH

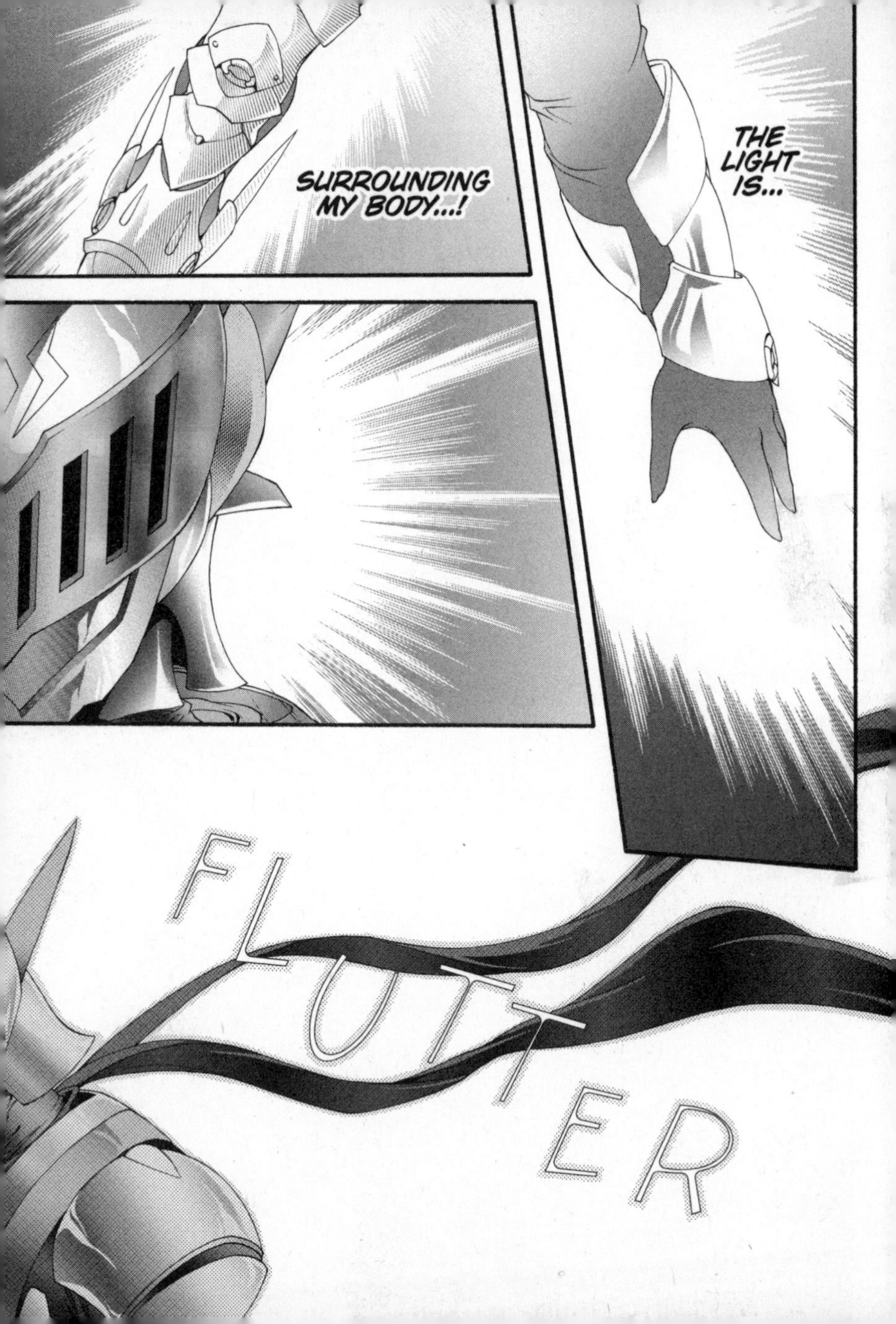
THE LIGHT IS...
SURROUNDING MY BODY...!
FLUTTER

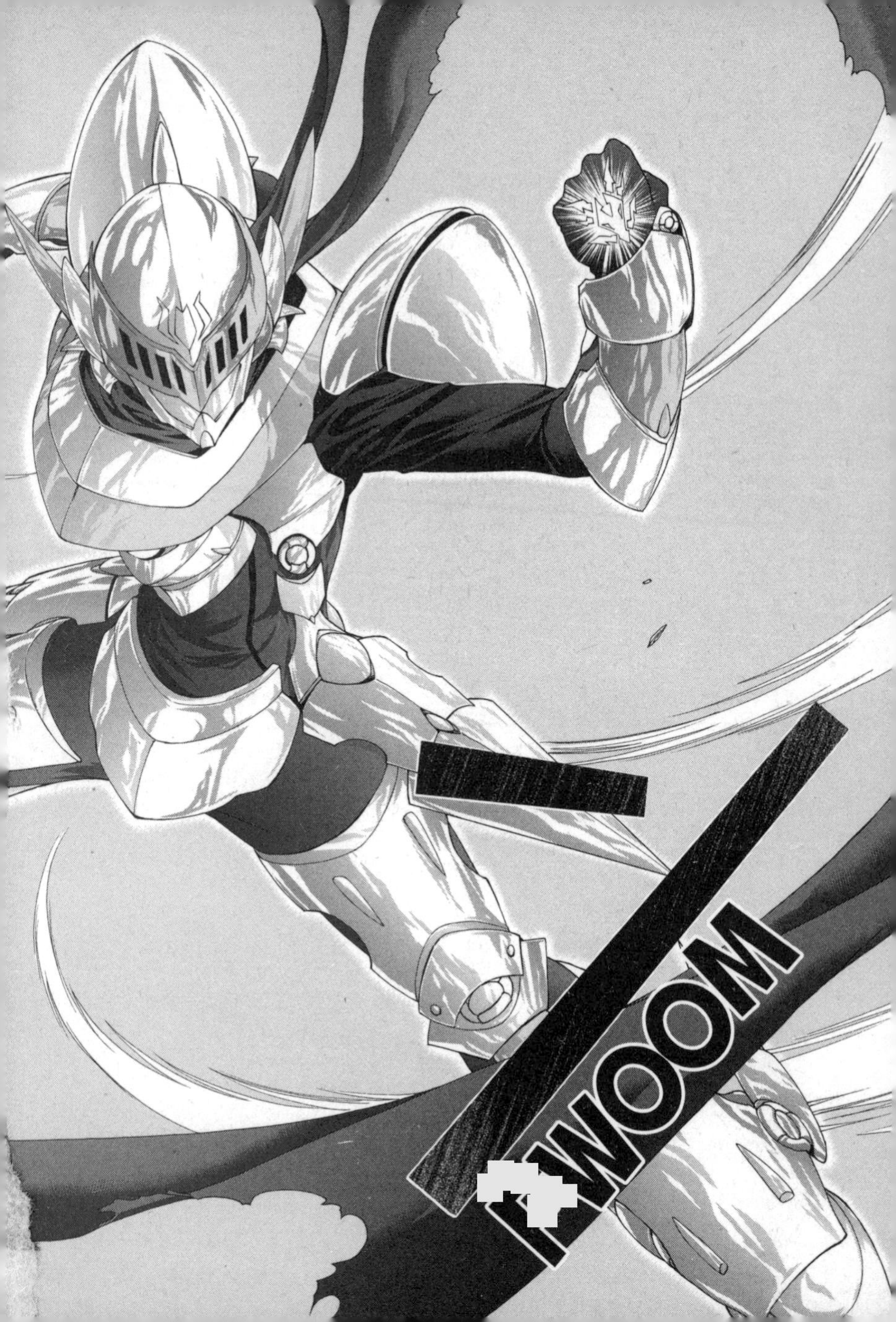
WOOM

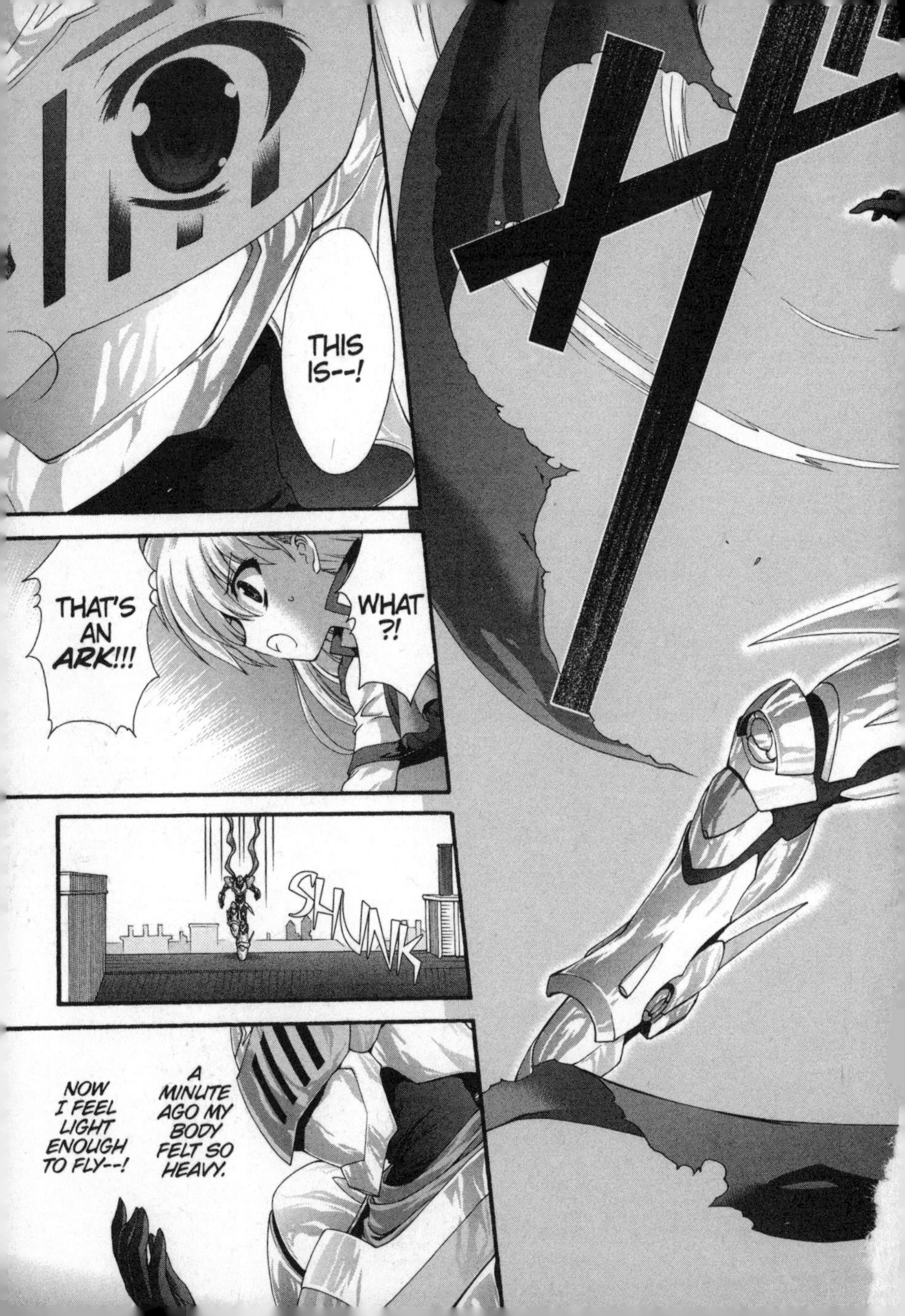
THIS IS--!
WHAT?!
THAT'S AN ARK!!!
SHUNK
A MINUTE AGO MY BODY FELT SO HEAVY.
NOW I FEEL LIGHT ENOUGH TO FLY--!

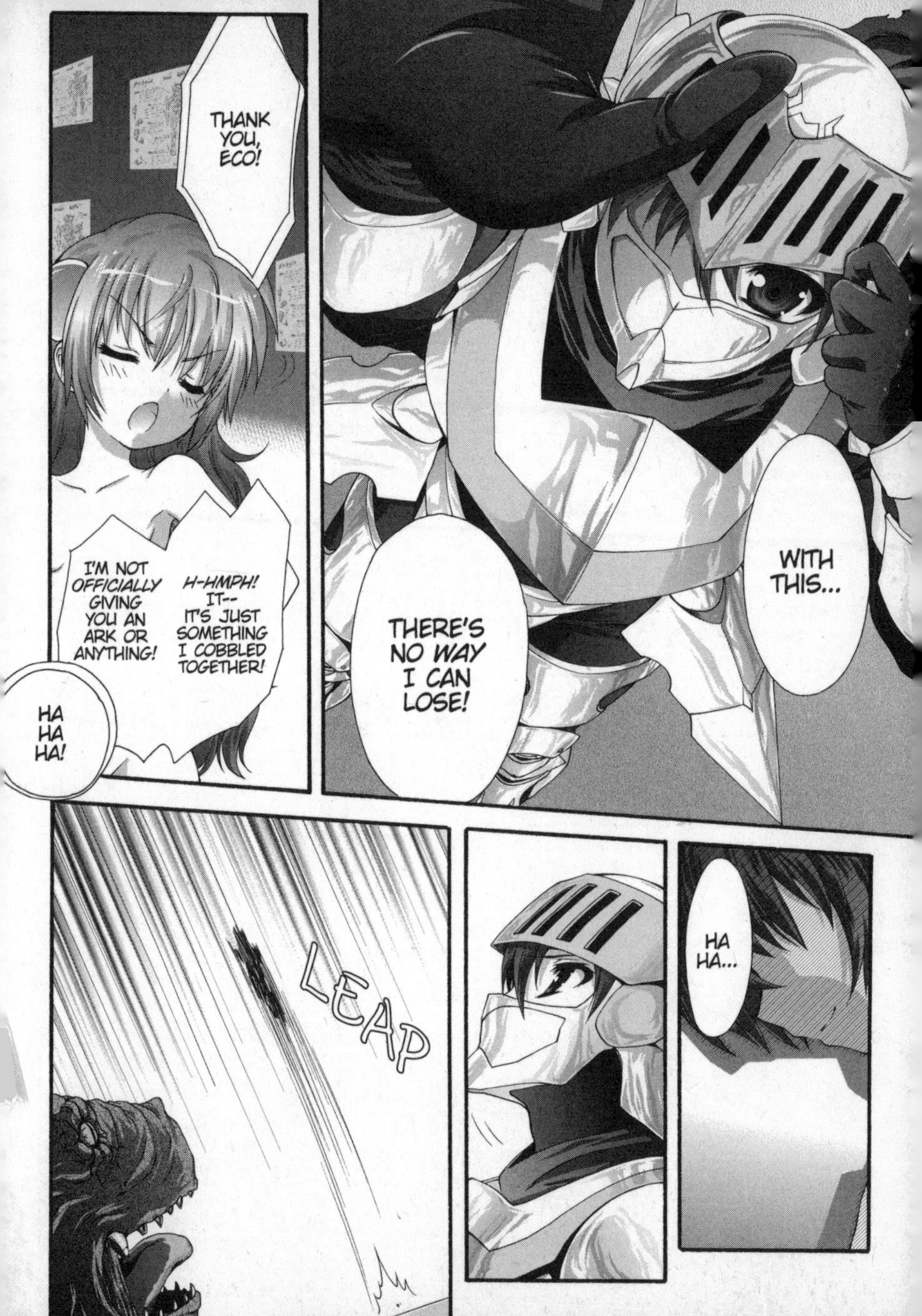
WITH THIS...
THERE'S NO WAY I CAN LOSE!
THANK YOU, ECO!
H-HMPH! IT-- IT'S JUST SOMETHING I COBBLED TOGETHER!
I'M NOT OFFICIALLY GIVING YOU AN ARK OR ANYTHING!
HA HA HA!
HA HA...
LEAP

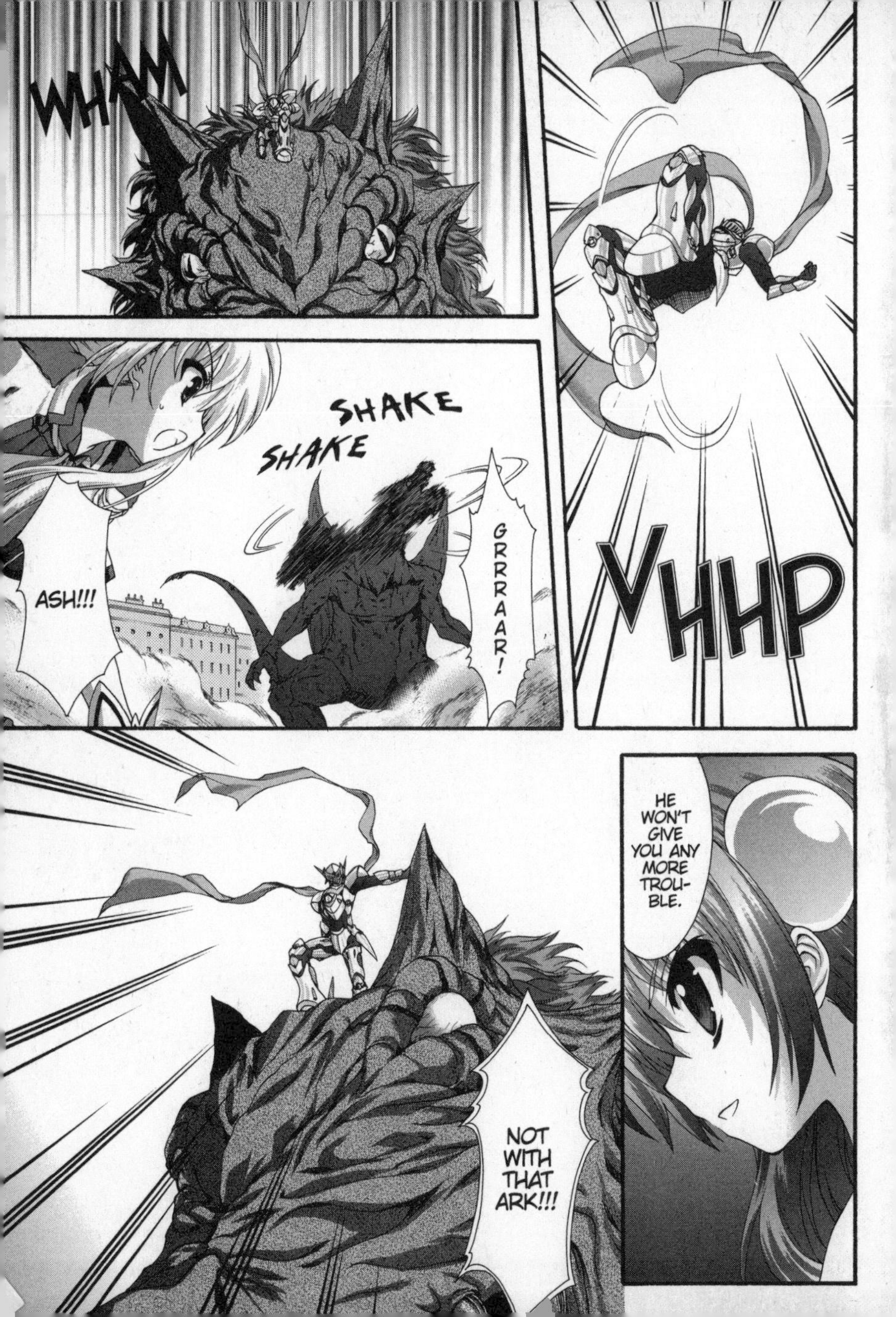
VHHP
WHAM
SHAKE
SHAKE
GRRRAAR!
ASH!!!
HE WON'T GIVE YOU ANY MORE TROUBLE.
NOT WITH THAT ARK!!!

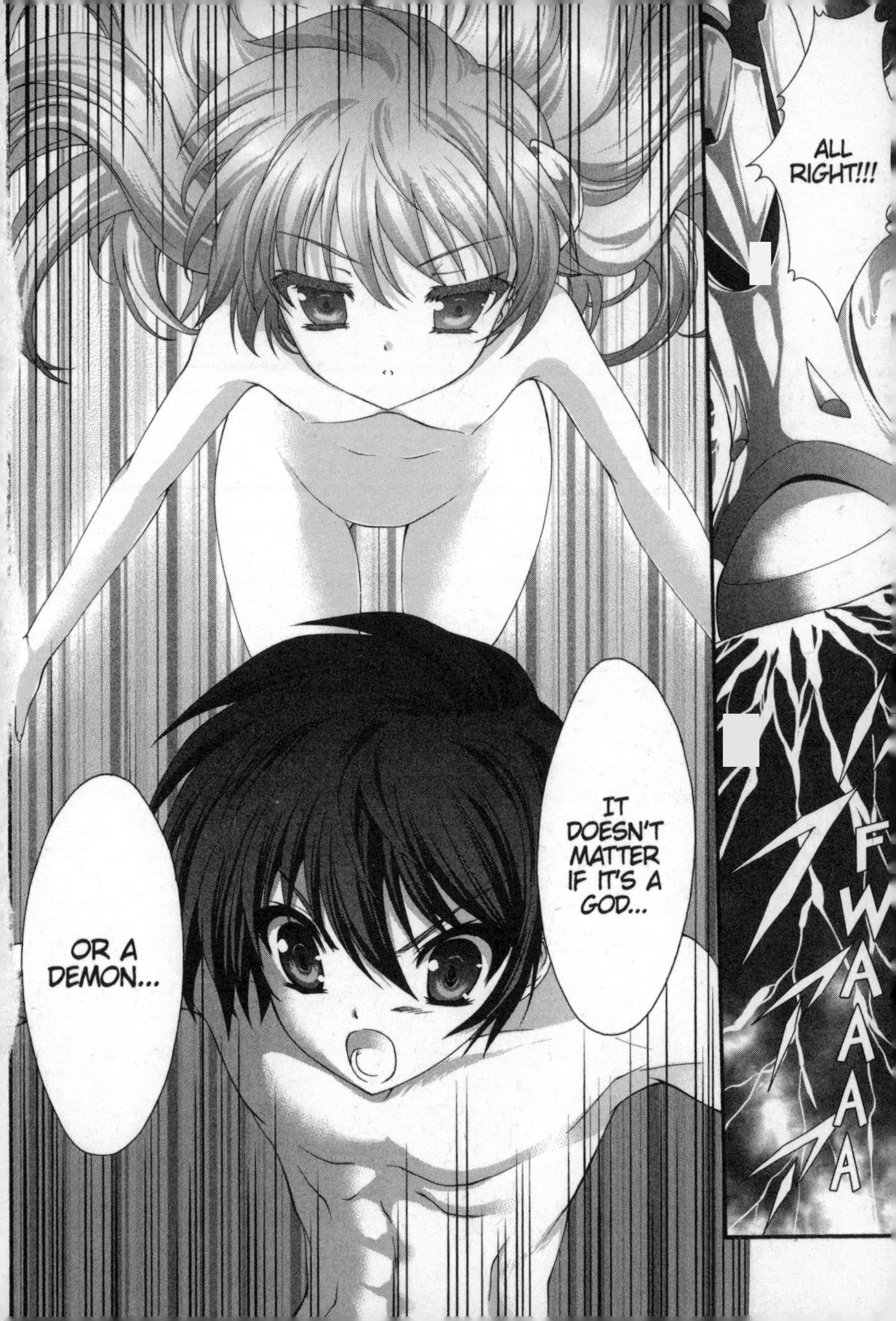
ALL RIGHT!!!
FWAAAA
IT DOESN'T MATTER IF IT'S A GOD...
OR A DEMON...

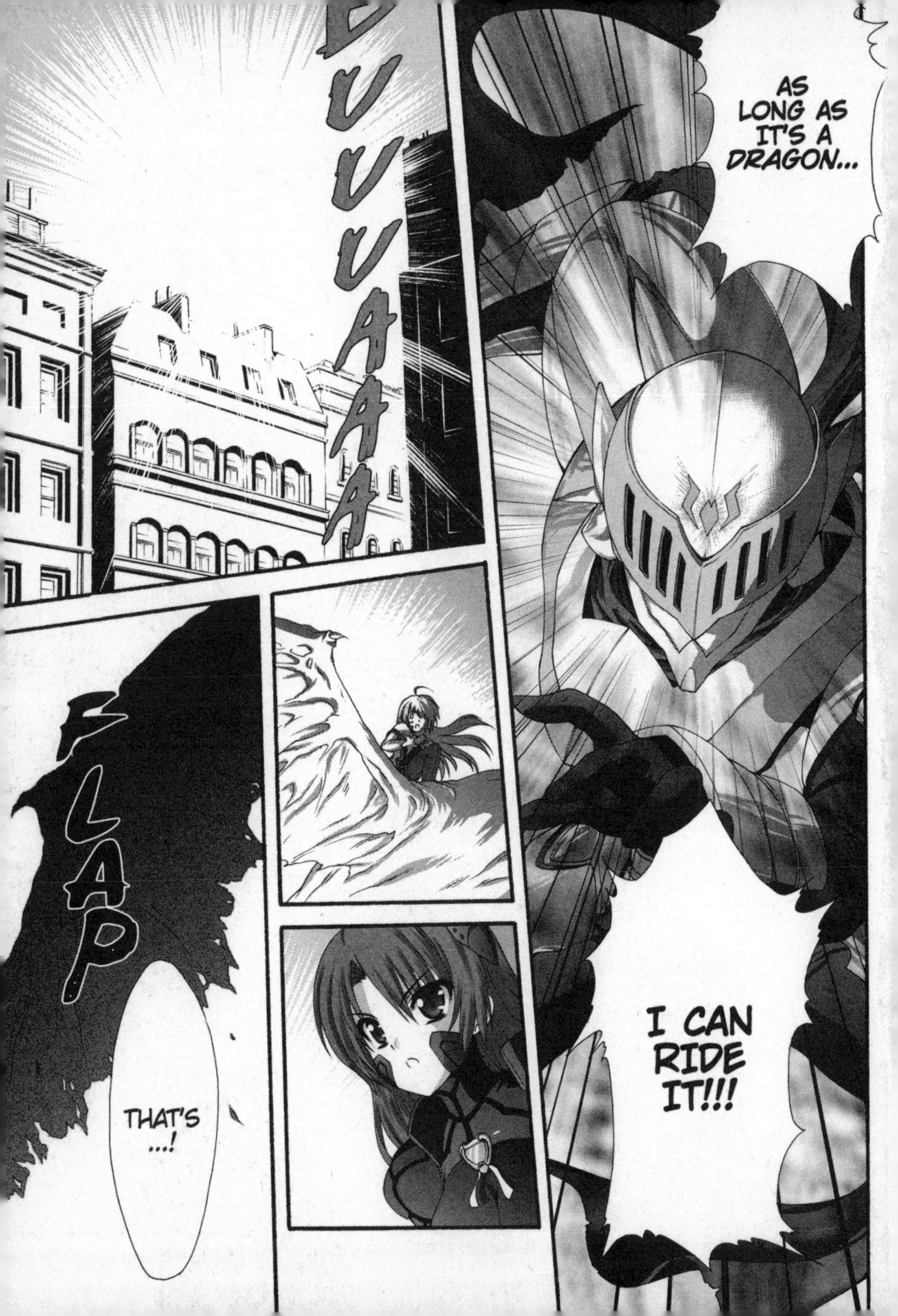
AS LONG AS IT'S A DRAGON...
I CAN RIDE IT!!!
DUUUAAA
FLAP
THAT'S ...!

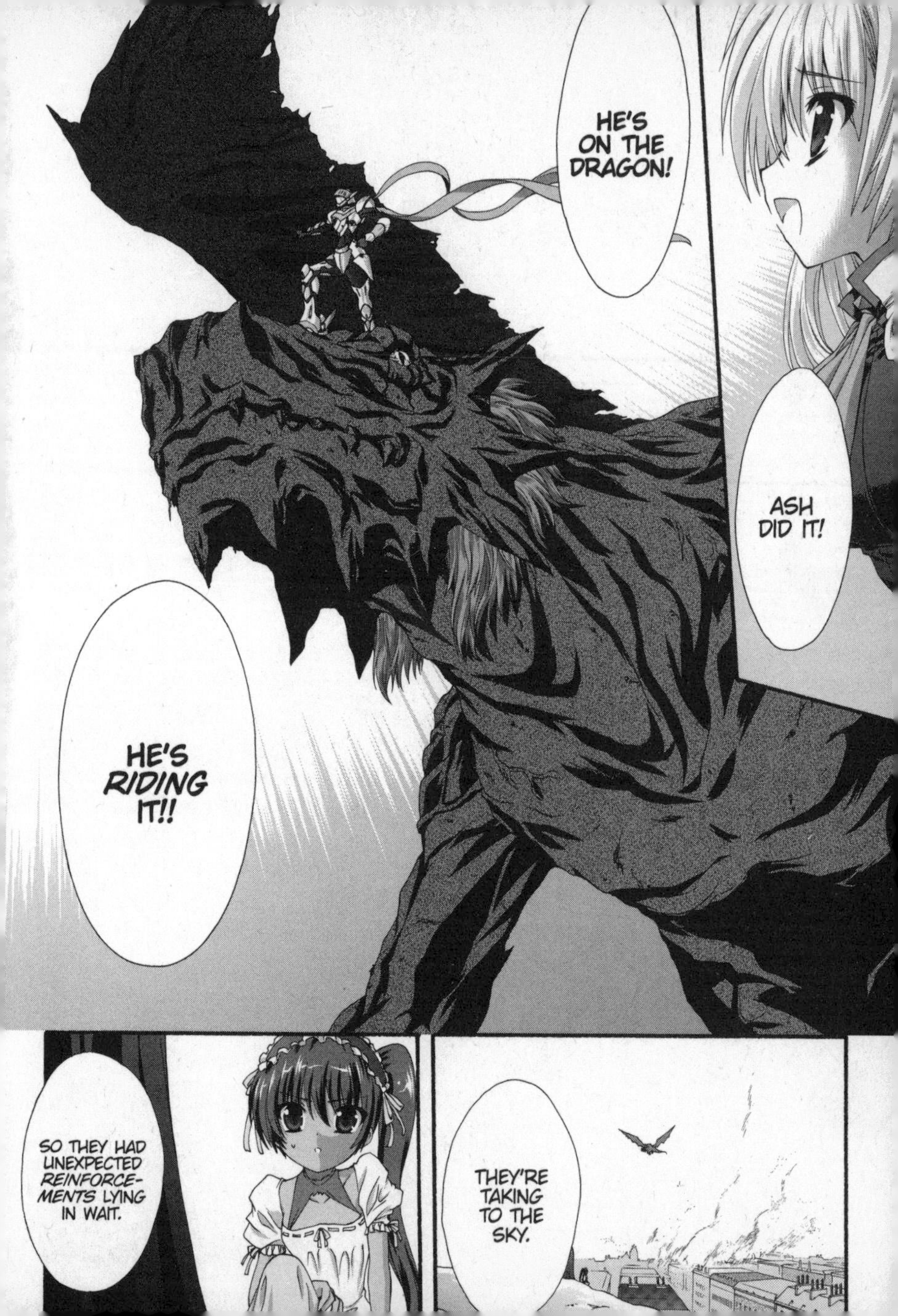
HE'S ON THE DRAGON!
ASH DID IT!
HE'S *RIDING* IT!!
THEY'RE TAKING TO THE SKY.
SO THEY HAD UNEXPECTED *REINFORCE-MENTS* LYING IN WAIT.

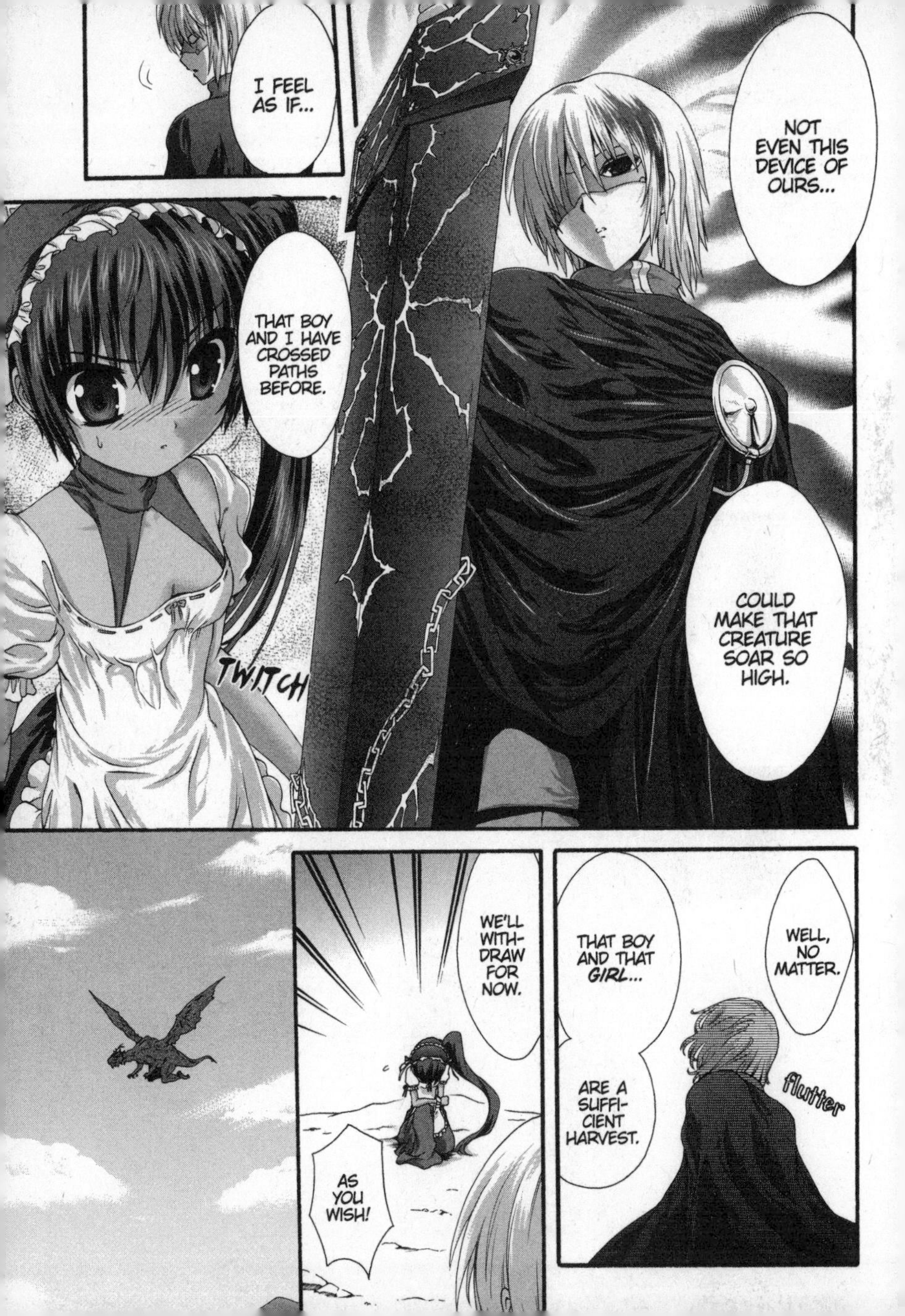
NOT EVEN THIS DEVICE OF OURS...
COULD MAKE THAT CREATURE SOAR SO HIGH.
I FEEL AS IF...
THAT BOY AND I HAVE CROSSED PATHS BEFORE.
TWITCH
WELL, NO MATTER.
THAT BOY AND THAT *GIRL*...
ARE A SUFFI-CIENT HARVEST.
flutter
WE'LL WITH-DRAW FOR NOW.
AS YOU WISH!

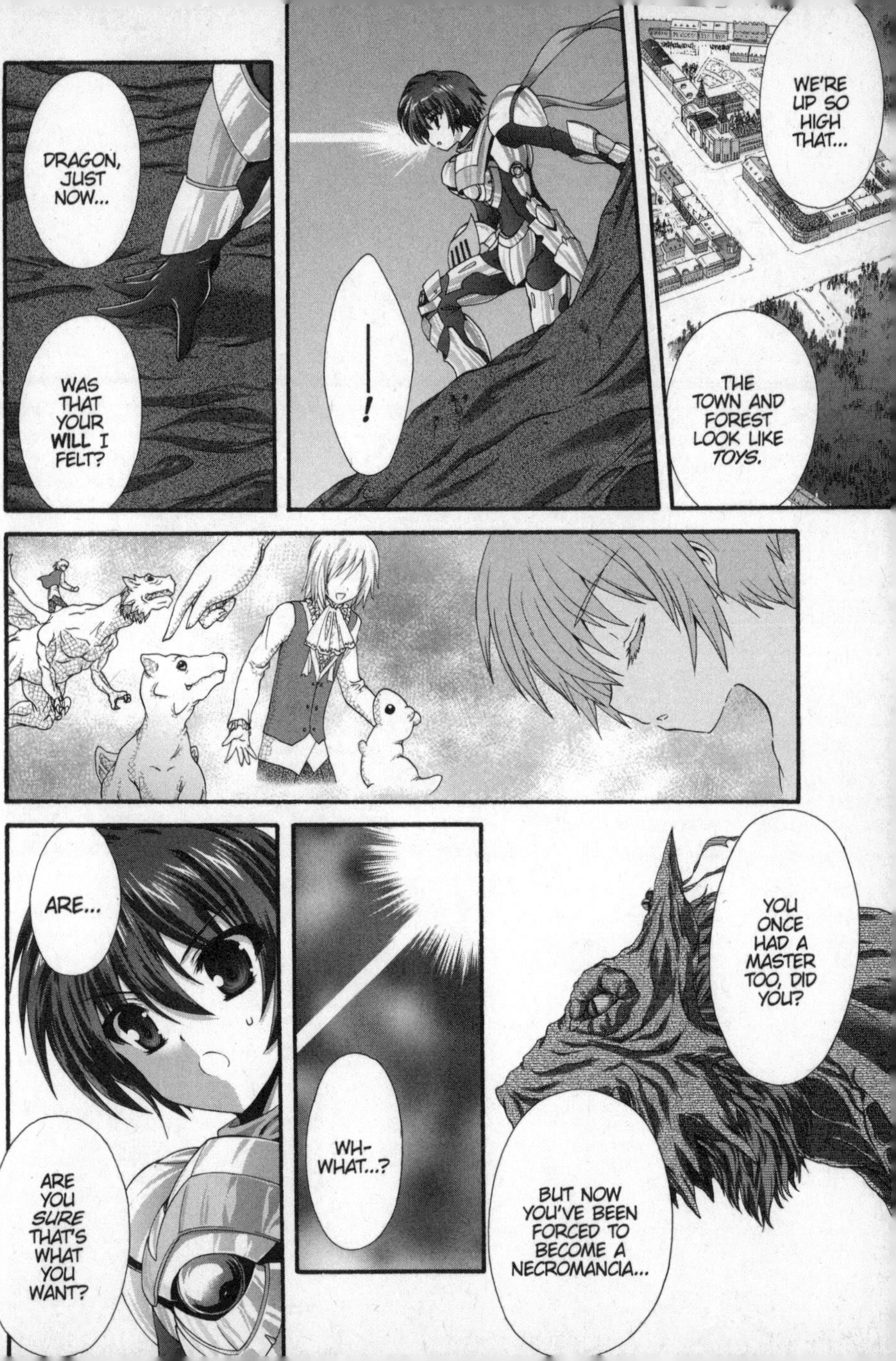
WE'RE UP SO HIGH THAT...
THE TOWN AND FOREST LOOK LIKE *TOYS.*
--!
DRAGON, JUST NOW...
WAS THAT YOUR WILL I FELT?
YOU ONCE HAD A MASTER TOO, DID YOU?
BUT NOW YOU'VE BEEN FORCED TO BECOME A NECROMANCIA...
WH-WHAT...?
ARE...
ARE YOU *SURE* THAT'S WHAT YOU WANT?

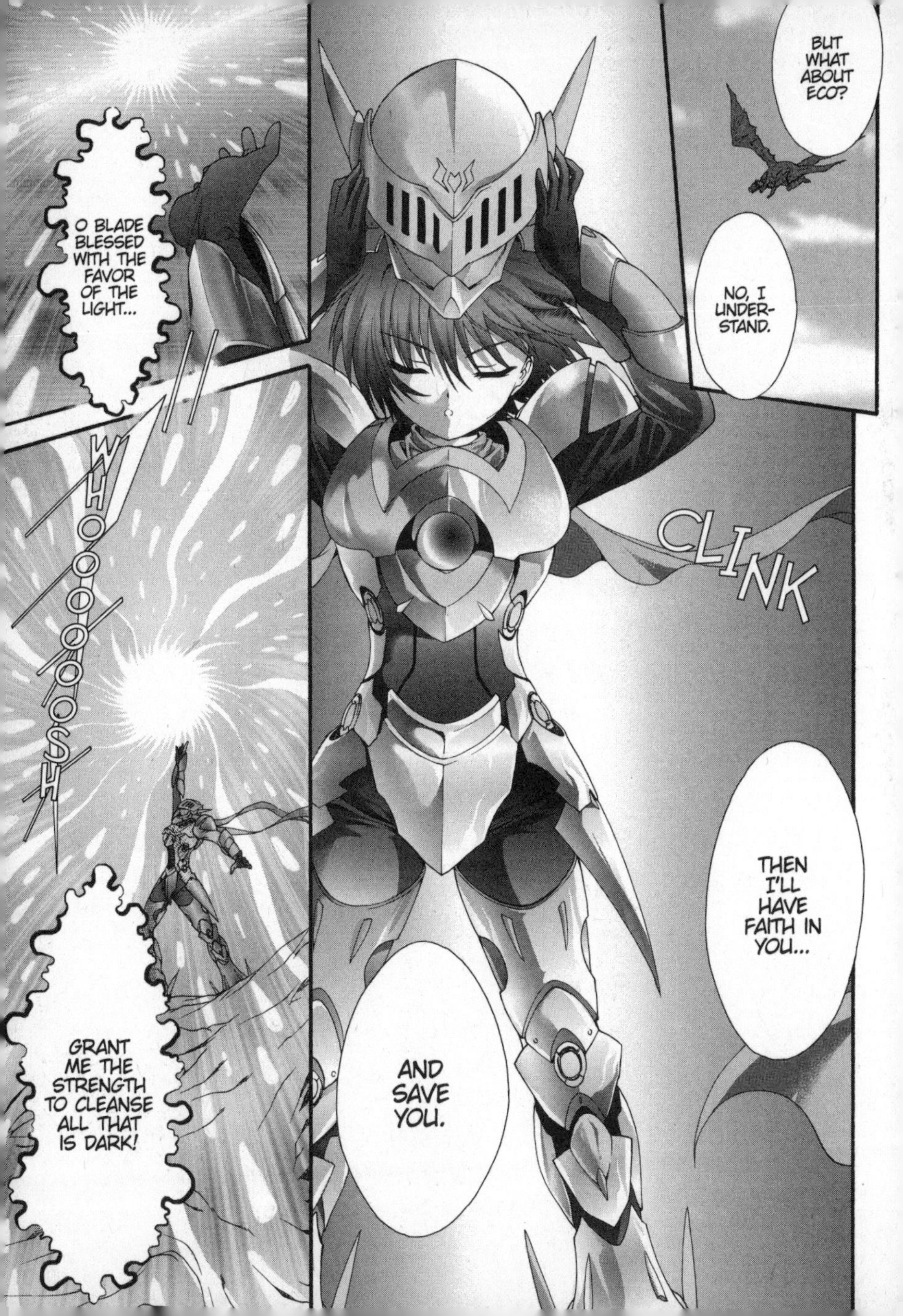
BUT WHAT ABOUT ECO?
NO, I UNDER-STAND.
CLINK
THEN I'LL HAVE FAITH IN YOU...
AND SAVE YOU.
O BLADE BLESSED WITH THE FAVOR OF THE LIGHT...
WHOOOOOOOSH
GRANT ME THE STRENGTH TO CLEANSE ALL THAT IS DARK!

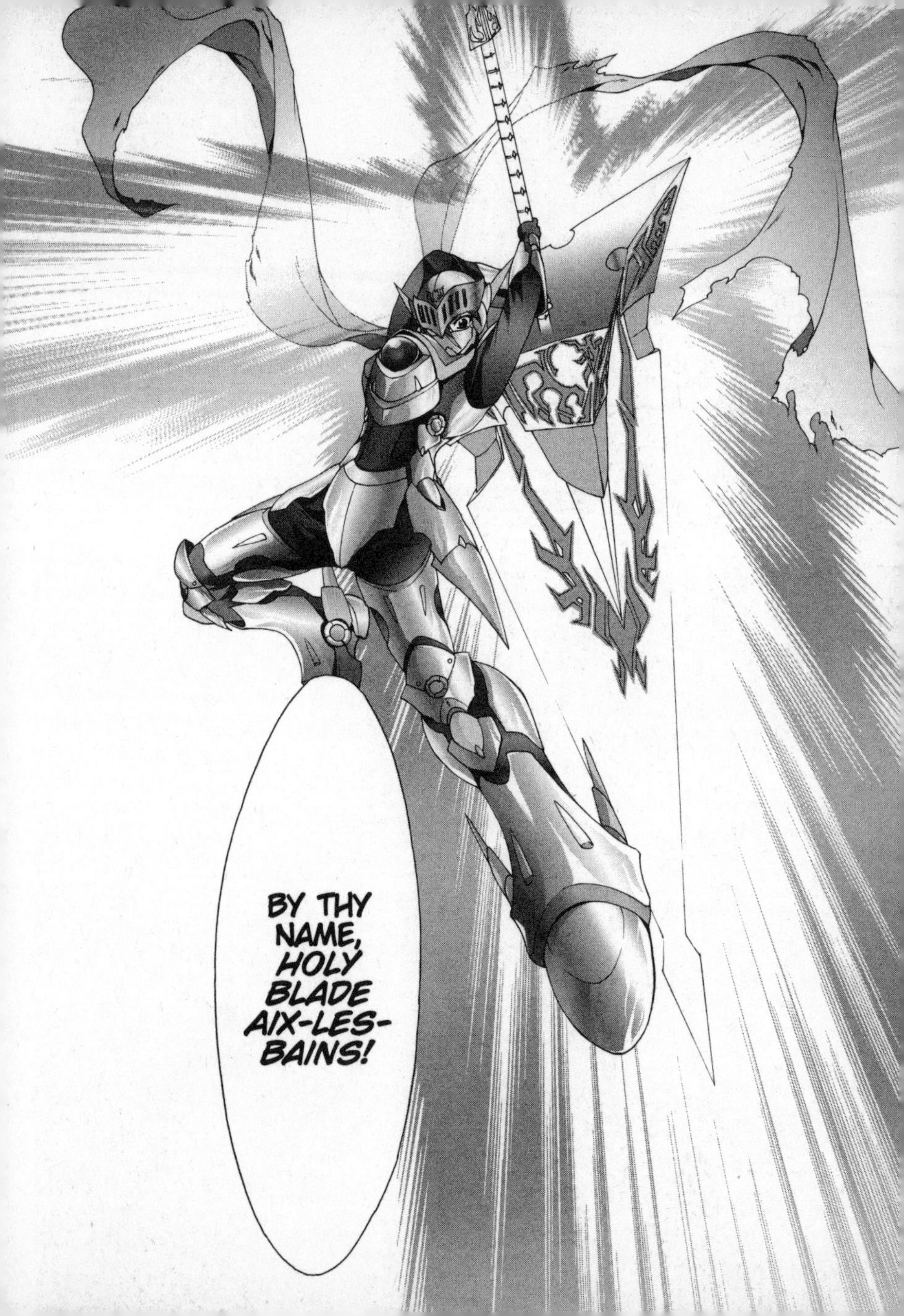
BY THY NAME, HOLY BLADE AIX-LES-BAINS!

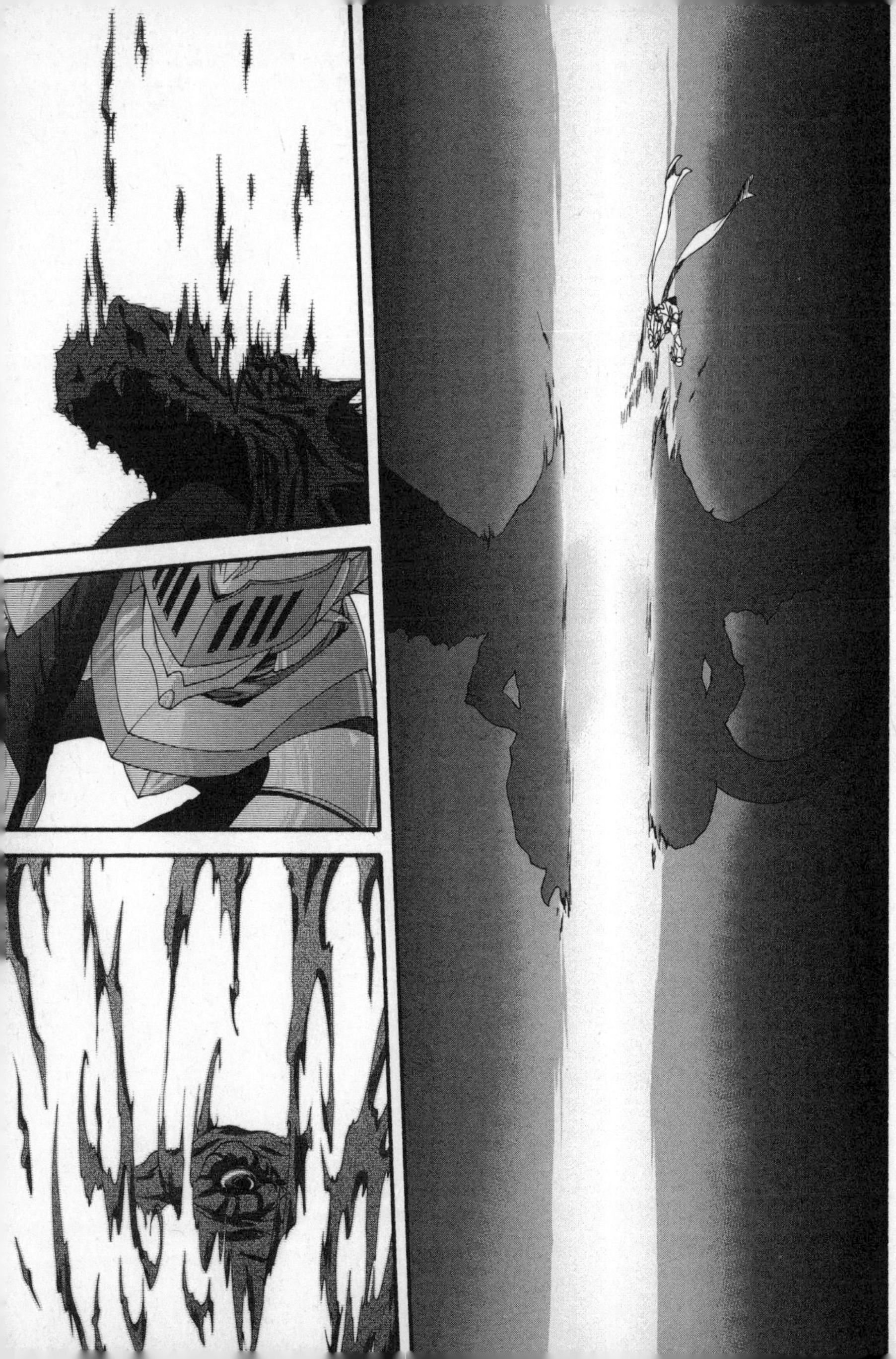

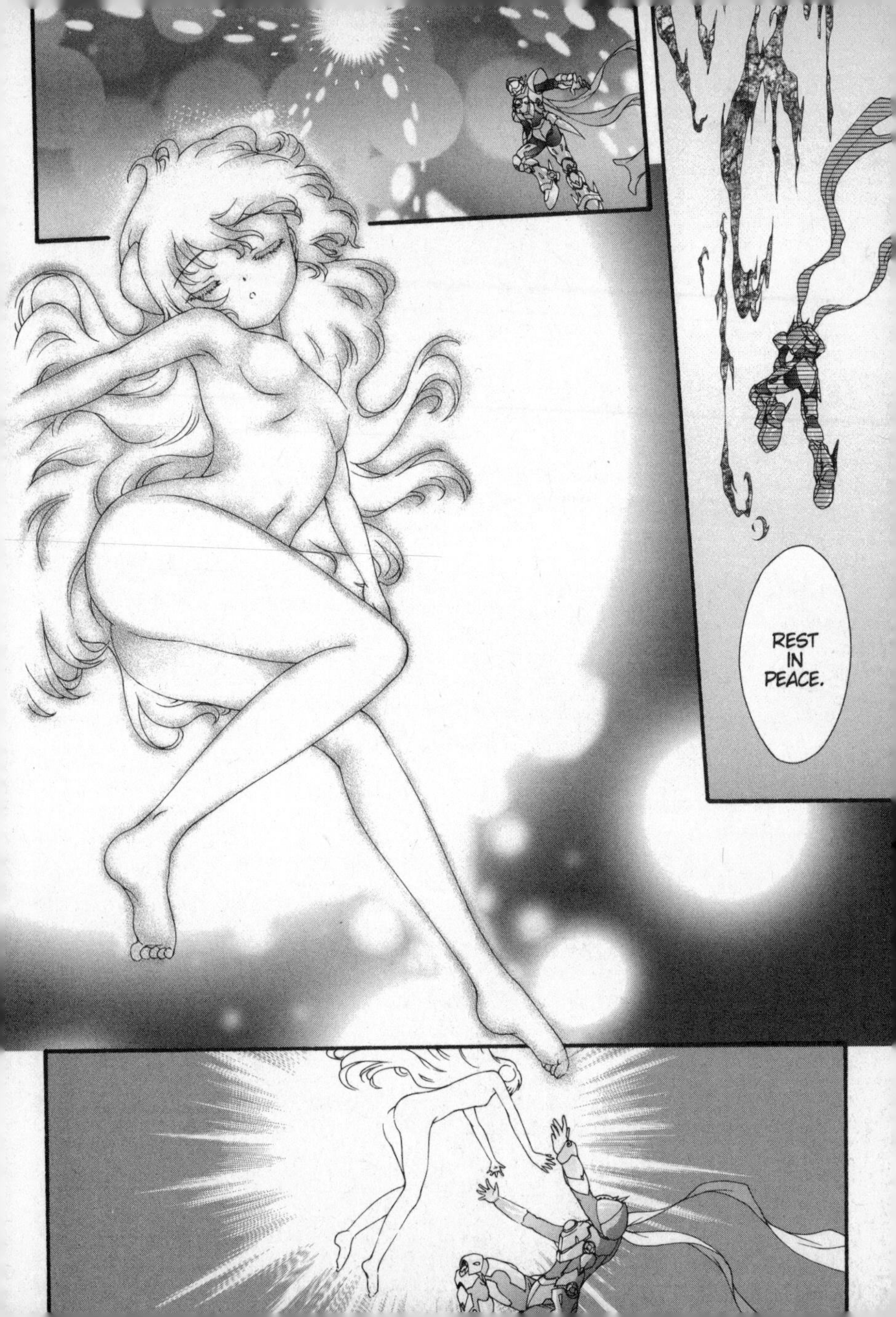
REST IN PEACE.

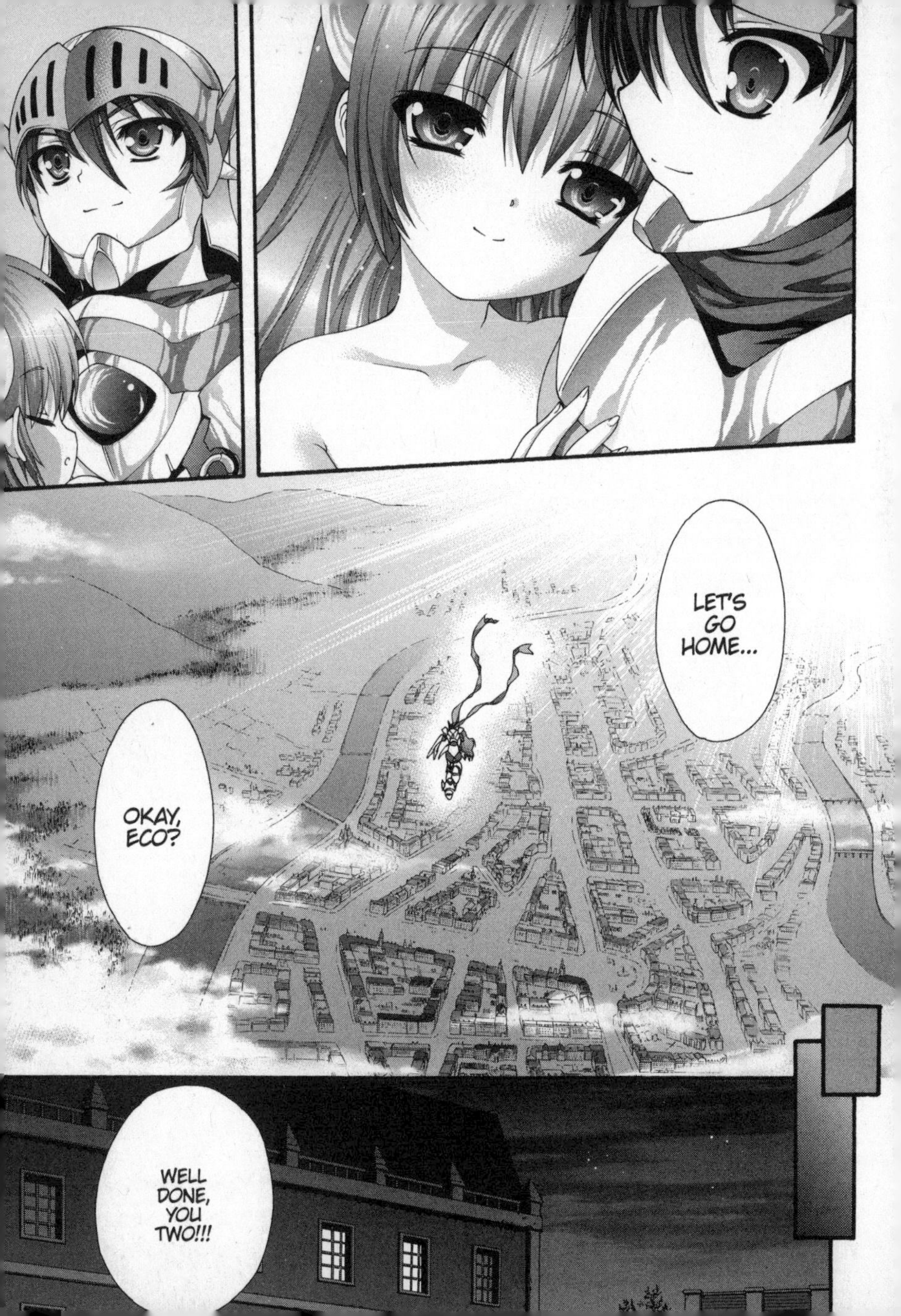
LET'S GO HOME...
OKAY, ECO?
WELL DONE, YOU TWO!!!

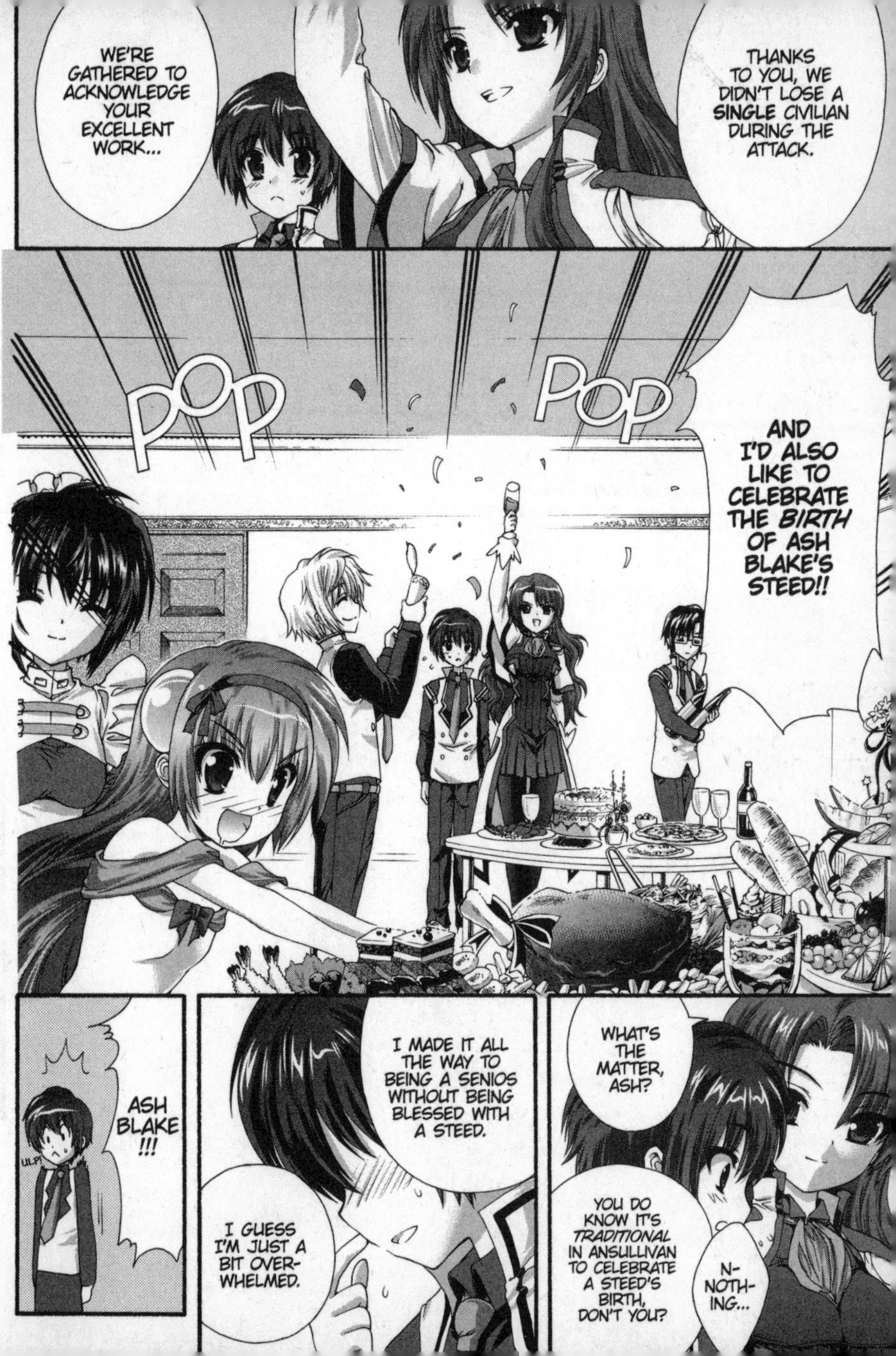
THANKS TO YOU, WE DIDN'T LOSE A SINGLE CIVILIAN DURING THE ATTACK.
WE'RE GATHERED TO ACKNOWLEDGE YOUR EXCELLENT WORK...
POP
POP
AND I'D ALSO LIKE TO CELEBRATE THE *BIRTH* OF ASH BLAKE'S STEED!!
WHAT'S THE MATTER, ASH?
N-NOTHING...
YOU DO KNOW IT'S *TRADITIONAL* IN ANSULLIVAN TO CELEBRATE A STEED'S BIRTH, DON'T YOU?
I MADE IT ALL THE WAY TO BEING A SENIOS WITHOUT BEING BLESSED WITH A STEED.
I GUESS I'M JUST A BIT OVER-WHELMED.
ASH BLAKE!!!
ULP!

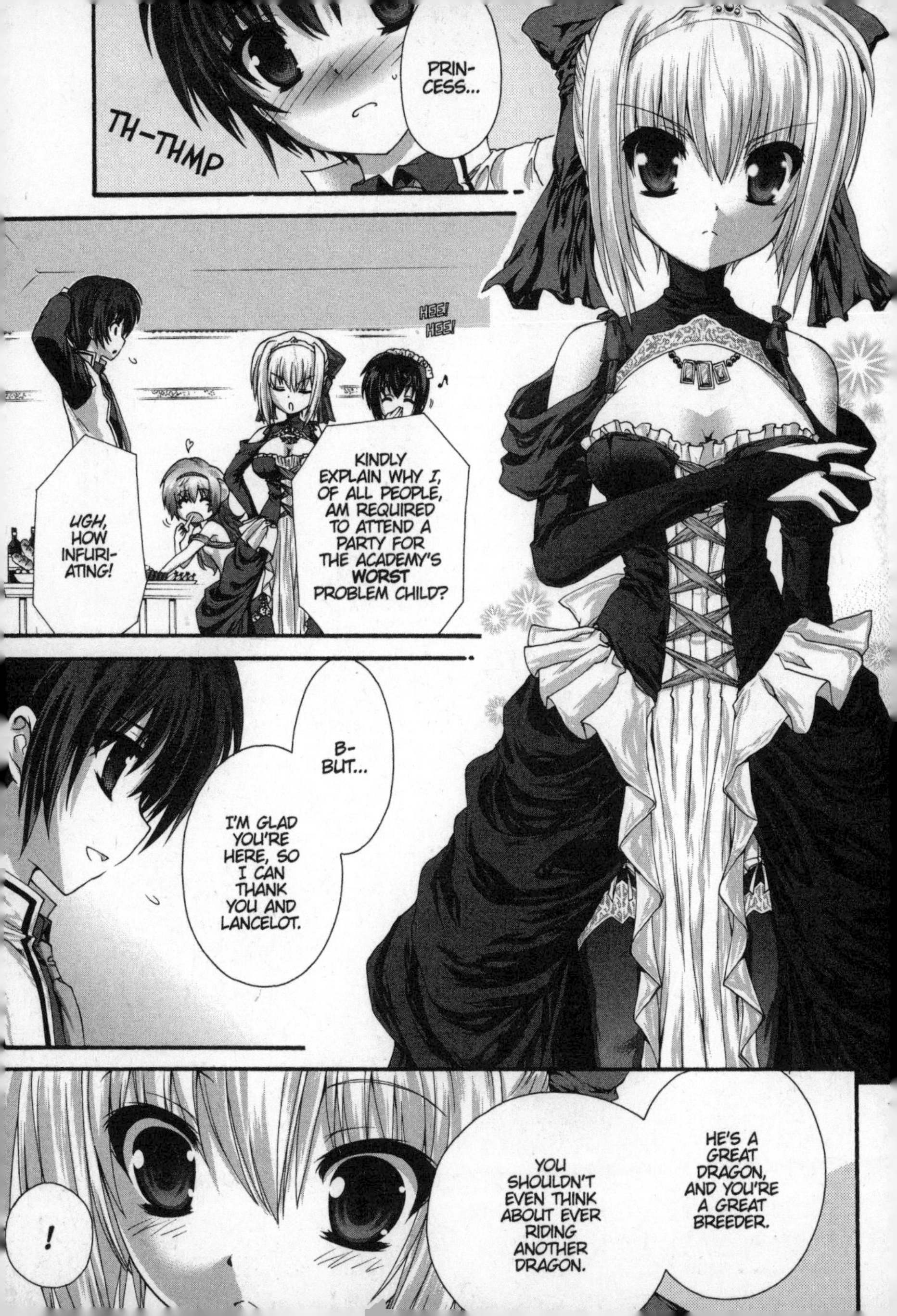
PRIN-CESS...
TH-THMP
HEE! HEE!
KINDLY EXPLAIN WHY *I*, OF ALL PEOPLE, AM REQUIRED TO ATTEND A PARTY FOR THE ACADEMY'S **WORST** PROBLEM CHILD?
UGH, HOW INFURI-ATING!
B-BUT...
I'M GLAD YOU'RE HERE, SO I CAN THANK YOU AND LANCELOT.
HE'S A GREAT DRAGON, AND YOU'RE A GREAT BREEDER.
YOU SHOULDN'T EVEN THINK ABOUT EVER RIDING ANOTHER DRAGON.
!

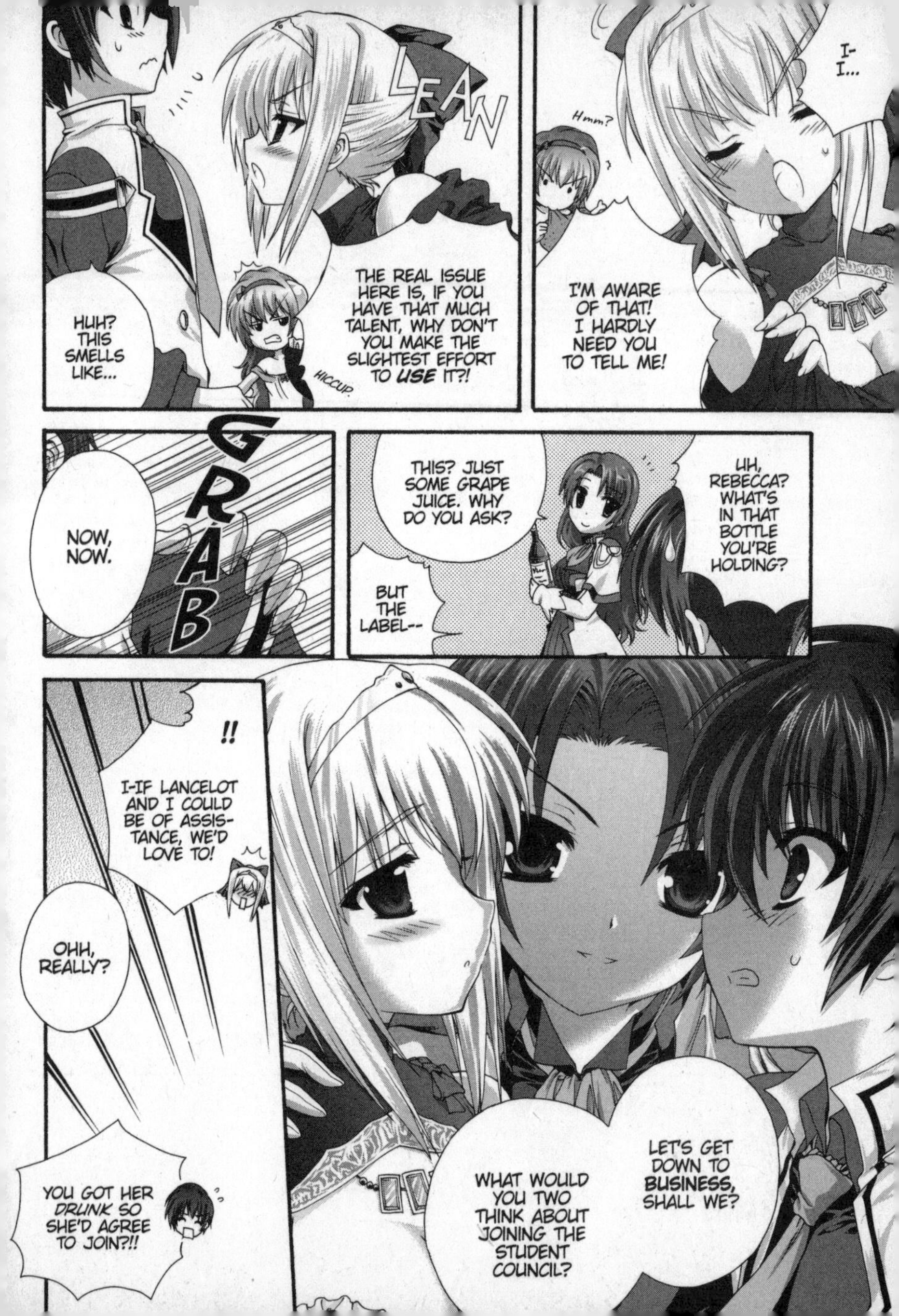
I-
I...
Hmm?
I'M AWARE OF THAT! I HARDLY NEED YOU TO TELL ME!
LEAN
THE REAL ISSUE HERE IS, IF YOU HAVE THAT MUCH TALENT, WHY DON'T YOU MAKE THE SLIGHTEST EFFORT TO *USE* IT?!
HUH? THIS SMELLS LIKE...
HICCUP.
UH, REBECCA? WHAT'S IN THAT BOTTLE YOU'RE HOLDING?
THIS? JUST SOME GRAPE JUICE. WHY DO YOU ASK?
BUT THE LABEL--
GRAB
NOW, NOW.
LET'S GET DOWN TO **BUSINESS,** SHALL WE?
WHAT WOULD YOU TWO THINK ABOUT JOINING THE STUDENT COUNCIL?
!!
I-IF LANCELOT AND I COULD BE OF ASSIS-TANCE, WE'D LOVE TO!
OHH, REALLY?
YOU GOT HER *DRUNK* SO SHE'D AGREE TO JOIN?!!

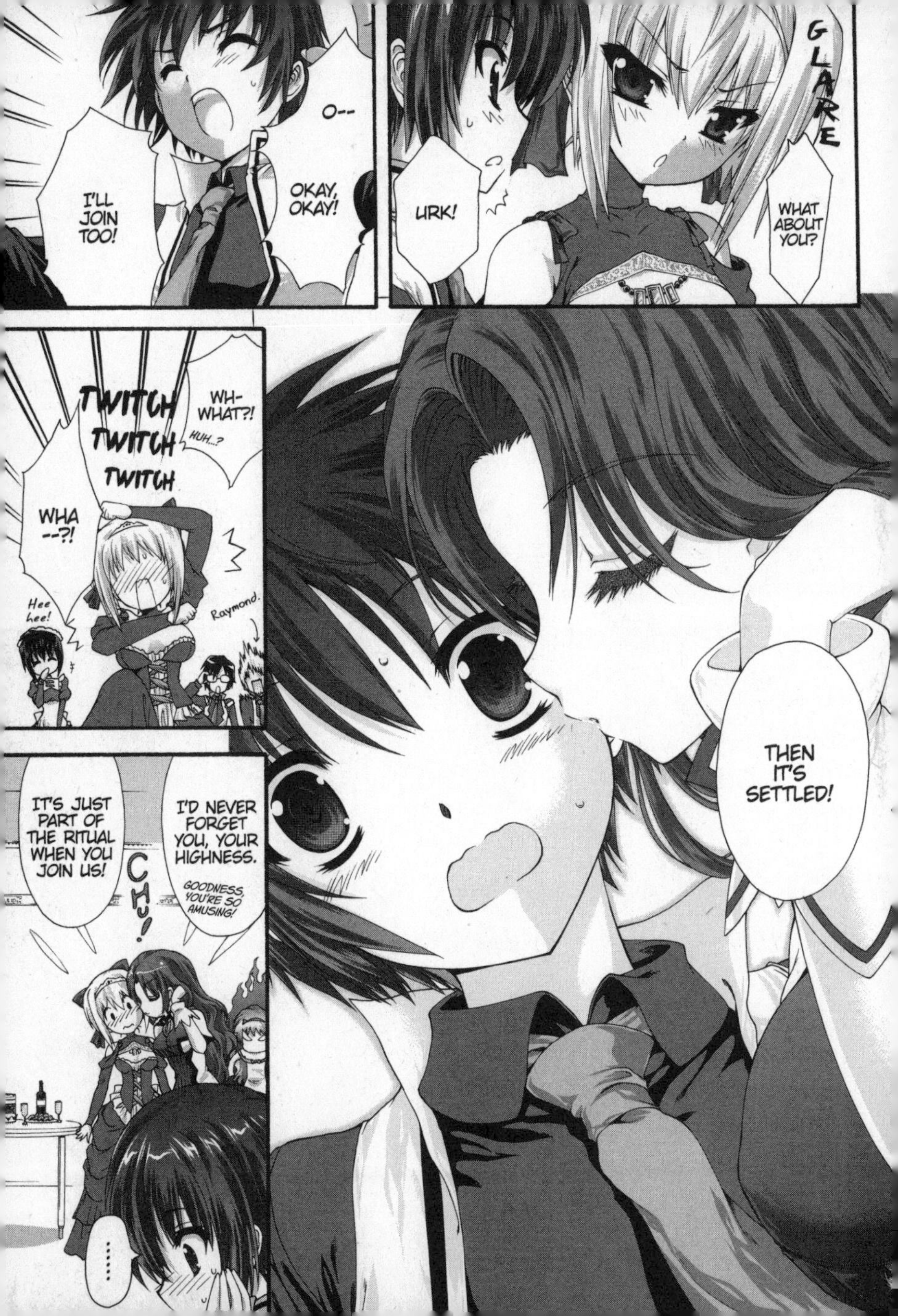
GLARE
WHAT ABOUT YOU?
URK!
O--
OKAY, OKAY!
I'LL JOIN TOO!
THEN IT'S SETTLED!
WH-WHAT?!
HUH...?
TWITCH
TWITCH
TWITCH
WHA--?!
Raymond.
Hee hee!
I'D NEVER FORGET YOU, YOUR HIGHNESS.
GOODNESS, YOU'RE SO AMUSING!
IT'S JUST PART OF THE RITUAL WHEN YOU JOIN US!
CHU!
......

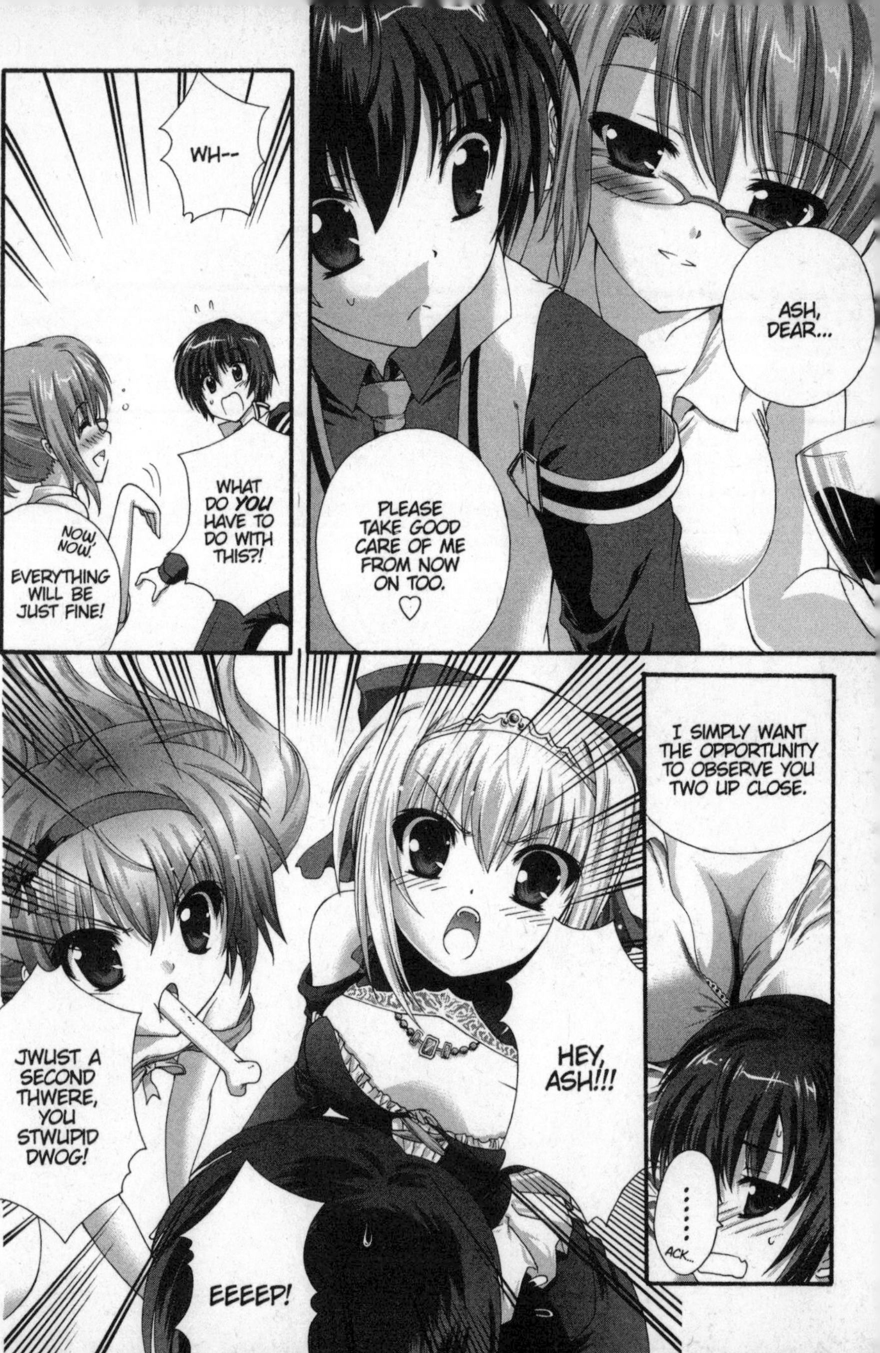
ASH, DEAR...
PLEASE TAKE GOOD CARE OF ME FROM NOW ON TOO. ♡
WH--
WHAT DO *YOU* HAVE TO DO WITH THIS?!
NOW, NOW!
EVERYTHING WILL BE JUST FINE!
I SIMPLY WANT THE OPPORTUNITY TO OBSERVE YOU TWO UP CLOSE.
......
ACK...
HEY, ASH!!!
JWUST A SECOND THWERE, YOU STWUPID DWOG!
EEEEP!

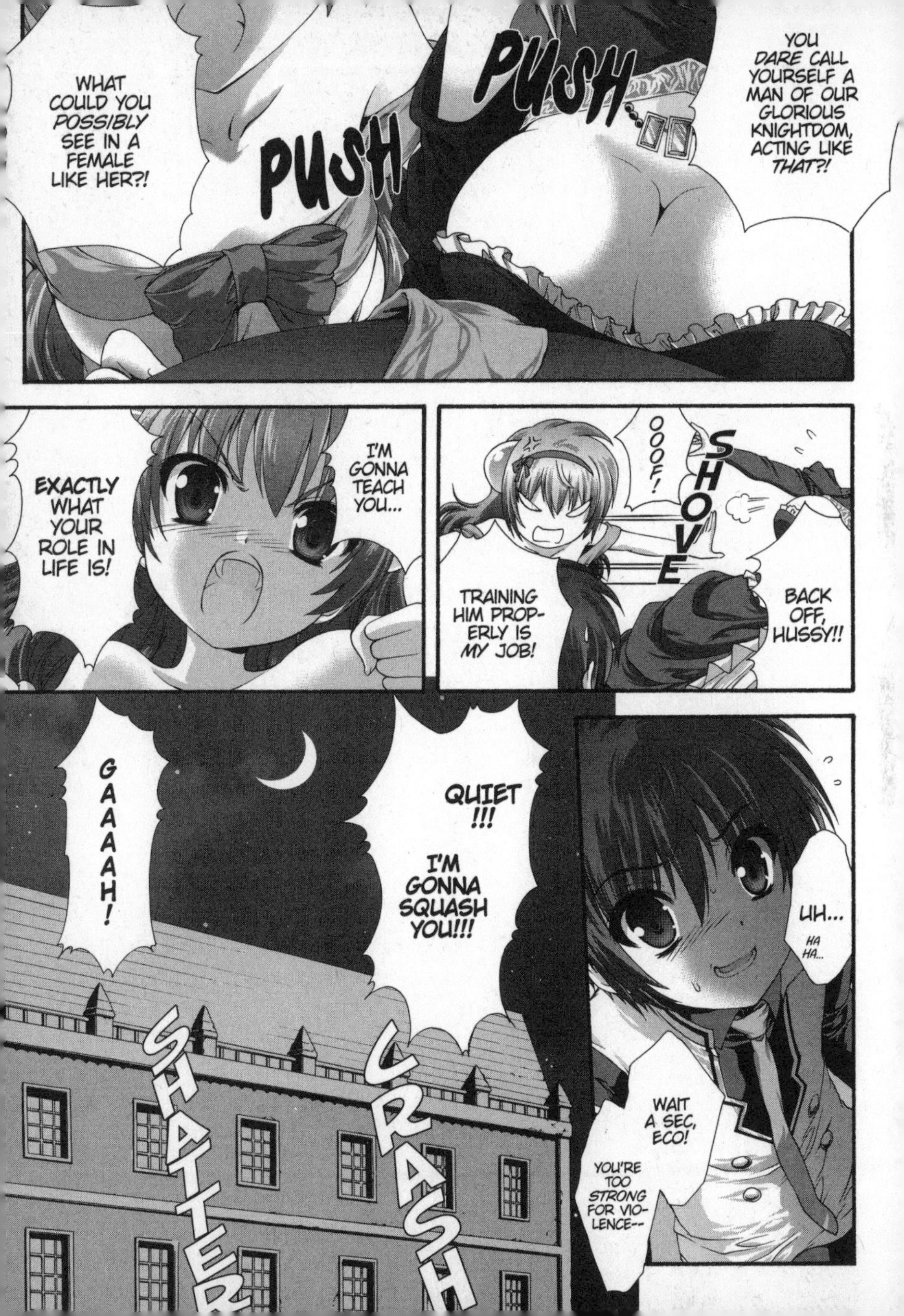
YOU DARE CALL YOURSELF A MAN OF OUR GLORIOUS KNIGHTDOM, ACTING LIKE THAT?!
PUSH
PUSH
WHAT COULD YOU POSSIBLY SEE IN A FEMALE LIKE HER?!
SHOVE
OOOF!
BACK OFF, HUSSY!!
TRAINING HIM PROPERLY IS MY JOB!
I'M GONNA TEACH YOU...
EXACTLY WHAT YOUR ROLE IN LIFE IS!
UH...
HA HA...
WAIT A SEC, ECO!
YOU'RE TOO STRONG FOR VIOLENCE--
QUIET!!!
I'M GONNA SQUASH YOU!!!
GAAAAAH!
CRASH
SHATTER

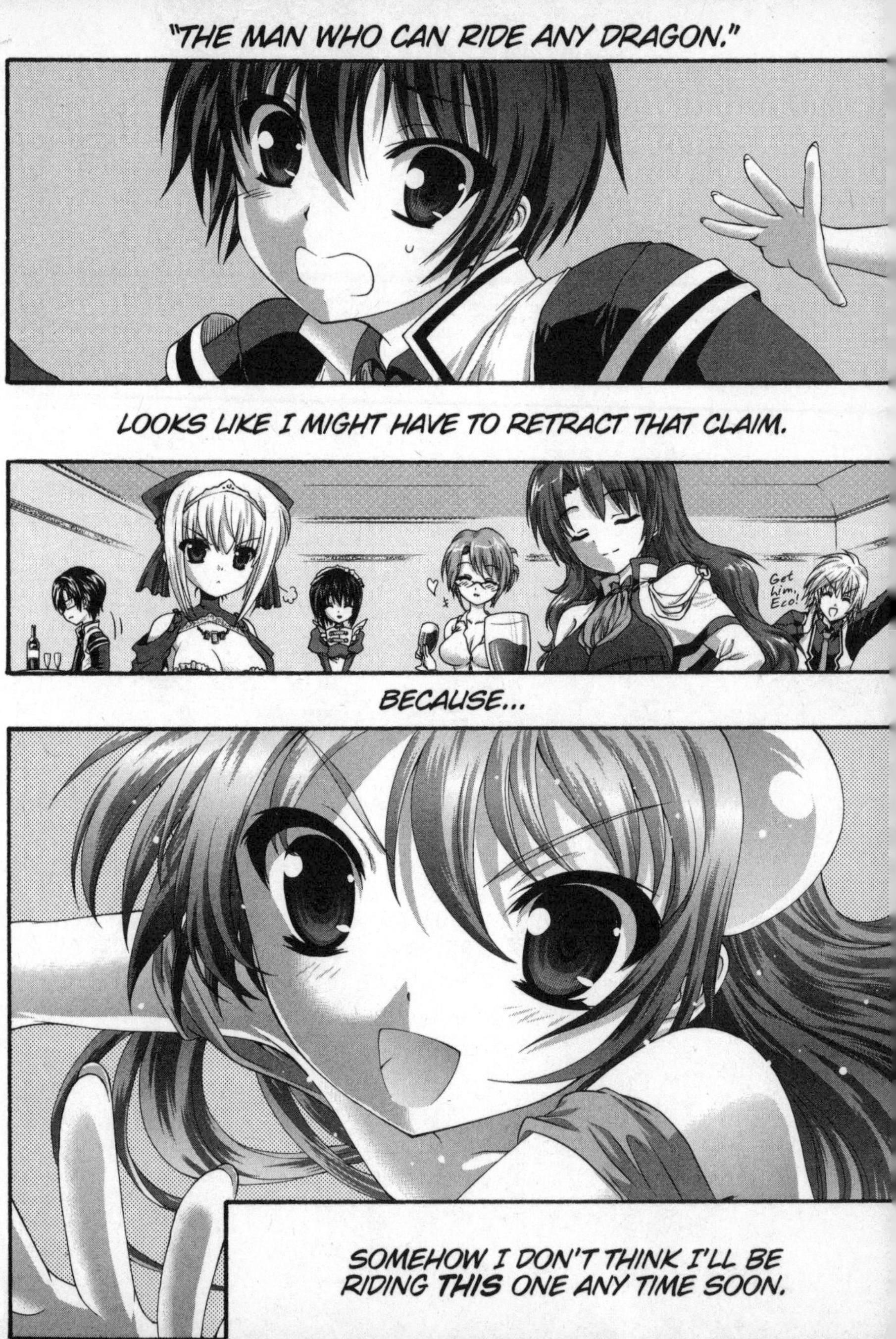
"THE MAN WHO CAN RIDE ANY DRAGON."
LOOKS LIKE I MIGHT HAVE TO RETRACT THAT CLAIM.
Get him, Eco!
BECAUSE...
SOMEHOW I DON'T THINK I'LL BE RIDING THIS ONE ANY TIME SOON.

DRAGONAR
ACADEMY

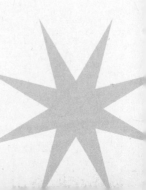

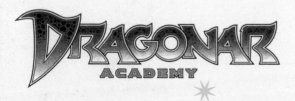

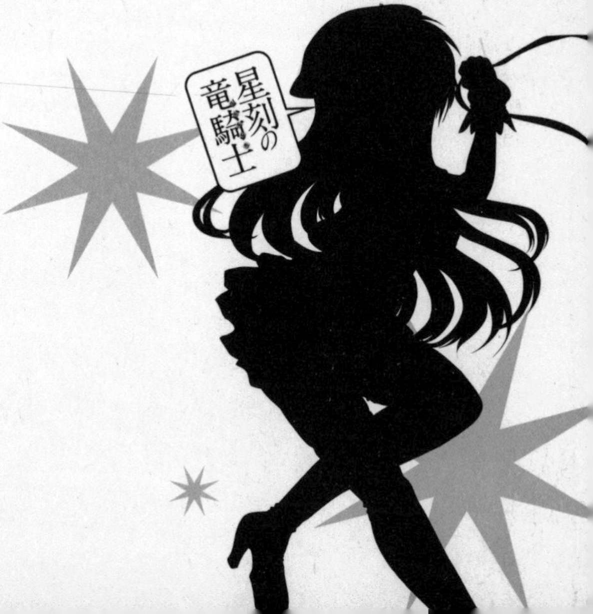
星刻の竜騎士

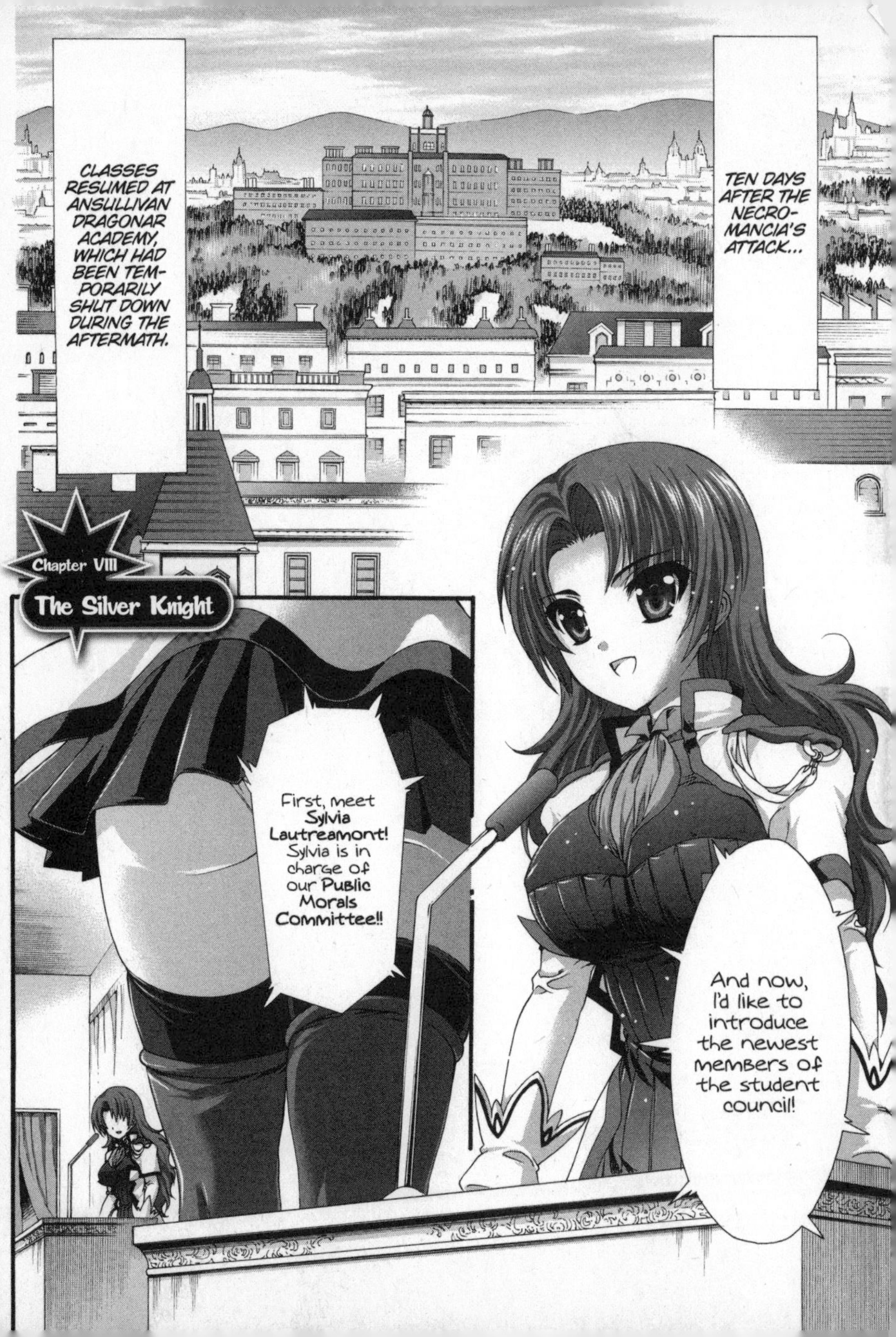
TEN DAYS AFTER THE NECRO-MANCIA'S ATTACK...
CLASSES RESUMED AT ANSULLIVAN DRAGONAR ACADEMY, WHICH HAD BEEN TEM-PORARILY SHUT DOWN DURING THE AFTERMATH.
Chapter VIII
The Silver Knight
And now, I'd like to introduce the newest members of the student council!
First, meet Sylvia Lautreamont! Sylvia is in charge of our Public Morals Committee!!

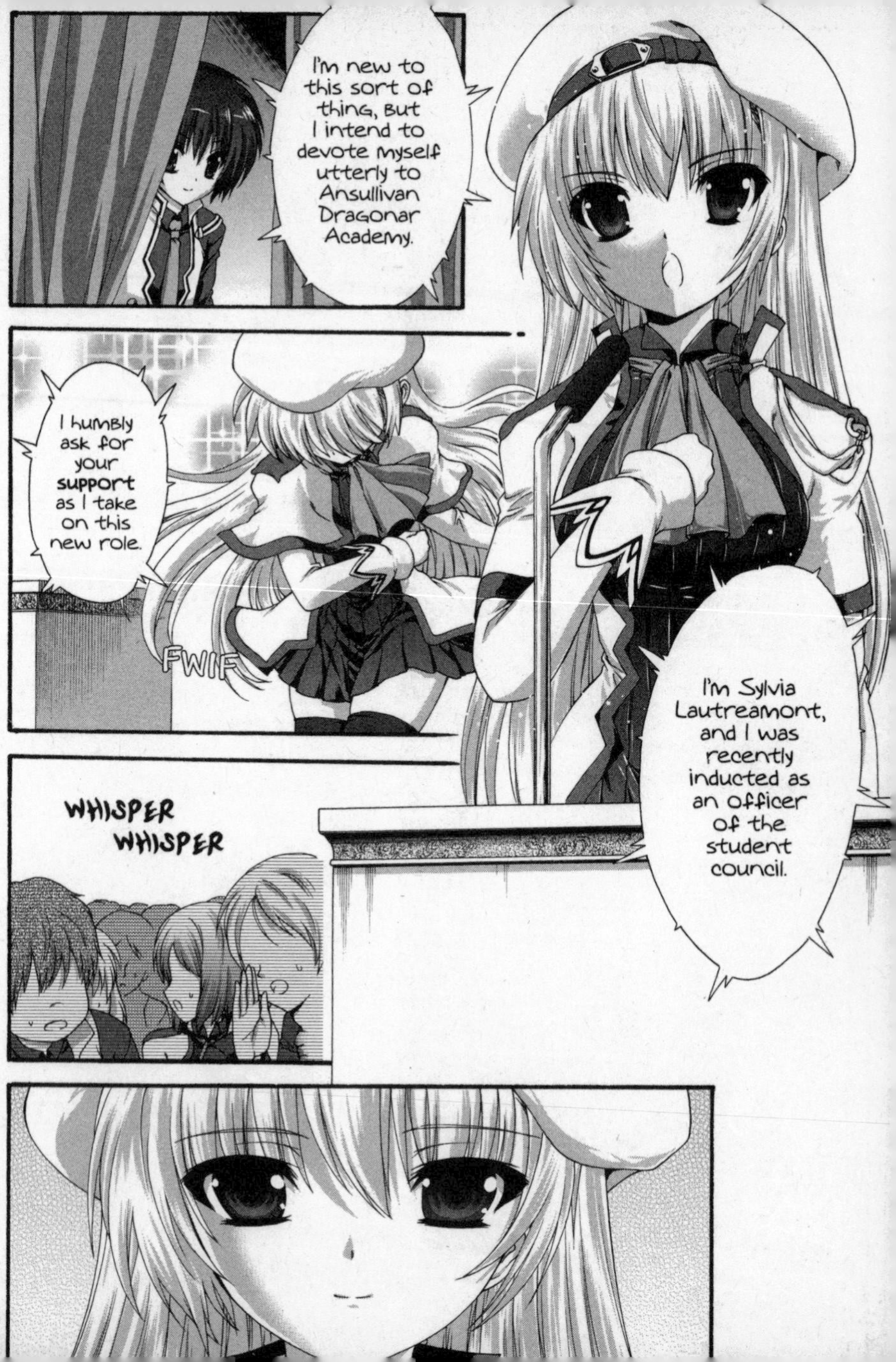
I'm Sylvia Lautreamont, and I was recently inducted as an officer of the student council.
I'm new to this sort of thing, but I intend to devote myself utterly to Ansullivan Dragonar Academy.
I humbly ask for your **support** as I take on this new role.
FWIF
WHISPER WHISPER

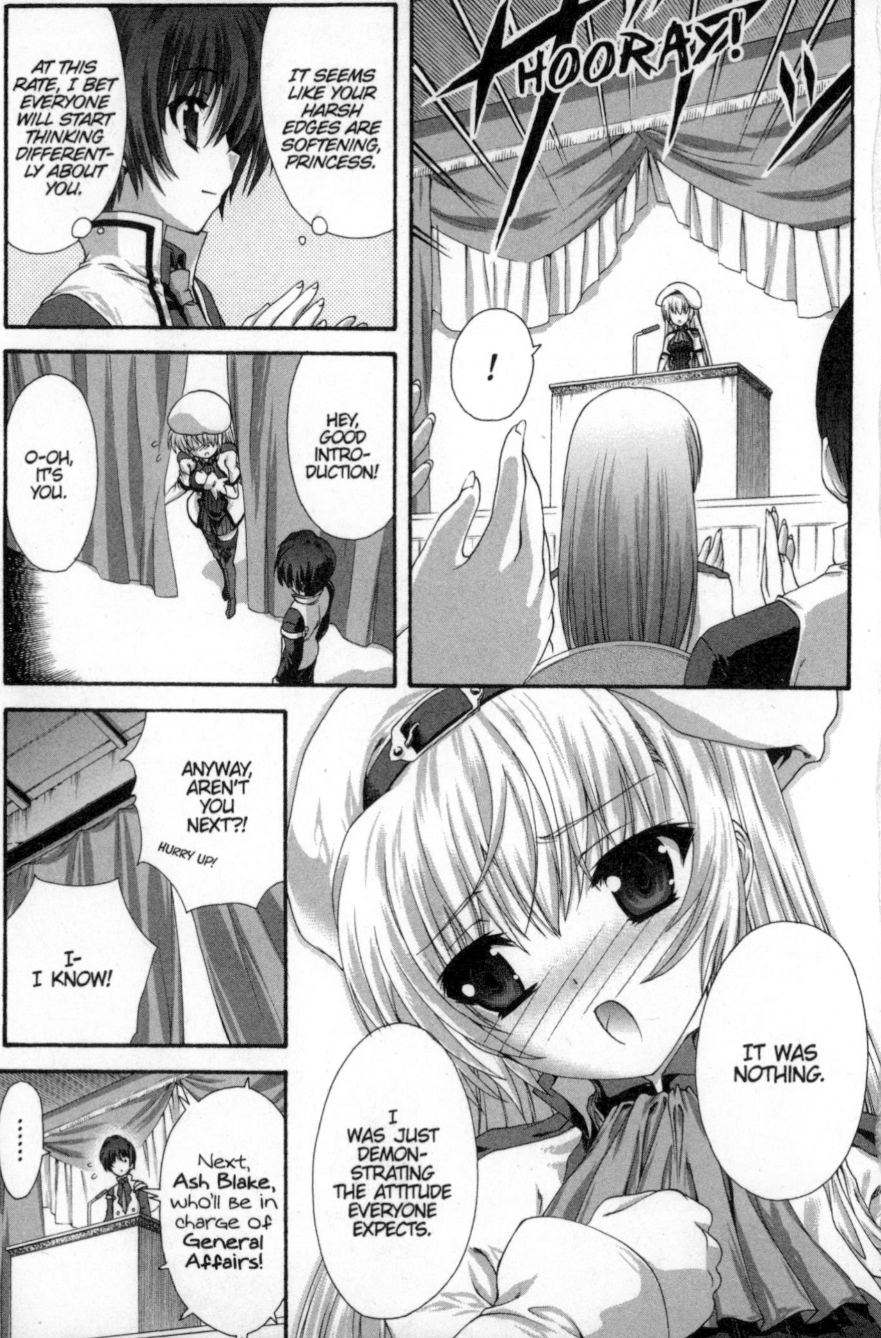
HOORAY!
!
IT SEEMS LIKE YOUR HARSH EDGES ARE SOFTENING, PRINCESS.
AT THIS RATE, I BET EVERYONE WILL START THINKING DIFFERENTLY ABOUT YOU.
HEY, GOOD INTRODUCTION!
O-OH, IT'S YOU.
IT WAS NOTHING.
I WAS JUST DEMONSTRATING THE ATTITUDE EVERYONE EXPECTS.
ANYWAY, AREN'T YOU NEXT?!
HURRY UP!
I- I KNOW!
Next, Ash Blake, who'll be in charge of General Affairs!
......

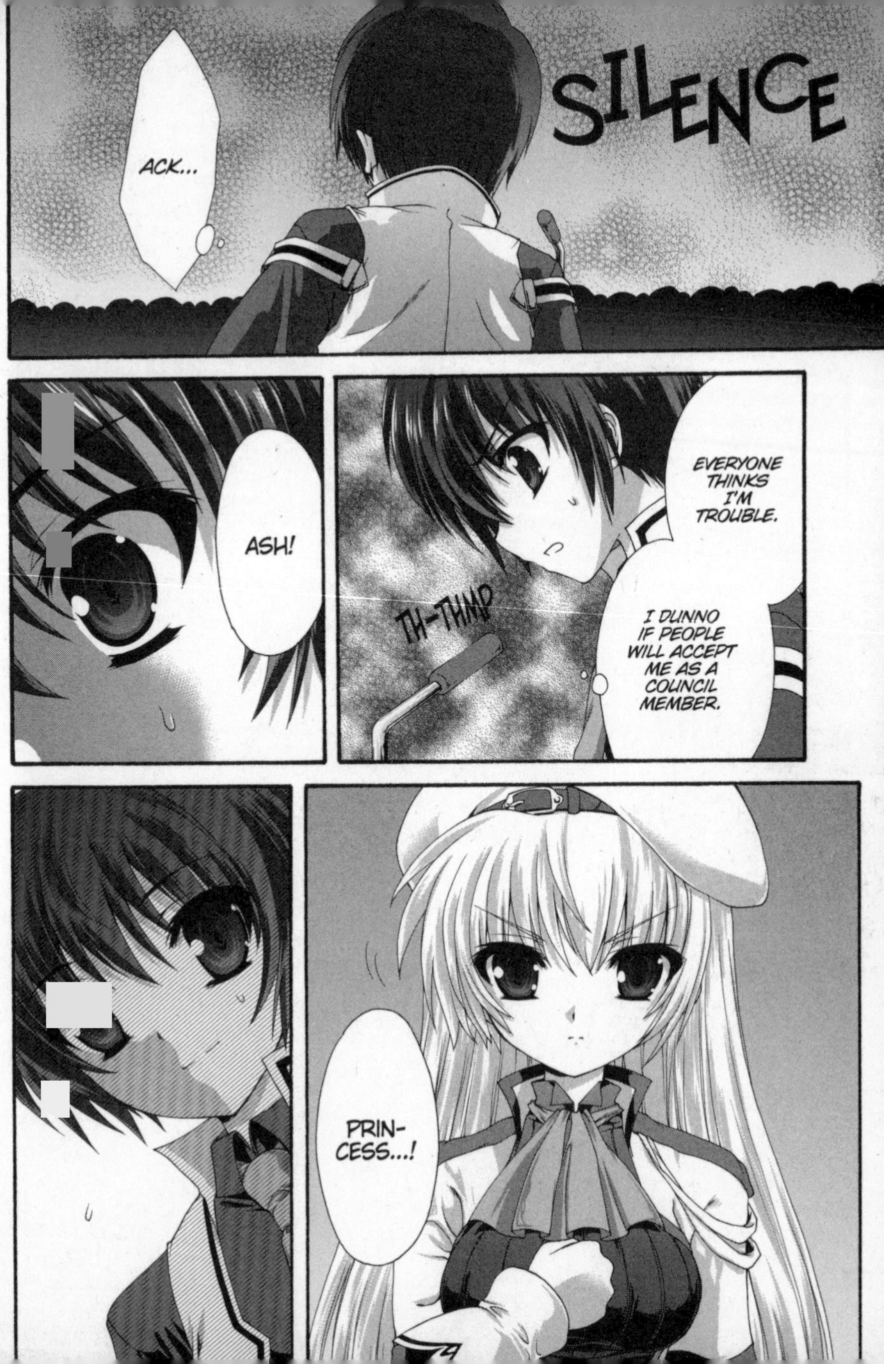
SILENCE
ACK...
EVERYONE THINKS I'M TROUBLE.
I DUNNO IF PEOPLE WILL ACCEPT ME AS A COUNCIL MEMBER.
TH-THMP
ASH!
PRIN-CESS...!

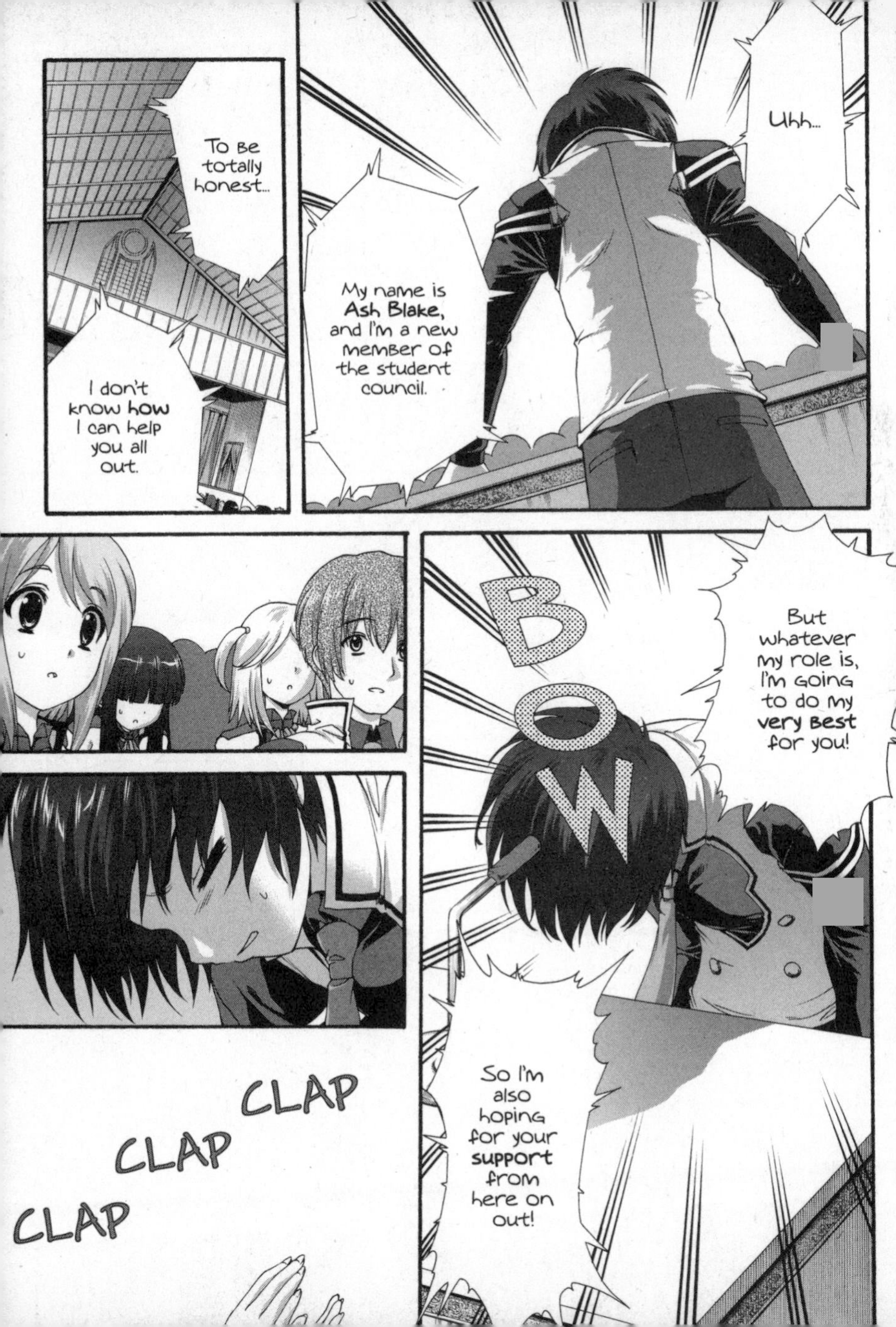
Uhh...
My name is Ash Blake, and I'm a new member of the student council.
To be totally honest...
I don't know how I can help you all out.
BOW
But whatever my role is, I'm going to do my very best for you!
So I'm also hoping for your support from here on out!
CLAP
CLAP
CLAP

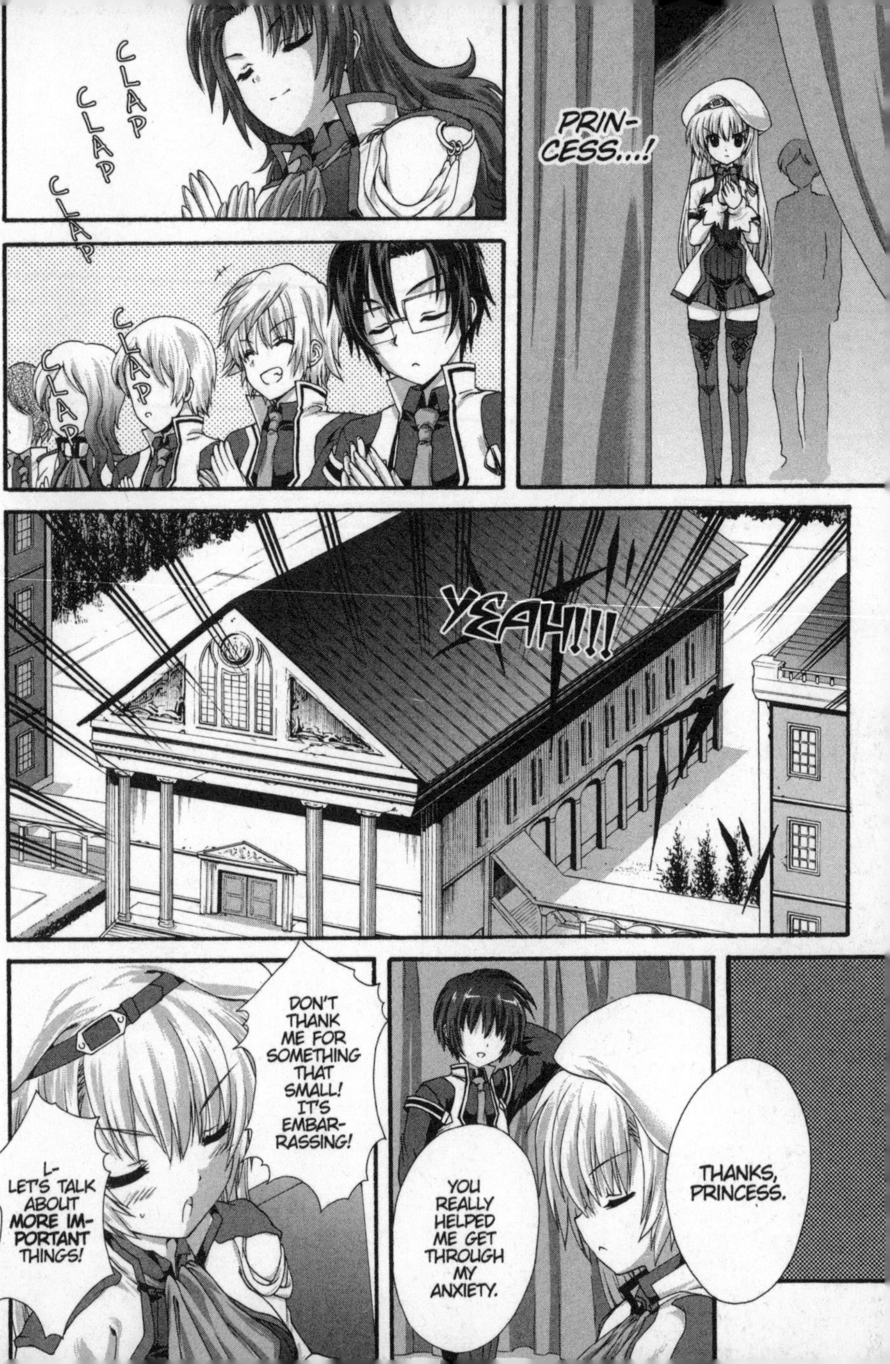
PRIN-CESS...!
CLAP
CLAP
CLAP
CLAP
CLAP
YEAH!!!
THANKS, PRINCESS.
YOU REALLY HELPED ME GET THROUGH MY ANXIETY.
DON'T THANK ME FOR SOMETHING THAT SMALL! IT'S EMBARRASSING!
L-LET'S TALK ABOUT MORE IM-PORTANT THINGS!

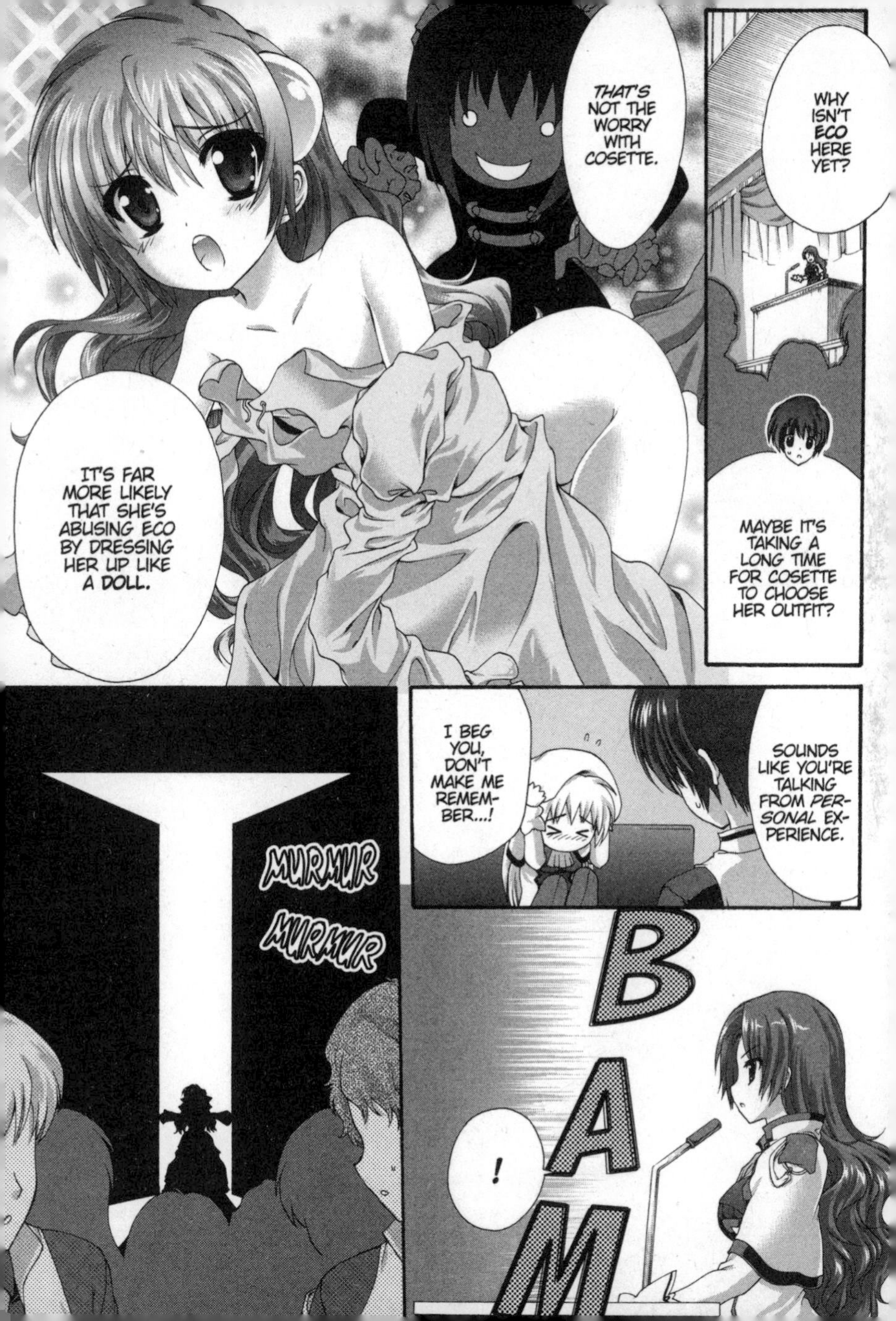
WHY ISN'T ECO HERE YET?
MAYBE IT'S TAKING A LONG TIME FOR COSETTE TO CHOOSE HER OUTFIT?
THAT'S NOT THE WORRY WITH COSETTE.
IT'S FAR MORE LIKELY THAT SHE'S ABUSING ECO BY DRESSING HER UP LIKE A DOLL.
SOUNDS LIKE YOU'RE TALKING FROM PERSONAL EXPERIENCE.
I BEG YOU, DON'T MAKE ME REMEMBER...!
BAM
!
MURMUR
MURMUR

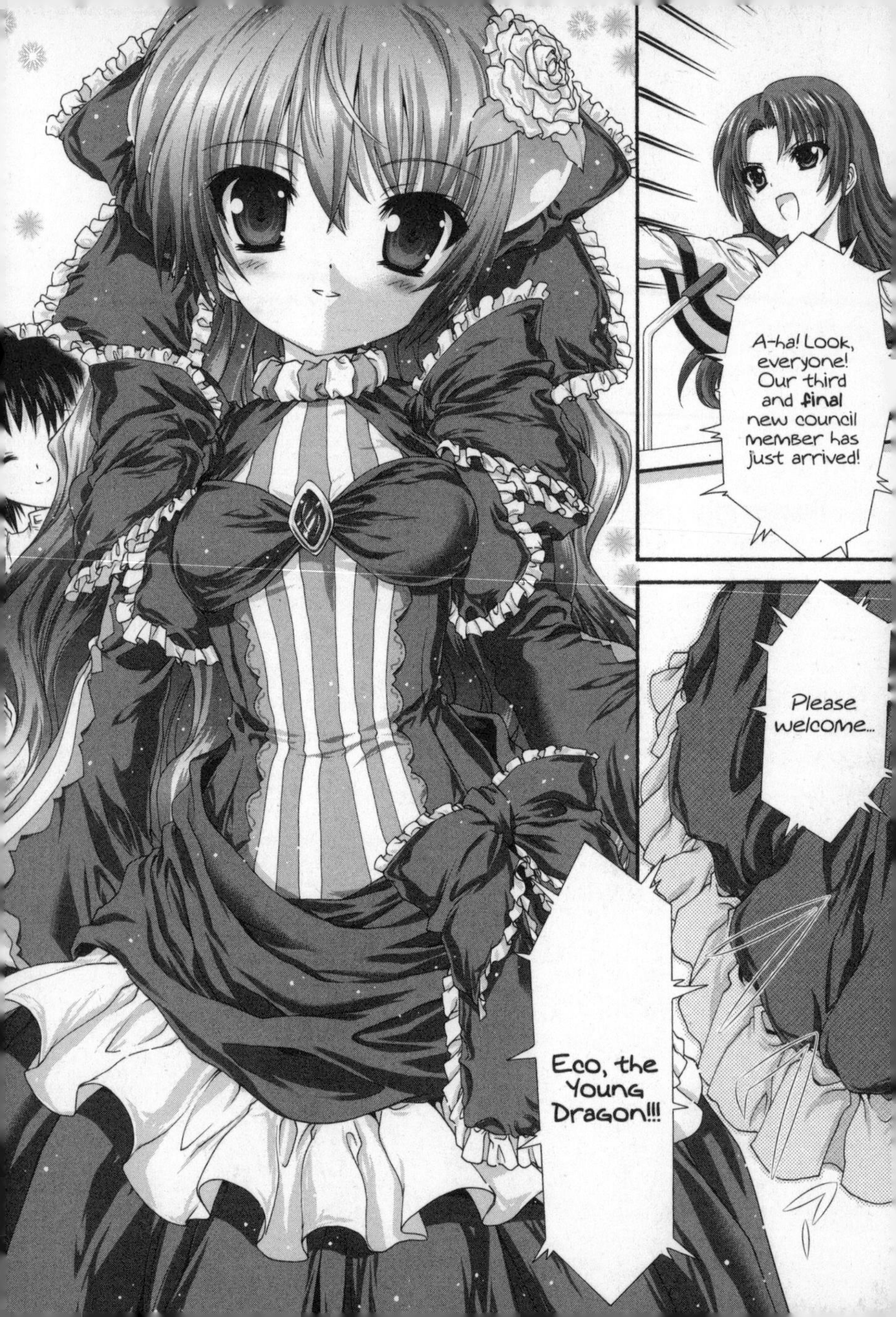
A-ha! Look, everyone! Our third and final new council member has just arrived!
Please welcome...
Eco, the Young Dragon!!!

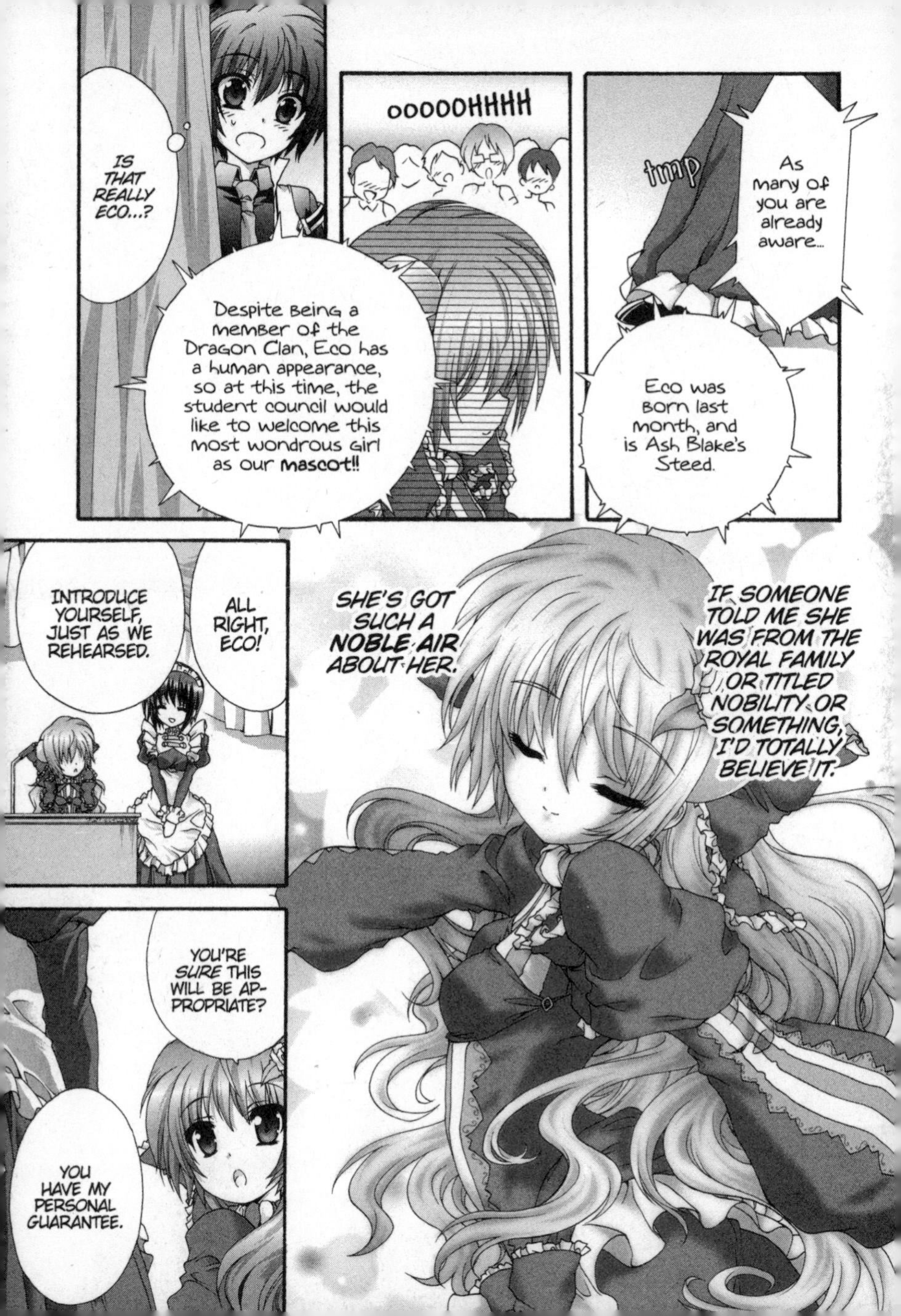
tmp
As many of you are already aware...
Eco was born last month, and is Ash Blake's Steed.
OOOOOHHHH
Despite being a member of the Dragon Clan, Eco has a human appearance, so at this time, the student council would like to welcome this most wondrous girl as our **mascot**!!
IS THAT REALLY ECO...?
IF SOMEONE TOLD ME SHE WAS FROM THE ROYAL FAMILY OR TITLED NOBILITY OR SOMETHING, I'D TOTALLY BELIEVE IT.
SHE'S GOT SUCH A NOBLE AIR ABOUT HER.
ALL RIGHT, ECO!
INTRODUCE YOURSELF, JUST AS WE REHEARSED.
YOU'RE *SURE* THIS WILL BE AP-PROPRIATE?
YOU HAVE MY PERSONAL GUARANTEE.

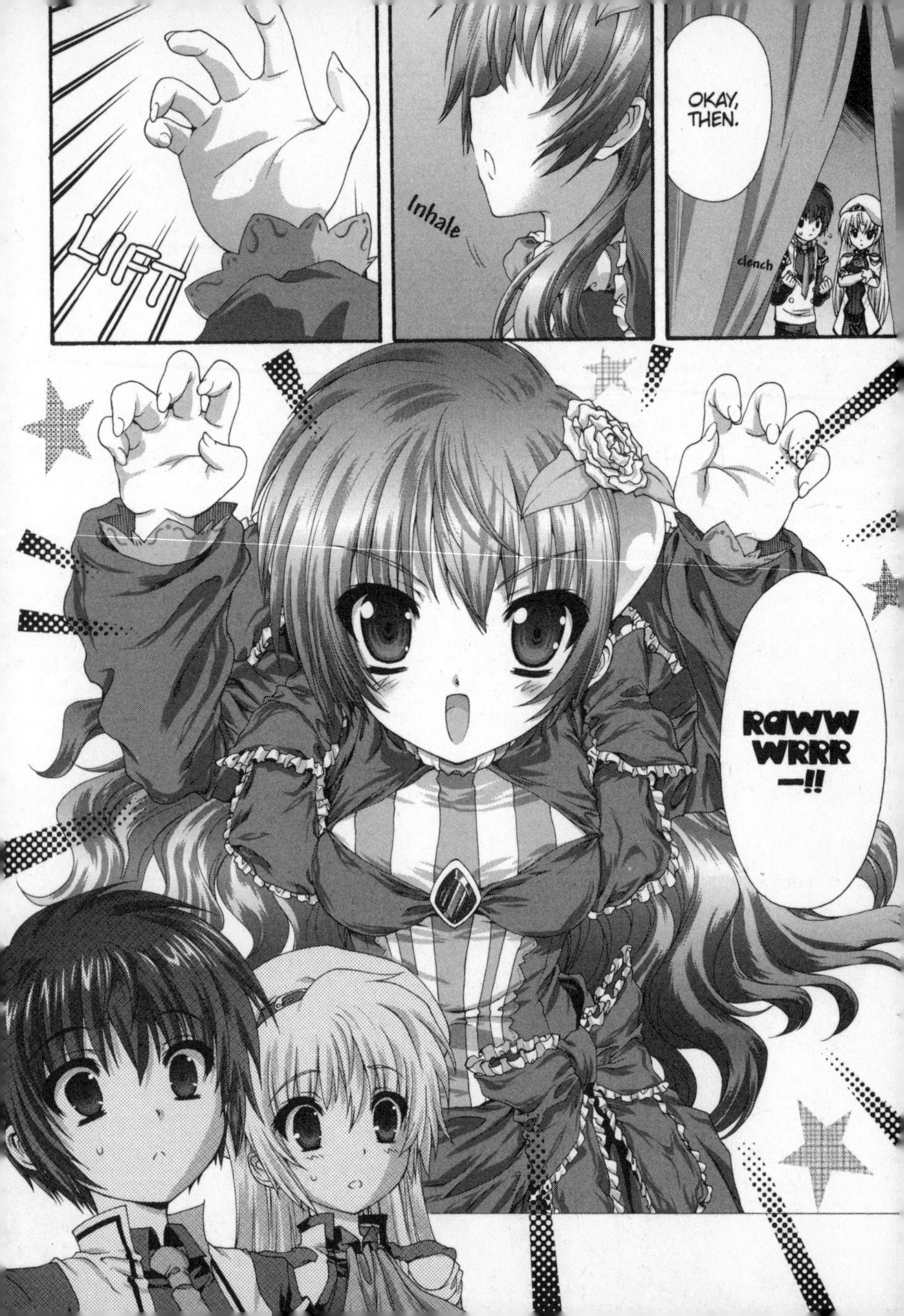
OKAY, THEN.
clench
Inhale
LIFT
RAWW WRRR —!!

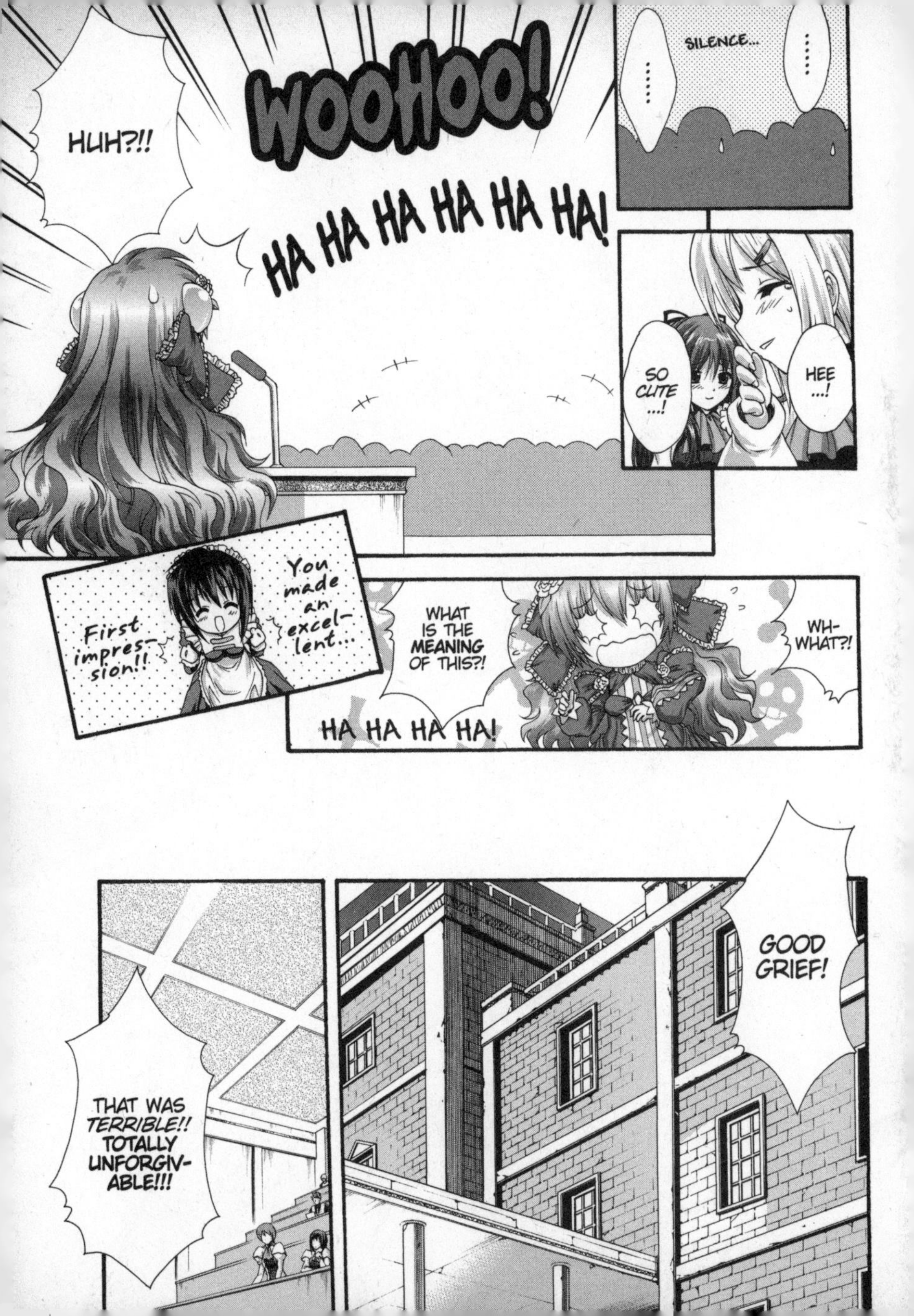
......
SILENCE...
......
HEE ...!
SO CUTE ...!
WOOHOO!
HUH?!!
HA HA HA HA HA HA HA!
WH- WHAT?!
WHAT IS THE MEANING OF THIS?!
HA HA HA HA!
You made an excel- lent...
First impres- sion!!
GOOD GRIEF!
THAT WAS TERRIBLE!! TOTALLY UNFORGIV- ABLE!!!

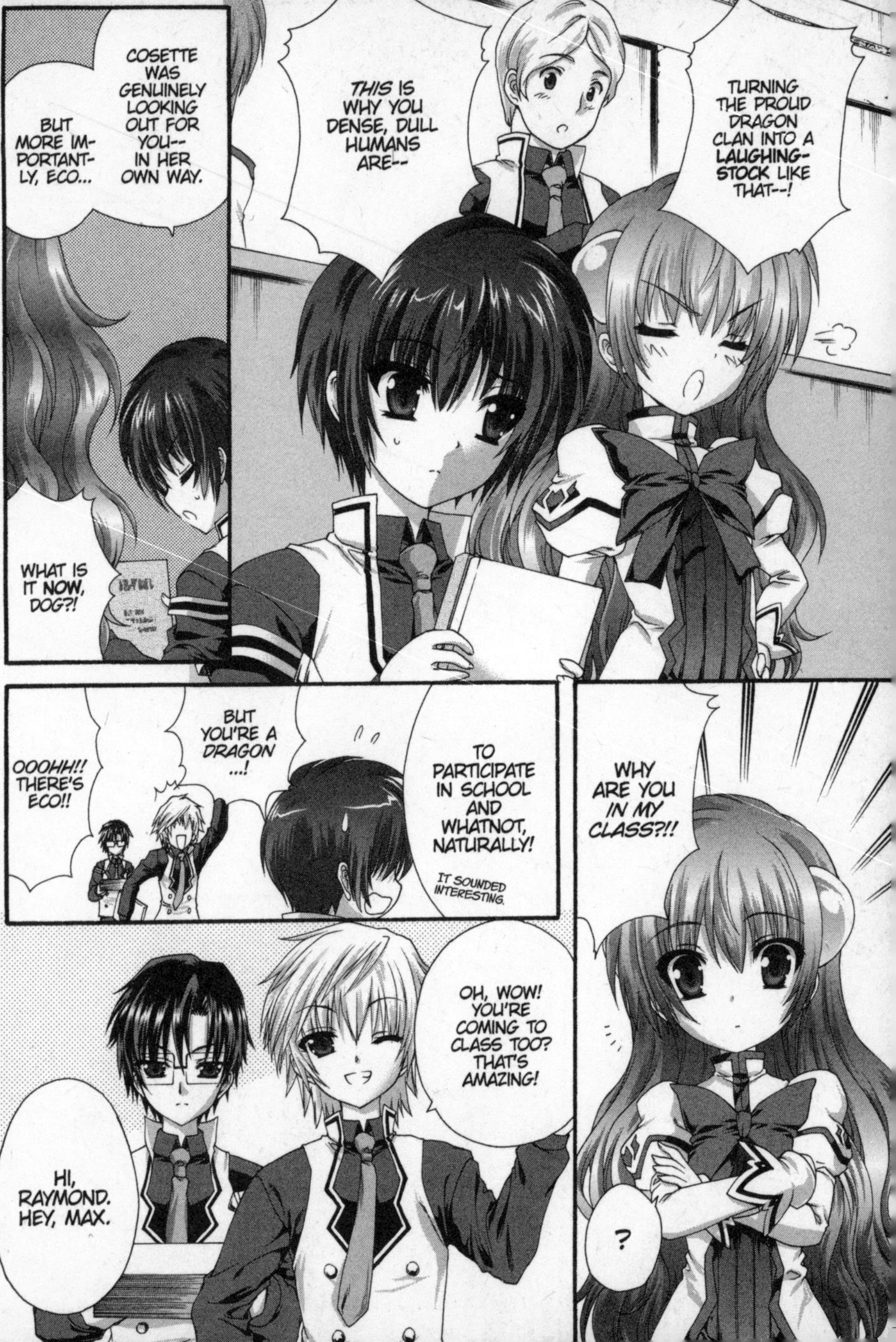
TURNING THE PROUD DRAGON CLAN INTO A LAUGHING-STOCK LIKE THAT--!
*THIS* IS WHY YOU DENSE, DULL HUMANS ARE--
COSETTE WAS GENUINELY LOOKING OUT FOR YOU-- IN HER OWN WAY.
BUT MORE IM-PORTANT-LY, ECO...
WHAT IS IT NOW, DOG?!
WHY ARE YOU *IN MY CLASS*?!!
?
TO PARTICIPATE IN SCHOOL AND WHATNOT, NATURALLY!
IT SOUNDED INTERESTING.
BUT YOU'RE A *DRAGON* ...!
OOOHH!! THERE'S ECO!!
OH, WOW! YOU'RE COMING TO CLASS TOO? THAT'S AMAZING!
HI, RAYMOND. HEY, MAX.

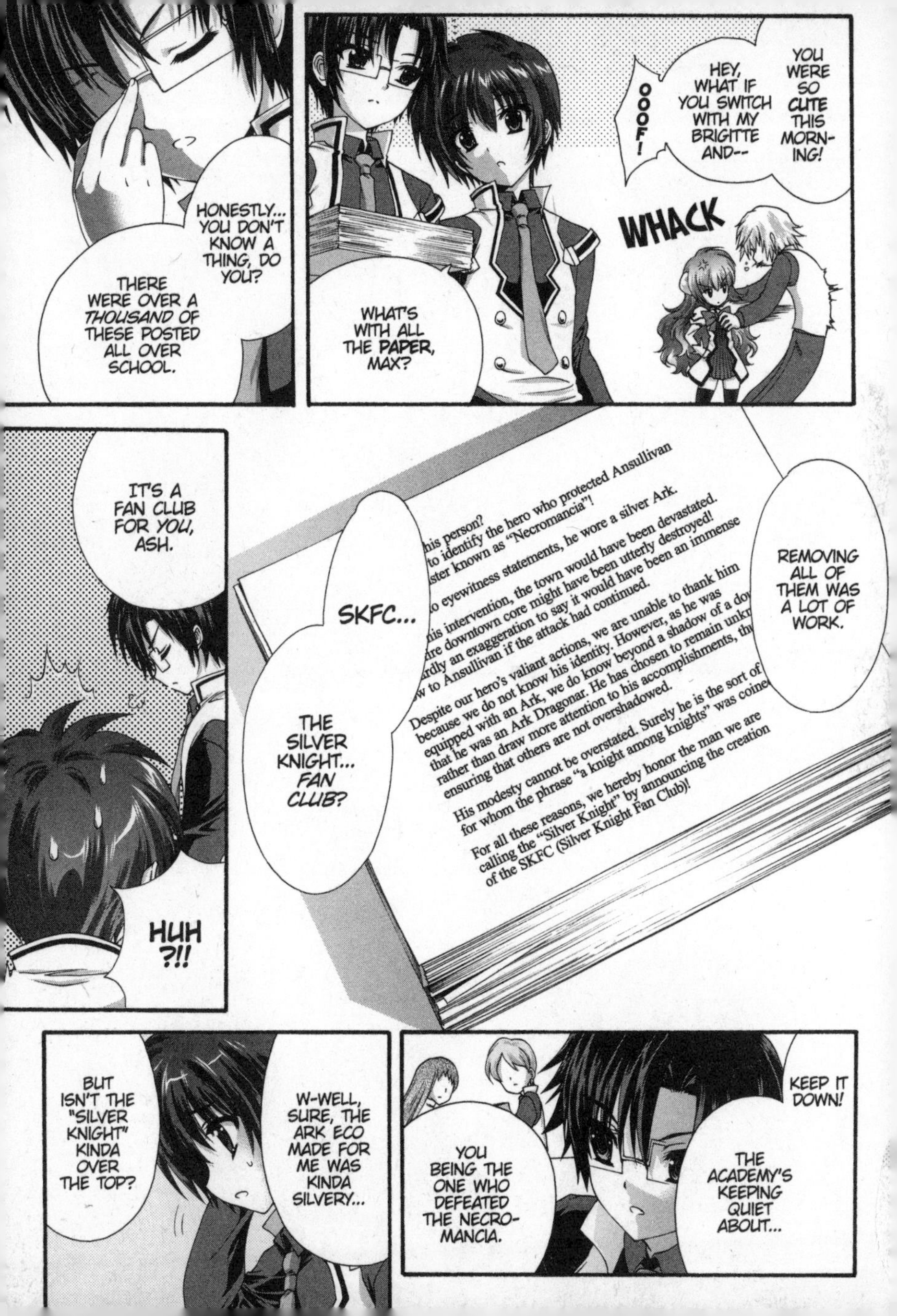
YOU WERE SO CUTE THIS MORNING!
HEY, WHAT IF YOU SWITCH WITH MY BRIGITTE AND--
OOOF!
WHACK
WHAT'S WITH ALL THE PAPER, MAX?
HONESTLY... YOU DON'T KNOW A THING, DO YOU?
THERE WERE OVER A THOUSAND OF THESE POSTED ALL OVER SCHOOL.
REMOVING ALL OF THEM WAS A LOT OF WORK.
his person?
to identify the hero who protected Ansullivan
ster known as "Necromancia"!
o eyewitness statements, he wore a silver Ark.
his intervention, the town would have been devastated.
ire downtown core might have been utterly destroyed!
rdly an exaggeration to say it would have been an immense
w to Ansullivan if the attack had continued.
Despite our hero's valiant actions, we are unable to thank him
because we do not know his identity. However, as he was
equipped with an Ark, we do know beyond a shadow of a do
that he was an Ark Dragonar. He has chosen to remain unkn
rather than draw more attention to his accomplishments, th
ensuring that others are not overshadowed.
His modesty cannot be overstated. Surely he is the sort of
for whom the phrase "a knight among knights" was coine
For all these reasons, we hereby honor the man we are
calling the "Silver Knight" by announcing the creation
of the SKFC (Silver Knight Fan Club)!
SKFC...
THE SILVER KNIGHT... FAN CLUB?
IT'S A FAN CLUB FOR YOU, ASH.
HUH?!!
KEEP IT DOWN!
THE ACADEMY'S KEEPING QUIET ABOUT...
YOU BEING THE ONE WHO DEFEATED THE NECROMANCIA.
W-WELL, SURE, THE ARK ECO MADE FOR ME WAS KINDA SILVERY...
BUT ISN'T THE "SILVER KNIGHT" KINDA OVER THE TOP?

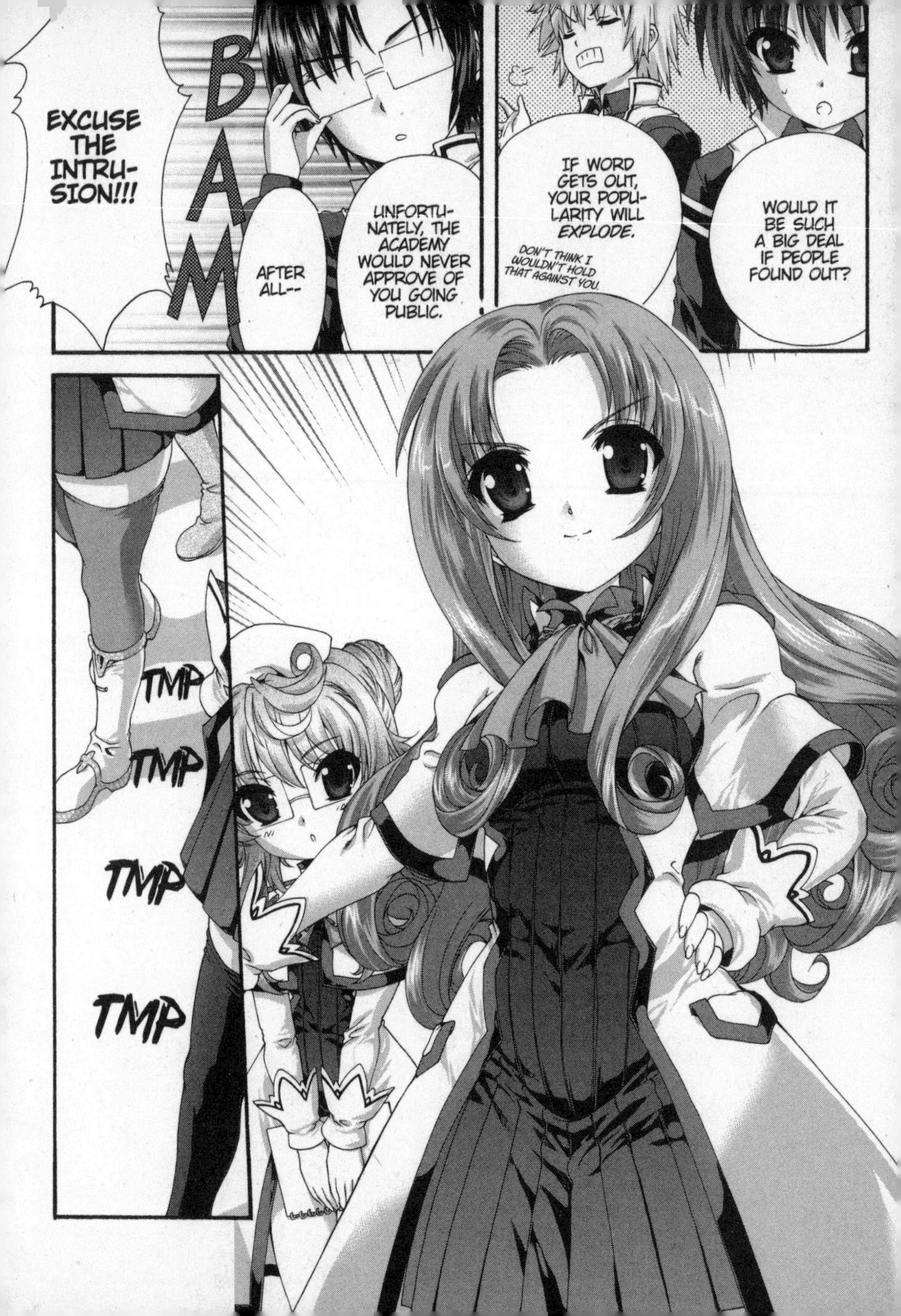

WOULD IT BE SUCH A BIG DEAL IF PEOPLE FOUND OUT?
IF WORD GETS OUT, YOUR POPULARITY WILL EXPLODE.
DON'T THINK I WOULDN'T HOLD THAT AGAINST YOU.
UNFORTUNATELY, THE ACADEMY WOULD NEVER APPROVE OF YOU GOING PUBLIC.
AFTER ALL--
BAM
EXCUSE THE INTRUSION!!!
TMP
TMP
TMP
TMP

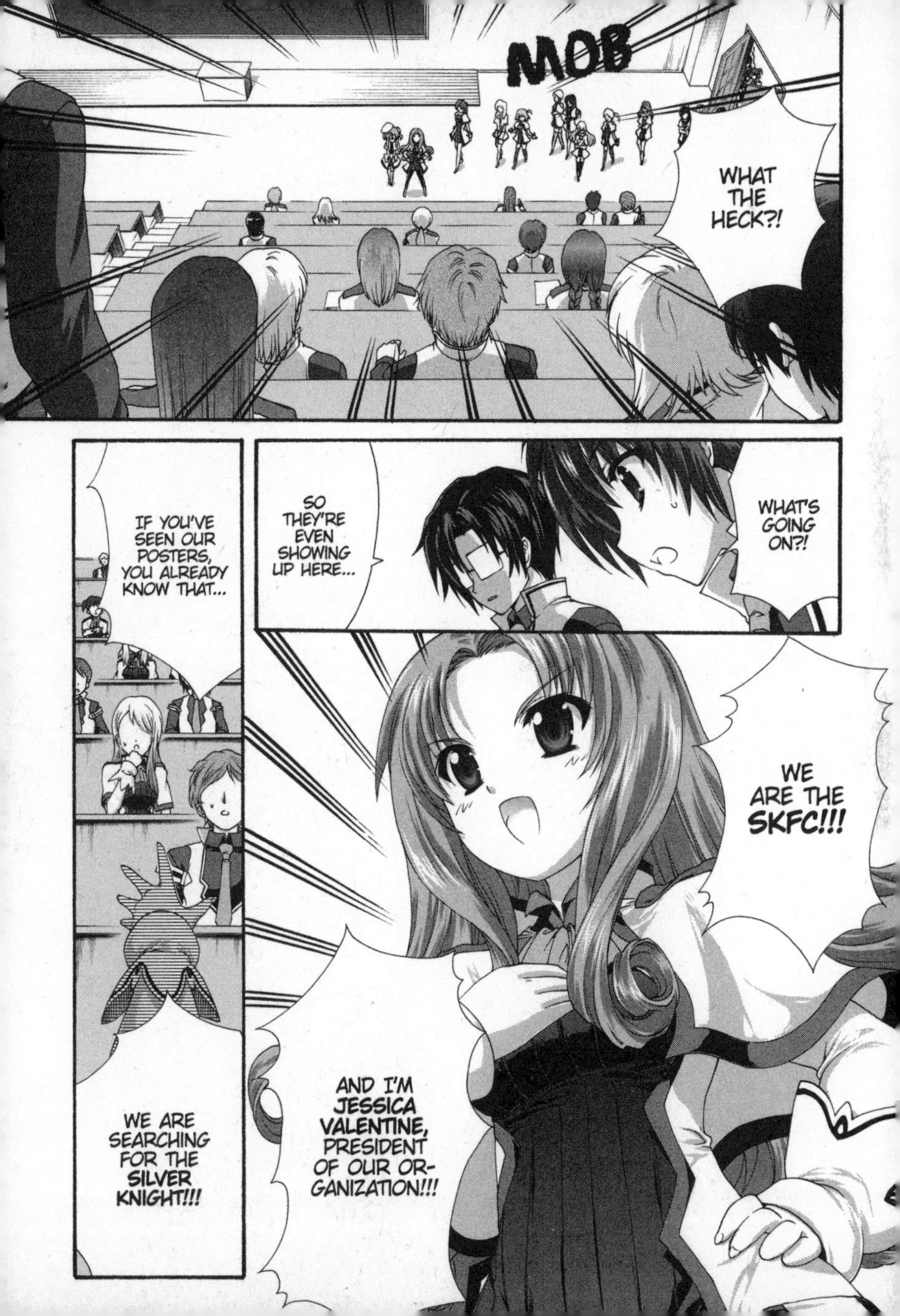
MOB
WHAT THE HECK?!
WHAT'S GOING ON?!
SO THEY'RE EVEN SHOWING UP HERE...
WE ARE THE SKFC!!!
AND I'M JESSICA VALENTINE, PRESIDENT OF OUR OR-GANIZATION!!!
IF YOU'VE SEEN OUR POSTERS, YOU ALREADY KNOW THAT...
WE ARE SEARCHING FOR THE SILVER KNIGHT!!!

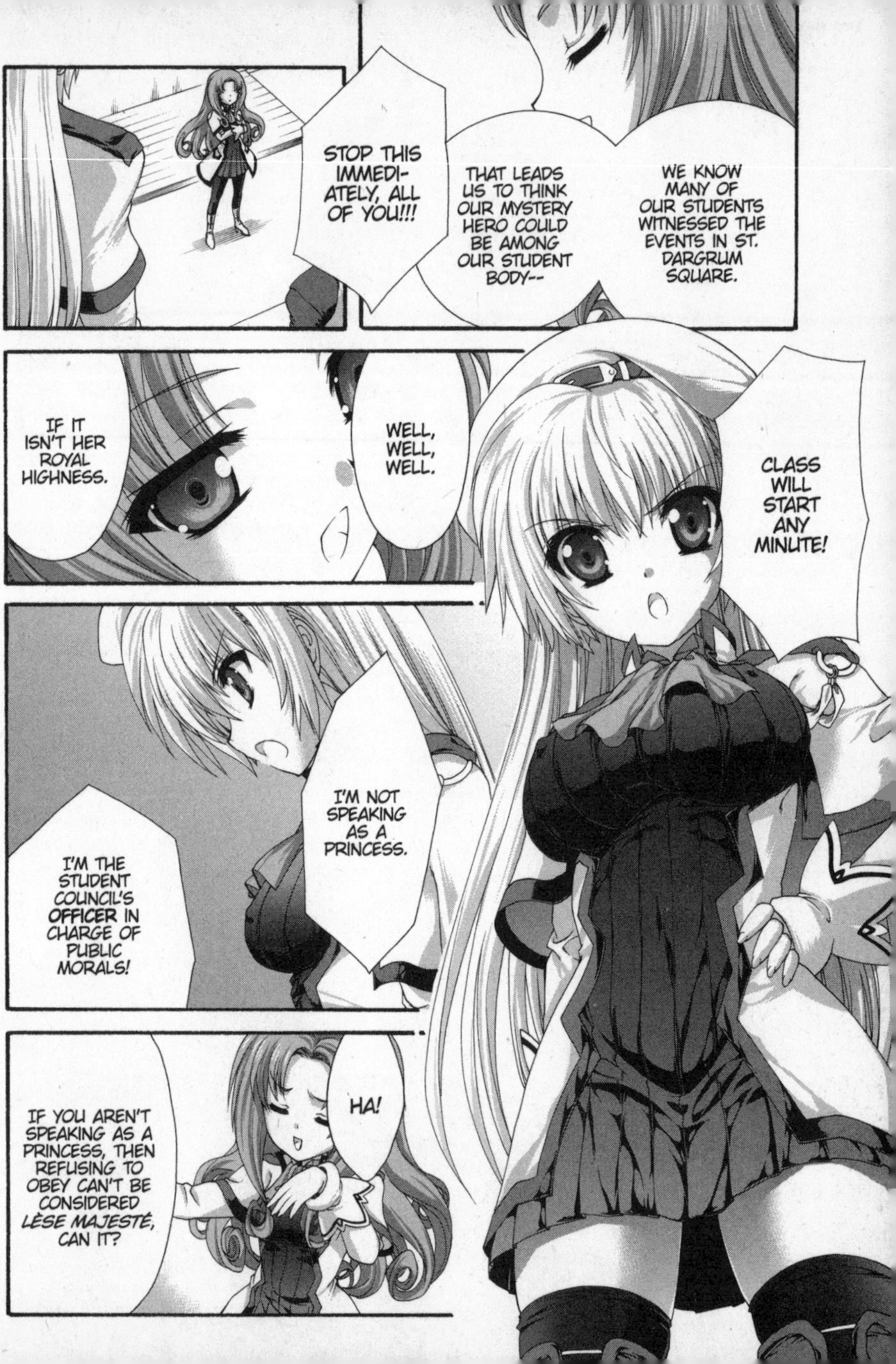
WE KNOW MANY OF OUR STUDENTS WITNESSED THE EVENTS IN ST. DARGRUM SQUARE.
THAT LEADS US TO THINK OUR MYSTERY HERO COULD BE AMONG OUR STUDENT BODY--
STOP THIS IMMEDI-ATELY, ALL OF YOU!!!
CLASS WILL START ANY MINUTE!
WELL, WELL, WELL.
IF IT ISN'T HER ROYAL HIGHNESS.
I'M NOT SPEAKING AS A PRINCESS.
I'M THE STUDENT COUNCIL'S **OFFICER** IN CHARGE OF PUBLIC MORALS!
HA!
IF YOU AREN'T SPEAKING AS A PRINCESS, THEN REFUSING TO OBEY CAN'T BE CONSIDERED *LÈSE MAJESTÉ*, CAN IT?

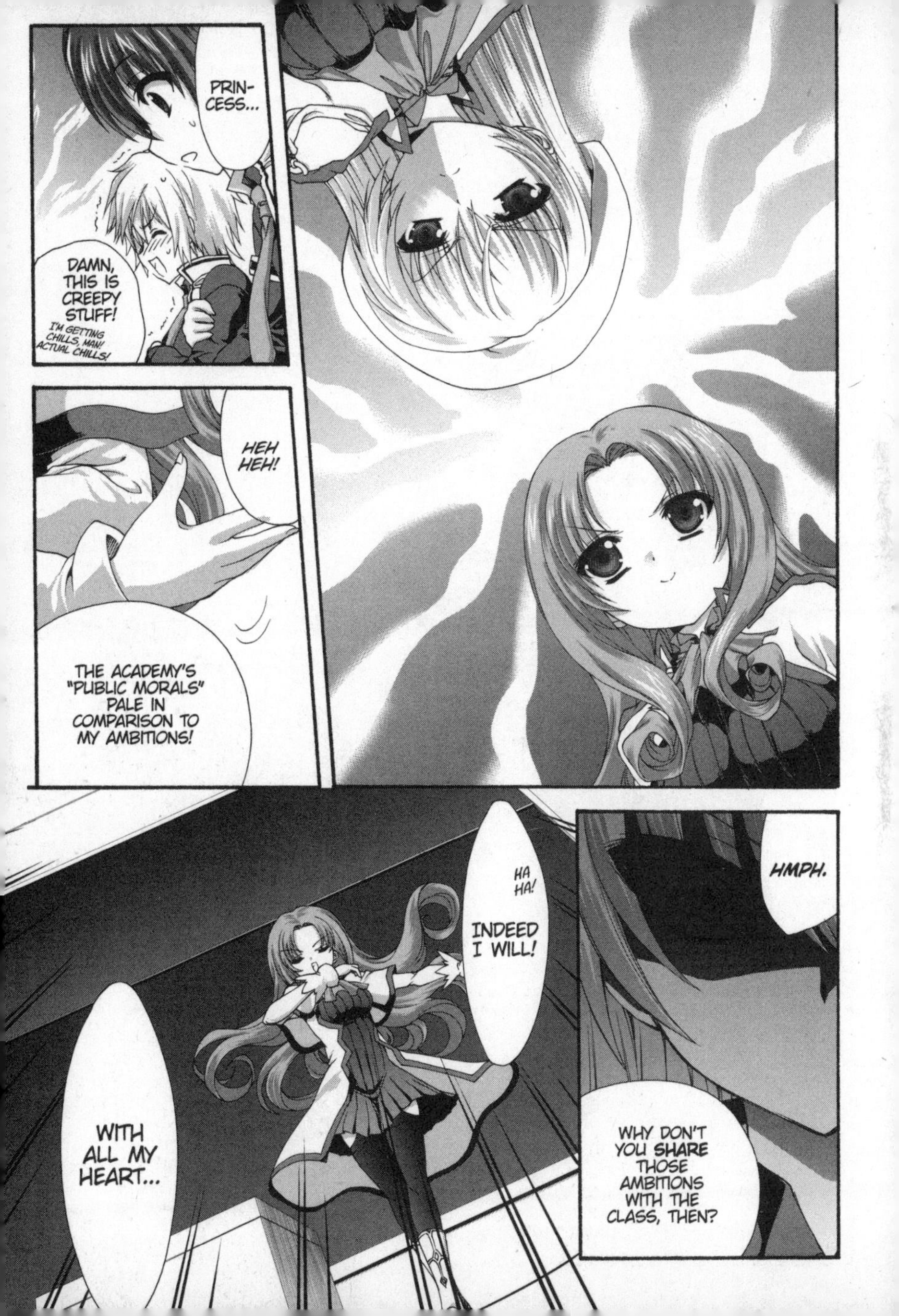
PRIN-CESS...
DAMN, THIS IS CREEPY STUFF!
I'M GETTING CHILLS, MAN! ACTUAL CHILLS!
HEH HEH!
THE ACADEMY'S "PUBLIC MORALS" PALE IN COMPARISON TO MY AMBITIONS!
HMPH.
WHY DON'T YOU **SHARE** THOSE AMBITIONS WITH THE CLASS, THEN?
HA HA!
INDEED I WILL!
WITH ALL MY HEART...

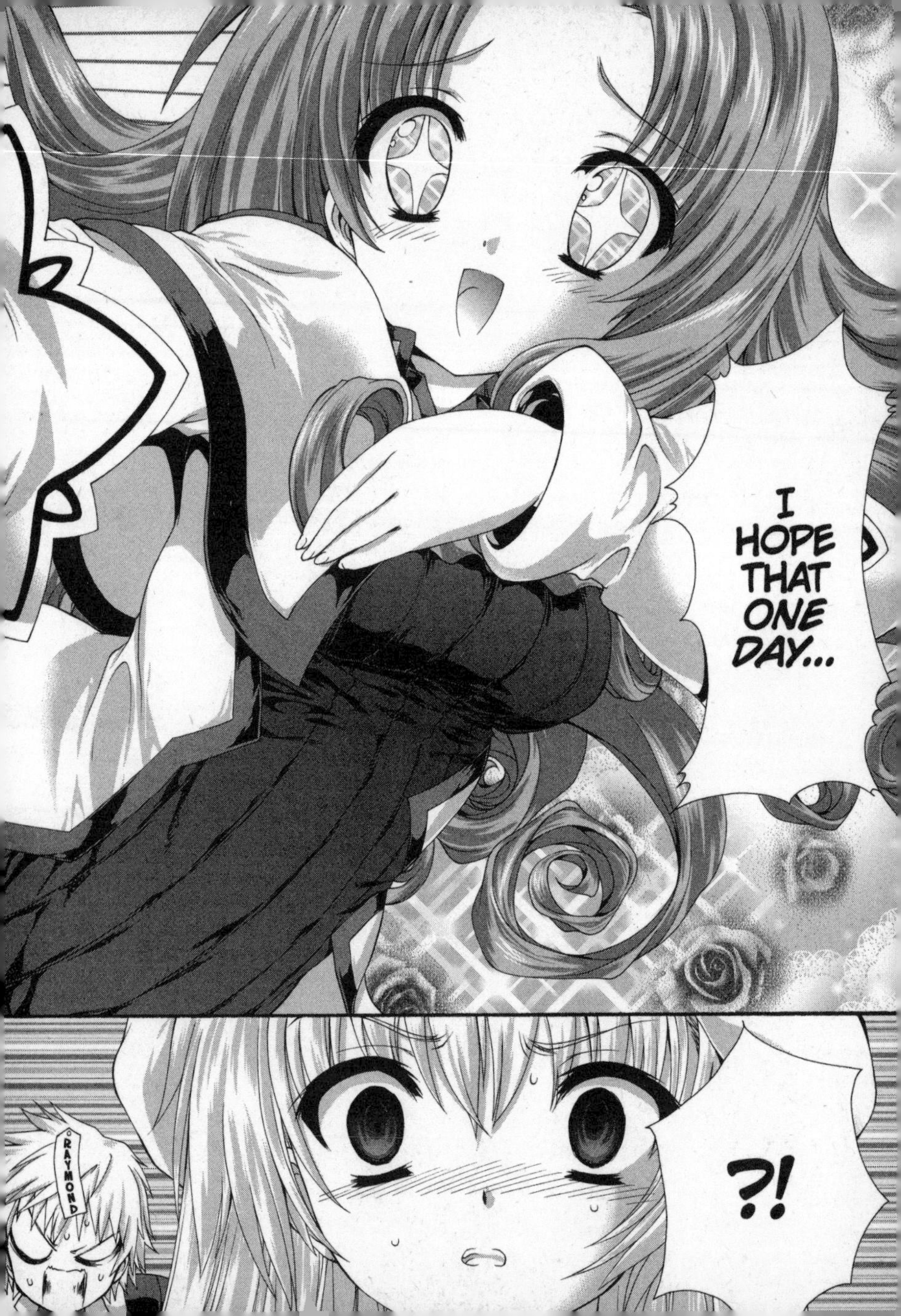
I HOPE THAT ONE DAY...
?!
RAYMOND

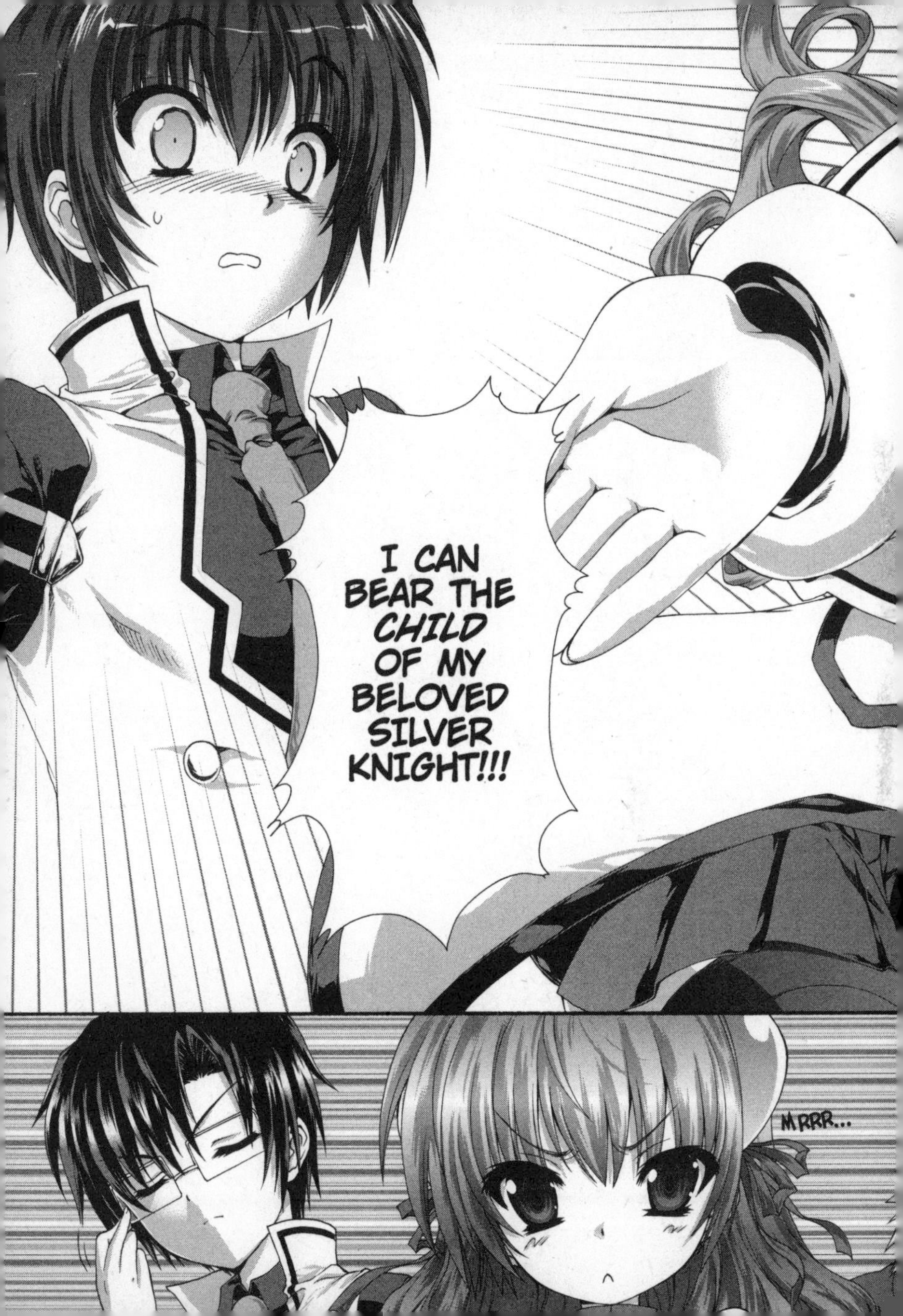
I CAN BEAR THE CHILD OF MY BELOVED SILVER KNIGHT!!!
MRRR...

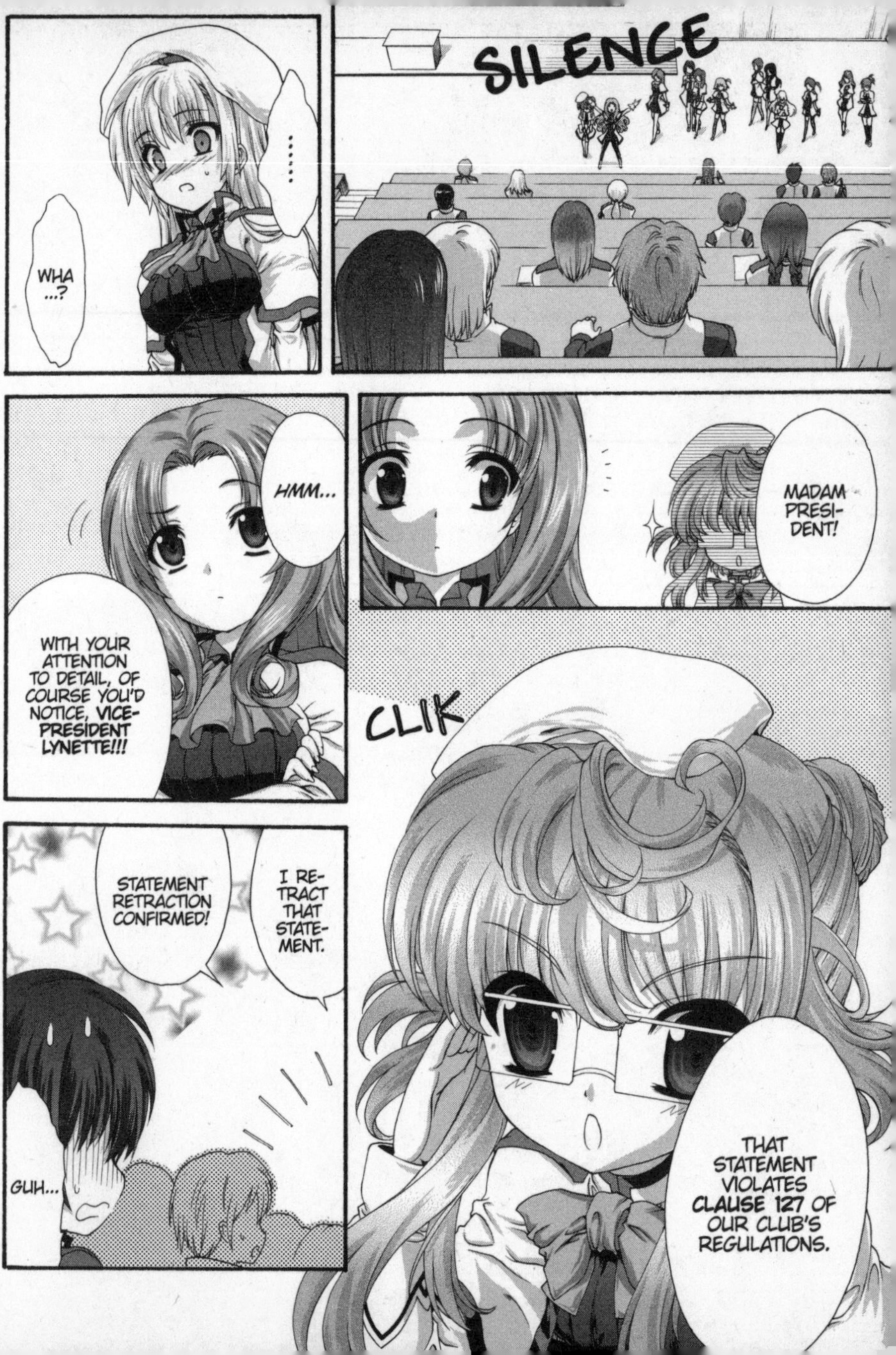
SILENCE
......
WHA ...?
MADAM PRESI-DENT!
HMM...
WITH YOUR ATTENTION TO DETAIL, OF COURSE YOU'D NOTICE, VICE-PRESIDENT LYNETTE!!!
CLIK
THAT STATEMENT VIOLATES CLAUSE 127 OF OUR CLUB'S REGULATIONS.
I RE-TRACT THAT STATE-MENT.
STATEMENT RETRACTION CONFIRMED!
GUH...

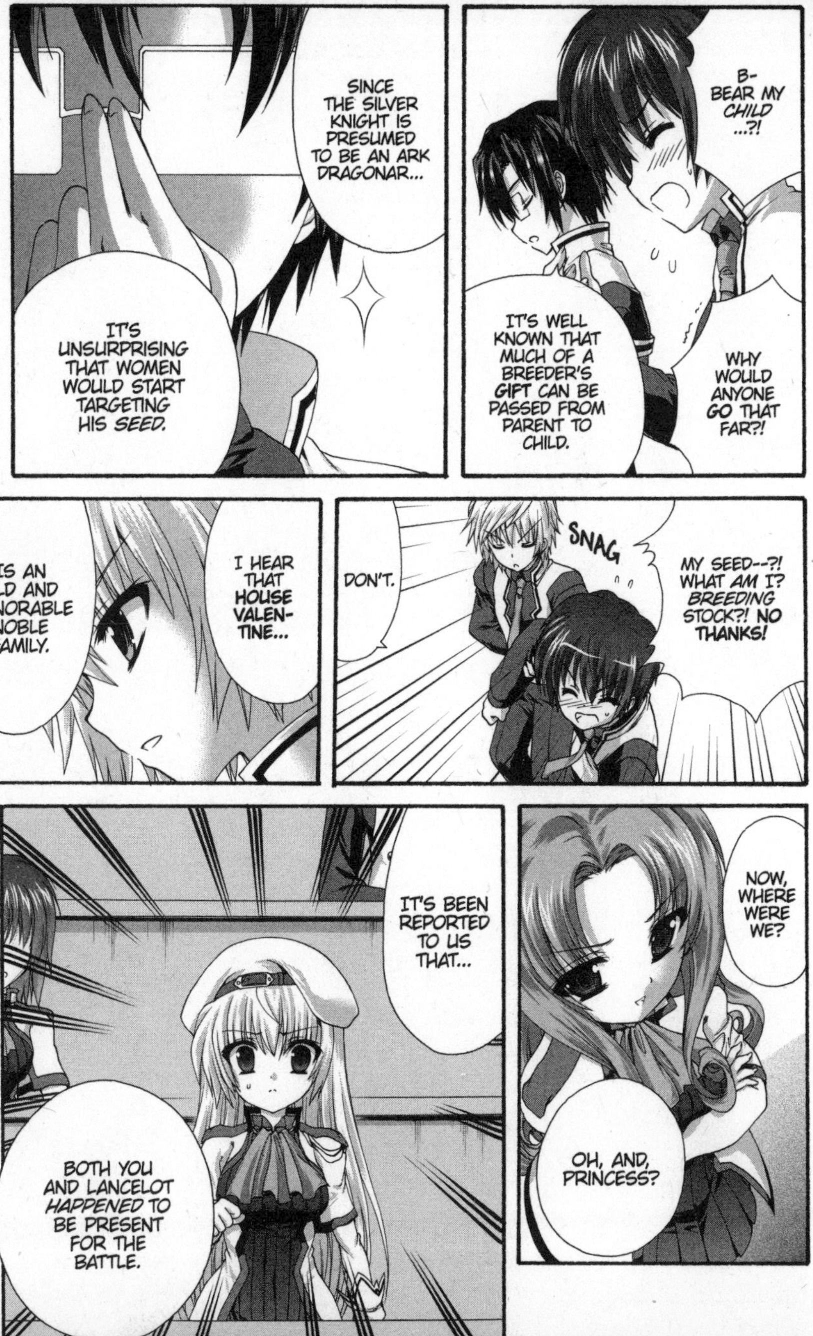
B- BEAR MY CHILD ...?!
WHY WOULD ANYONE GO THAT FAR?!
IT'S WELL KNOWN THAT MUCH OF A BREEDER'S GIFT CAN BE PASSED FROM PARENT TO CHILD.
SINCE THE SILVER KNIGHT IS PRESUMED TO BE AN ARK DRAGONAR...
IT'S UNSURPRISING THAT WOMEN WOULD START TARGETING HIS SEED.
MY SEED--?! WHAT AM I? BREEDING STOCK?! NO THANKS!
SNAG
DON'T.
I HEAR THAT HOUSE VALENTINE...
IS AN OLD AND HONORABLE NOBLE FAMILY.
NOW, WHERE WERE WE?
OH, AND, PRINCESS?
IT'S BEEN REPORTED TO US THAT...
BOTH YOU AND LANCELOT HAPPENED TO BE PRESENT FOR THE BATTLE.

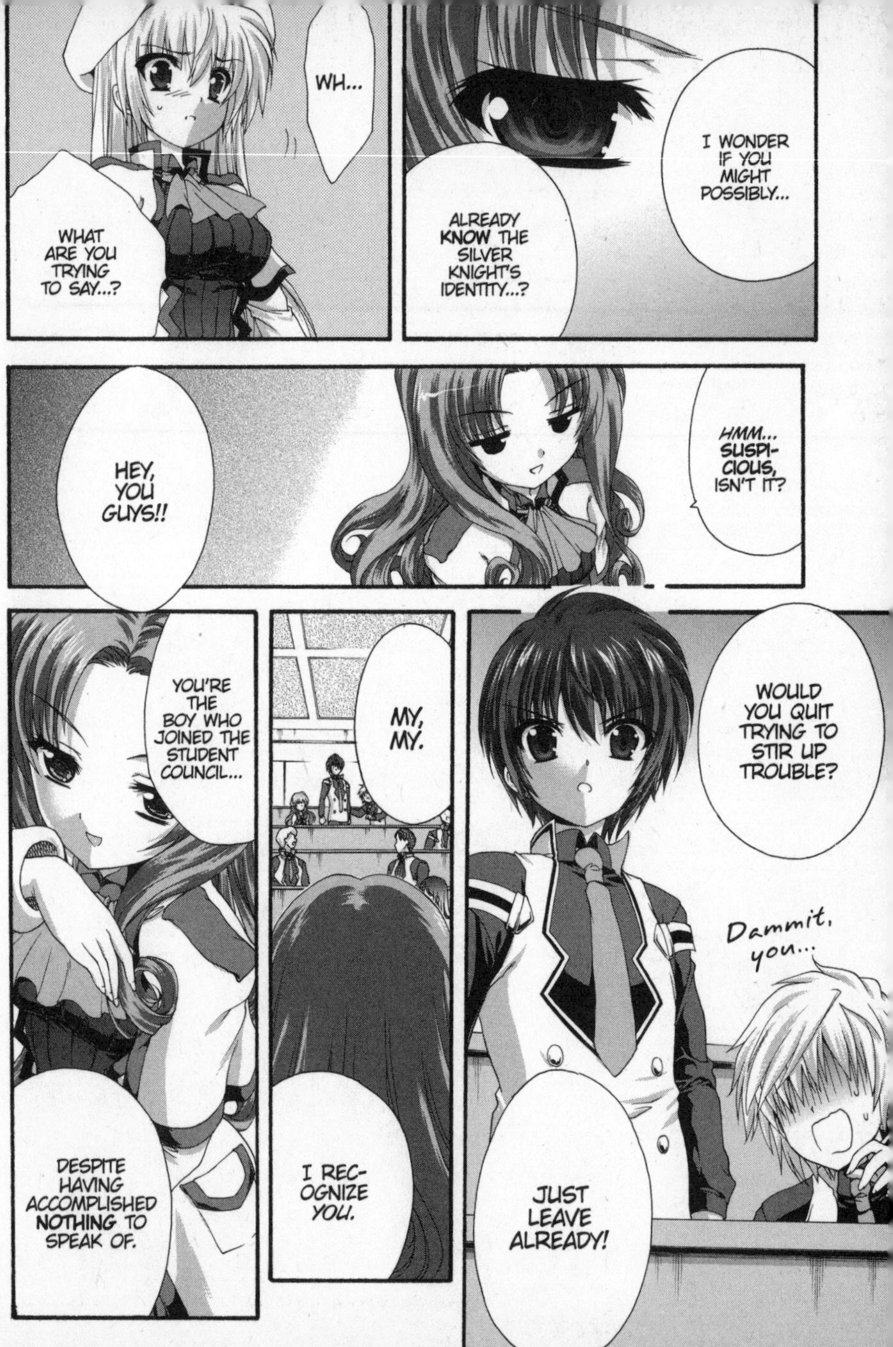
I WONDER IF YOU MIGHT POSSIBLY...
ALREADY KNOW THE SILVER KNIGHT'S IDENTITY...?
WH...
WHAT ARE YOU TRYING TO SAY...?
HMM... SUSPICIOUS, ISN'T IT?
HEY, YOU GUYS!!
WOULD YOU QUIT TRYING TO STIR UP TROUBLE?
Dammit, you...
JUST LEAVE ALREADY!
MY, MY.
I RECOGNIZE YOU.
YOU'RE THE BOY WHO JOINED THE STUDENT COUNCIL...
DESPITE HAVING ACCOMPLISHED NOTHING TO SPEAK OF.

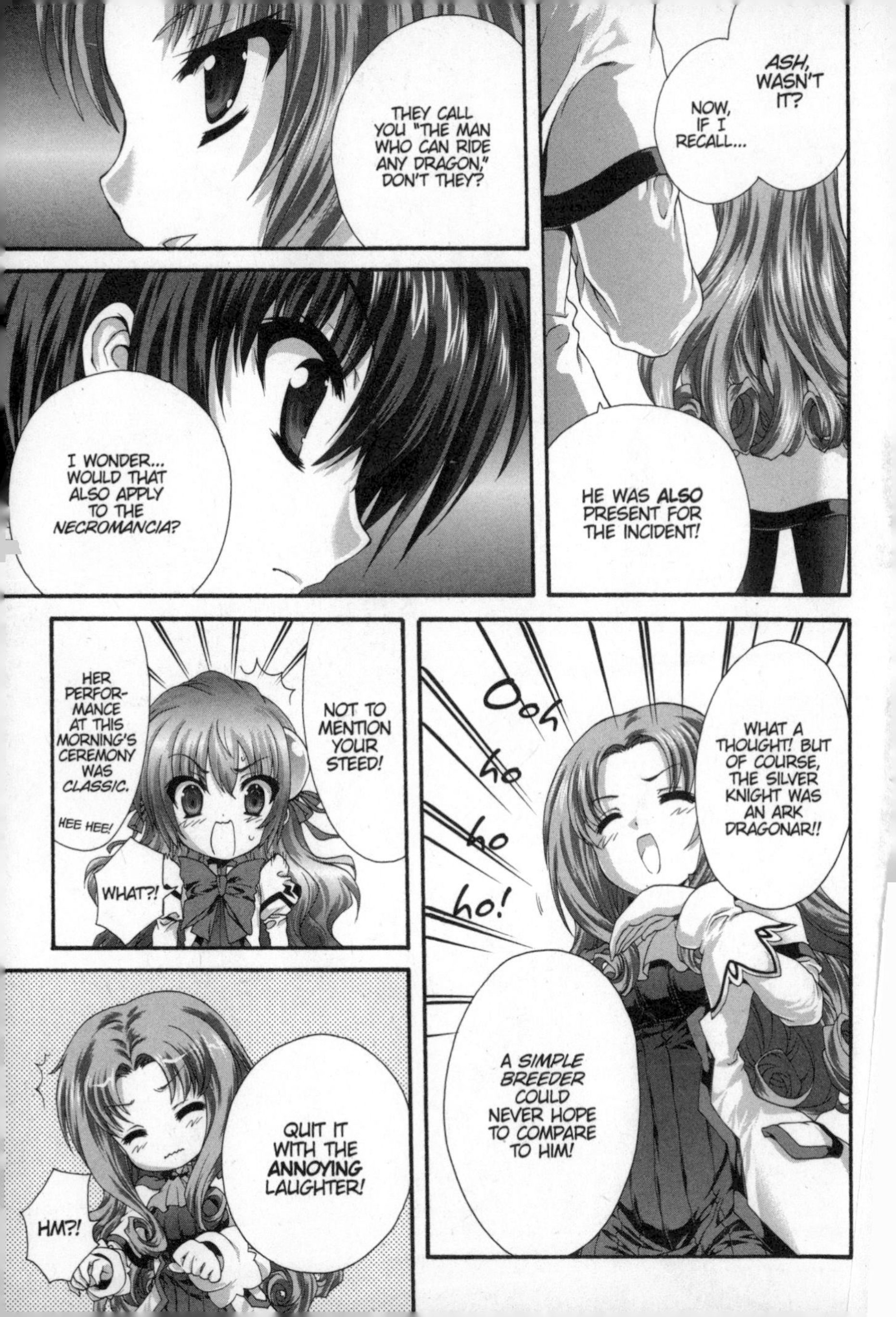
ASH, WASN'T IT?
NOW, IF I RECALL...
HE WAS ALSO PRESENT FOR THE INCIDENT!
THEY CALL YOU "THE MAN WHO CAN RIDE ANY DRAGON," DON'T THEY?
I WONDER... WOULD THAT ALSO APPLY TO THE NECROMANCIA?
WHAT A THOUGHT! BUT OF COURSE, THE SILVER KNIGHT WAS AN ARK DRAGONAR!!
Ooh ho ho ho!
A SIMPLE BREEDER COULD NEVER HOPE TO COMPARE TO HIM!
NOT TO MENTION YOUR STEED!
HER PERFORMANCE AT THIS MORNING'S CEREMONY WAS CLASSIC.
HEE HEE!
WHAT?!
QUIT IT WITH THE ANNOYING LAUGHTER!
HM?!

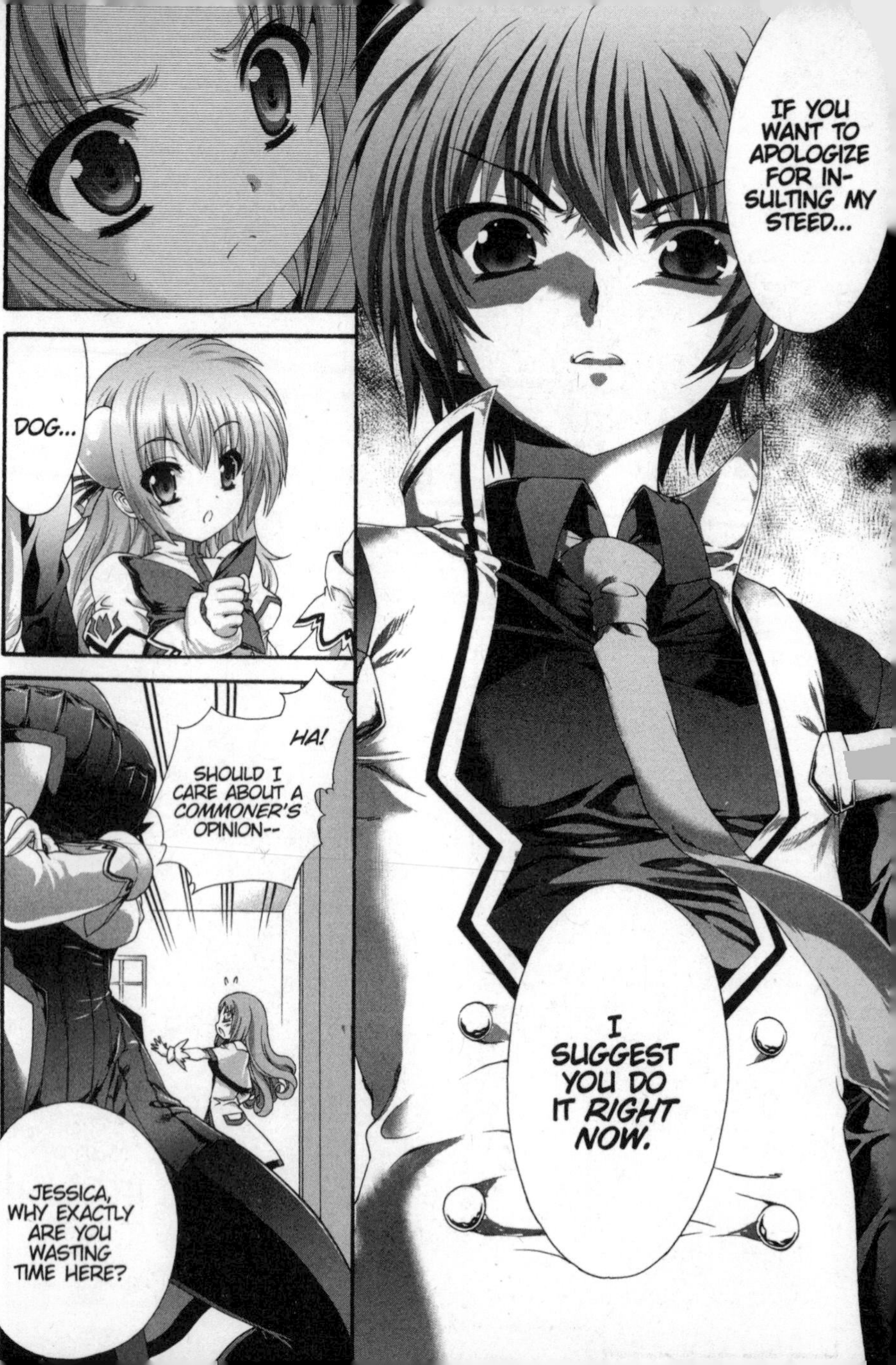
IF YOU WANT TO APOLOGIZE FOR IN-SULTING MY STEED...
I SUGGEST YOU DO IT *RIGHT NOW.*
DOG...
HA!
SHOULD I CARE ABOUT A COMMONER'S OPINION--
JESSICA, WHY EXACTLY ARE YOU WASTING TIME HERE?

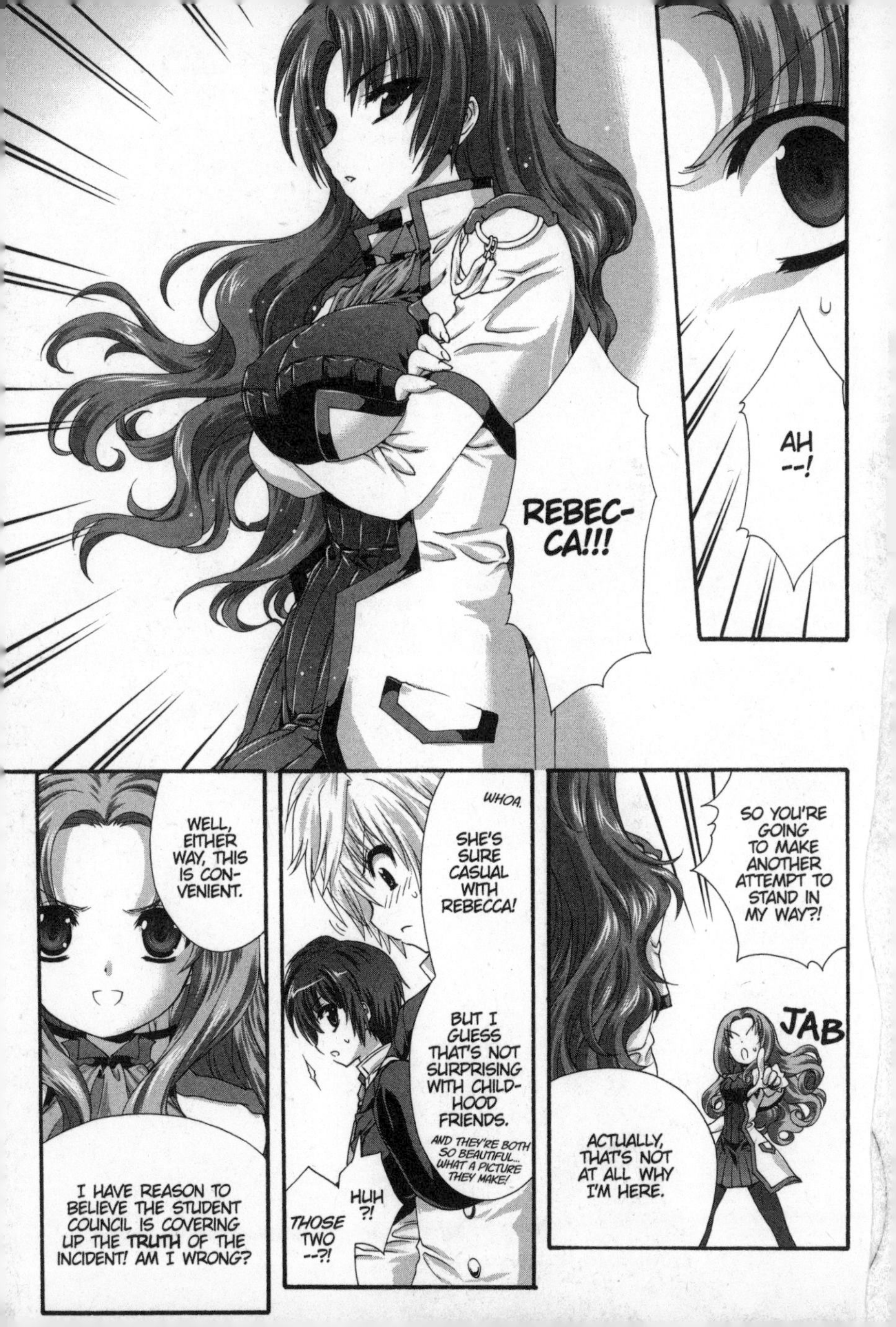
AH --!
REBEC-CA!!!
SO YOU'RE GOING TO MAKE ANOTHER ATTEMPT TO STAND IN MY WAY?!
JAB
ACTUALLY, THAT'S NOT AT ALL WHY I'M HERE.
WHOA.
SHE'S SURE CASUAL WITH REBECCA!
BUT I GUESS THAT'S NOT SURPRISING WITH CHILD-HOOD FRIENDS.
AND THEY'RE BOTH SO BEAUTIFUL... WHAT A PICTURE THEY MAKE!
HUH ?!
THOSE TWO --?!
WELL, EITHER WAY, THIS IS CON-VENIENT.
I HAVE REASON TO BELIEVE THE STUDENT COUNCIL IS COVERING UP THE TRUTH OF THE INCIDENT! AM I WRONG?

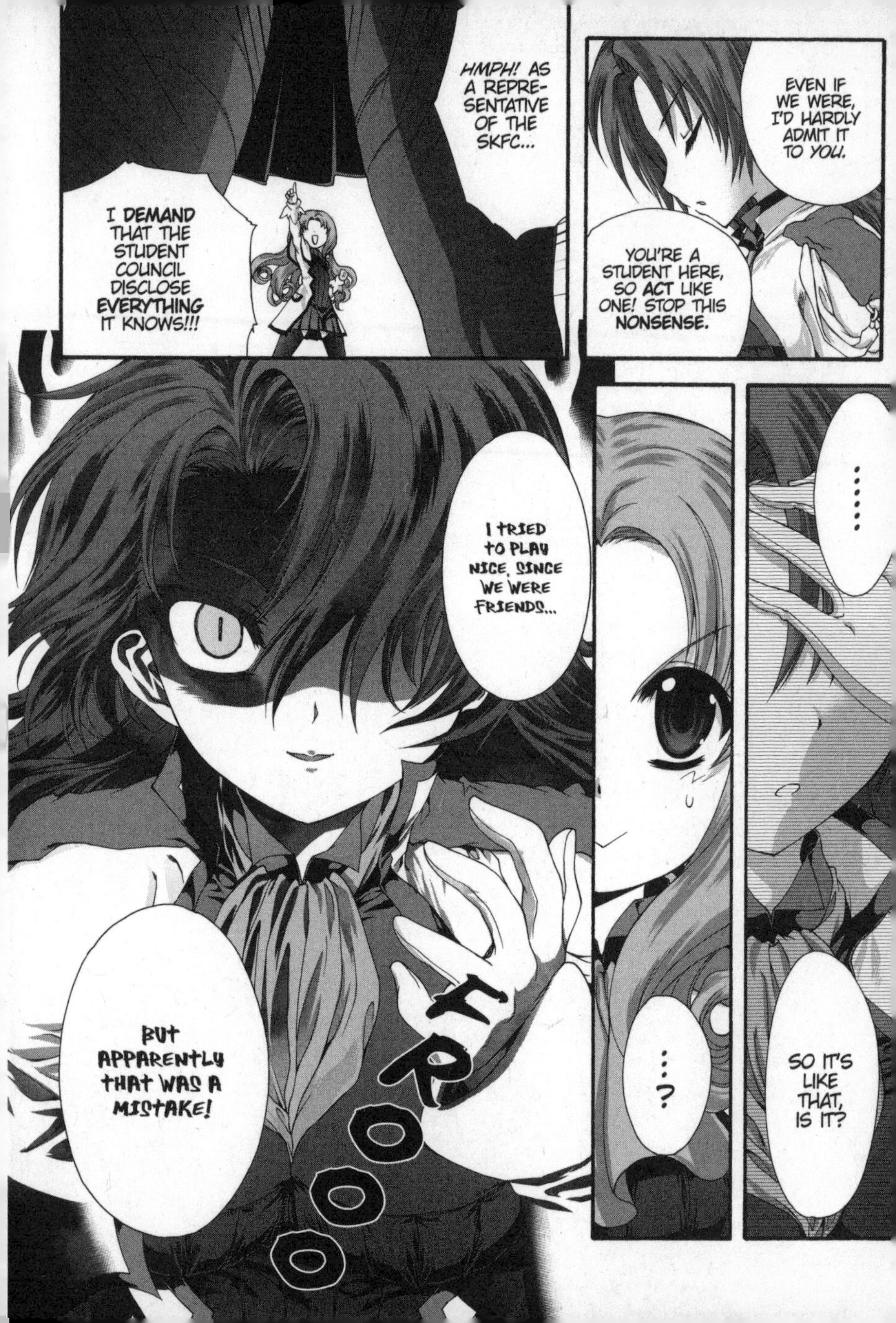
EVEN IF WE WERE, I'D HARDLY ADMIT IT TO *YOU*.
YOU'RE A STUDENT HERE, SO **ACT** LIKE ONE! STOP THIS **NONSENSE**.
*HMPH!* AS A REPRESENTATIVE OF THE SKFC...
I **DEMAND** THAT THE STUDENT COUNCIL DISCLOSE **EVERYTHING** IT KNOWS!!!
......
SO IT'S LIKE THAT, IS IT?
...?
I TRIED TO PLAY NICE, SINCE WE WERE FRIENDS...
BUT APPARENTLY THAT WAS A MISTAKE!
FROOO

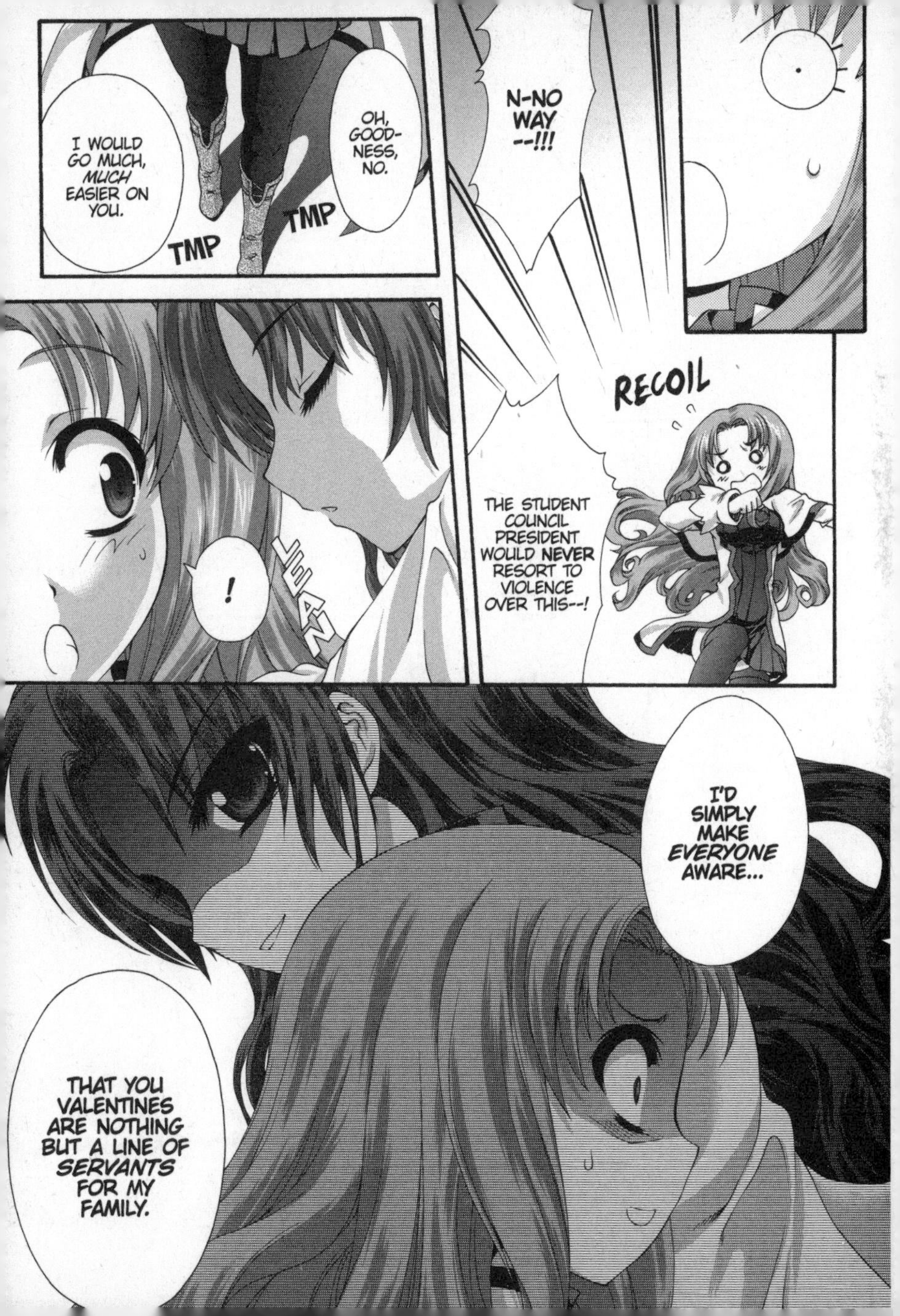
N-NO WAY--!!!
OH, GOODNESS, NO.
TMP
I WOULD GO MUCH, MUCH EASIER ON YOU.
TMP
RECOIL
THE STUDENT COUNCIL PRESIDENT WOULD NEVER RESORT TO VIOLENCE OVER THIS--!
!
I'D SIMPLY MAKE EVERYONE AWARE...
THAT YOU VALENTINES ARE NOTHING BUT A LINE OF SERVANTS FOR MY FAMILY.

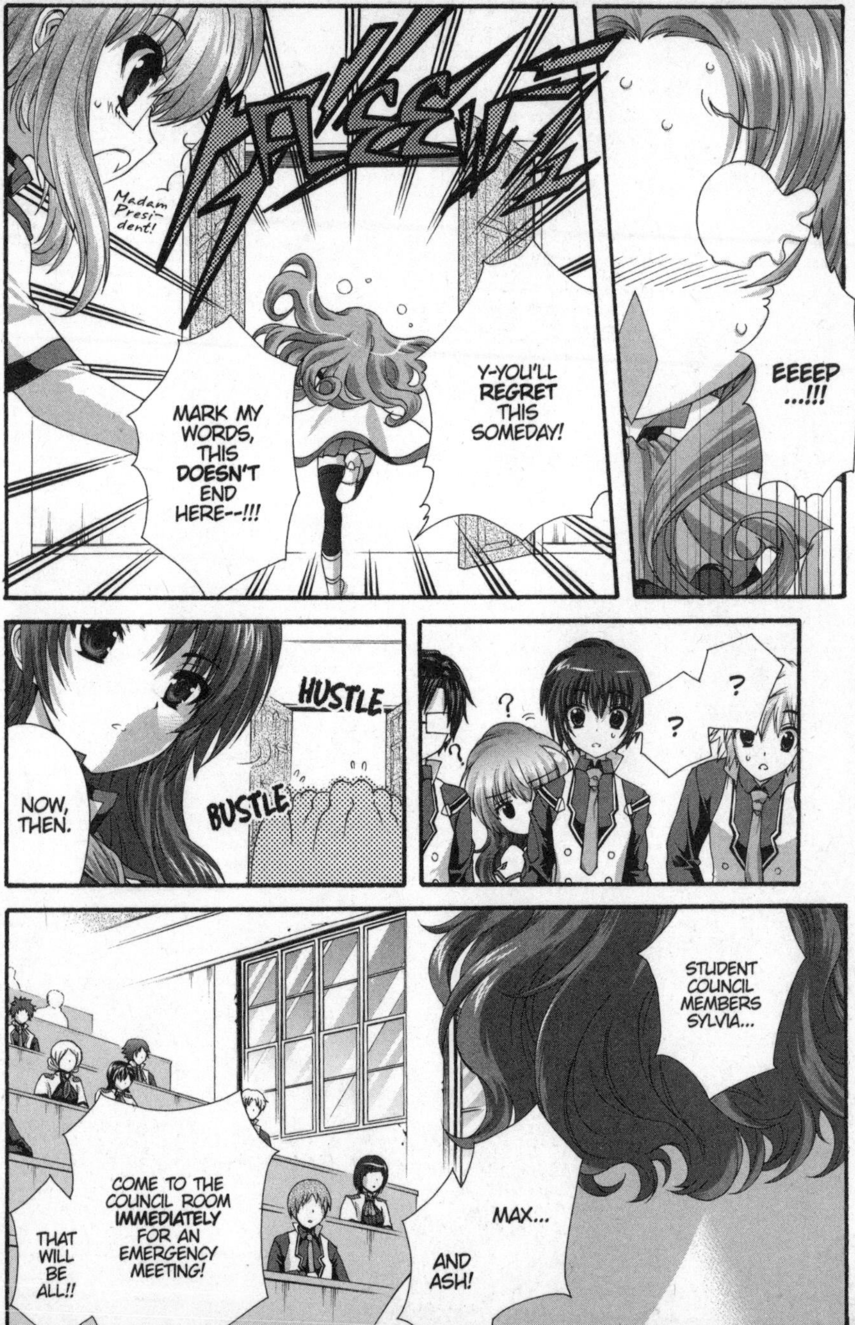
EEEEP ...!!!
Y-YOU'LL REGRET THIS SOMEDAY!
MARK MY WORDS, THIS DOESN'T END HERE--!!!
Madam Presi-dent!
?
?
?
?
HUSTLE
BUSTLE
NOW, THEN.
STUDENT COUNCIL MEMBERS SYLVIA...
MAX...
AND ASH!
COME TO THE COUNCIL ROOM IMMEDIATELY FOR AN EMERGENCY MEETING!
THAT WILL BE ALL!!

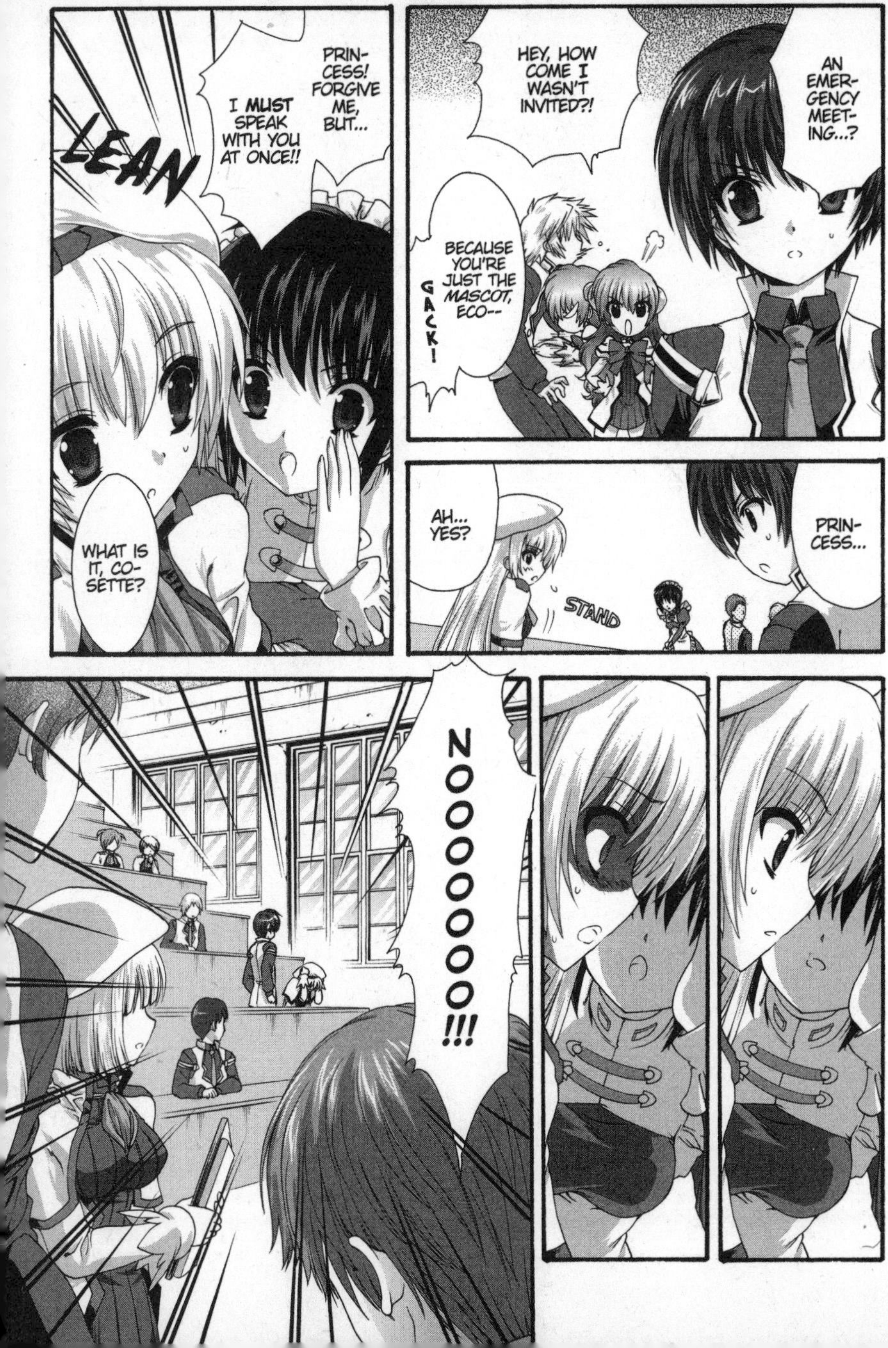
AN EMER-GENCY MEET-ING...?
HEY, HOW COME I WASN'T INVITED?!
BECAUSE YOU'RE JUST THE MASCOT, ECO--
GACK!
PRIN-CESS...
AH... YES?
STAND
PRIN-CESS! FORGIVE ME, BUT...
I MUST SPEAK WITH YOU AT ONCE!!
LEAN
WHAT IS IT, CO-SETTE?
NOOOOOOOOO!!!

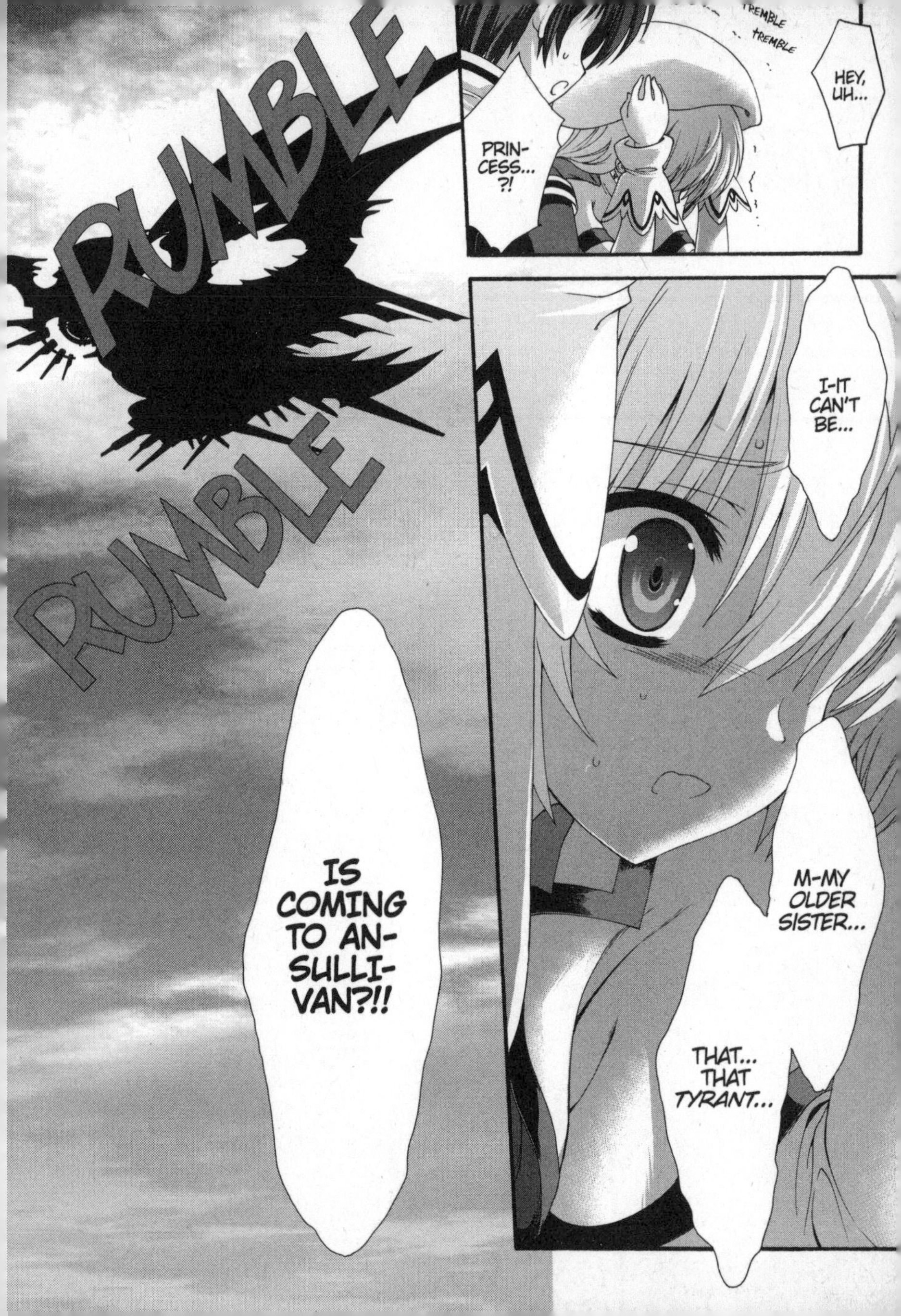
TREMBLE TREMBLE
HEY, UH...
PRIN-CESS...?!
I-IT CAN'T BE...
M-MY OLDER SISTER...
THAT... THAT *TYRANT*...
RUMBLE
RUMBLE
IS COMING TO AN-SULLI-VAN?!!

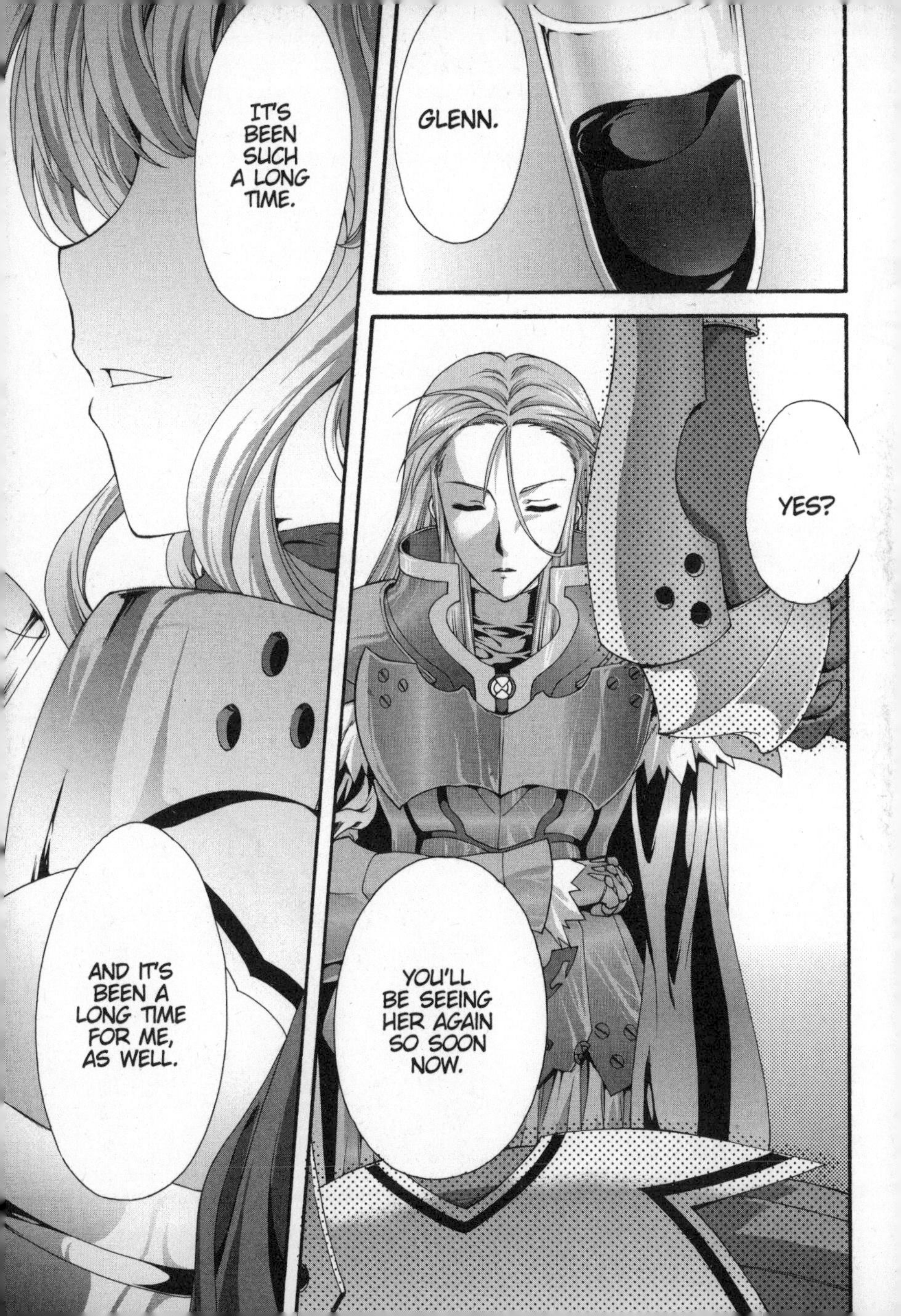
GLENN.
YES?
YOU'LL BE SEEING HER AGAIN SO SOON NOW.
IT'S BEEN SUCH A LONG TIME.
AND IT'S BEEN A LONG TIME FOR ME, AS WELL.

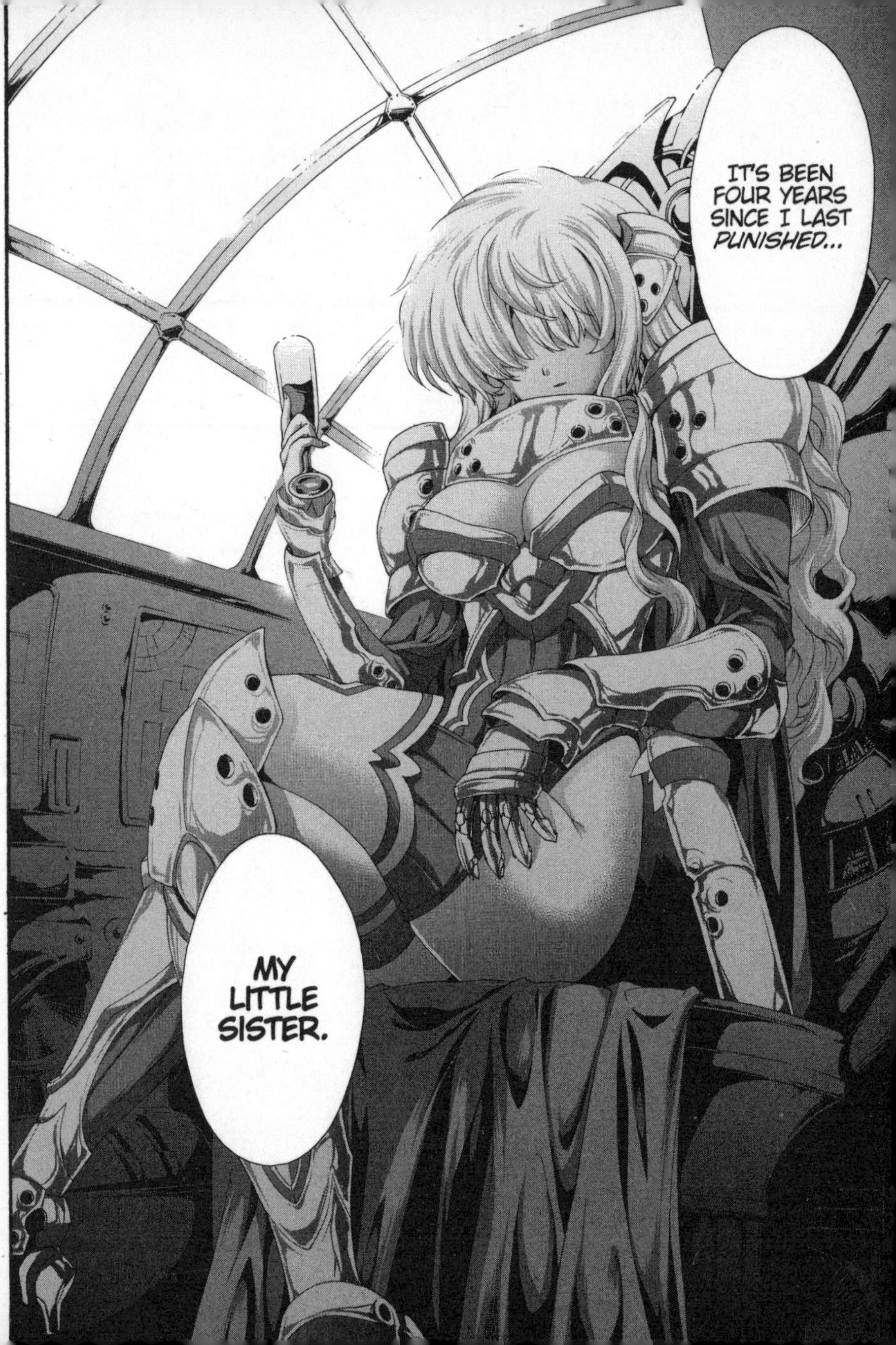
IT'S BEEN FOUR YEARS SINCE I LAST *PUNISHED*...
MY LITTLE SISTER.

DRAGONAR
ACADEMY

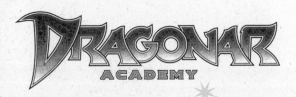

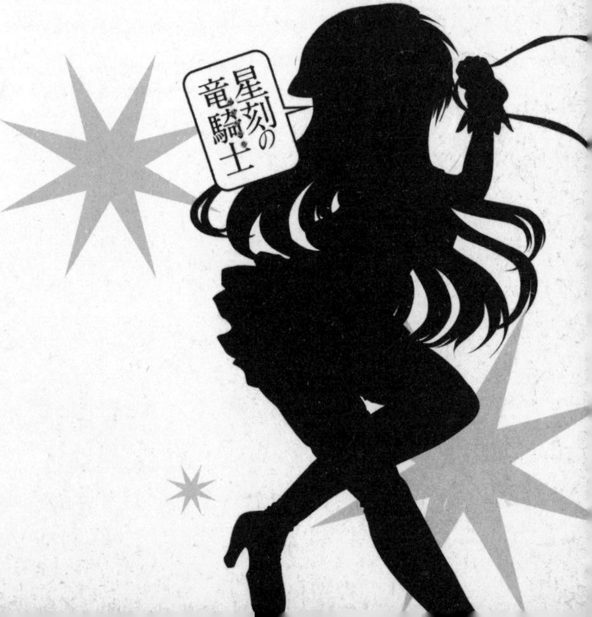
星刻の竜騎士

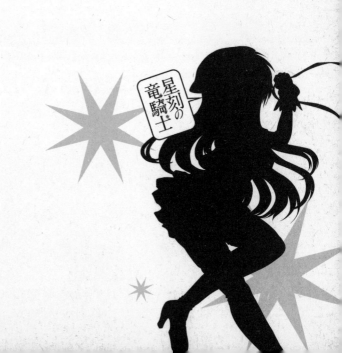

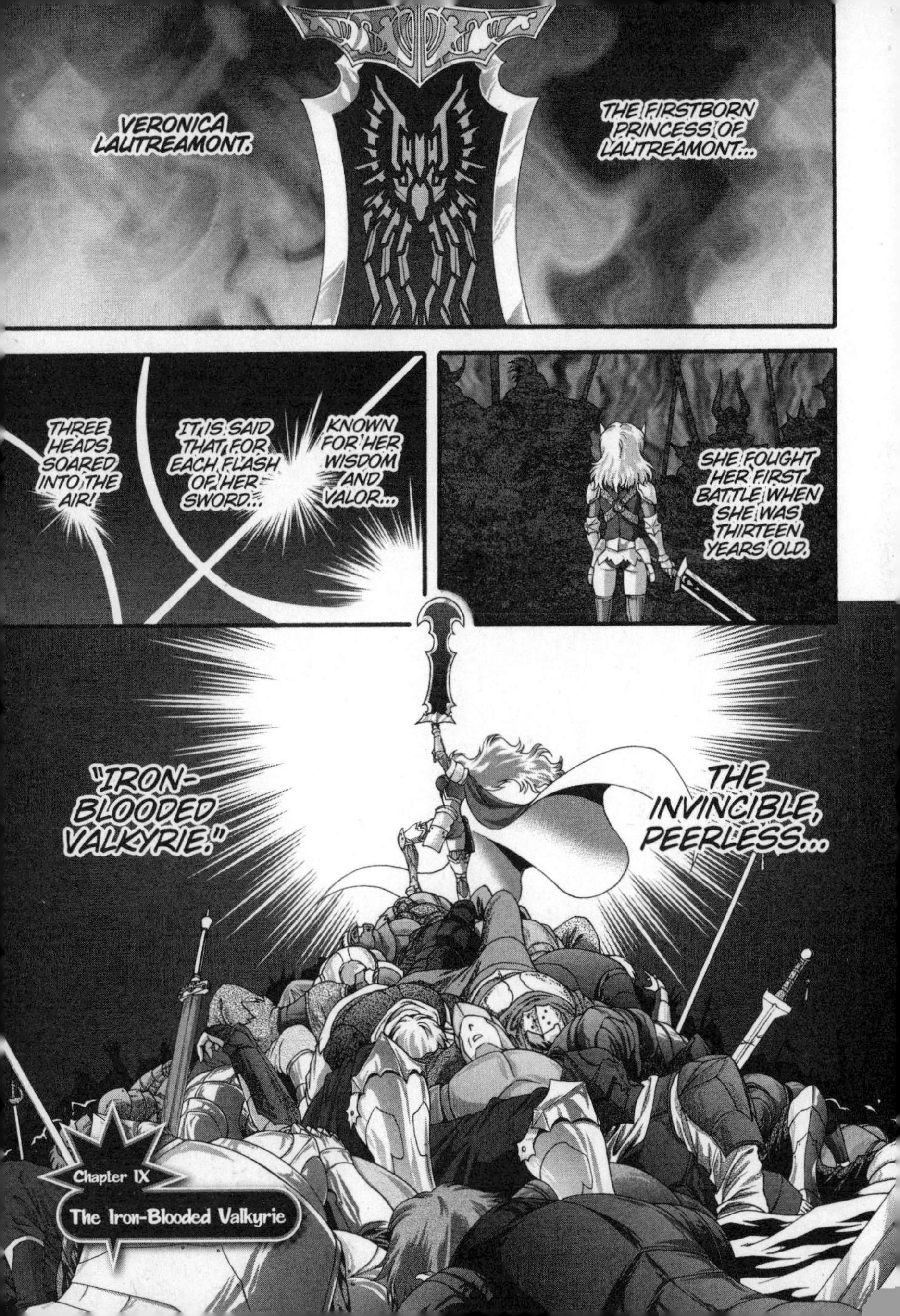
THE FIRSTBORN PRINCESS OF LAUTREAMONT...
VERONICA LAUTREAMONT.
SHE FOUGHT HER FIRST BATTLE WHEN SHE WAS THIRTEEN YEARS OLD.
KNOWN FOR HER WISDOM AND VALOR...
IT IS SAID THAT FOR EACH FLASH OF HER SWORD...
THREE HEADS SOARED INTO THE AIR!
THE INVINCIBLE, PEERLESS...
"IRON-BLOODED VALKYRIE."
Chapter IX
The Iron-Blooded Valkyrie

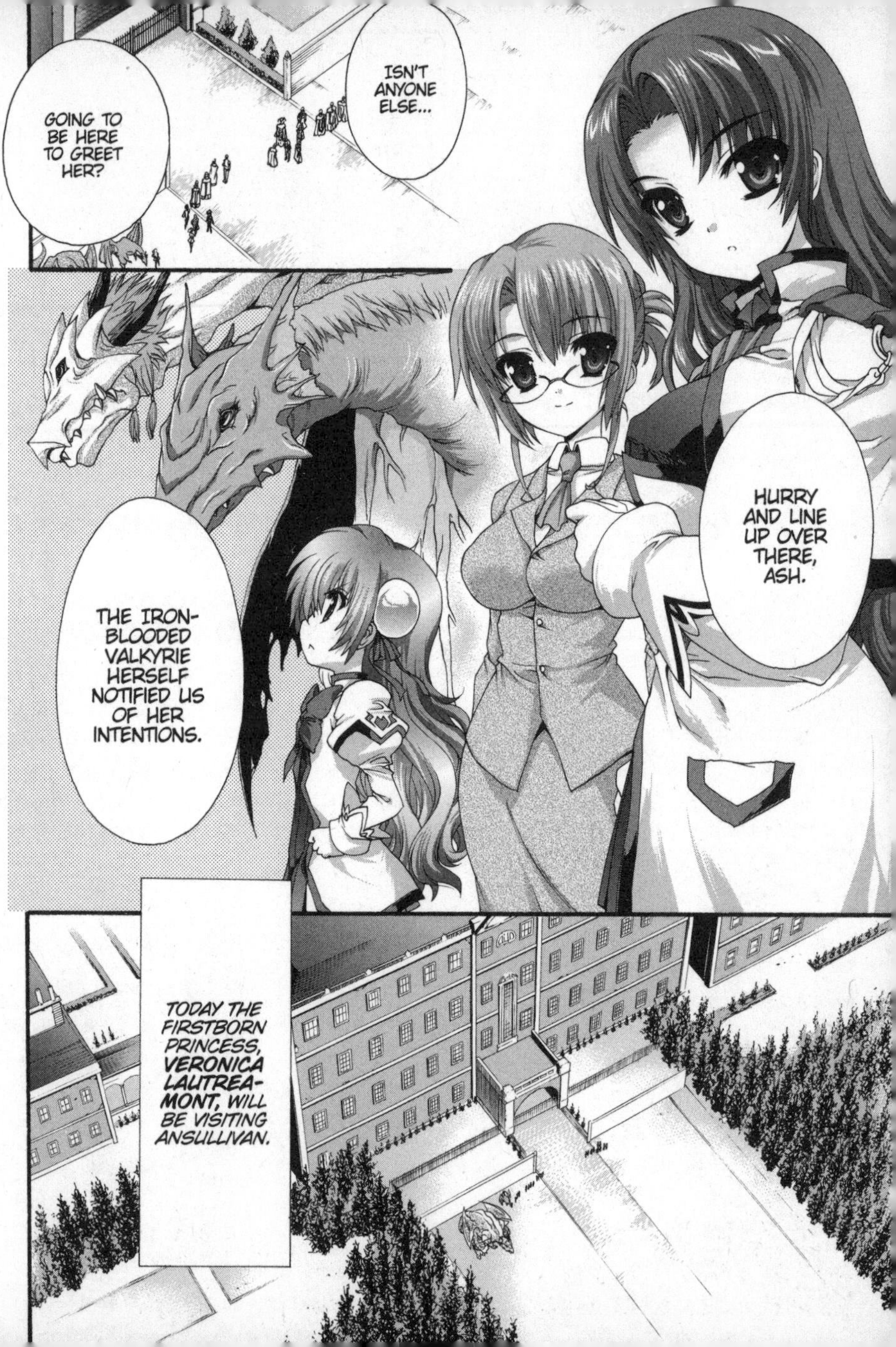
ISN'T ANYONE ELSE...
GOING TO BE HERE TO GREET HER?
HURRY AND LINE UP OVER THERE, ASH.
THE IRON-BLOODED VALKYRIE HERSELF NOTIFIED US OF HER INTENTIONS.
TODAY THE FIRSTBORN PRINCESS, VERONICA LAUTREAMONT, WILL BE VISITING ANSULLIVAN.

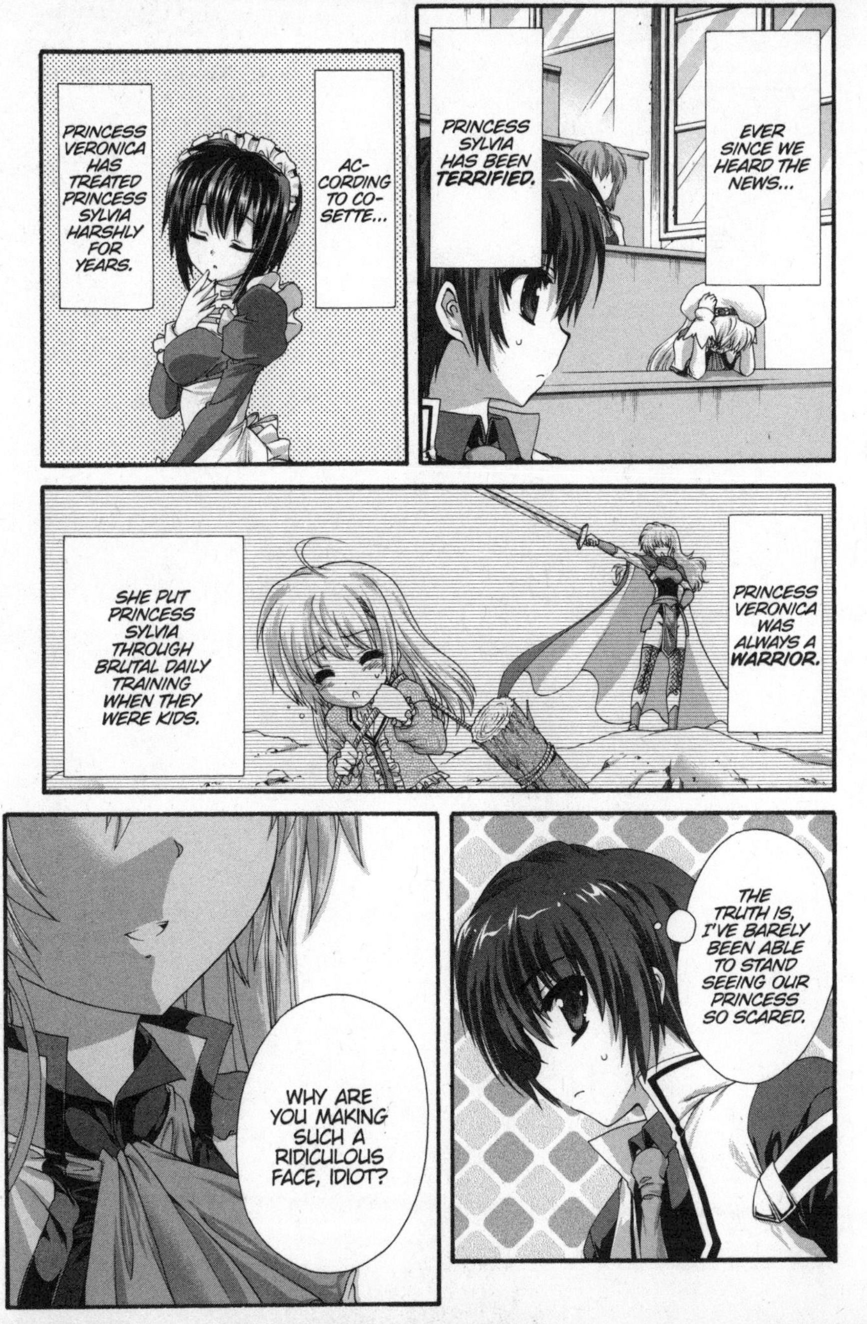
EVER SINCE WE HEARD THE NEWS...
PRINCESS SYLVIA HAS BEEN TERRIFIED.
AC-CORDING TO CO-SETTE...
PRINCESS VERONICA HAS TREATED PRINCESS SYLVIA HARSHLY FOR YEARS.
PRINCESS VERONICA WAS ALWAYS A WARRIOR.
SHE PUT PRINCESS SYLVIA THROUGH BRUTAL DAILY TRAINING WHEN THEY WERE KIDS.
THE TRUTH IS, I'VE BARELY BEEN ABLE TO STAND SEEING OUR PRINCESS SO SCARED.
WHY ARE YOU MAKING SUCH A RIDICULOUS FACE, IDIOT?

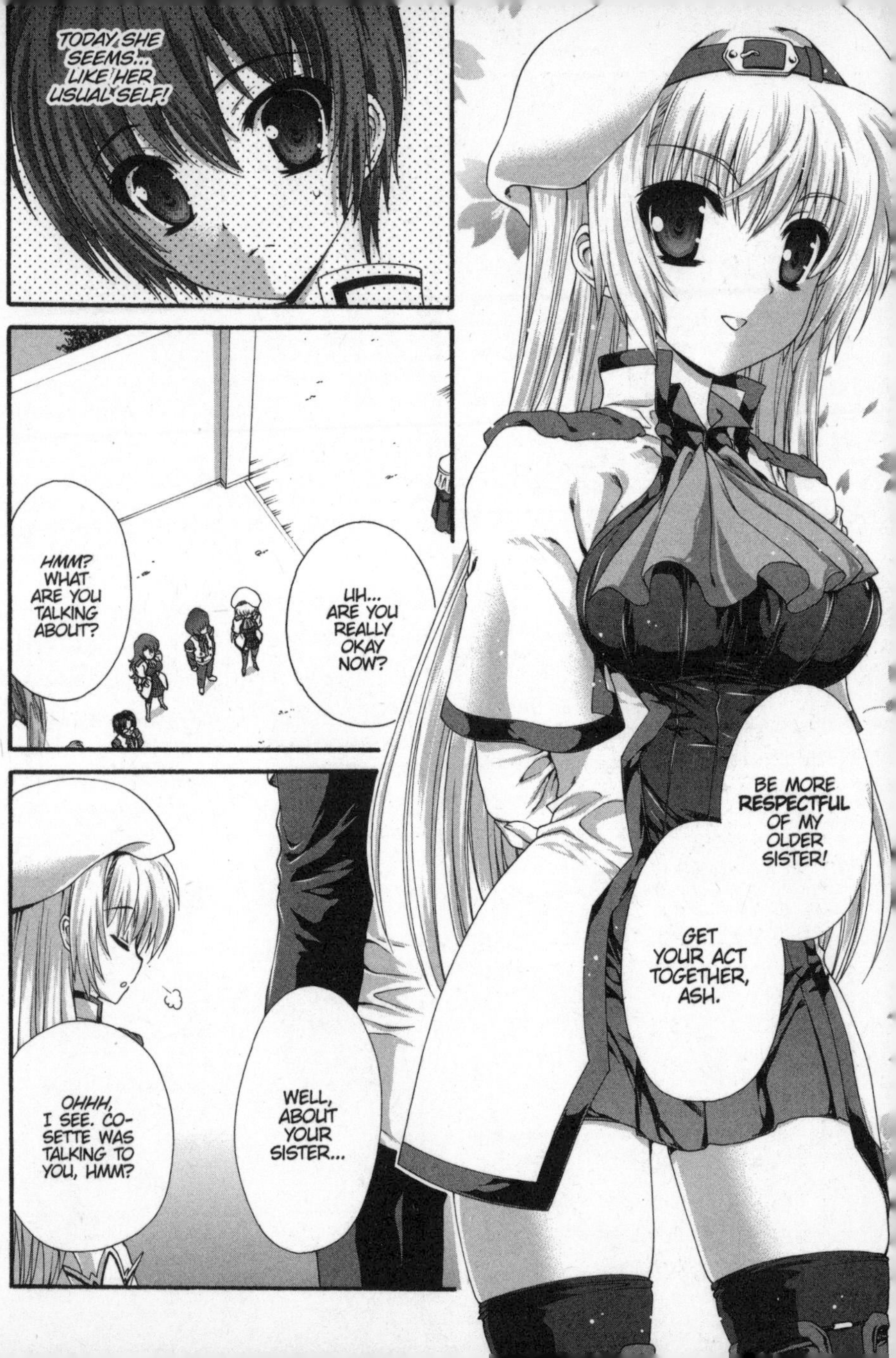
BE MORE RESPECTFUL OF MY OLDER SISTER!
GET YOUR ACT TOGETHER, ASH.
TODAY, SHE SEEMS... LIKE HER USUAL SELF!
UH... ARE YOU REALLY OKAY NOW?
HMM? WHAT ARE YOU TALKING ABOUT?
WELL, ABOUT YOUR SISTER...
OHHH, I SEE. CO-SETTE WAS TALKING TO YOU, HMM?

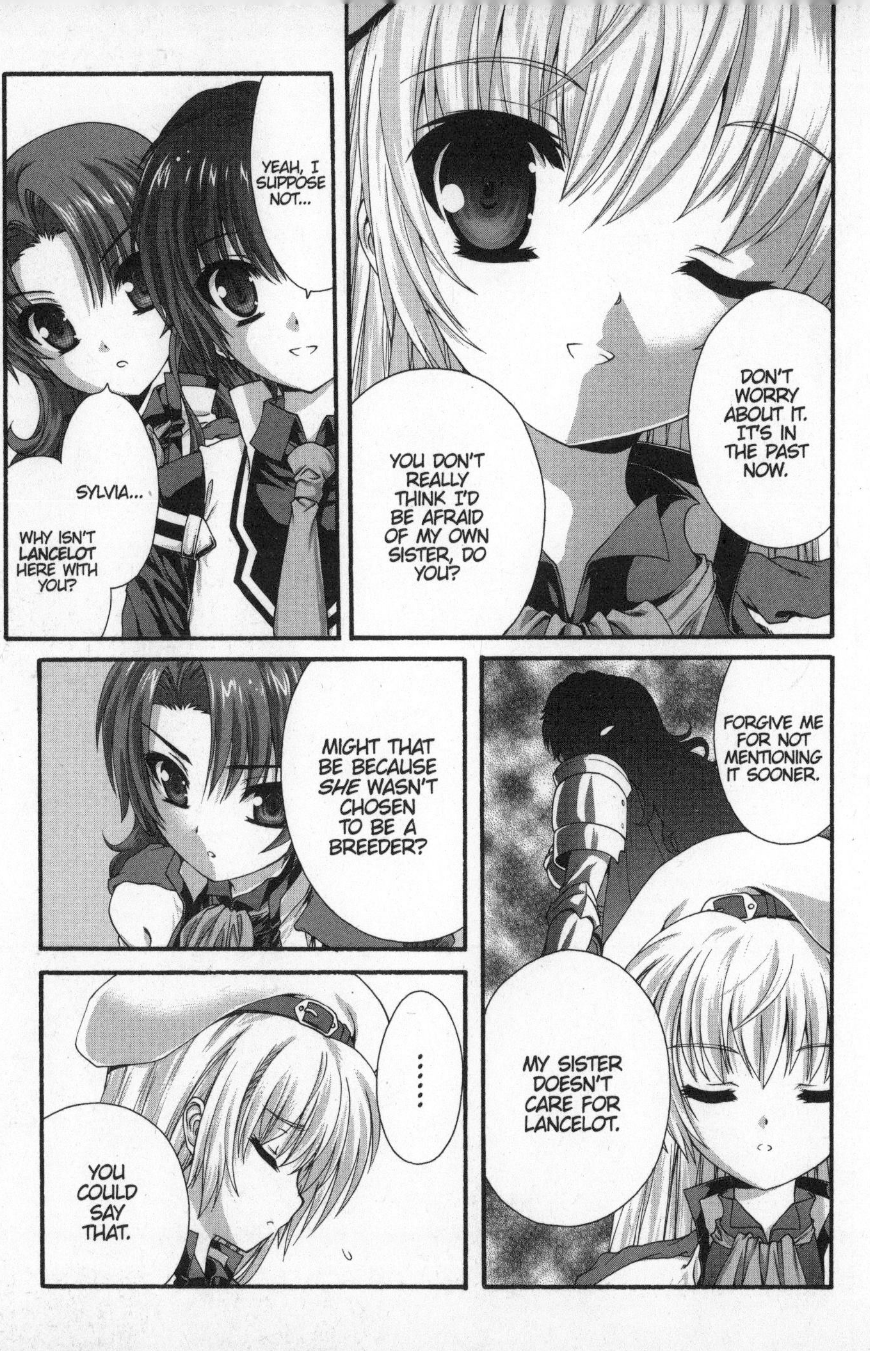
DON'T WORRY ABOUT IT. IT'S IN THE PAST NOW.
YOU DON'T REALLY THINK I'D BE AFRAID OF MY OWN SISTER, DO YOU?
YEAH, I SUPPOSE NOT...
SYLVIA...
WHY ISN'T LANCELOT HERE WITH YOU?
FORGIVE ME FOR NOT MENTIONING IT SOONER.
MY SISTER DOESN'T CARE FOR LANCELOT.
MIGHT THAT BE BECAUSE *SHE* WASN'T CHOSEN TO BE A BREEDER?
......
YOU COULD SAY THAT.

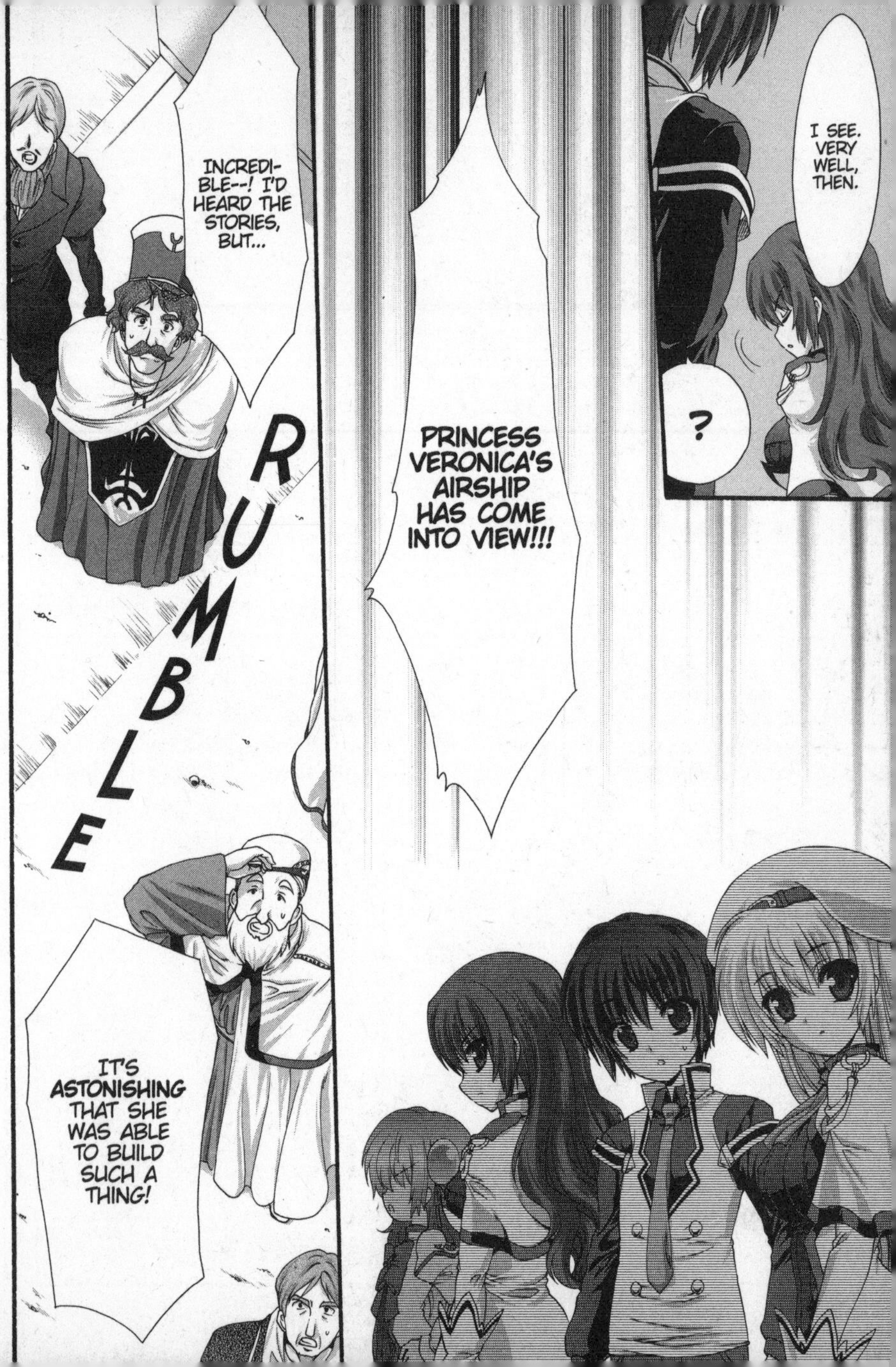
I SEE. VERY WELL, THEN.
?
PRINCESS VERONICA'S AIRSHIP HAS COME INTO VIEW!!!
INCREDI-BLE--! I'D HEARD THE STORIES, BUT...
RUMBLE
IT'S ASTONISHING THAT SHE WAS ABLE TO BUILD SUCH A THING!

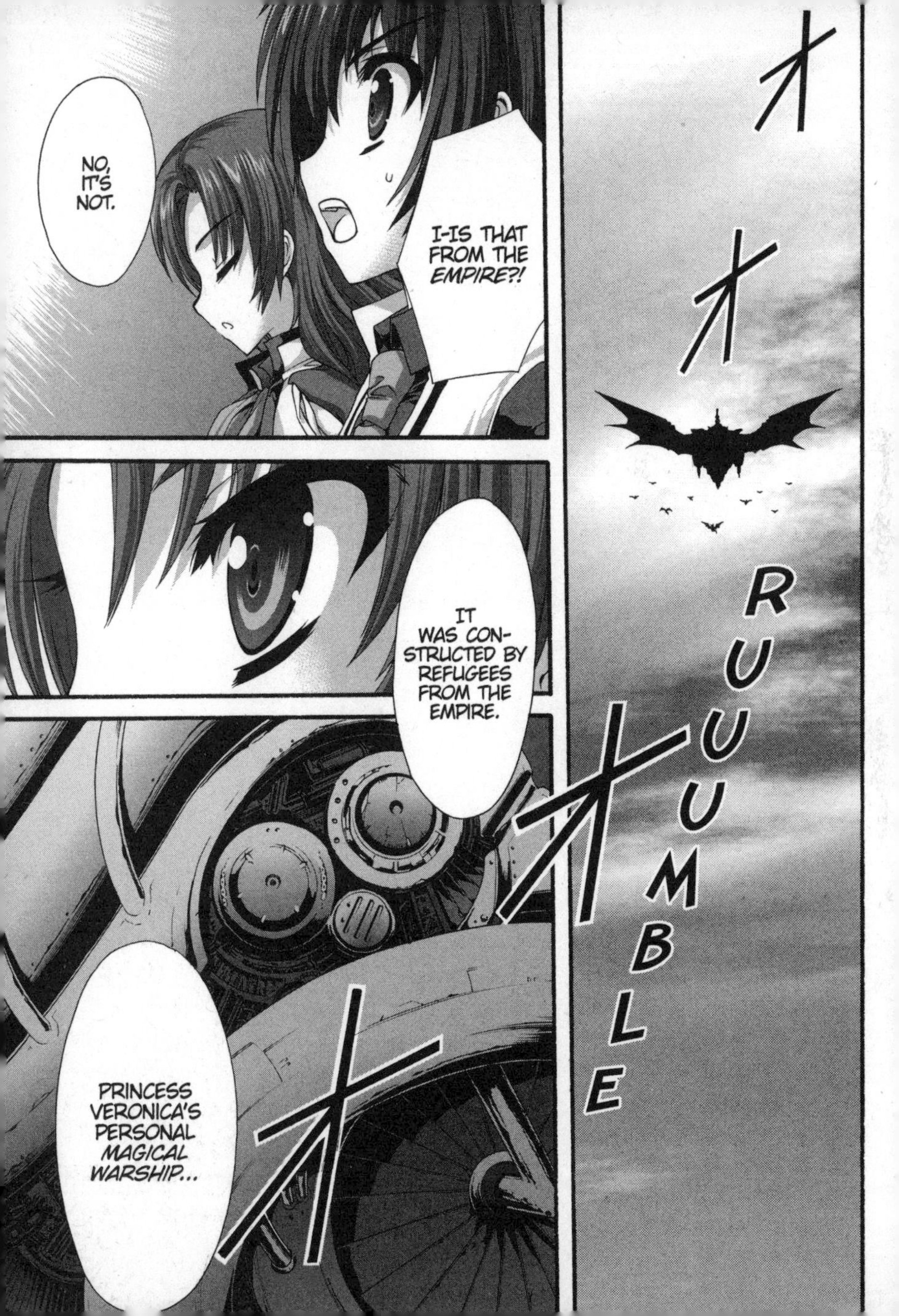
RUUUMBLE
I-IS THAT FROM THE EMPIRE?!
NO, IT'S NOT.
IT WAS CONSTRUCTED BY REFUGEES FROM THE EMPIRE.
PRINCESS VERONICA'S PERSONAL MAGICAL WARSHIP...

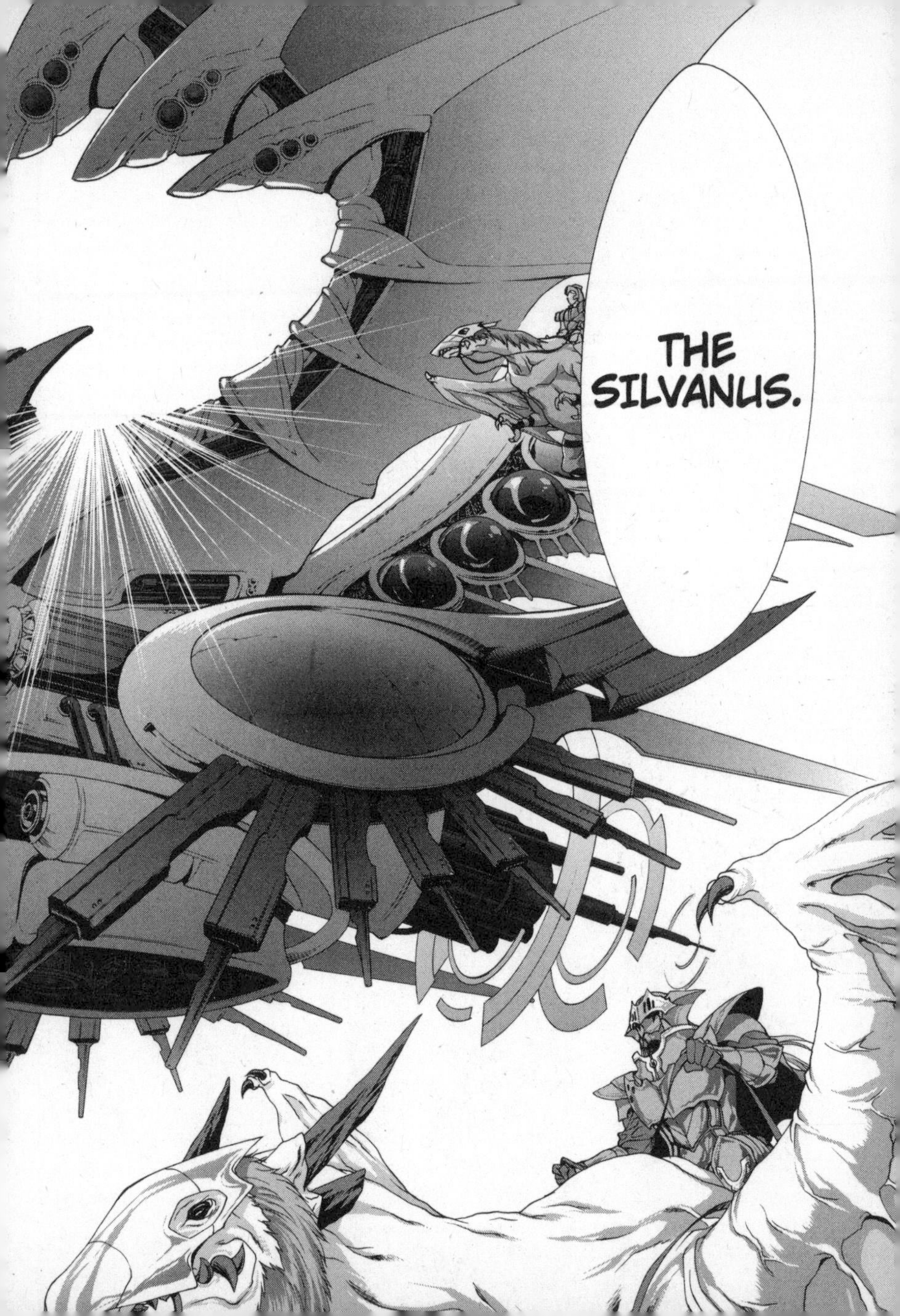
THE SILVANUS.

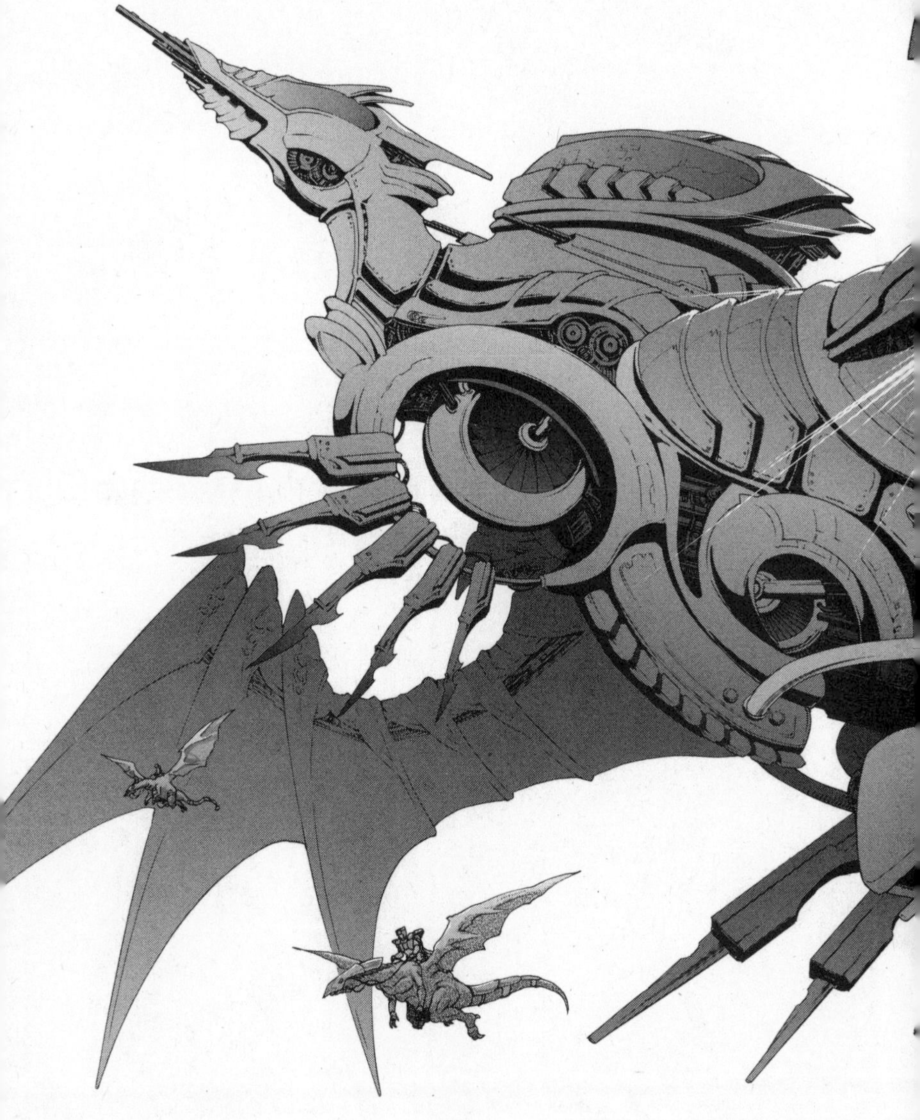

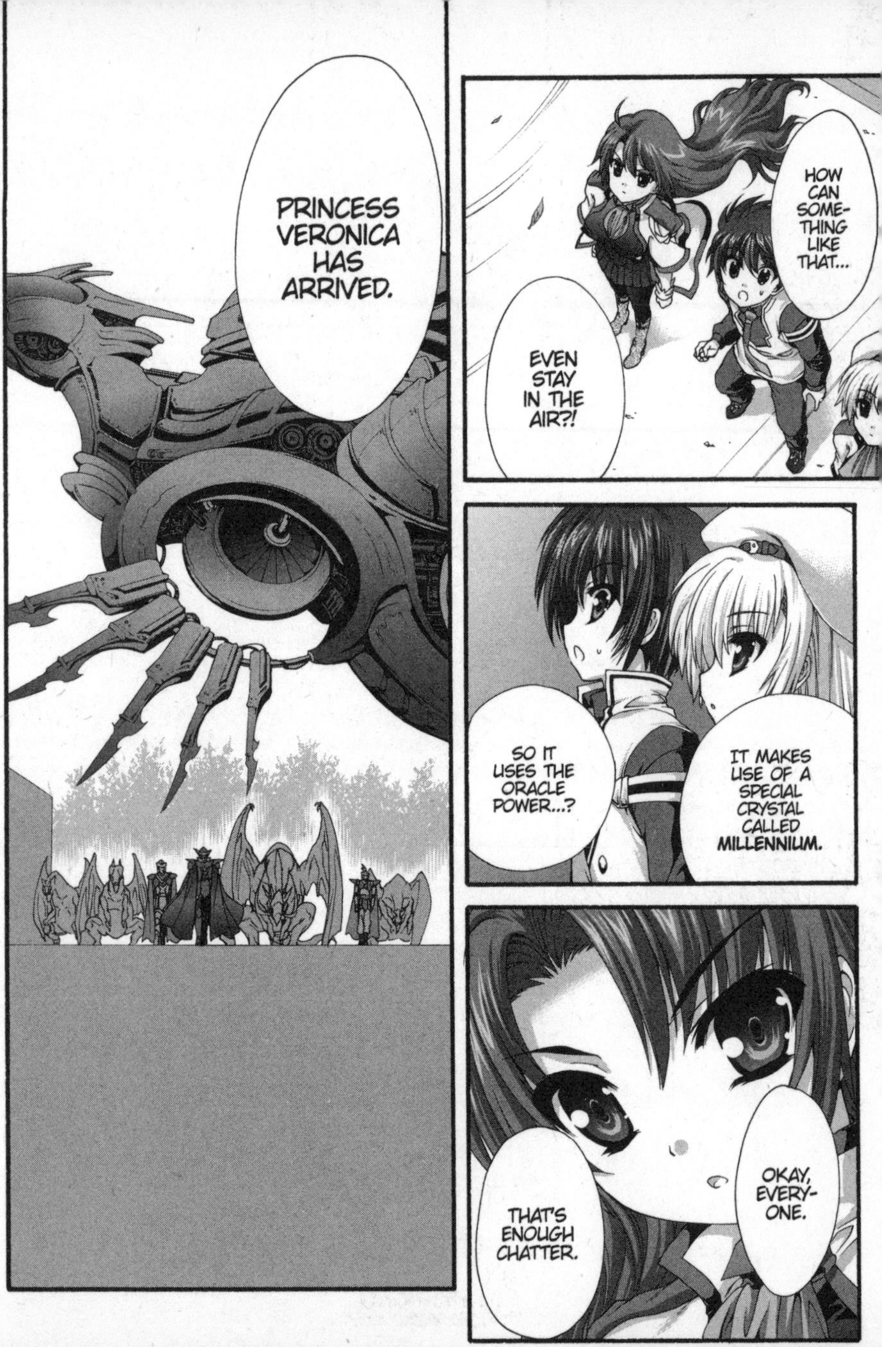
HOW CAN SOME-THING LIKE THAT...
EVEN STAY IN THE AIR?!
IT MAKES USE OF A SPECIAL CRYSTAL CALLED MILLENNIUM.
SO IT USES THE ORACLE POWER...?
OKAY, EVERY-ONE.
THAT'S ENOUGH CHATTER.
PRINCESS VERONICA HAS ARRIVED.

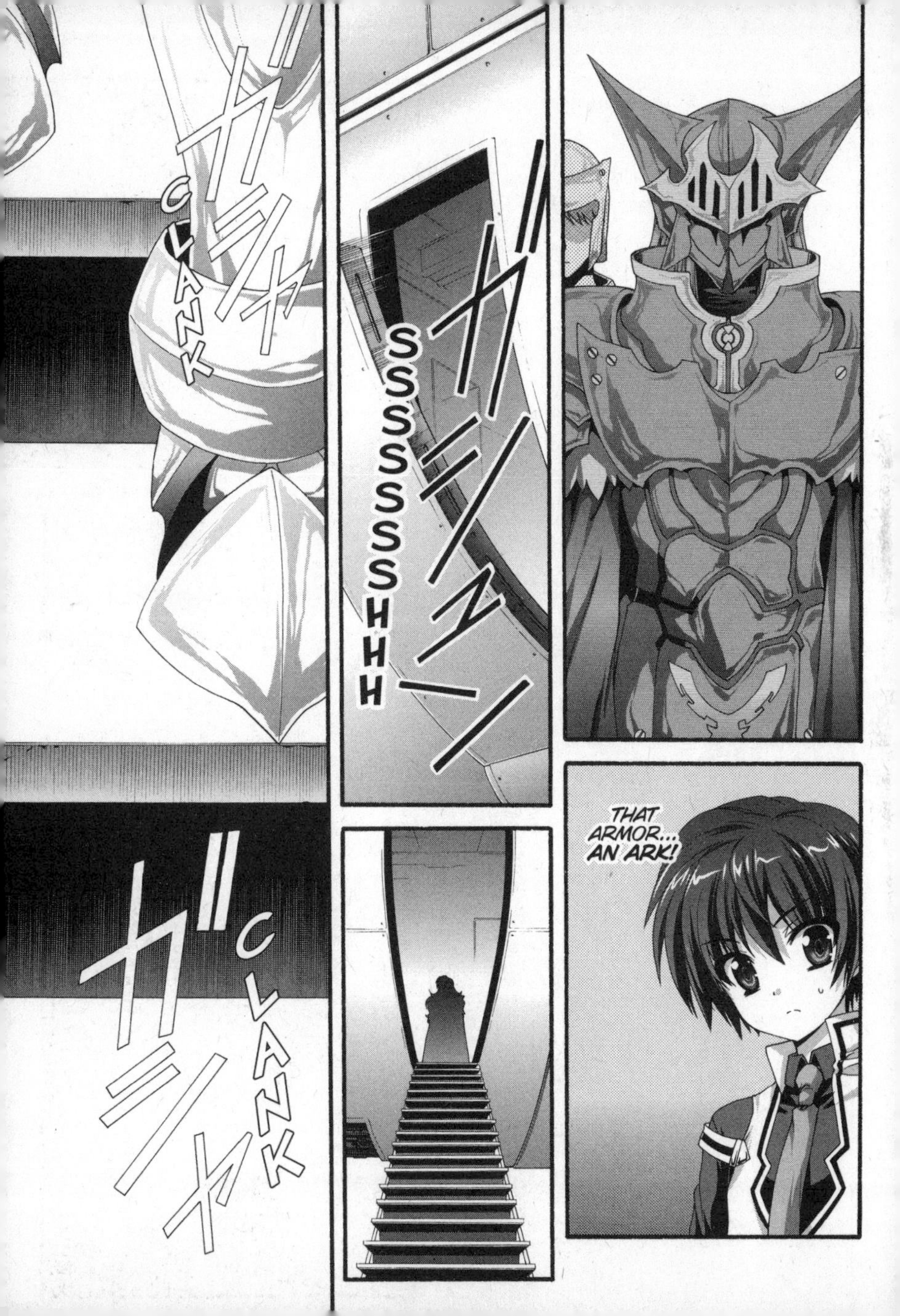
SSSSSSSSHHH
THAT ARMOR... AN ARK!
CLANK
CLANK

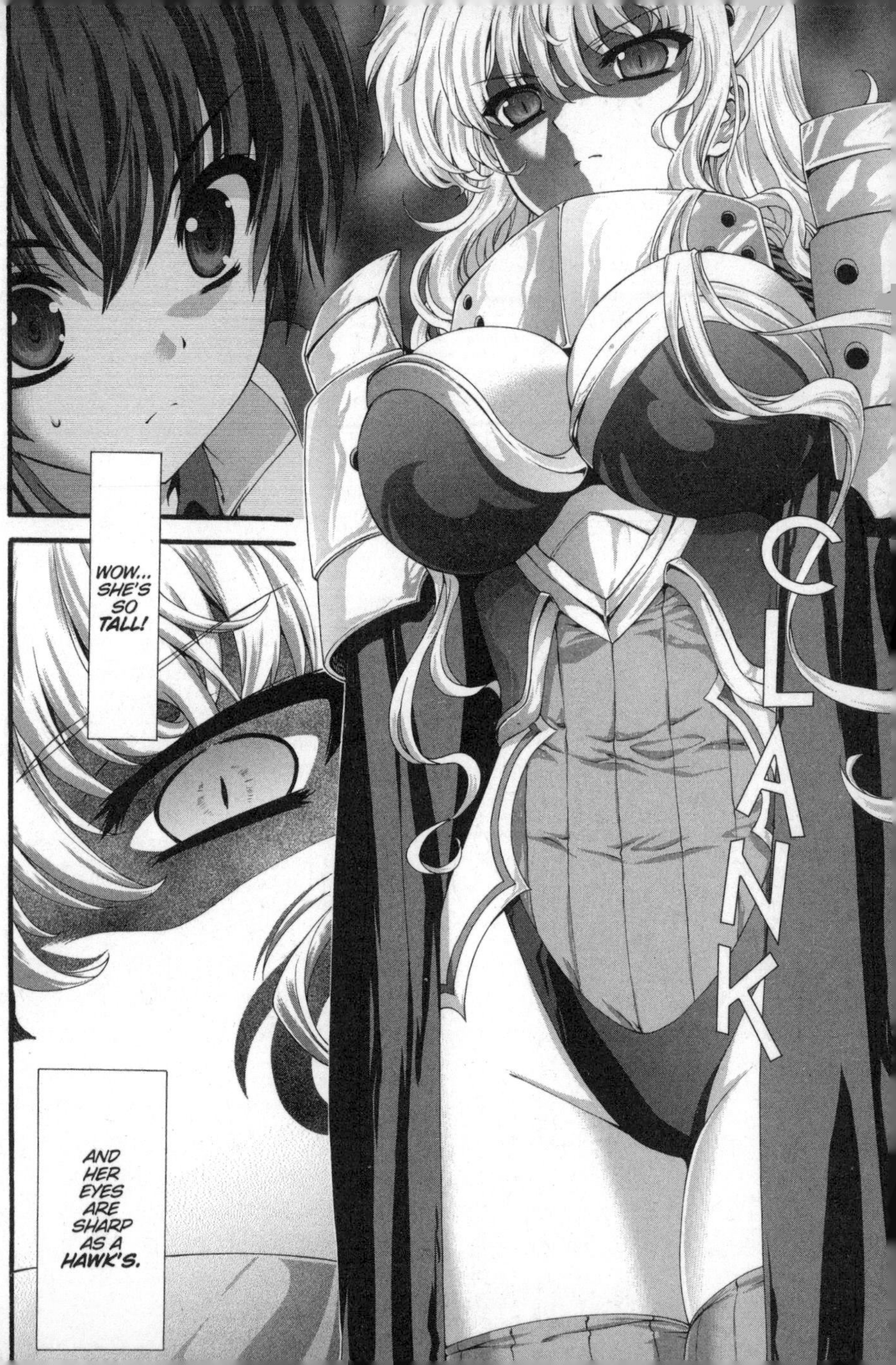
CLANK
WOW... SHE'S SO TALL!
AND HER EYES ARE SHARP AS A HAWK'S.

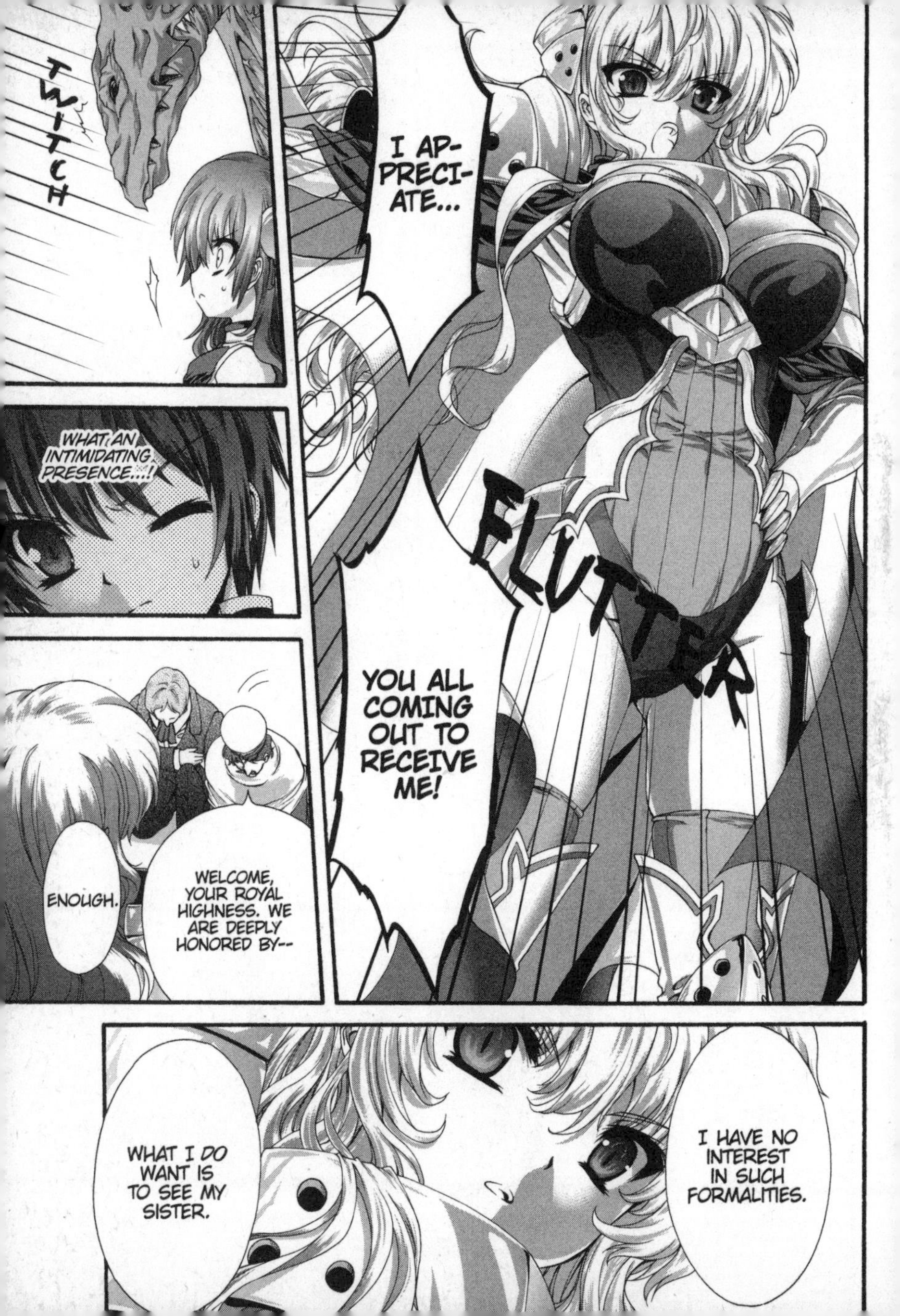
I AP-PRECI-ATE...
FLUTTER
YOU ALL COMING OUT TO RECEIVE ME!
TWITCH
WHAT AN INTIMIDATING PRESENCE...!
WELCOME, YOUR ROYAL HIGHNESS. WE ARE DEEPLY HONORED BY--
ENOUGH.
I HAVE NO INTEREST IN SUCH FORMALITIES.
WHAT I DO WANT IS TO SEE MY SISTER.

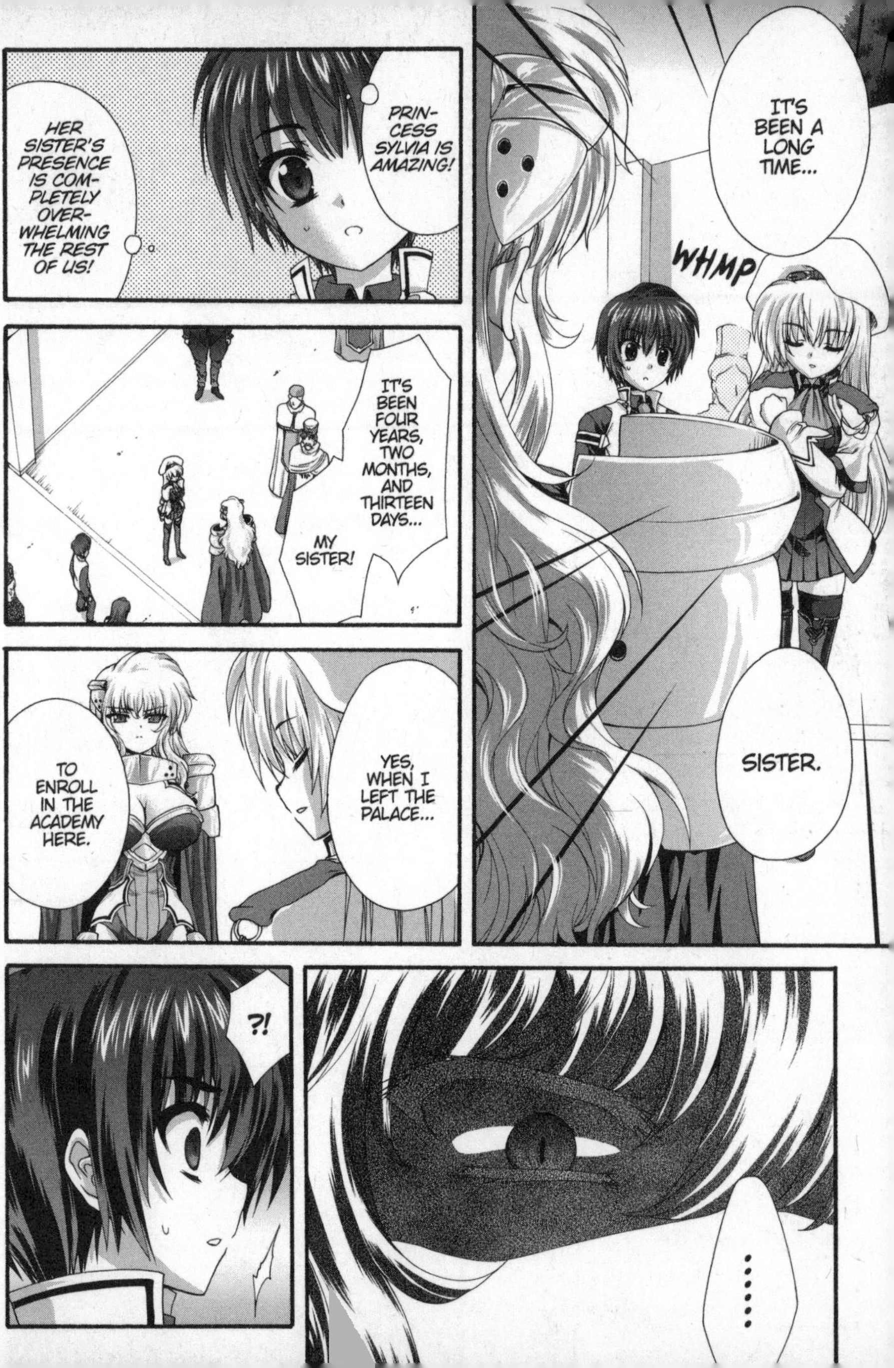
IT'S BEEN A LONG TIME...
WHMP
SISTER.
PRINCESS SYLVIA IS AMAZING!
HER SISTER'S PRESENCE IS COMPLETELY OVERWHELMING THE REST OF US!
IT'S BEEN FOUR YEARS, TWO MONTHS, AND THIRTEEN DAYS...
MY SISTER!
YES, WHEN I LEFT THE PALACE...
TO ENROLL IN THE ACADEMY HERE.
......
?!

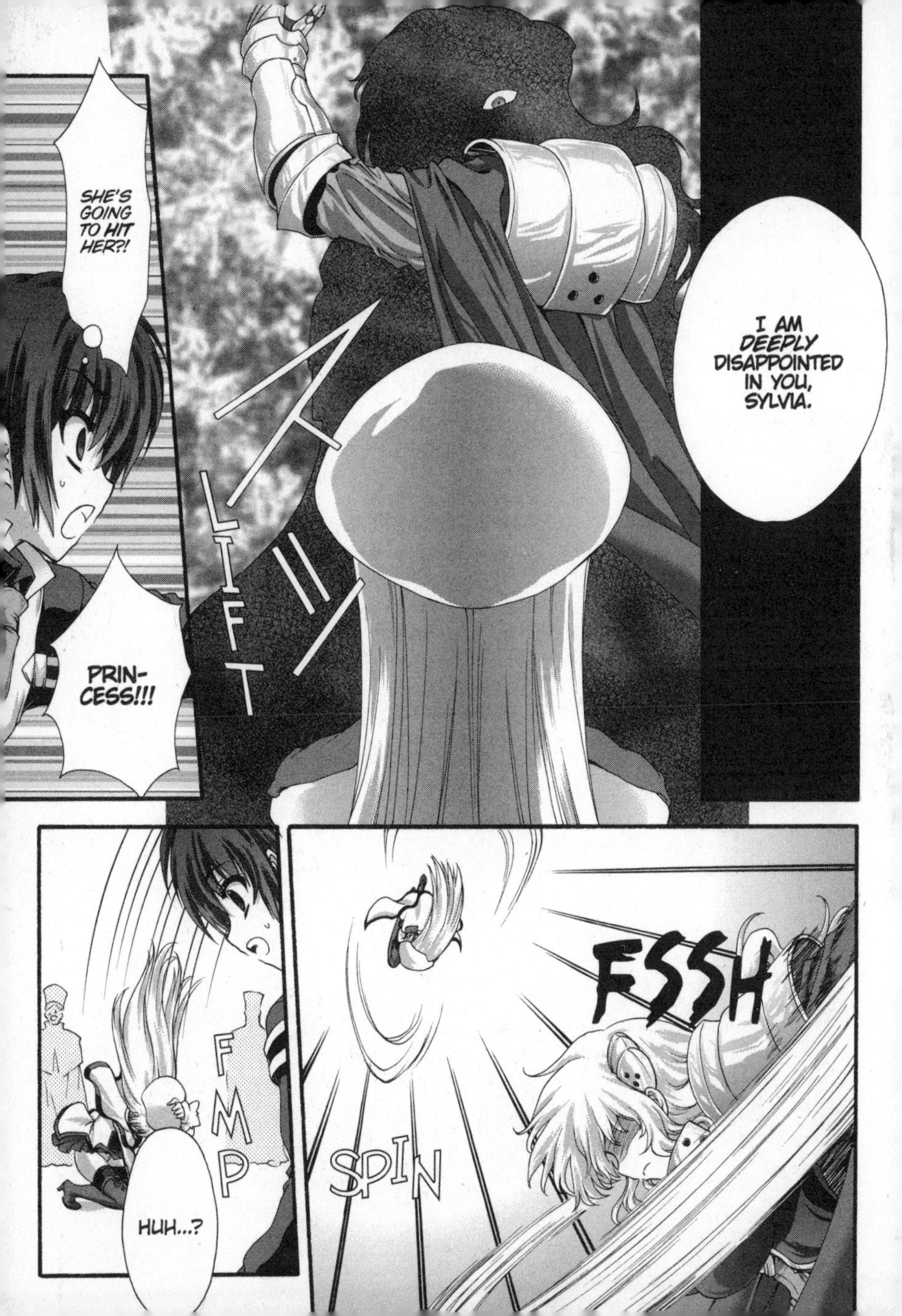
I AM DEEPLY DISAPPOINTED IN YOU, SYLVIA.
LIFT
SHE'S GOING TO HIT HER?!
PRIN-CESS!!!
FSSH
SPIN
FMP
HUH...?

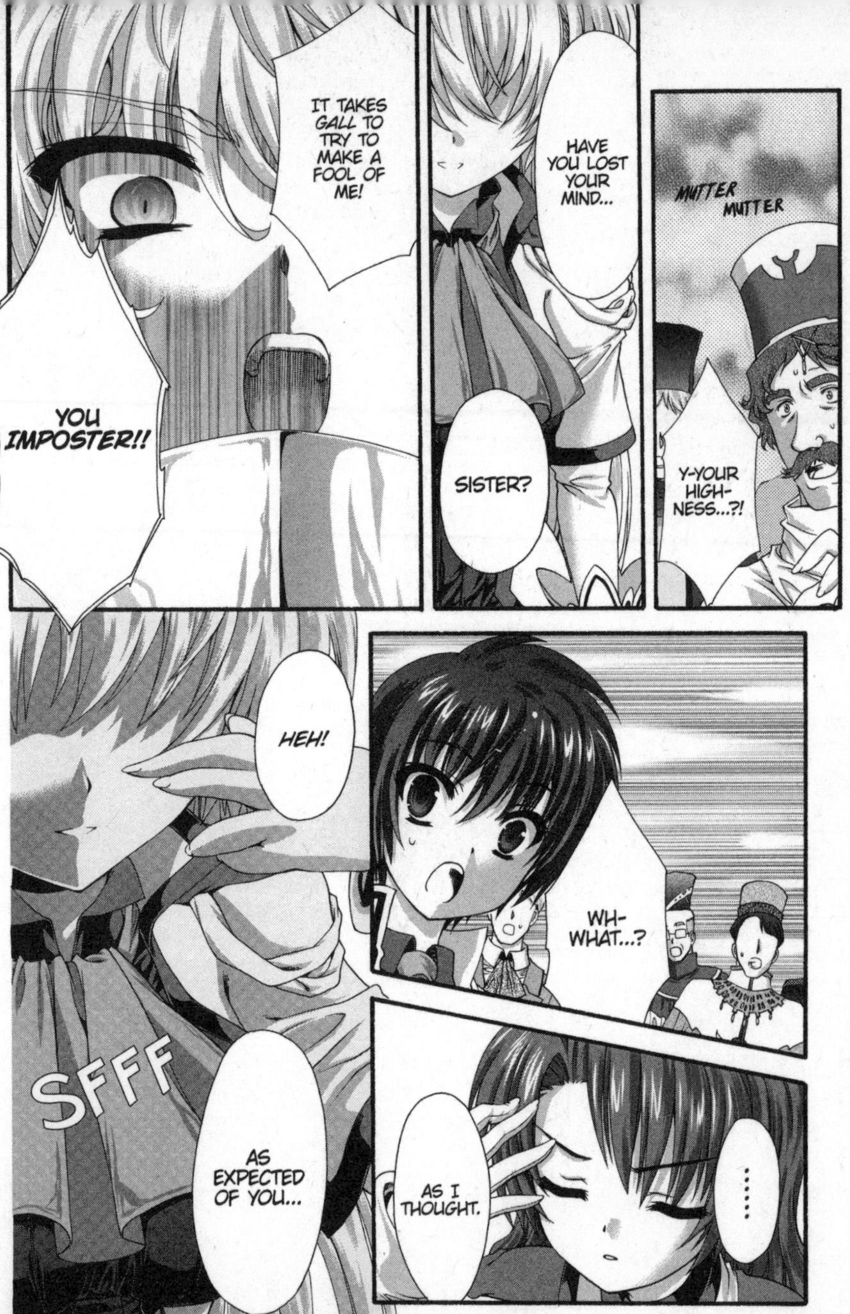
MUTTER MUTTER
Y-YOUR HIGHNESS...?!
HAVE YOU LOST YOUR MIND...
SISTER?
IT TAKES GALL TO TRY TO MAKE A FOOL OF ME!
YOU IMPOSTER!!
HEH!
WH-WHAT...?
......
AS I THOUGHT.
SFFF
AS EXPECTED OF YOU...

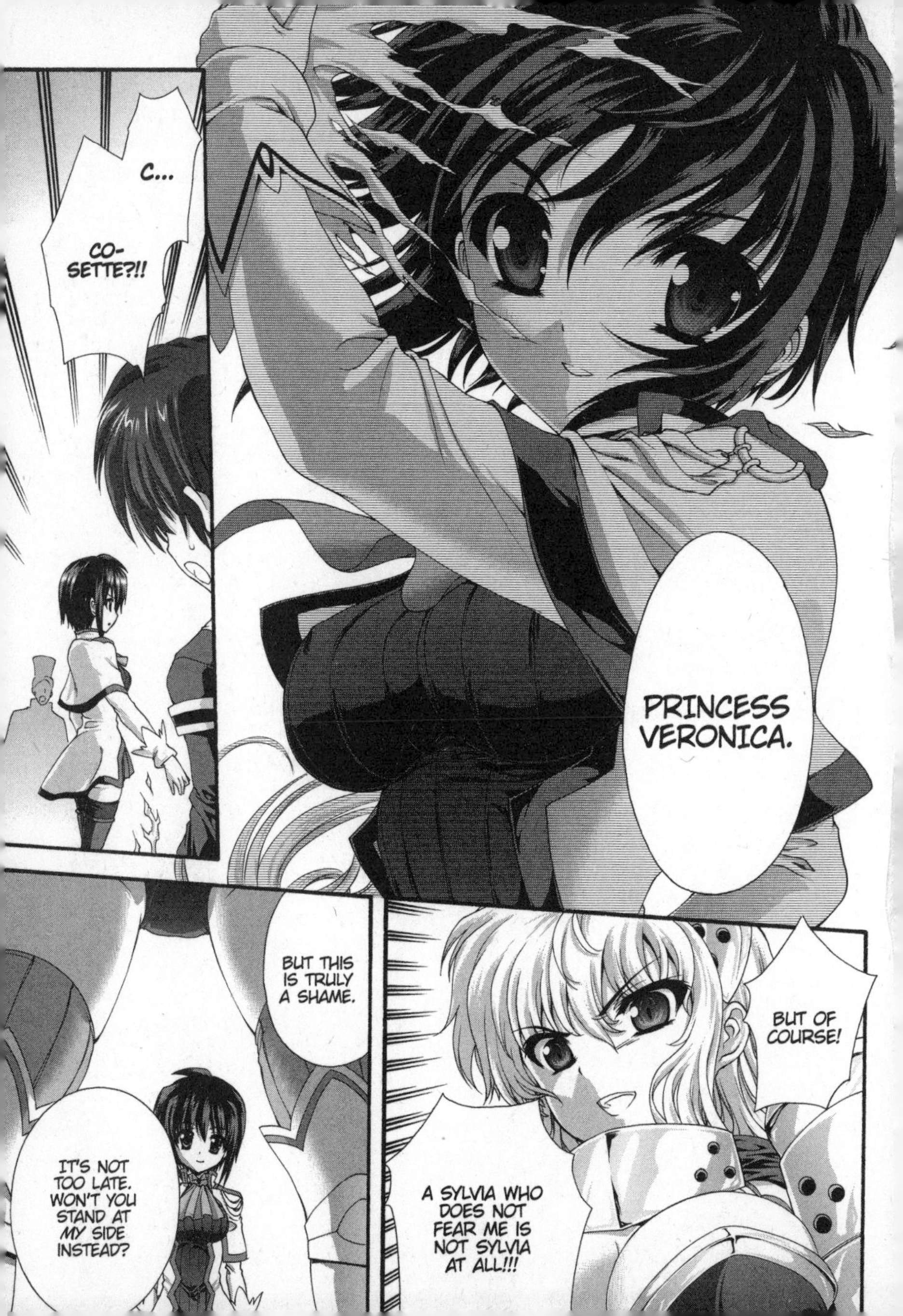
PRINCESS VERONICA.
C...
CO-SETTE?!!
BUT OF COURSE!
A SYLVIA WHO DOES NOT FEAR ME IS NOT SYLVIA AT ALL!!!
BUT THIS IS TRULY A SHAME.
IT'S NOT TOO LATE. WON'T YOU STAND AT MY SIDE INSTEAD?

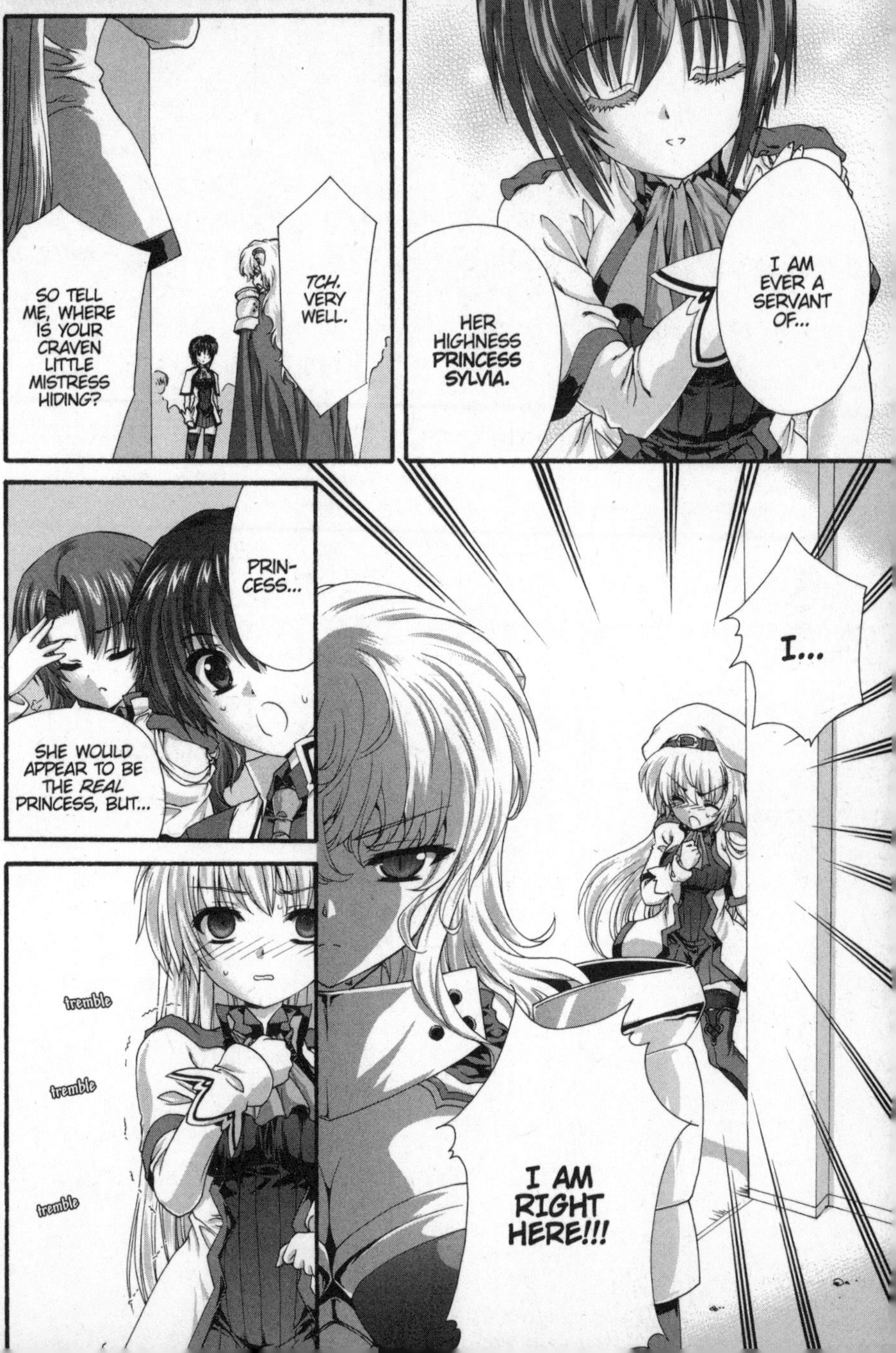
I AM EVER A SERVANT OF...
HER HIGHNESS PRINCESS SYLVIA.
TCH. VERY WELL.
SO TELL ME, WHERE IS YOUR CRAVEN LITTLE MISTRESS HIDING?
I...
I AM RIGHT HERE!!!
PRIN-CESS...
SHE WOULD APPEAR TO BE THE *REAL* PRINCESS, BUT...
tremble
tremble
tremble

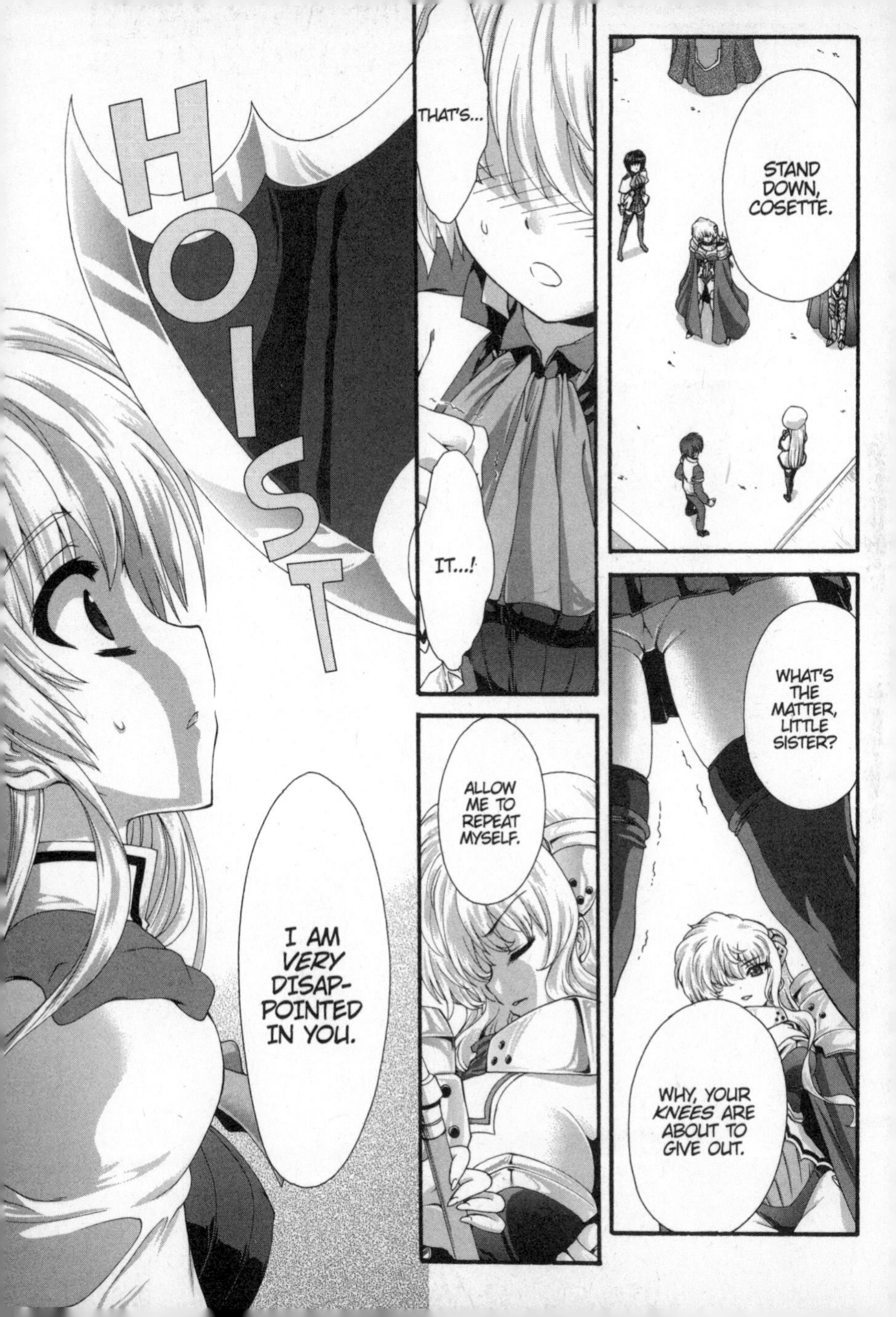
STAND DOWN, COSETTE.
THAT'S...
IT...!
WHAT'S THE MATTER, LITTLE SISTER?
WHY, YOUR KNEES ARE ABOUT TO GIVE OUT.
ALLOW ME TO REPEAT MYSELF.
HOIST
I AM VERY DISAP-POINTED IN YOU.

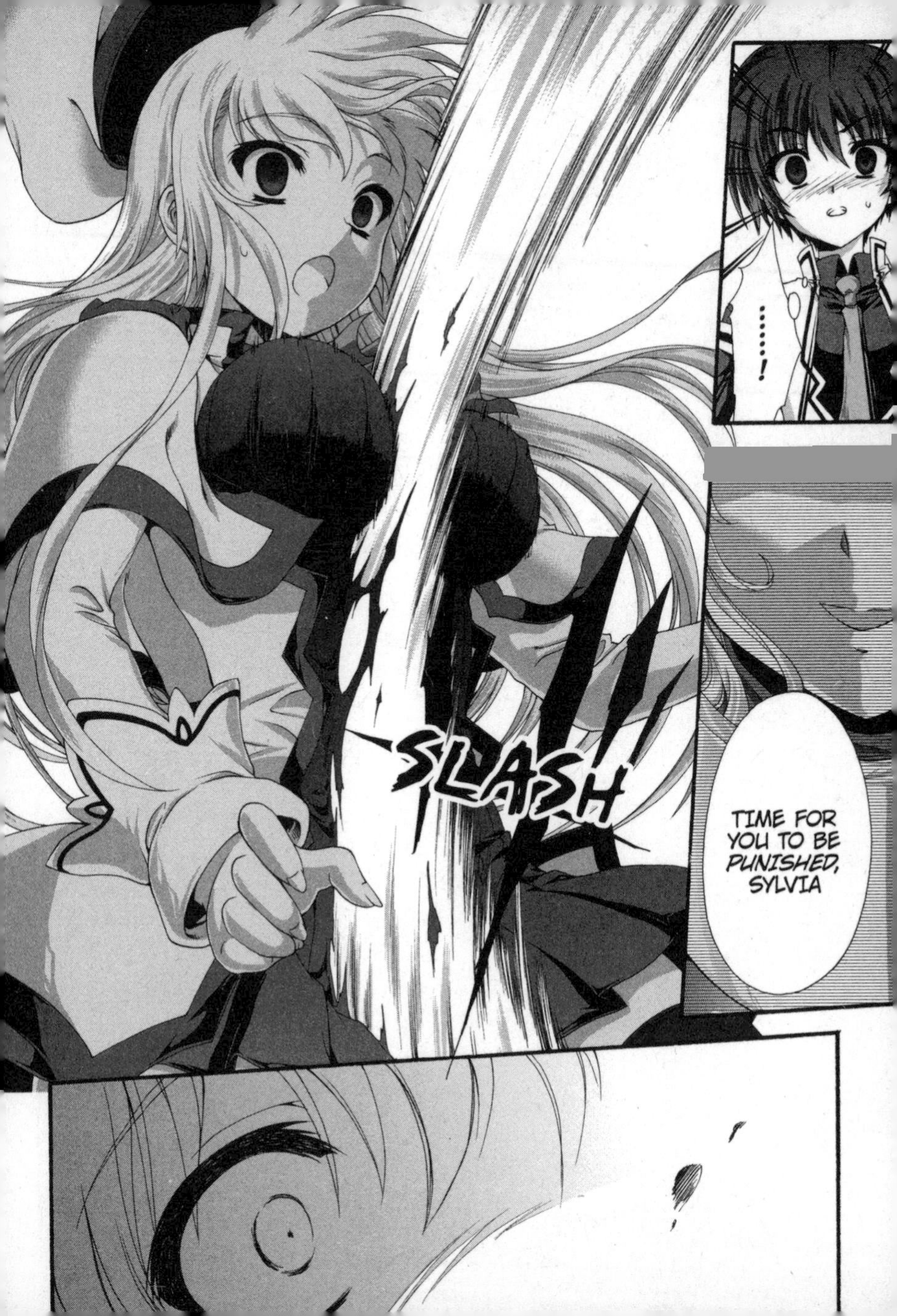
......!
TIME FOR YOU TO BE PUNISHED, SYLVIA
SLASH

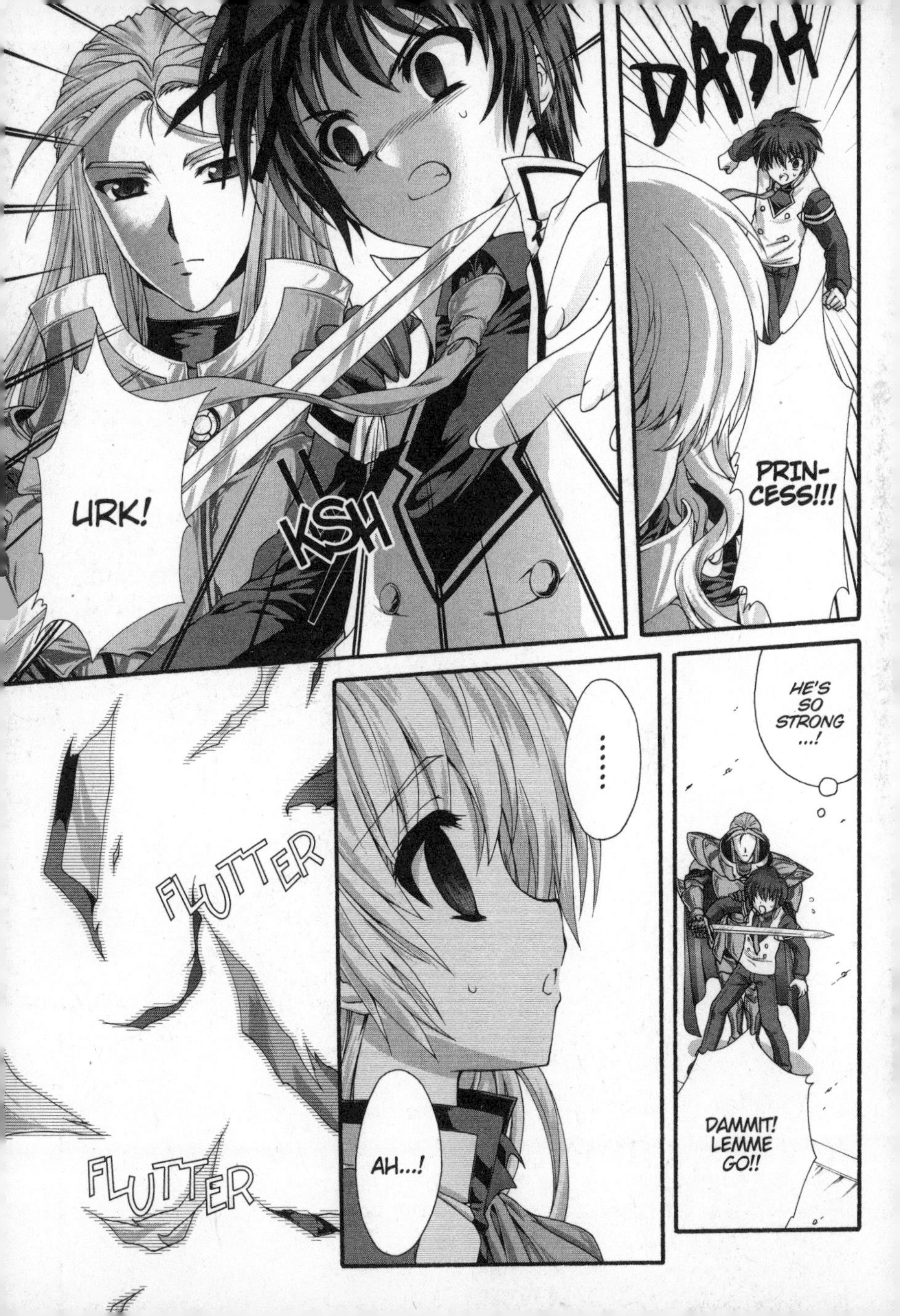
DASH
PRIN-
CESS!!!
URK!
KSH
HE'S SO STRONG...!
DAMMIT! LEMME GO!!
......
AH...!
FLUTTER
FLUTTER

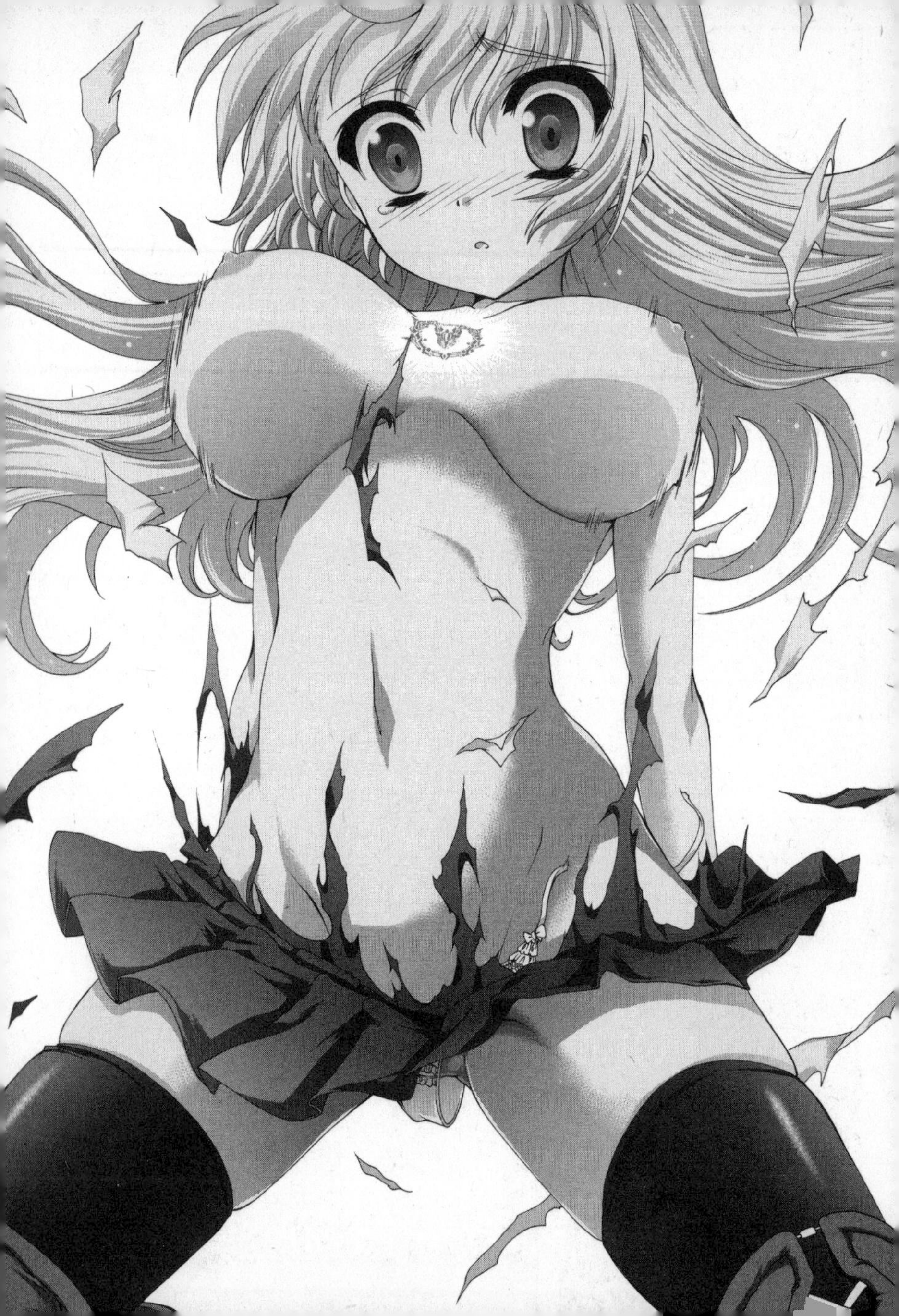

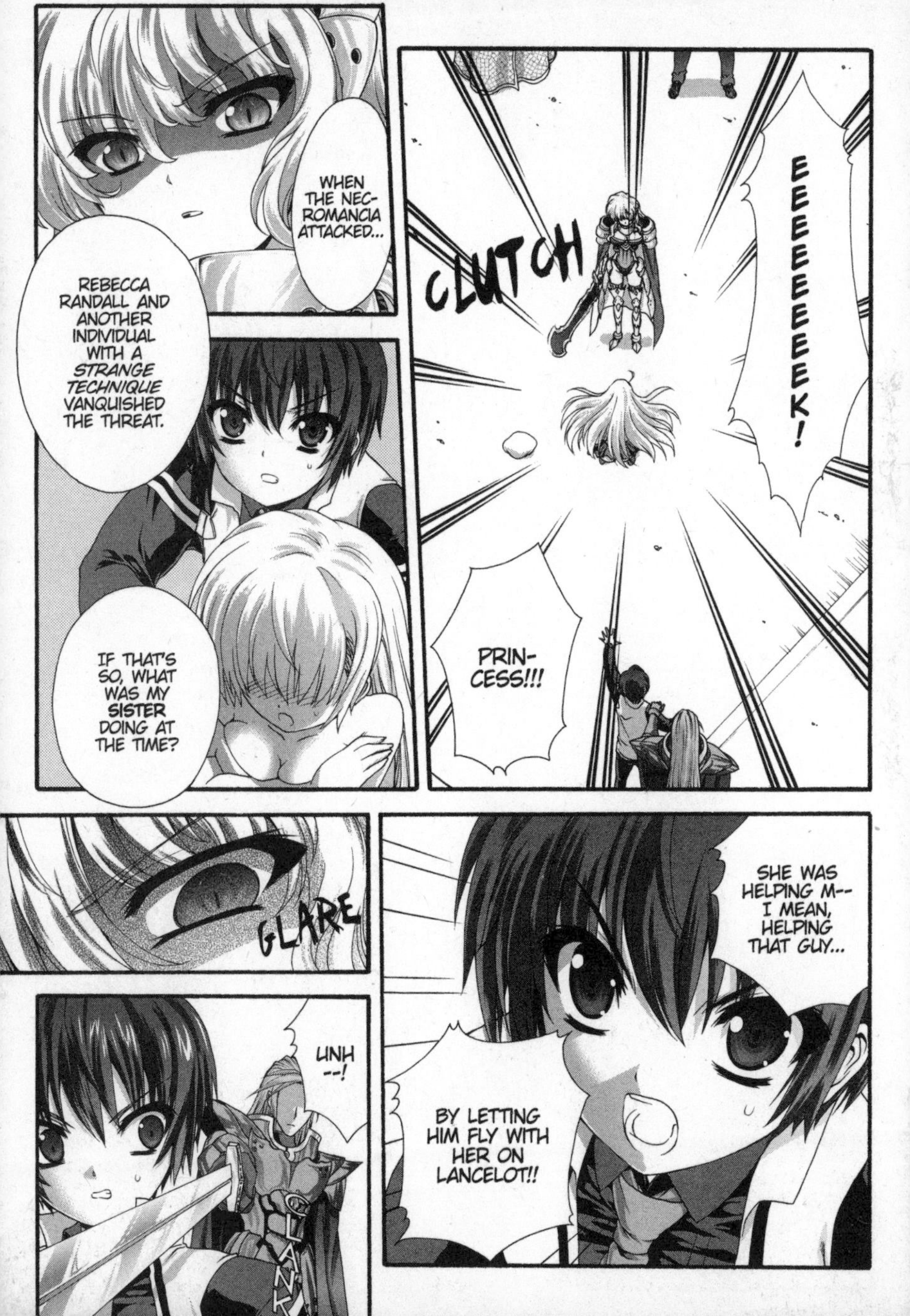
EEEEEEEEEEK!
CLUTCH
PRIN-CESS!!!
WHEN THE NEC-ROMANCIA ATTACKED...
REBECCA RANDALL AND ANOTHER INDIVIDUAL WITH A *STRANGE TECHNIQUE* VANQUISHED THE THREAT.
IF THAT'S SO, WHAT WAS MY **SISTER** DOING AT THE TIME?
SHE WAS HELPING M-- I MEAN, HELPING THAT GUY...
BY LETTING HIM FLY WITH HER ON LANCELOT!!
GLARE
UNH --!
CLANK

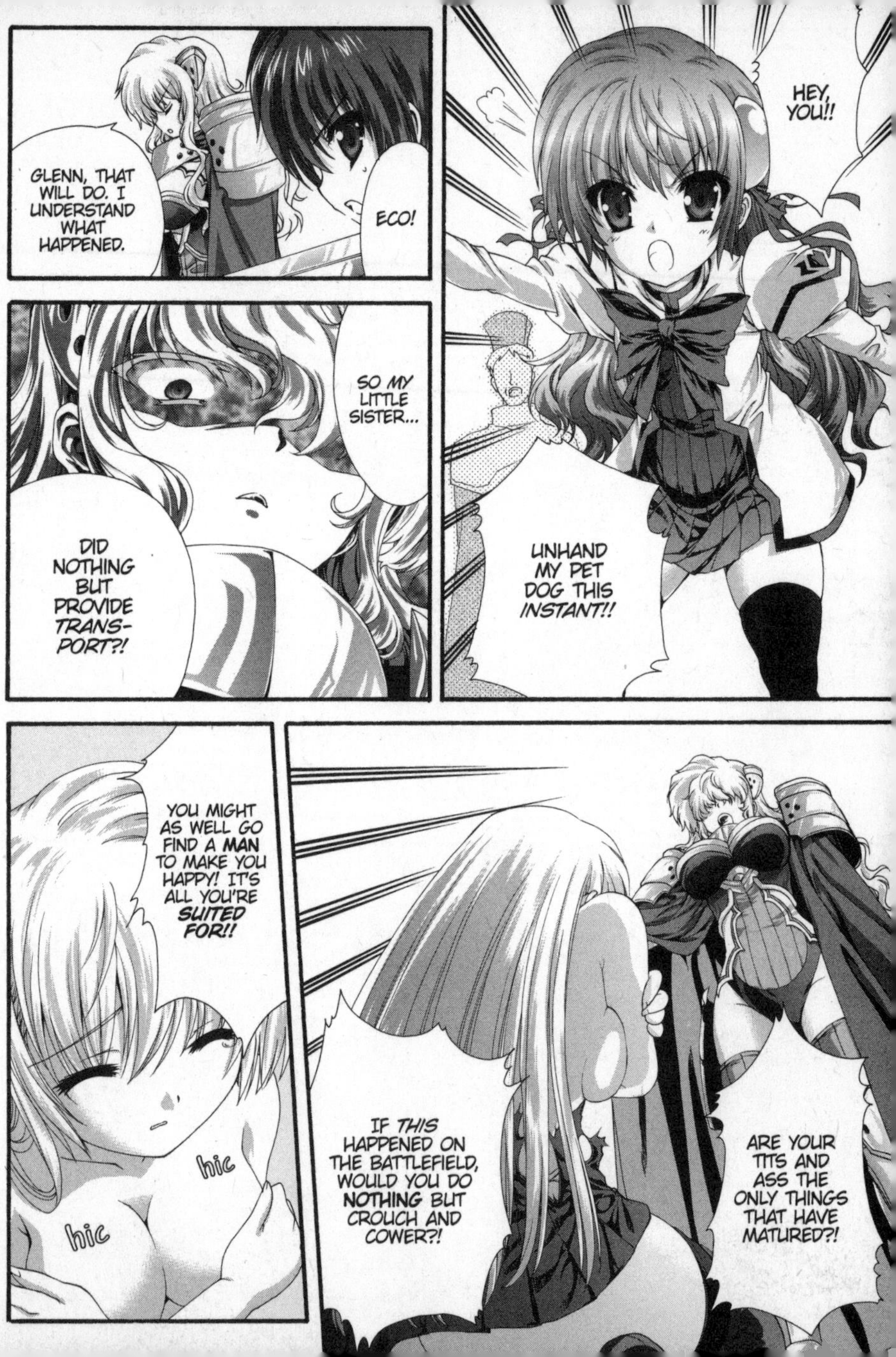
HEY, YOU!!
UNHAND MY PET DOG THIS INSTANT!!
ECO!
GLENN, THAT WILL DO. I UNDERSTAND WHAT HAPPENED.
SO MY LITTLE SISTER...
DID NOTHING BUT PROVIDE TRANS-PORT?!
ARE YOUR TITS AND ASS THE ONLY THINGS THAT HAVE MATURED?!
IF THIS HAPPENED ON THE BATTLEFIELD, WOULD YOU DO NOTHING BUT CROUCH AND COWER?!
YOU MIGHT AS WELL GO FIND A MAN TO MAKE YOU HAPPY! IT'S ALL YOU'RE SUITED FOR!!
hic
hic

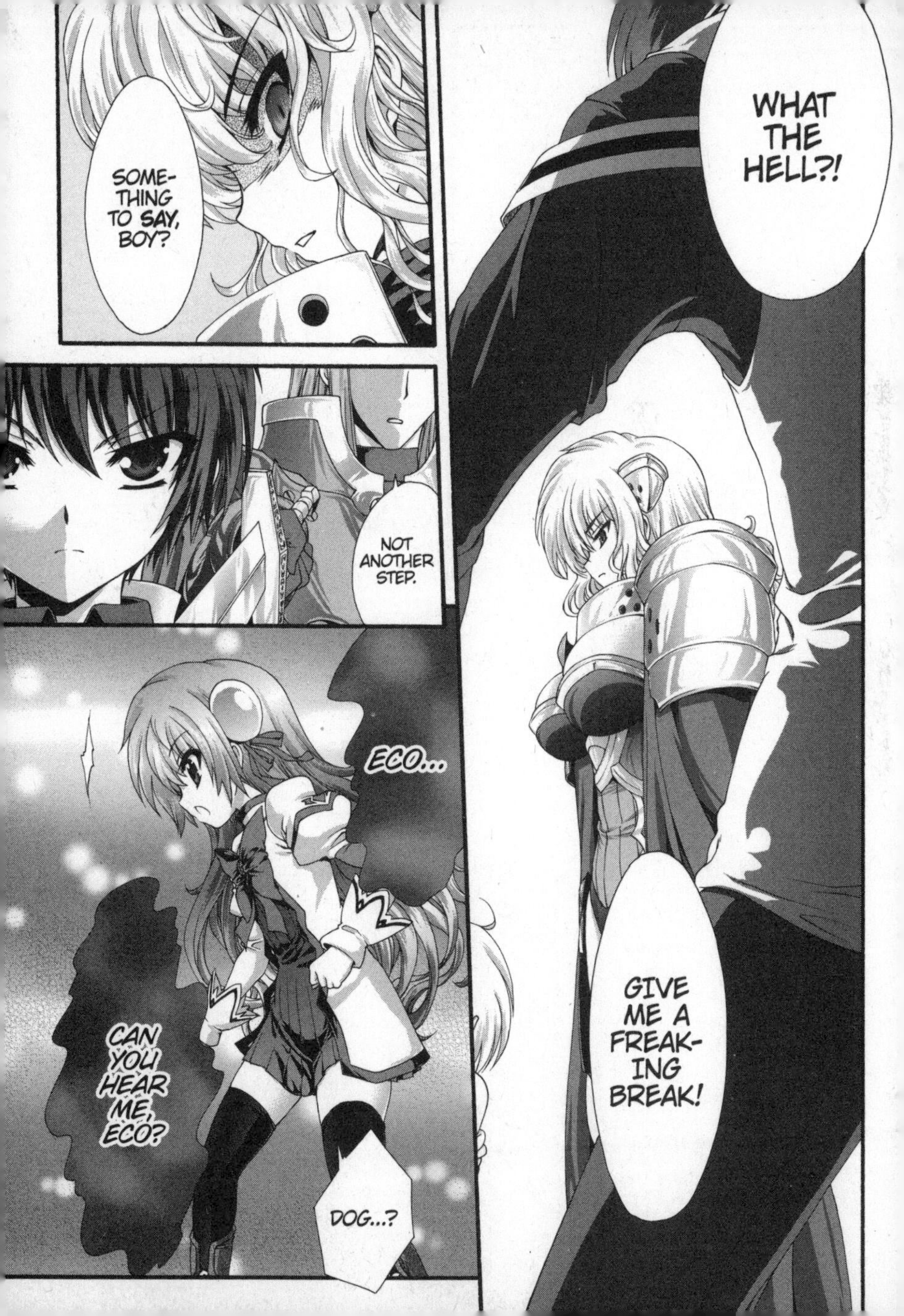
WHAT THE HELL?!
GIVE ME A FREAKING BREAK!
SOMETHING TO SAY, BOY?
NOT ANOTHER STEP.
ECO...
CAN YOU HEAR ME, ECO?
DOG...?

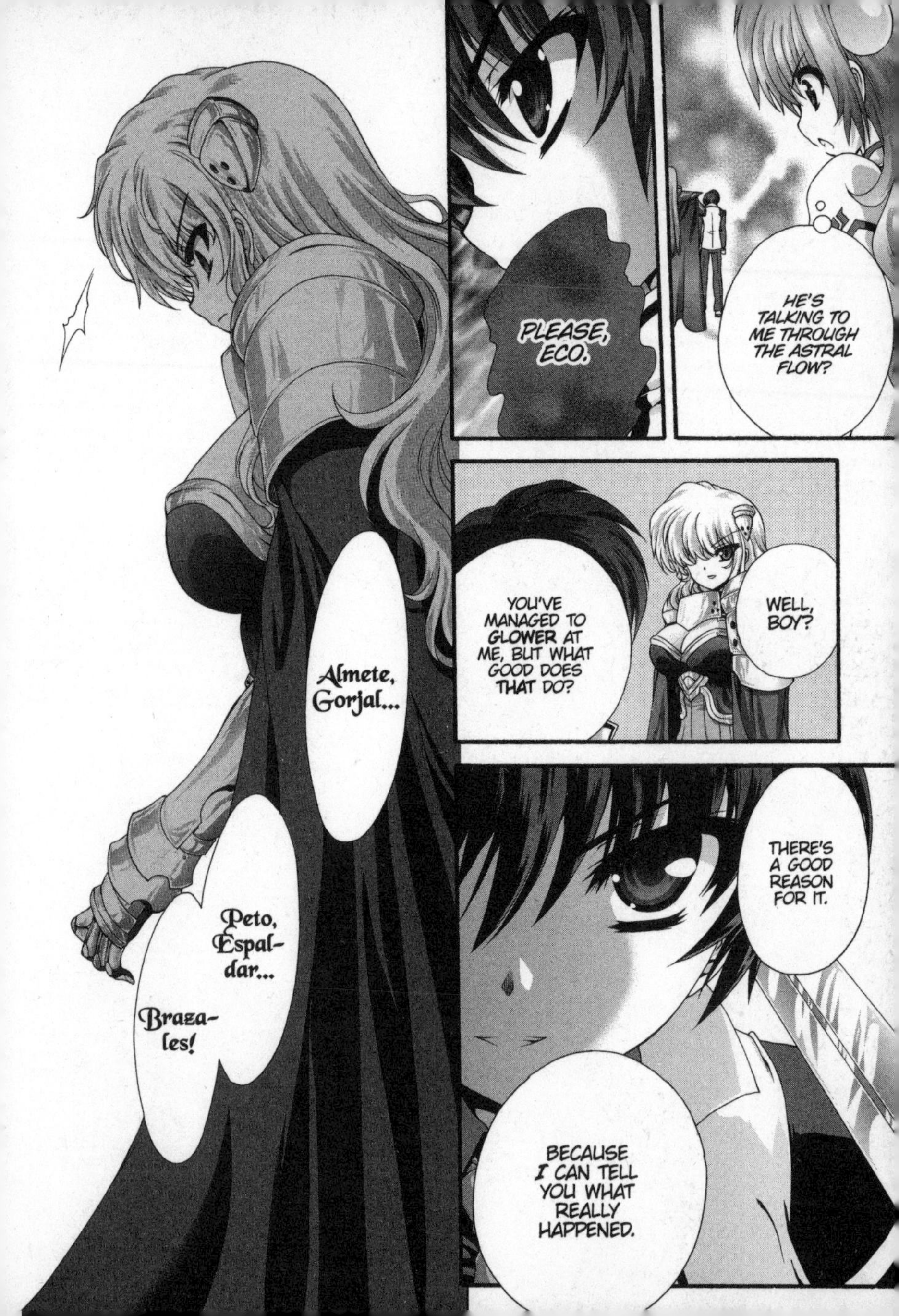
HE'S TALKING TO ME THROUGH THE ASTRAL FLOW?
PLEASE, ECO.
WELL, BOY?
YOU'VE MANAGED TO GLOWER AT ME, BUT WHAT GOOD DOES THAT DO?
THERE'S A GOOD REASON FOR IT.
BECAUSE I CAN TELL YOU WHAT REALLY HAPPENED.
Almete, Gorjal...
Peto, Espal-dar...
Braza-les!

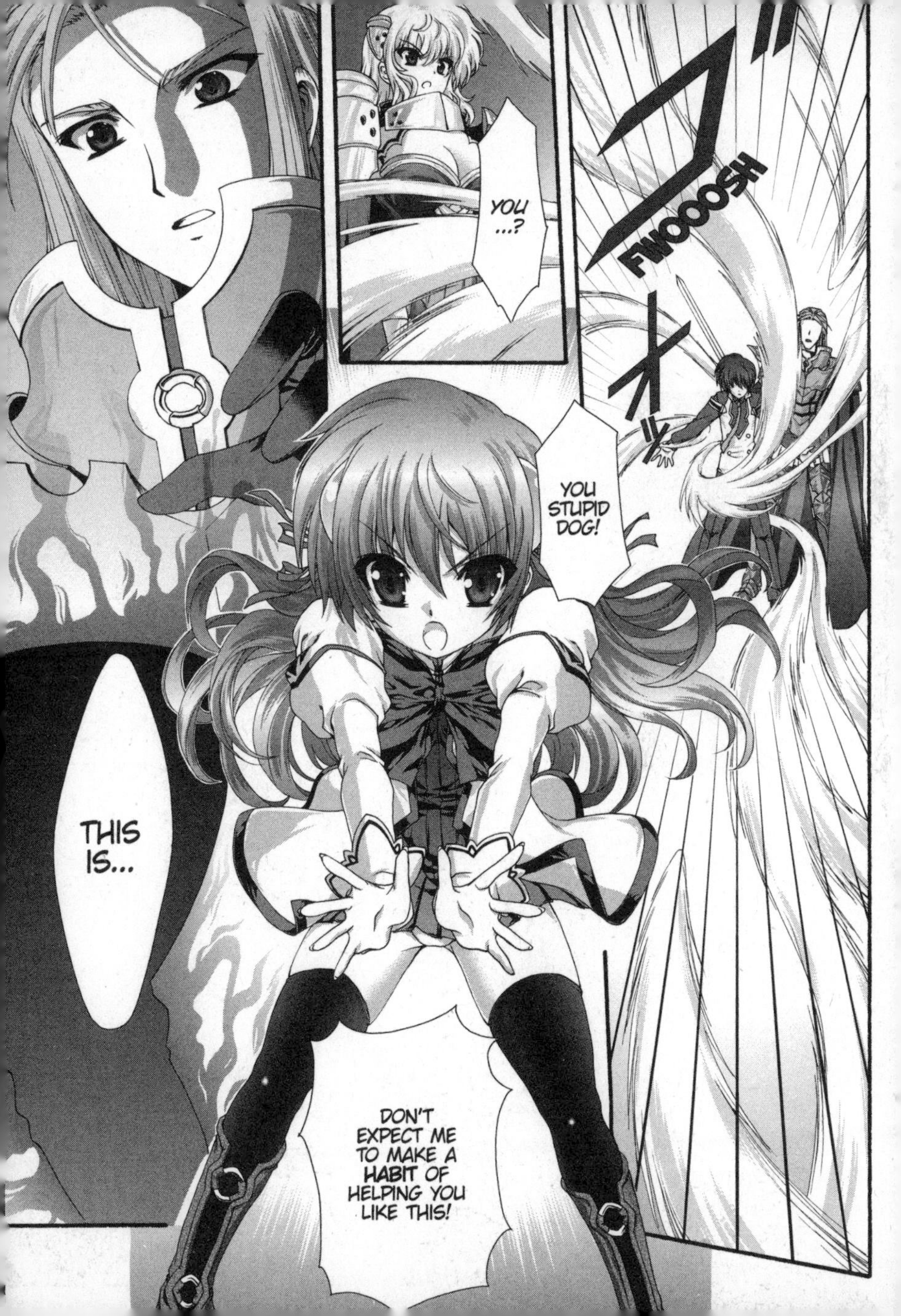
FWOOOSH
YOU ...?
THIS IS...
YOU STUPID DOG!
DON'T EXPECT ME TO MAKE A HABIT OF HELPING YOU LIKE THIS!

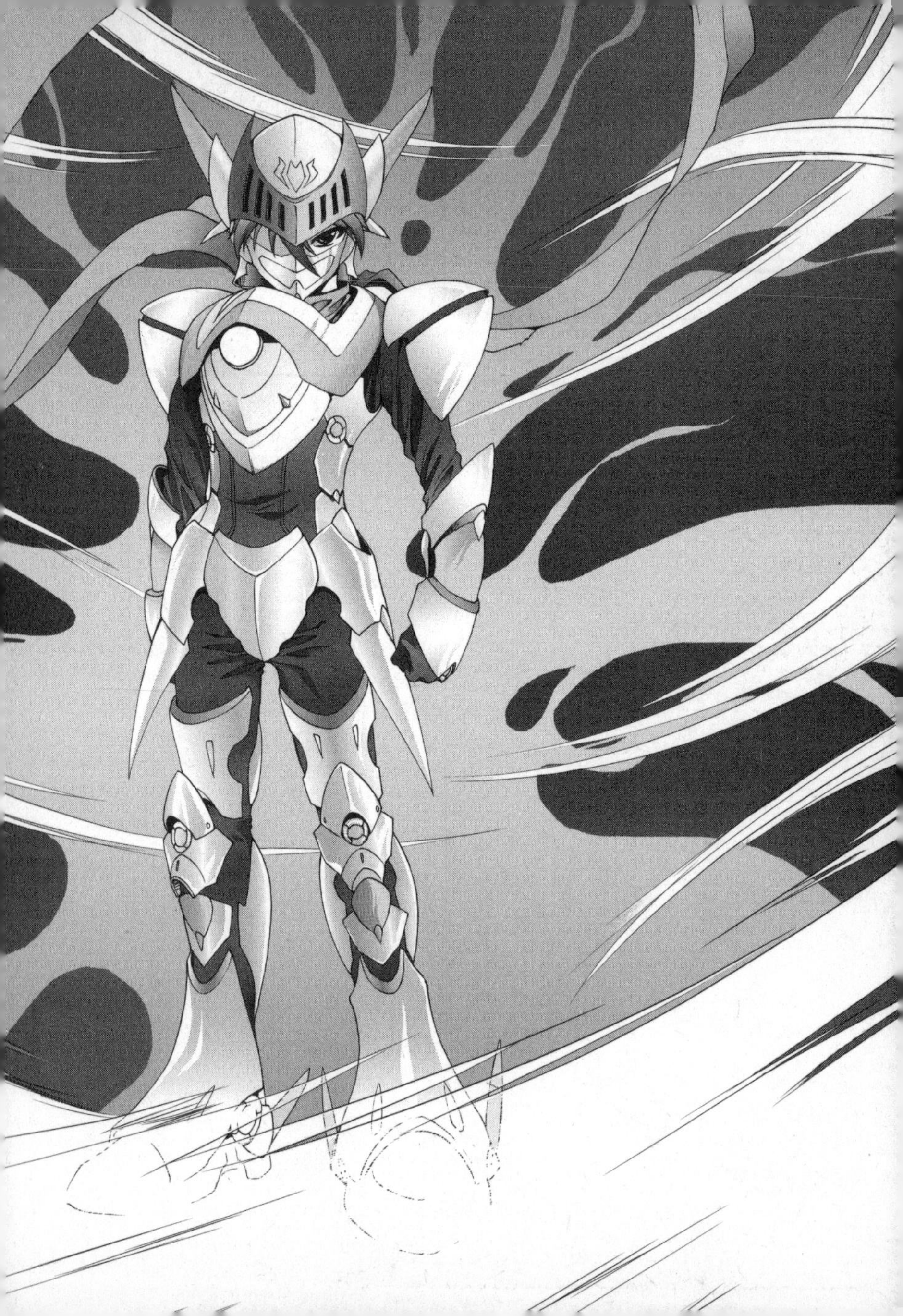

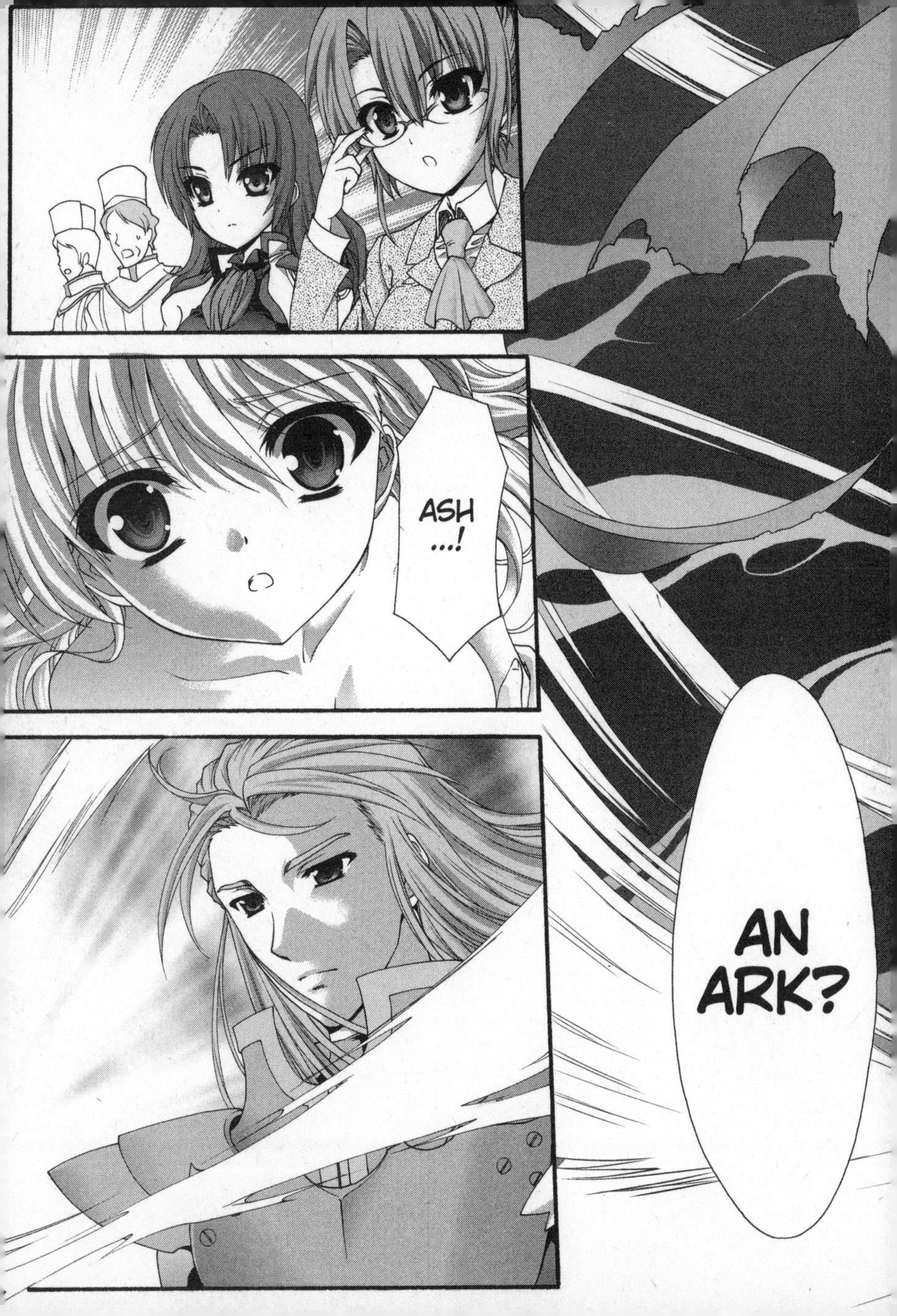
ASH ...!
AN ARK?

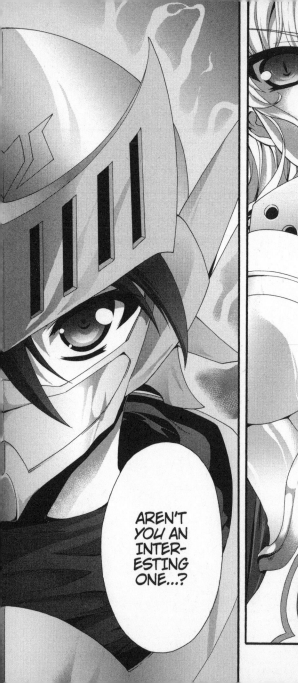

AREN'T YOU AN INTER- ESTING ONE...?

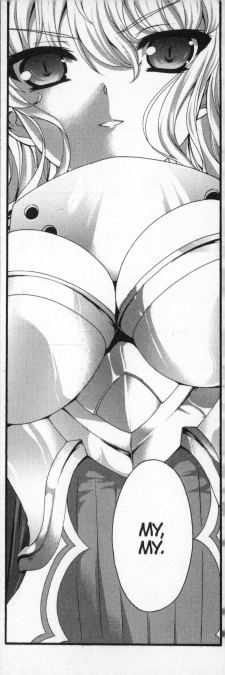

MY, MY.

DRAGONAR
ACADEMY

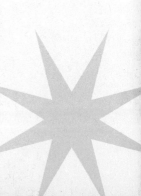

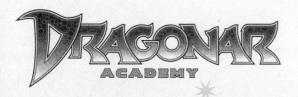

星刻の竜騎士

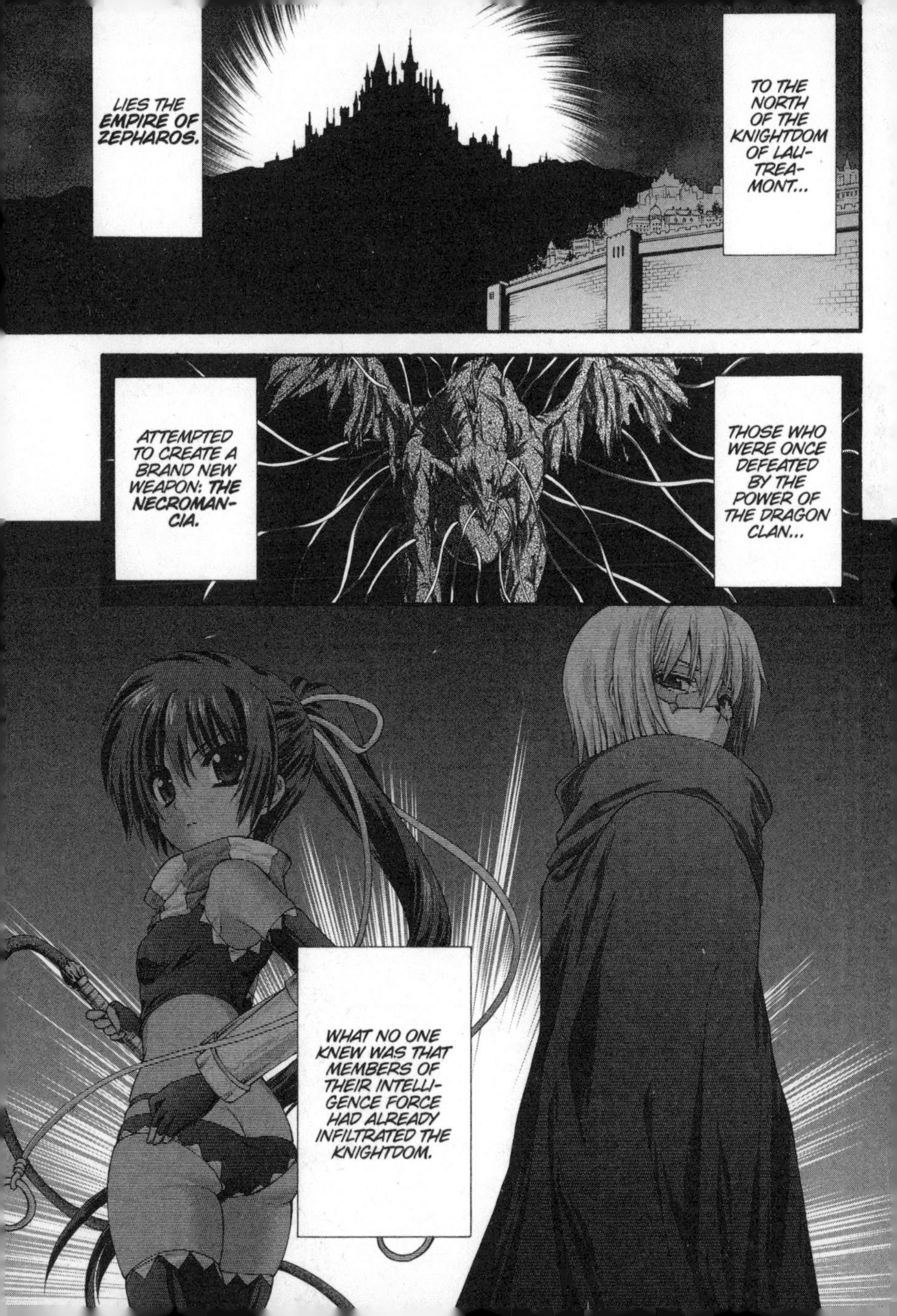
TO THE NORTH OF THE KNIGHTDOM OF LAU-TREA-MONT...
LIES THE EMPIRE OF ZEPHAROS.
THOSE WHO WERE ONCE DEFEATED BY THE POWER OF THE DRAGON CLAN...
ATTEMPTED TO CREATE A BRAND NEW WEAPON: THE NECROMAN-CIA.
WHAT NO ONE KNEW WAS THAT MEMBERS OF THEIR INTELLI-GENCE FORCE HAD ALREADY INFILTRATED THE KNIGHTDOM.

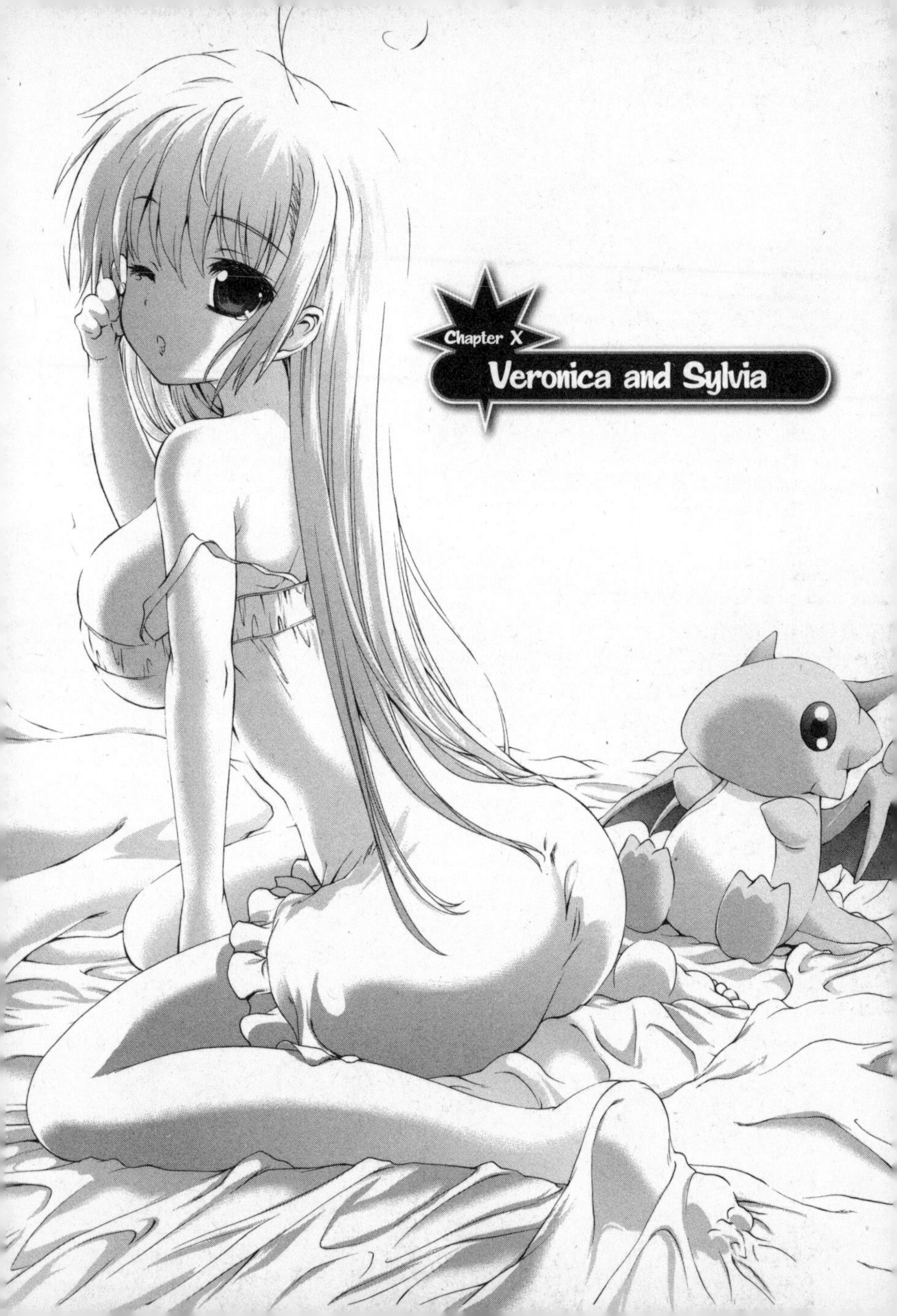
Chapter X
Veronica and Sylvia

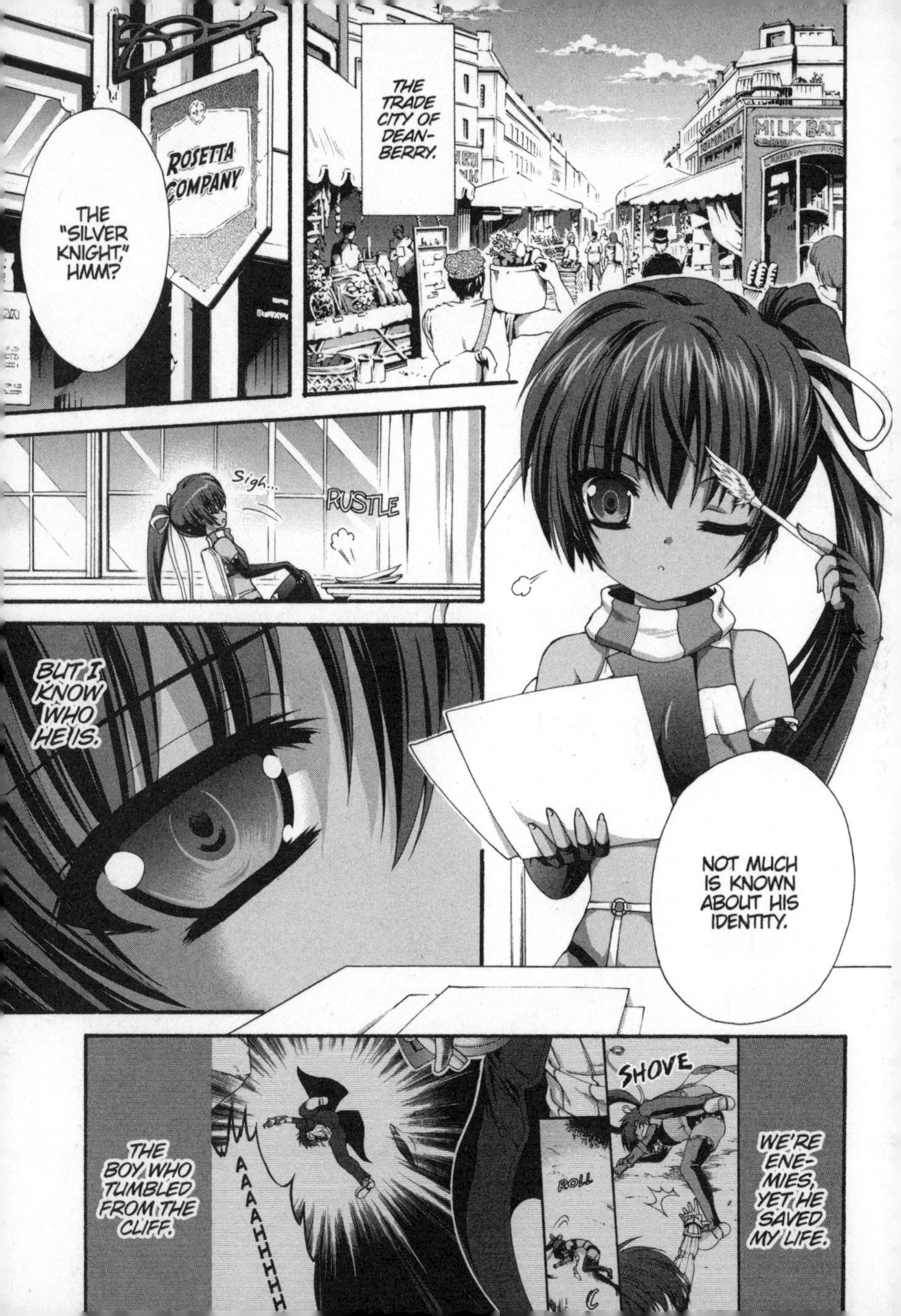
THE TRADE CITY OF DEAN-BERRY.
ROSETTA COMPANY
THE "SILVER KNIGHT," HMM?
NOT MUCH IS KNOWN ABOUT HIS IDENTITY.
Sigh...
RUSTLE
BUT I KNOW WHO HE IS.
WE'RE ENE-MIES, YET HE SAVED MY LIFE.
SHOVE
ROLL
AAAAHHHHH
THE BOY WHO TUMBLED FROM THE CLIFF.

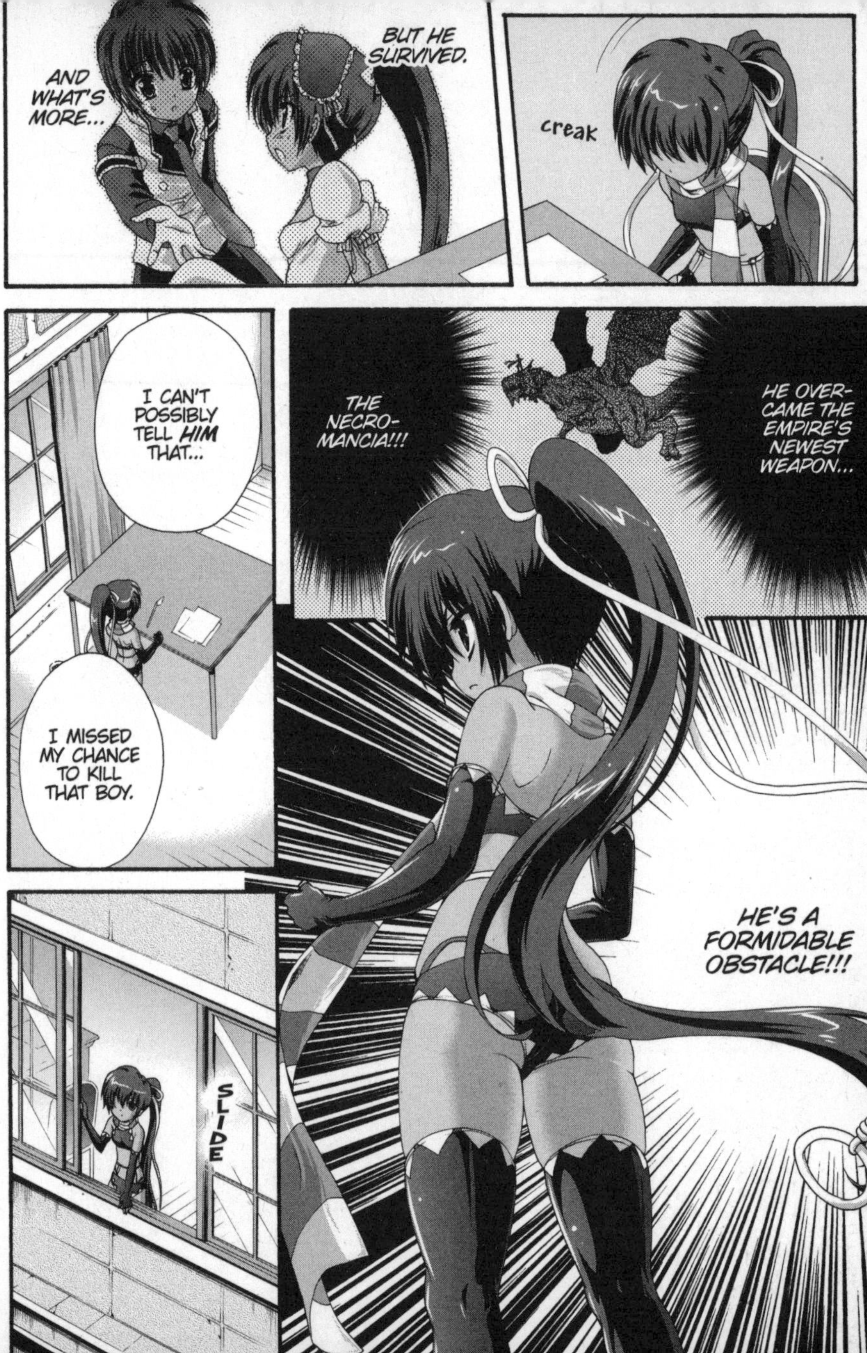
creak
BUT HE SURVIVED.
AND WHAT'S MORE...
HE OVERCAME THE EMPIRE'S NEWEST WEAPON...
THE NECROMANCIA!!!
HE'S A FORMIDABLE OBSTACLE!!!
I CAN'T POSSIBLY TELL *HIM* THAT...
I MISSED MY CHANCE TO KILL THAT BOY.
SLIDE

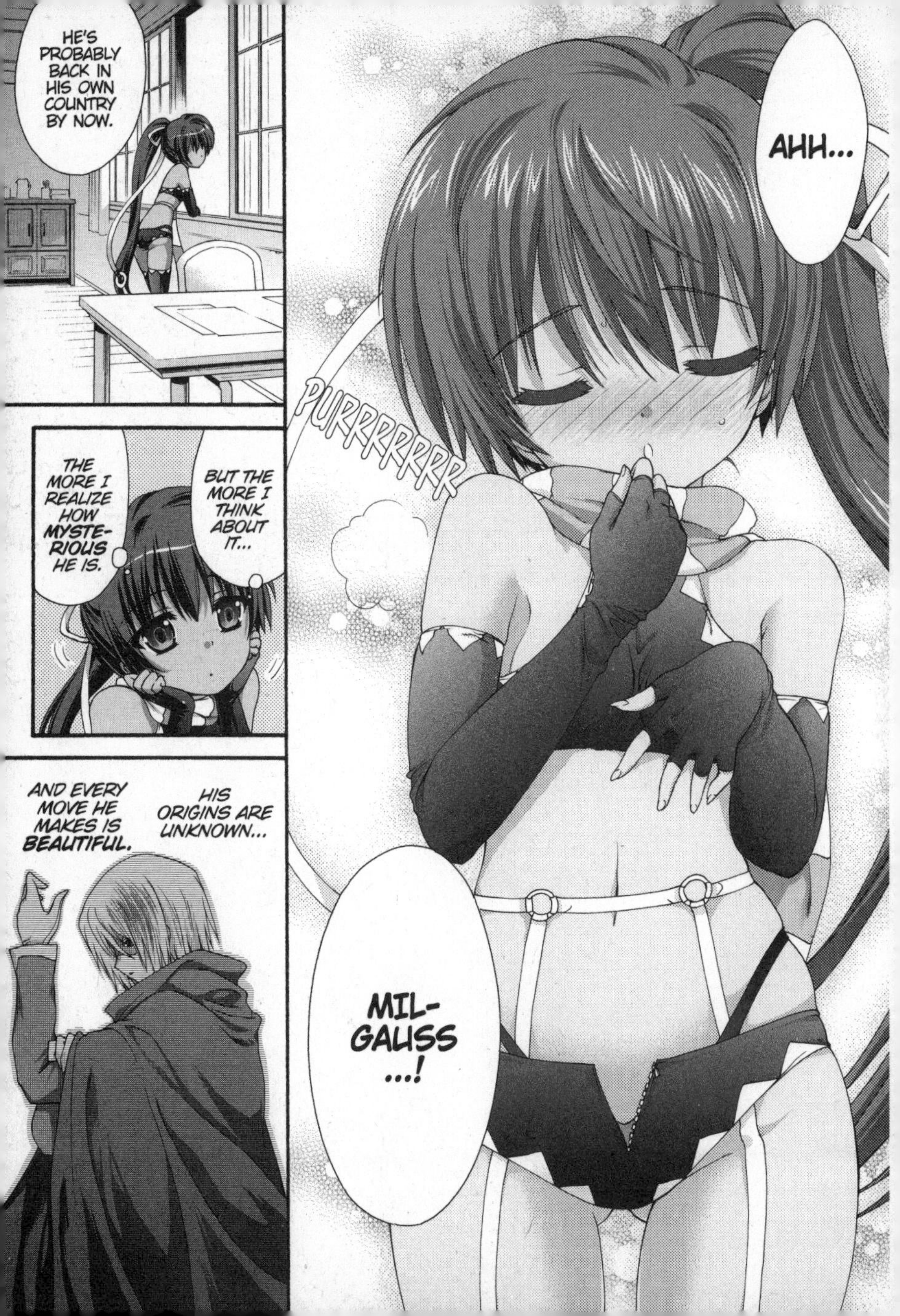
AHH...
PURRRRRRRR
MIL-GAUSS ...!
HE'S PROBABLY BACK IN HIS OWN COUNTRY BY NOW.
BUT THE MORE I THINK ABOUT IT...
THE MORE I REALIZE HOW MYSTERIOUS HE IS.
HIS ORIGINS ARE UNKNOWN...
AND EVERY MOVE HE MAKES IS BEAUTIFUL.

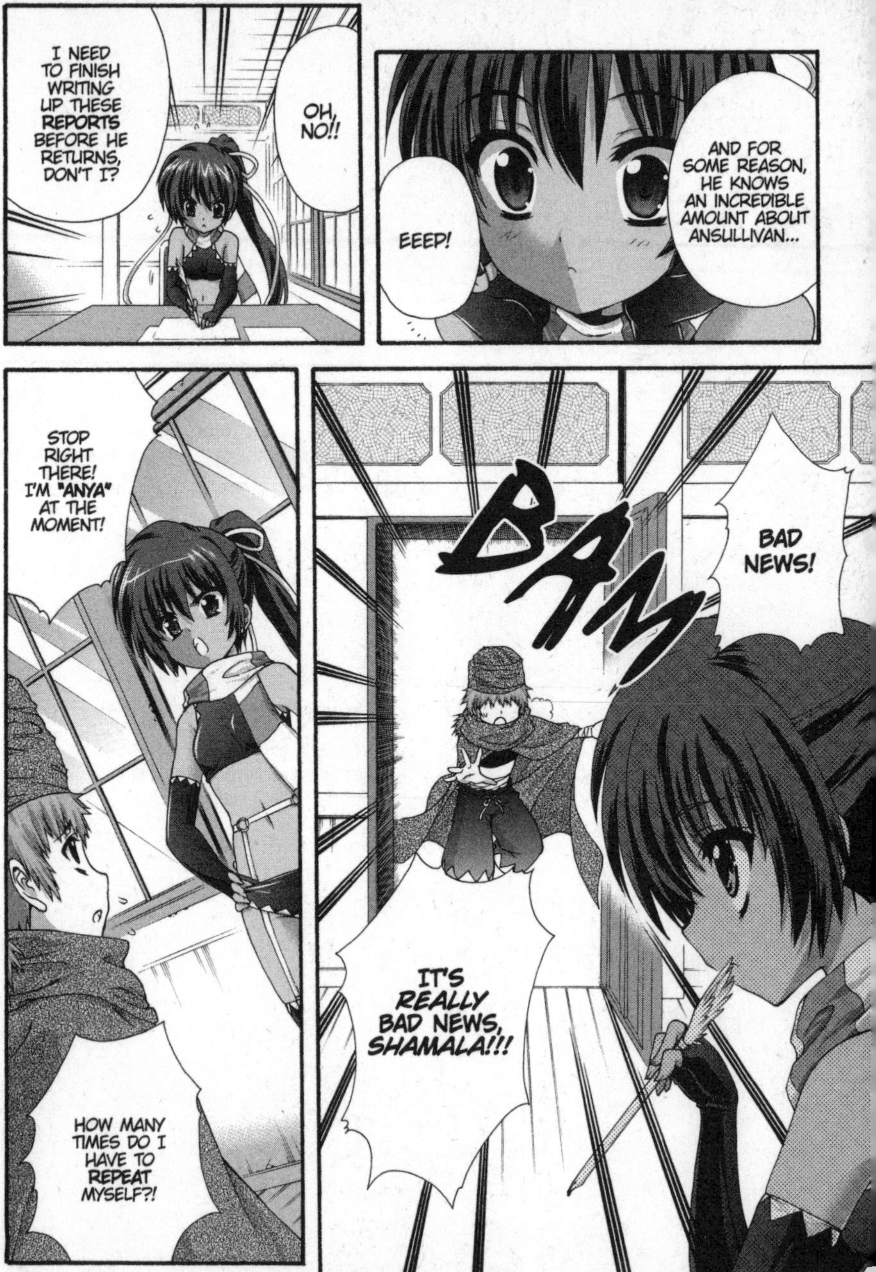
AND FOR SOME REASON, HE KNOWS AN INCREDIBLE AMOUNT ABOUT ANSULLIVAN...
EEEP!
I NEED TO FINISH WRITING UP THESE REPORTS BEFORE HE RETURNS, DON'T I?
OH, NO!!
BAD NEWS!
BAM
IT'S REALLY BAD NEWS, SHAMALA!!!
STOP RIGHT THERE! I'M "ANYA" AT THE MOMENT!
HOW MANY TIMES DO I HAVE TO REPEAT MYSELF?!

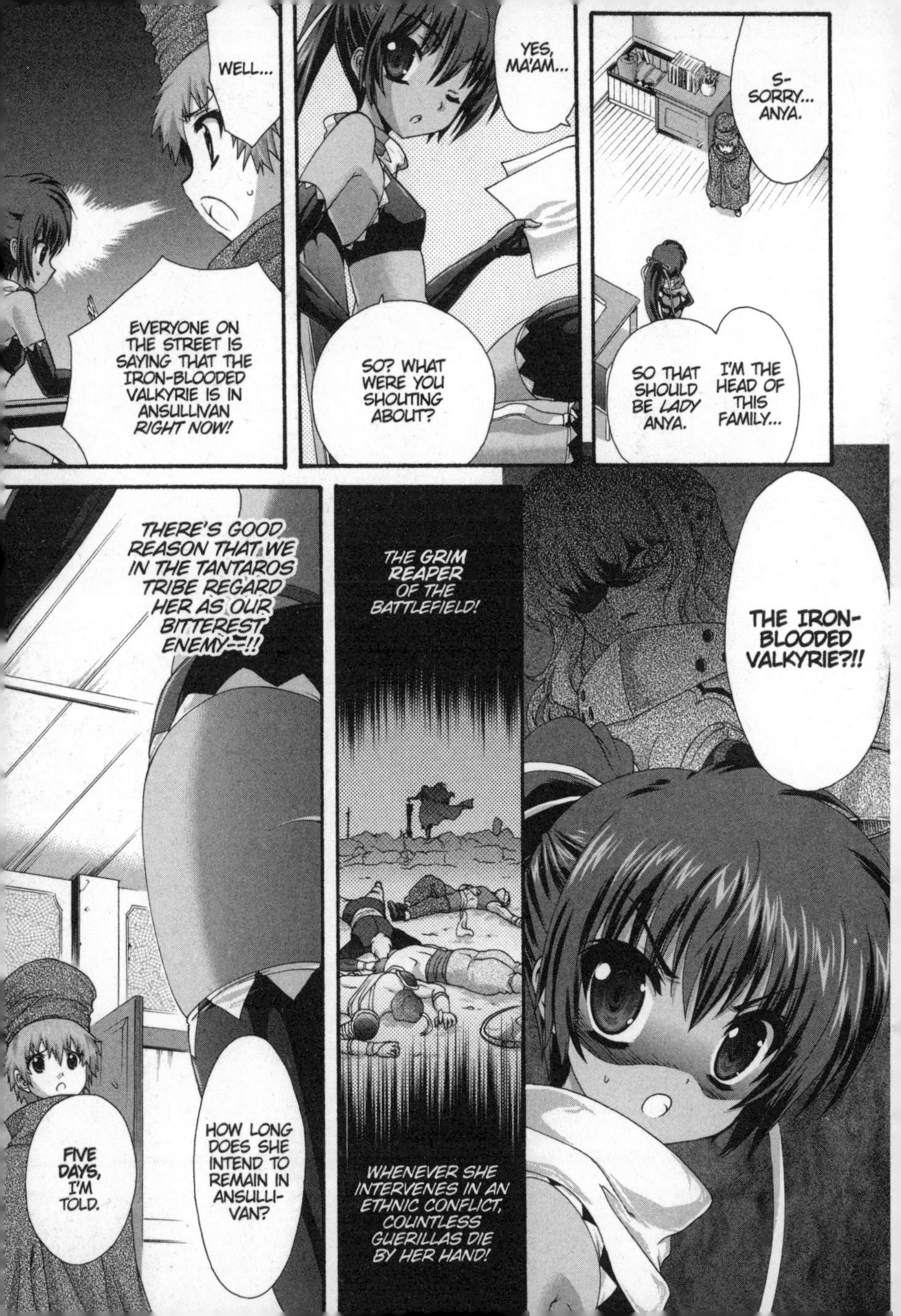
S-SORRY... ANYA.
I'M THE HEAD OF THIS FAMILY...
SO THAT SHOULD BE *LADY* ANYA.
YES, MA'AM...
SO? WHAT WERE YOU SHOUTING ABOUT?
WELL...
EVERYONE ON THE STREET IS SAYING THAT THE IRON-BLOODED VALKYRIE IS IN ANSULLIVAN *RIGHT NOW!*
THE IRON-BLOODED VALKYRIE?!!
THE GRIM REAPER OF THE BATTLEFIELD!
WHENEVER SHE INTERVENES IN AN ETHNIC CONFLICT, COUNTLESS GUERILLAS DIE BY HER HAND!
THERE'S GOOD REASON THAT WE IN THE TANTAROS TRIBE REGARD HER AS OUR BITTEREST ENEMY--!!
HOW LONG DOES SHE INTEND TO REMAIN IN ANSULLI-VAN?
FIVE DAYS, I'M TOLD.

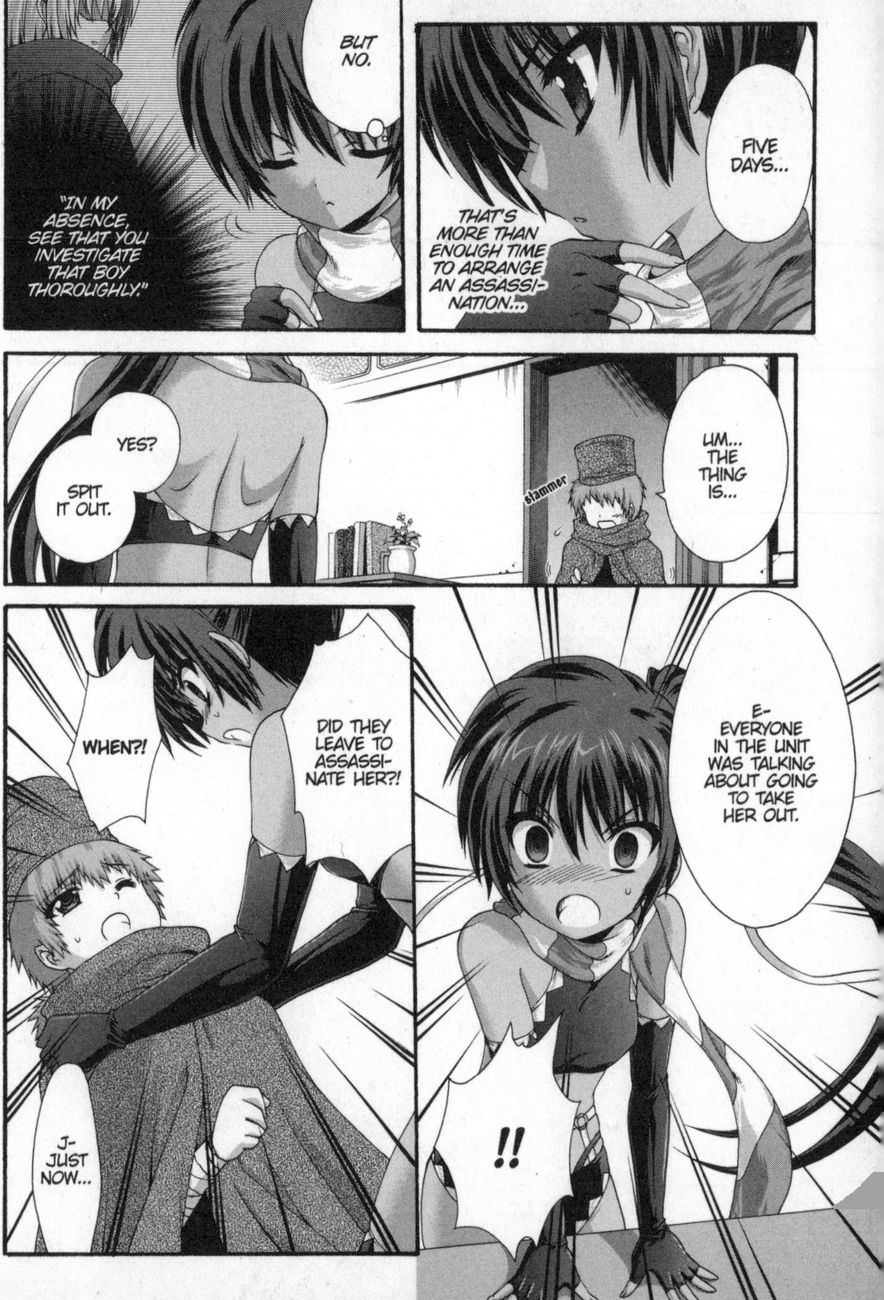
FIVE DAYS...
THAT'S MORE THAN ENOUGH TIME TO ARRANGE AN ASSASSI-NATION...
BUT NO.
"IN MY ABSENCE, SEE THAT YOU INVESTIGATE THAT BOY THOROUGHLY."
UM... THE THING IS...
stammer
YES?
SPIT IT OUT.
E-EVERYONE IN THE UNIT WAS TALKING ABOUT GOING TO TAKE HER OUT.
!!
DID THEY LEAVE TO ASSASSI-NATE HER?!
WHEN?!
J-JUST NOW...

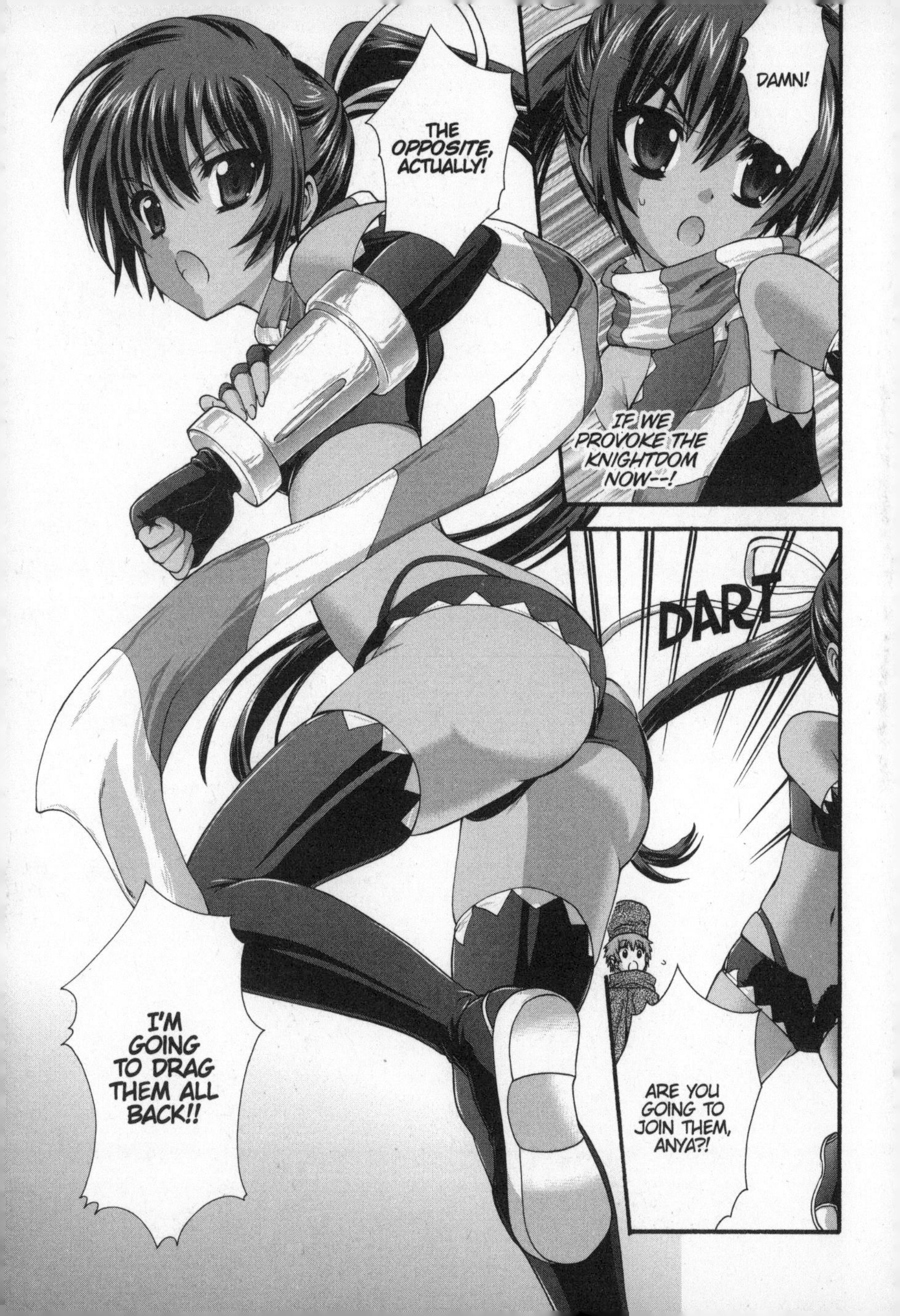
DAMN!
IF WE PROVOKE THE KNIGHTDOM NOW--!
DART
ARE YOU GOING TO JOIN THEM, ANYA?!
THE OPPOSITE, ACTUALLY!
I'M GOING TO DRAG THEM ALL BACK!!

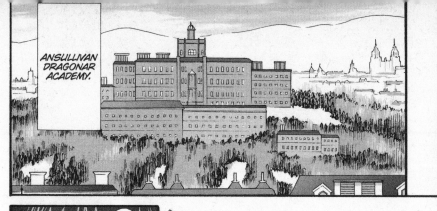

ANSULLIVAN DRAGONAR ACADEMY.

UH...

THE MAGIC WARSHIP SILVANUS.

PRIN- CESS VERON- ICA?

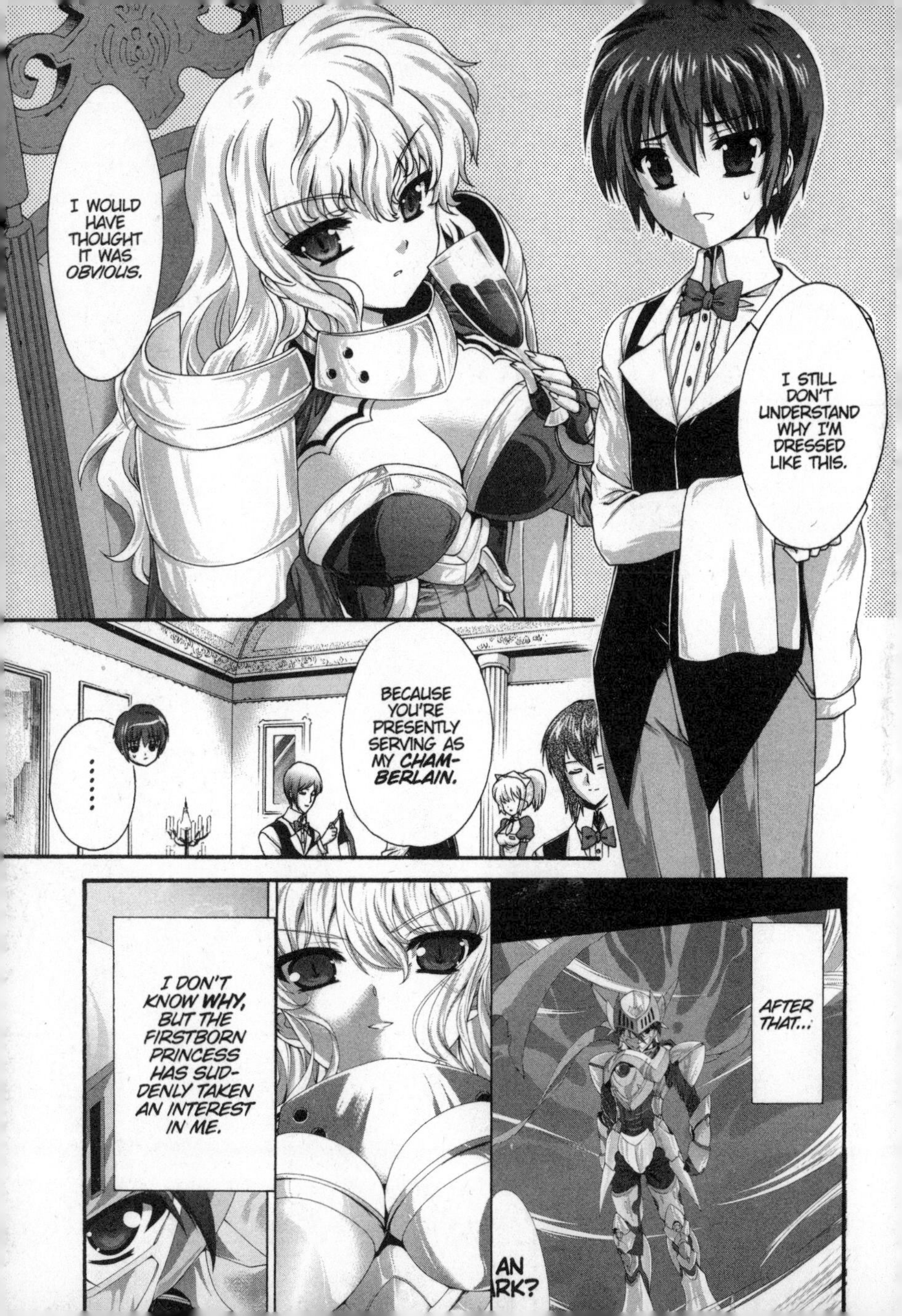
I STILL DON'T UNDERSTAND WHY I'M DRESSED LIKE THIS.
I WOULD HAVE THOUGHT IT WAS OBVIOUS.
BECAUSE YOU'RE PRESENTLY SERVING AS MY CHAMBERLAIN.
......
AFTER THAT...
I DON'T KNOW WHY, BUT THE FIRSTBORN PRINCESS HAS SUDDENLY TAKEN AN INTEREST IN ME.

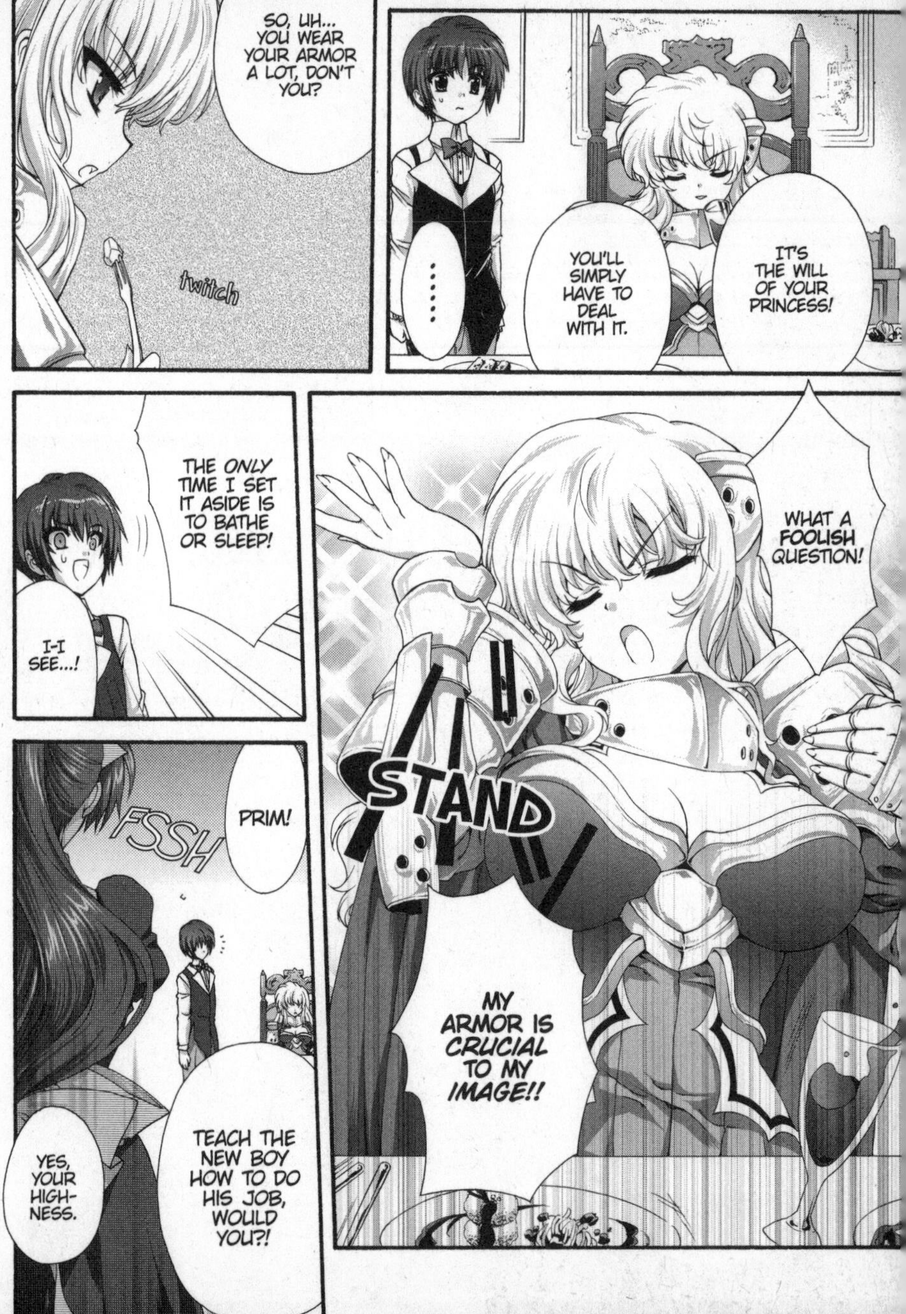
IT'S THE WILL OF YOUR PRINCESS!
YOU'LL SIMPLY HAVE TO DEAL WITH IT.
......
SO, UH... YOU WEAR YOUR ARMOR A LOT, DON'T YOU?
twitch
WHAT A FOOLISH QUESTION!
STAND
MY ARMOR IS CRUCIAL TO MY IMAGE!!
THE ONLY TIME I SET IT ASIDE IS TO BATHE OR SLEEP!
I-I SEE...!
PRIM!
FSSH
TEACH THE NEW BOY HOW TO DO HIS JOB, WOULD YOU?!
YES, YOUR HIGHNESS.

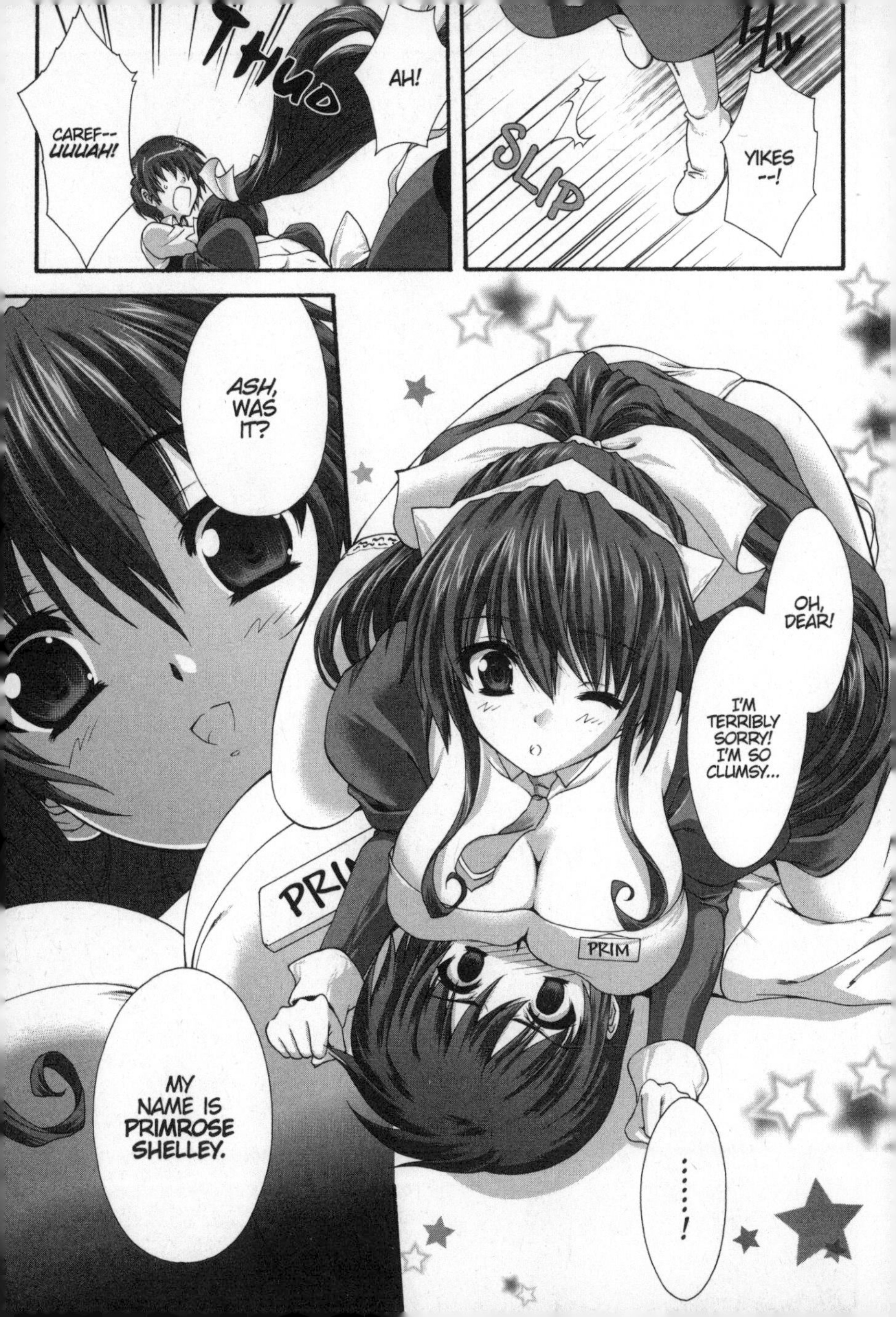
YIKES --!
SLIP
AH!
THUD
CAREF-- UUUAH!
OH, DEAR!
I'M TERRIBLY SORRY! I'M SO CLUMSY...
ASH, WAS IT?
PRIM
PRIM
......!
MY NAME IS PRIMROSE SHELLEY.

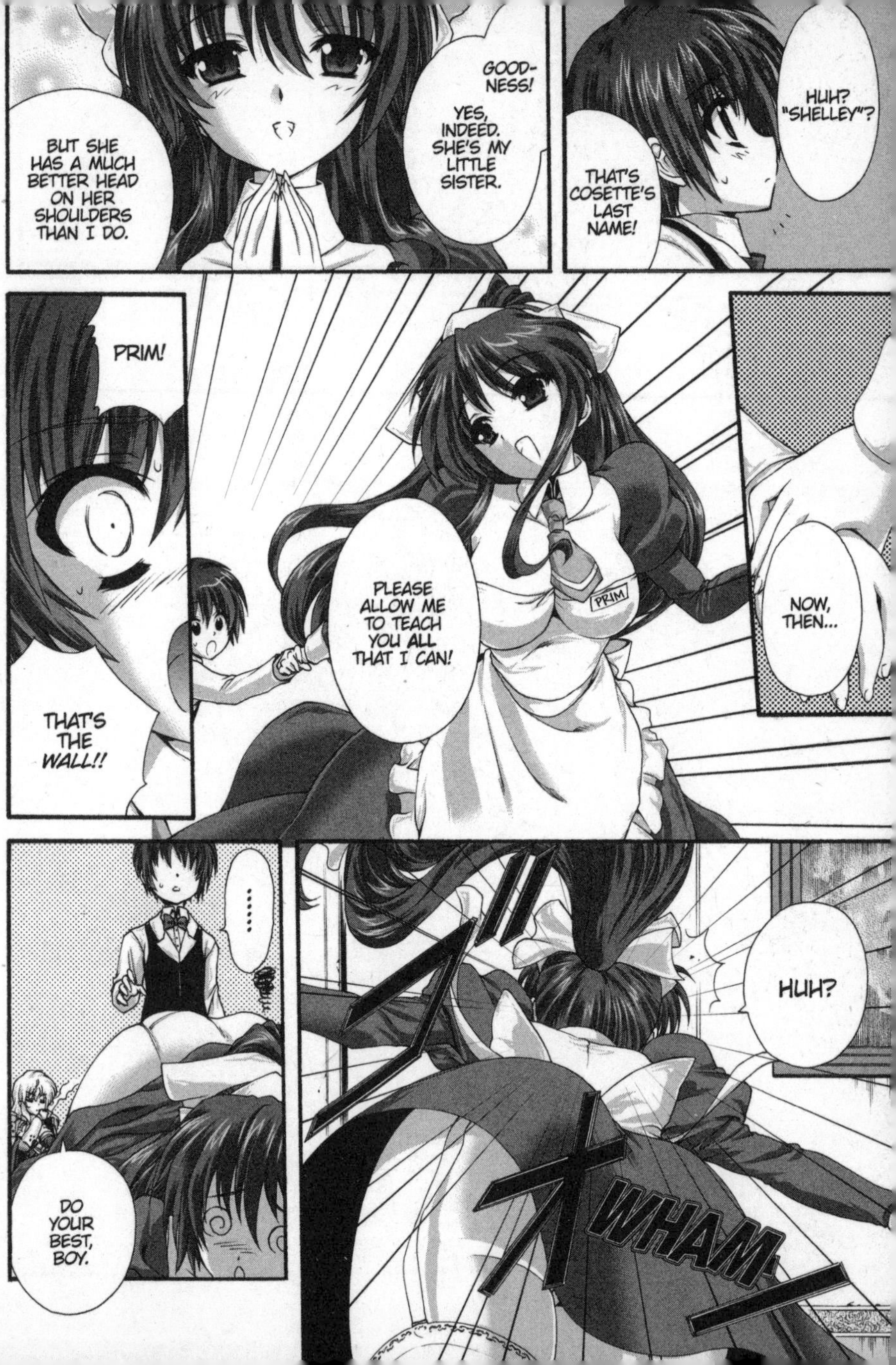
HUH? "SHELLEY"?
THAT'S COSETTE'S LAST NAME!
GOOD-NESS!
YES, INDEED. SHE'S MY LITTLE SISTER.
BUT SHE HAS A MUCH BETTER HEAD ON HER SHOULDERS THAN I DO.
NOW, THEN...
PRIM
PLEASE ALLOW ME TO TEACH YOU ALL THAT I CAN!
PRIM!
THAT'S THE WALL!!
HUH?
WHAM
......
DO YOUR BEST, BOY.

LALIN-
DRY.

wobble
wobble

GAH! STOP! I'LL TAKE CARE OF IT! JUST PUT IT DOWN!!

CRASH

COOK-
ING.

SMASH

Oh, no...!

CLEAN-
ING.

HUH?

GOODNESS! IT'S ALMOST THAT TIME!

THE PRINCESS IS CALLING US!

I'M STILL IN SCHOOL, ANYWAY!

CALLING US WHERE?!

I'M SO SORRY, ASH.

AT THIS RATE, I FEAR I'LL NEVER MAKE YOU A FINE CHAMBERLAIN.

SOB

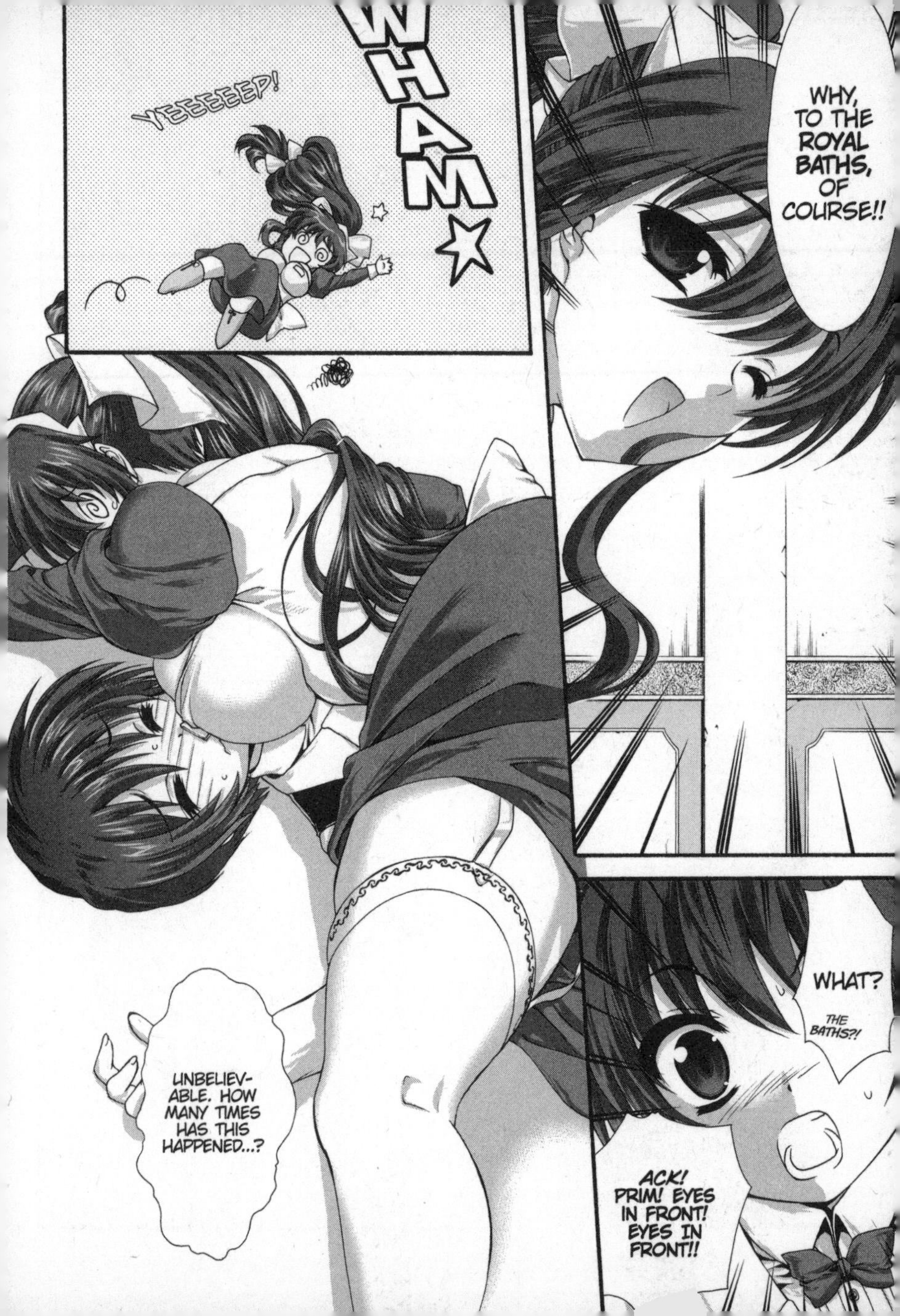
WHY, TO THE ROYAL BATHS, OF COURSE!!
WHAT?
THE BATHS?!
ACK! PRIM! EYES IN FRONT! EYES IN FRONT!!
WHAM
YEEEEEP!
UNBELIEV-ABLE. HOW MANY TIMES HAS THIS HAPPENED...?

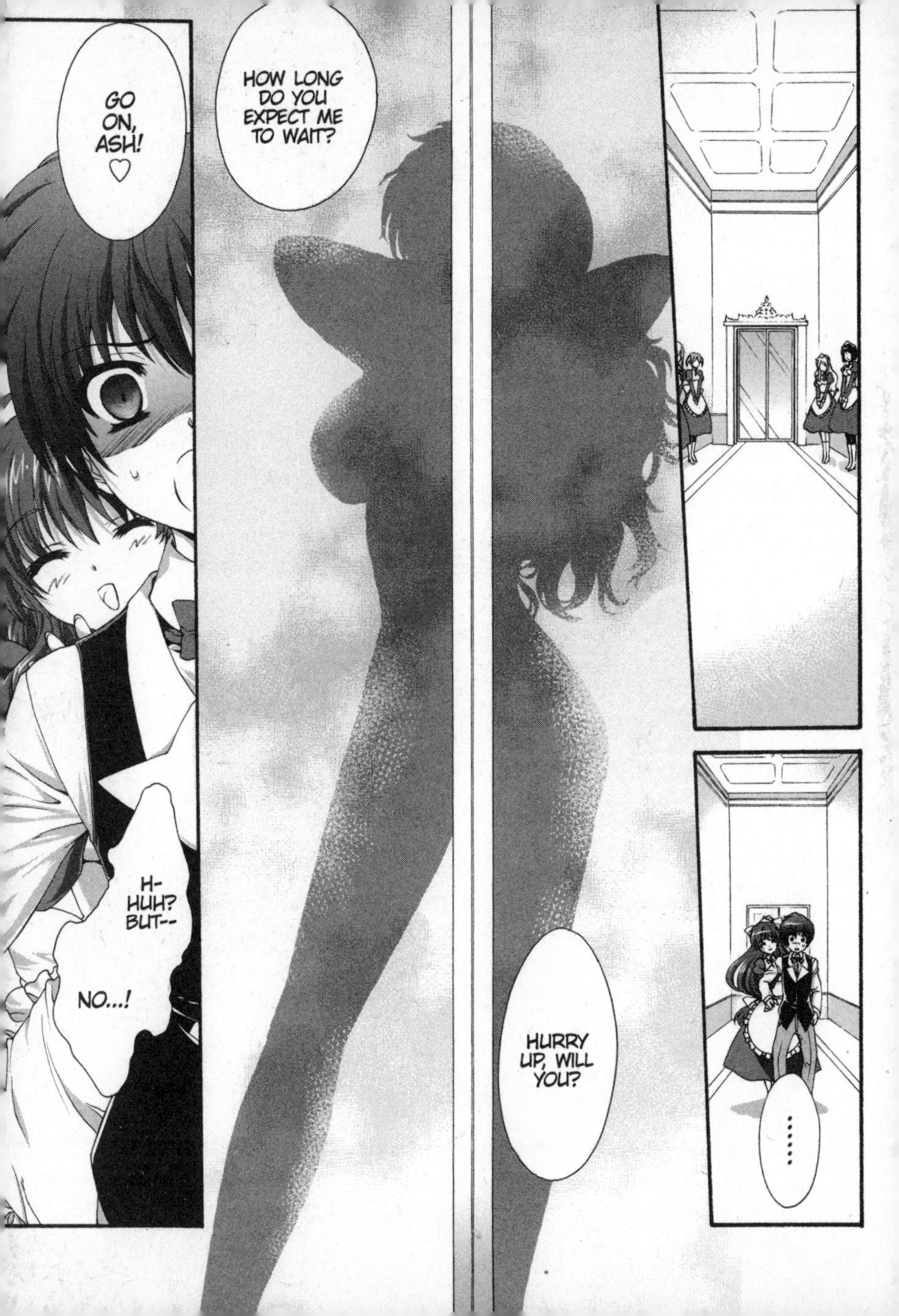
......
HURRY UP, WILL YOU?
HOW LONG DO YOU EXPECT ME TO WAIT?
GO ON, ASH! ♡
H-HUH? BUT--
NO...!

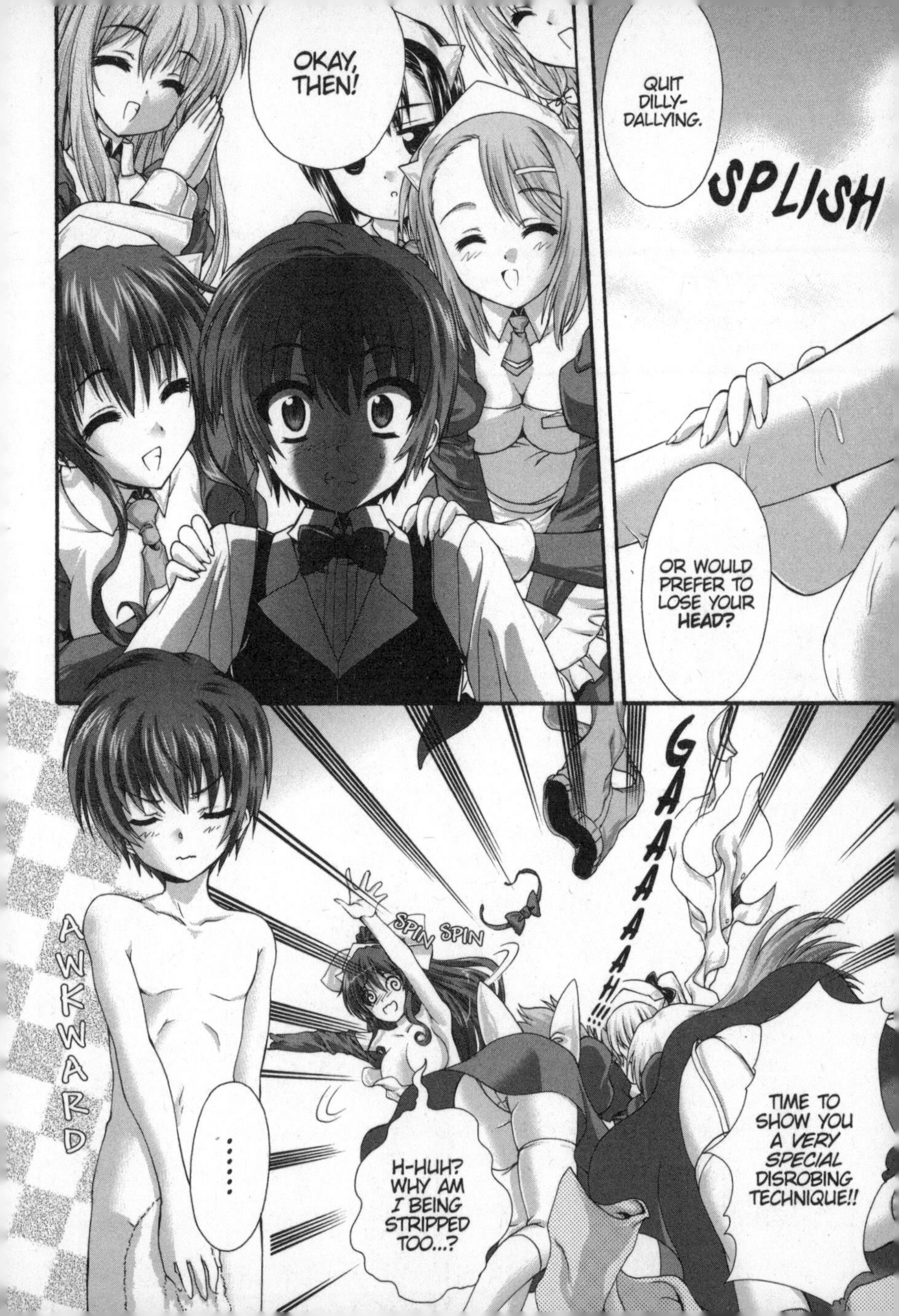

QUIT DILLY-DALLYING.
SPLISH
OR WOULD PREFER TO LOSE YOUR HEAD?
OKAY, THEN!
GAAAAAAAH!!!
TIME TO SHOW YOU A VERY SPECIAL DISROBING TECHNIQUE!!
SPIN SPIN
H-HUH? WHY AM I BEING STRIPPED TOO...?
......
AWKWARD

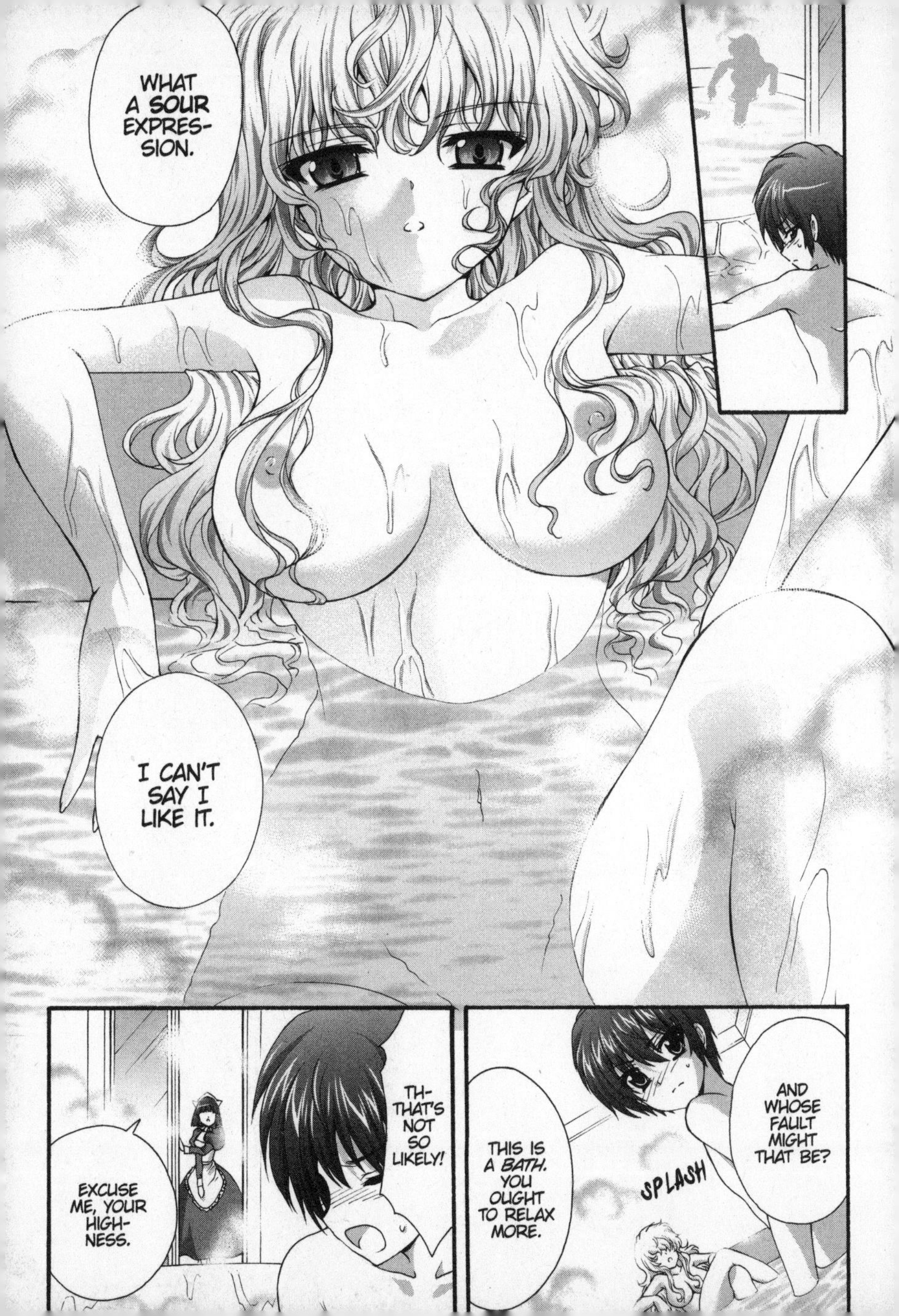
WHAT A SOUR EXPRES-SION.
I CAN'T SAY I LIKE IT.
AND WHOSE FAULT MIGHT THAT BE?
SPLASH
THIS IS A *BATH*. YOU OUGHT TO RELAX MORE.
TH-THAT'S NOT SO LIKELY!
EXCUSE ME, YOUR HIGH-NESS.

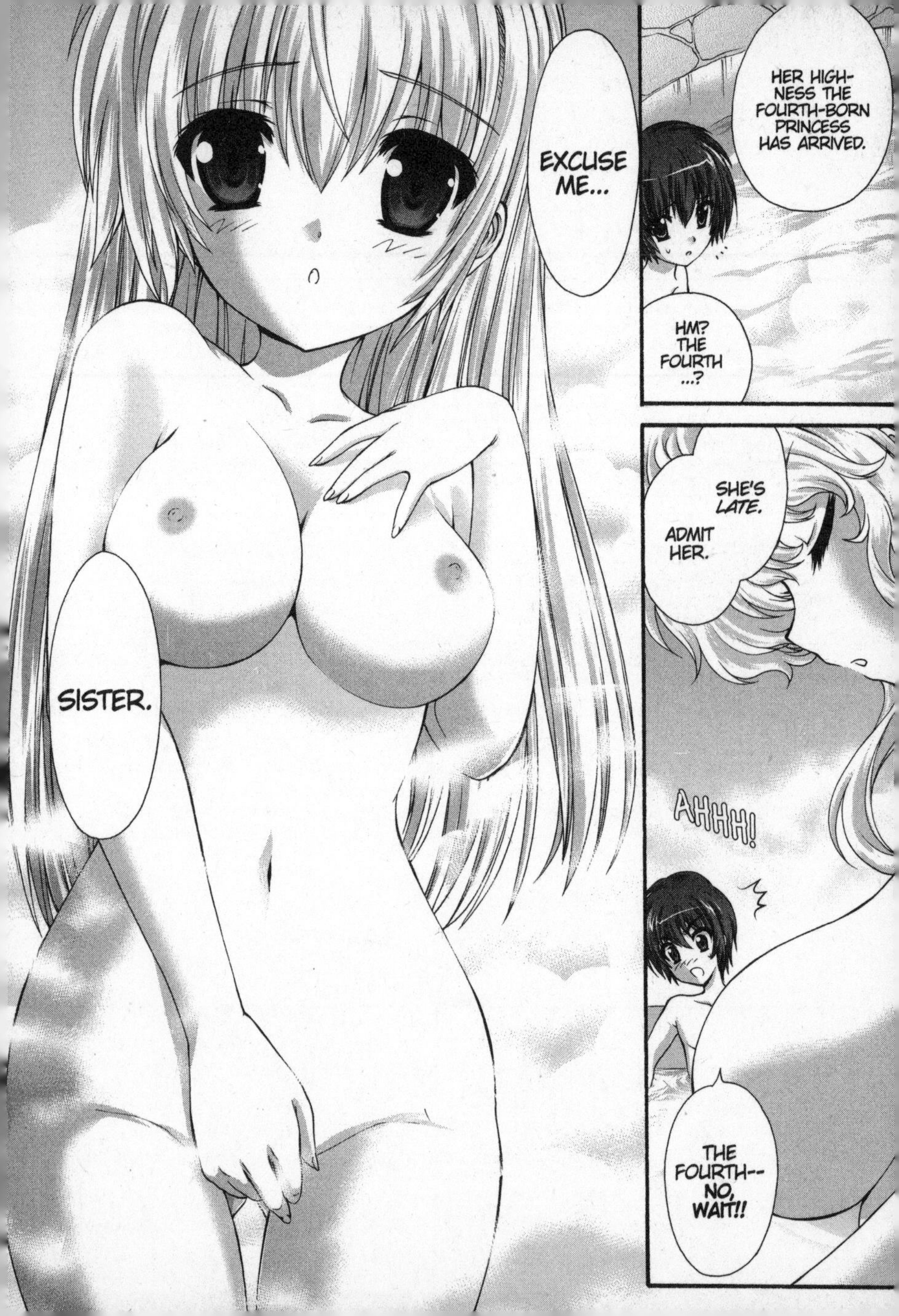
HER HIGH-NESS THE FOURTH-BORN PRINCESS HAS ARRIVED.
HM? THE FOURTH ...?
SHE'S LATE.
ADMIT HER.
AHHH!
THE FOURTH-- NO, WAIT!!
EXCUSE ME...
SISTER.

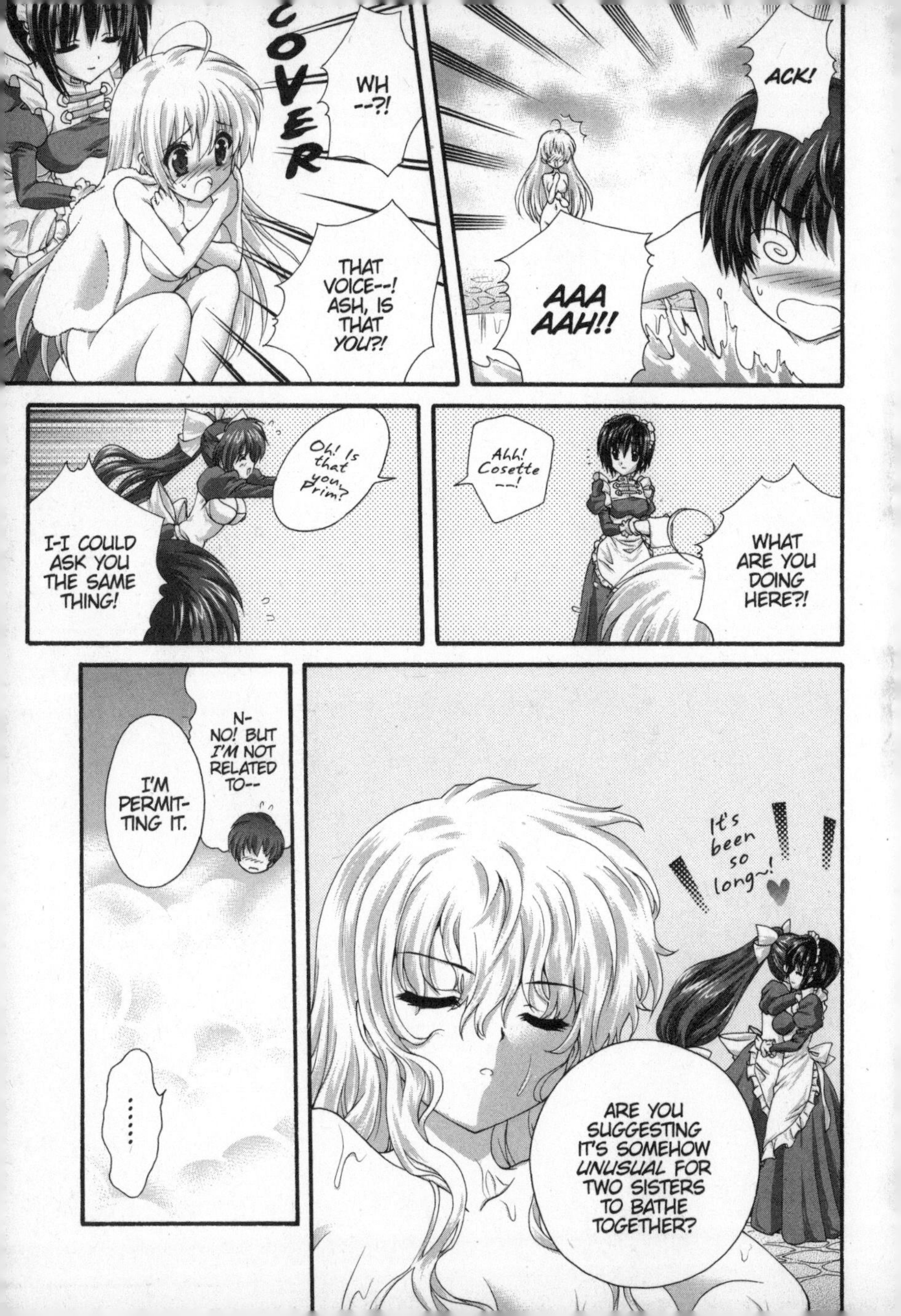
ACK!
AAA AAH!!
WH --?!
COVER
THAT VOICE--! ASH, IS THAT *YOU*?!
Ahh! Cosette--!
WHAT ARE YOU DOING HERE?!
Oh! Is that you, Prim?
I-I COULD ASK YOU THE SAME THING!
It's been so long~! ♥
ARE YOU SUGGESTING IT'S SOMEHOW *UNUSUAL* FOR TWO SISTERS TO BATHE TOGETHER?
N-NO! BUT *I'M* NOT RELATED TO--
I'M PERMIT-TING IT.
......

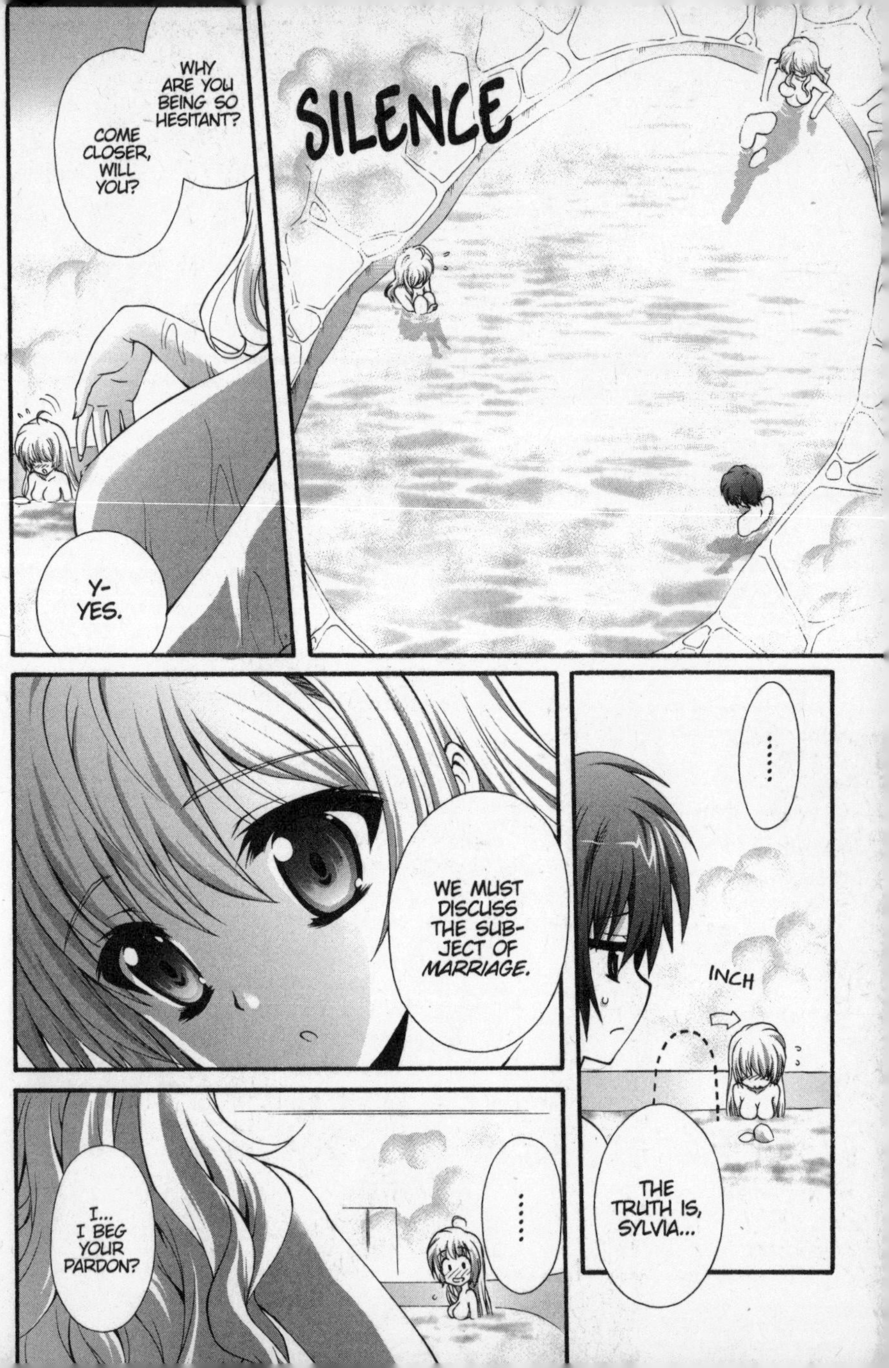
SILENCE
WHY ARE YOU BEING SO HESITANT?
COME CLOSER, WILL YOU?
Y-YES.
......
INCH
THE TRUTH IS, SYLVIA...
WE MUST DISCUSS THE SUBJECT OF MARRIAGE.
......
I... I BEG YOUR PARDON?

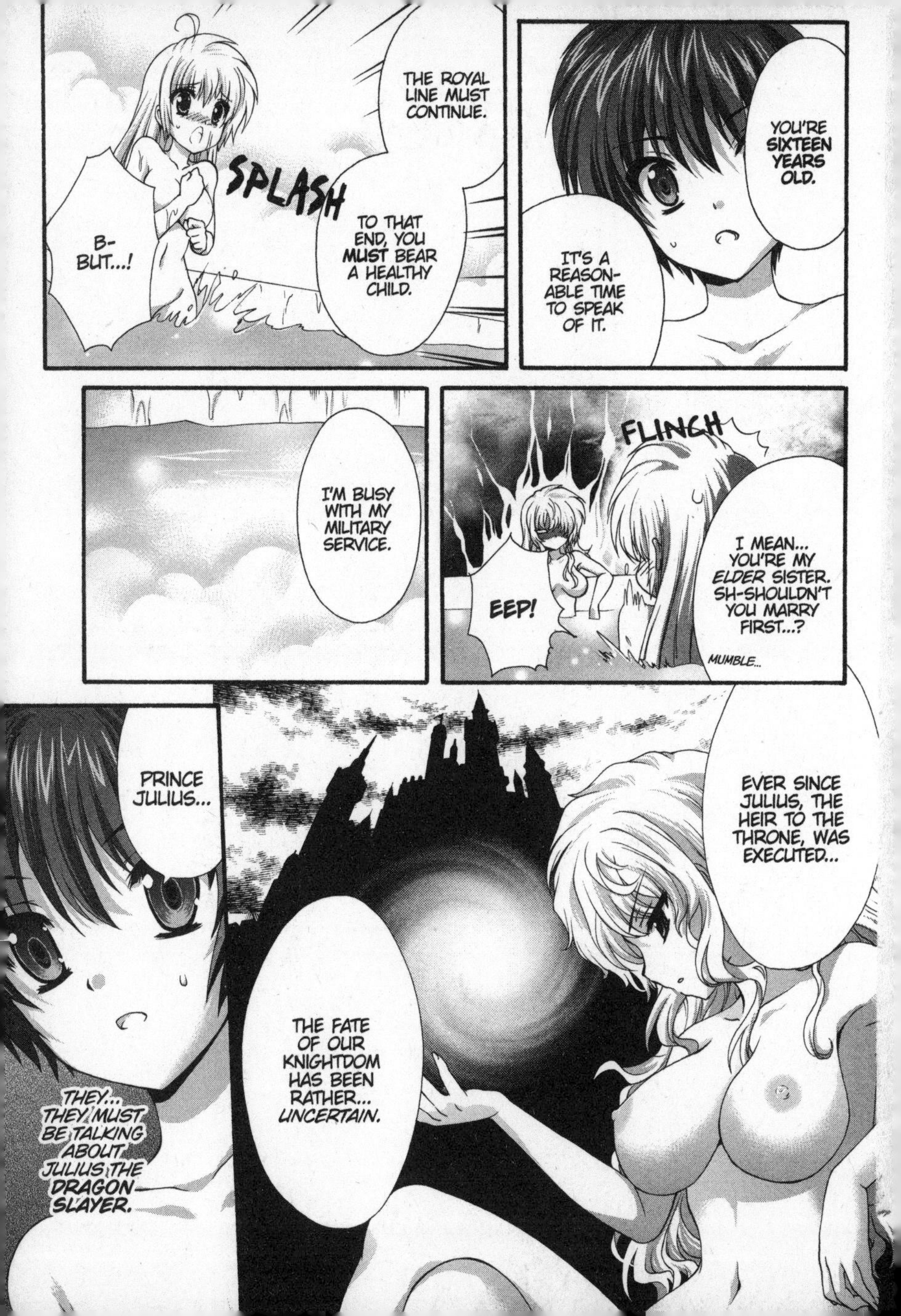
YOU'RE SIXTEEN YEARS OLD.
IT'S A REASON-ABLE TIME TO SPEAK OF IT.
THE ROYAL LINE MUST CONTINUE.
TO THAT END, YOU MUST BEAR A HEALTHY CHILD.
SPLASH
B-BUT...!
FLINCH
I MEAN... YOU'RE MY ELDER SISTER. SH-SHOULDN'T YOU MARRY FIRST...?
MUMBLE...
EEP!
I'M BUSY WITH MY MILITARY SERVICE.
EVER SINCE JULIUS, THE HEIR TO THE THRONE, WAS EXECUTED...
THE FATE OF OUR KNIGHTDOM HAS BEEN RATHER... UNCERTAIN.
PRINCE JULIUS...
THEY... THEY MUST BE TALKING ABOUT JULIUS THE DRAGON SLAYER.

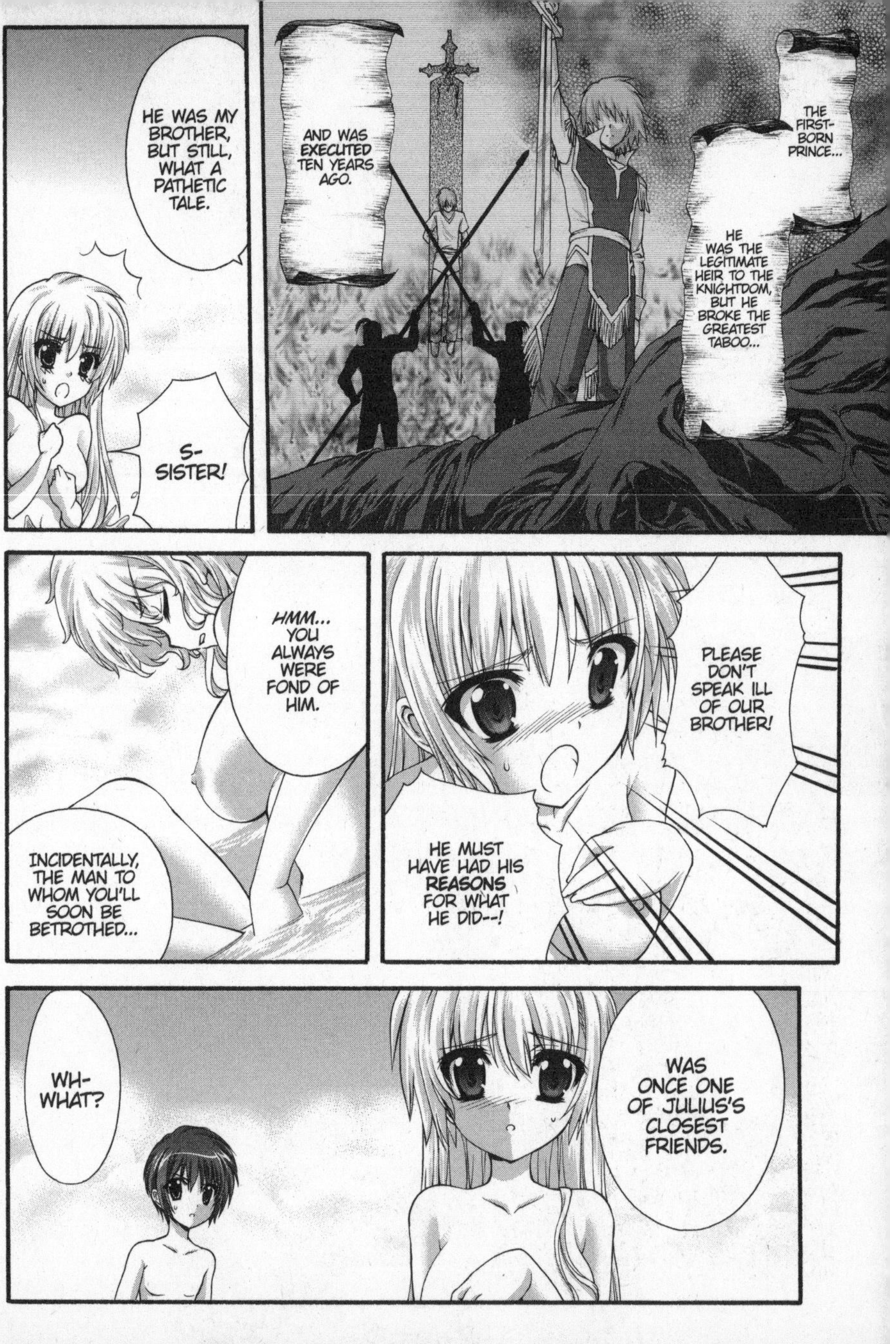
THE FIRST-BORN PRINCE...
HE WAS THE LEGITIMATE HEIR TO THE KNIGHTDOM, BUT HE BROKE THE GREATEST TABOO...
AND WAS EXECUTED TEN YEARS AGO.
HE WAS MY BROTHER, BUT STILL, WHAT A PATHETIC TALE.
S-SISTER!
PLEASE DON'T SPEAK ILL OF OUR BROTHER!
HE MUST HAVE HAD HIS REASONS FOR WHAT HE DID--!
HMM... YOU ALWAYS WERE FOND OF HIM.
INCIDENTALLY, THE MAN TO WHOM YOU'LL SOON BE BETROTHED...
WAS ONCE ONE OF JULIUS'S CLOSEST FRIENDS.
WH-WHAT?

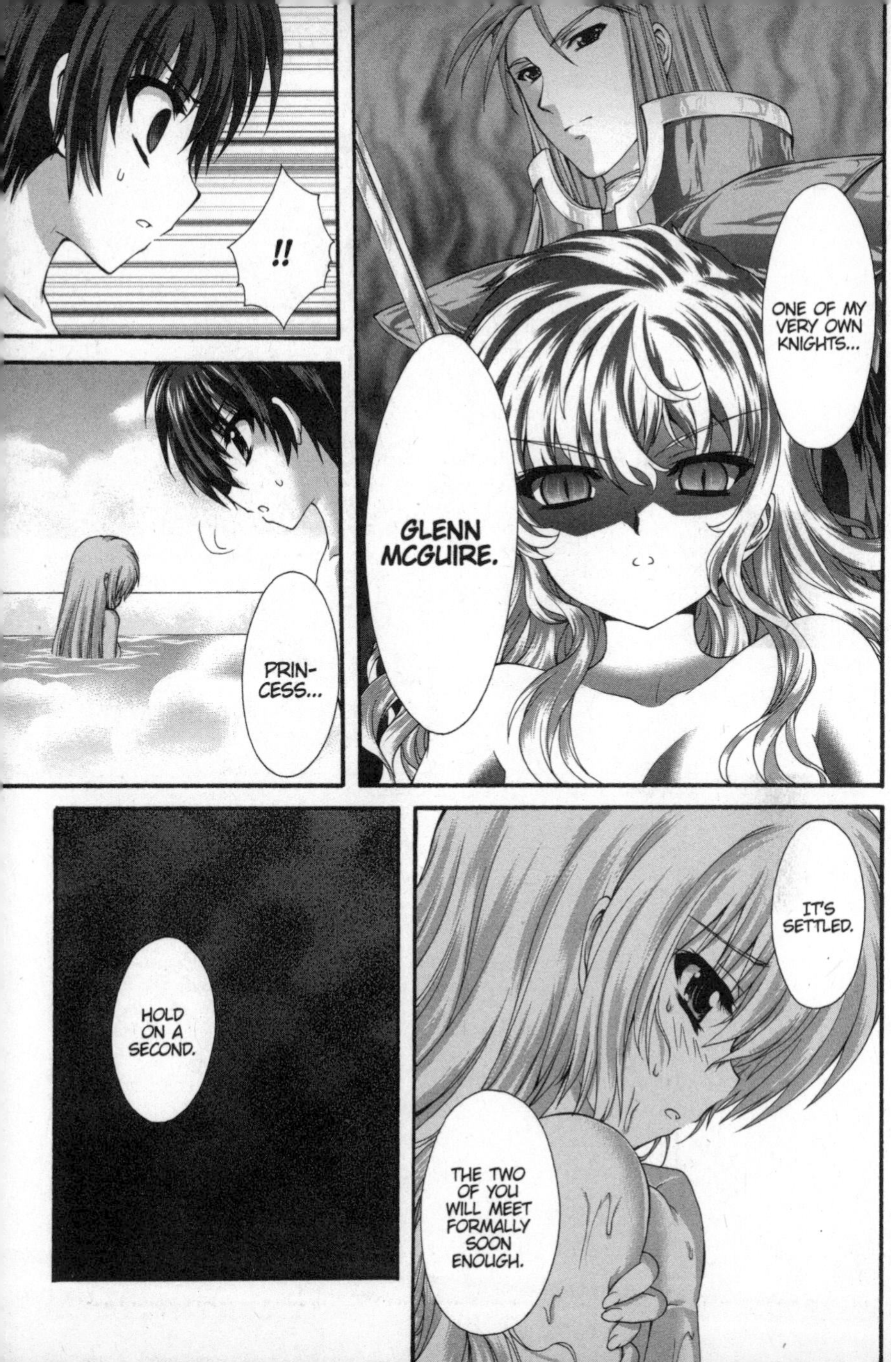
ONE OF MY VERY OWN KNIGHTS...
GLENN MCGUIRE.
!!
PRIN-CESS...
IT'S SETTLED.
THE TWO OF YOU WILL MEET FORMALLY SOON ENOUGH.
HOLD ON A SECOND.

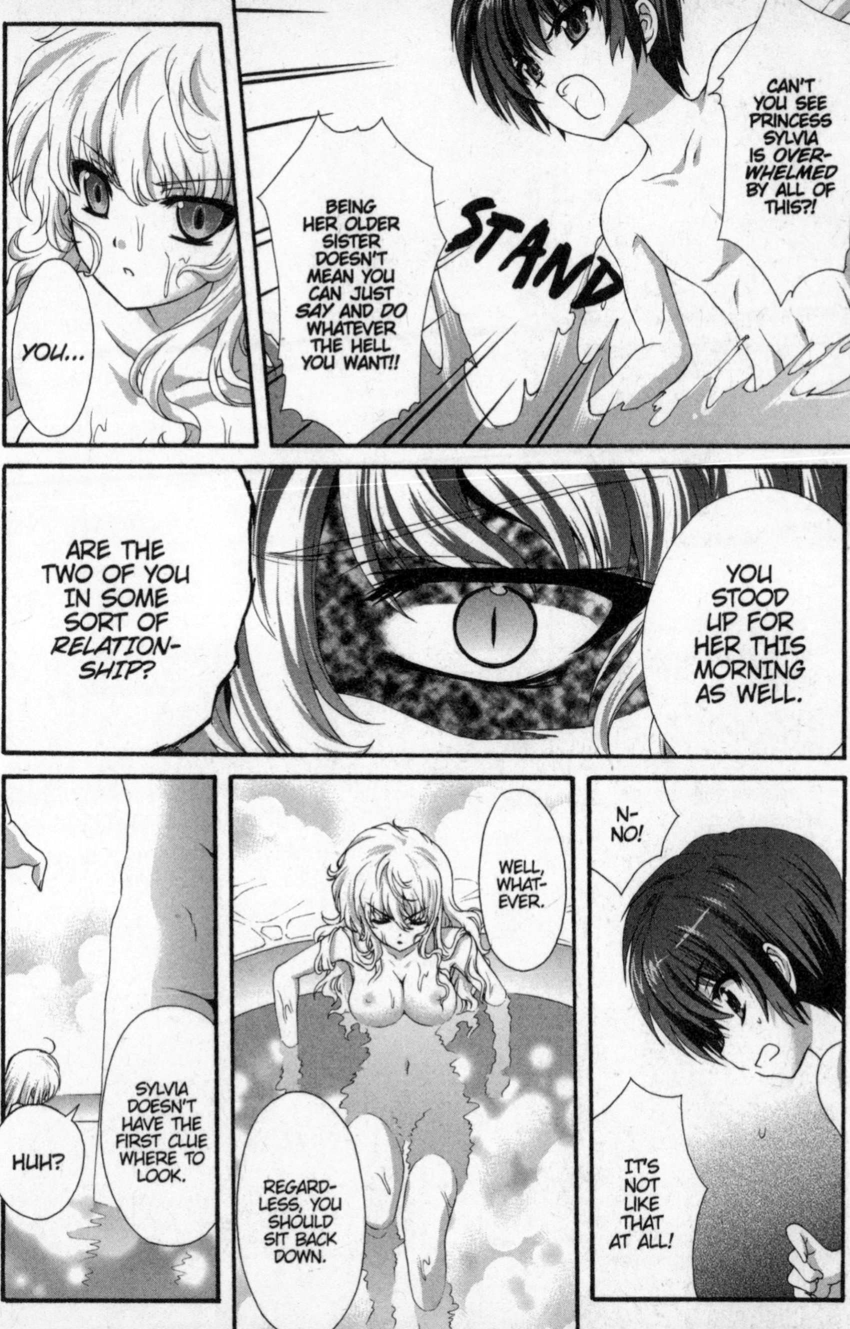
CAN'T YOU SEE PRINCESS SYLVIA IS *OVER-WHELMED* BY ALL OF THIS?!
BEING HER OLDER SISTER DOESN'T MEAN YOU CAN JUST *SAY* AND *DO* WHATEVER THE HELL YOU WANT!!
STAND
YOU...
YOU STOOD UP FOR HER THIS MORNING AS WELL.
ARE THE TWO OF YOU IN SOME SORT OF *RELATION-SHIP?*
N-NO!
IT'S NOT LIKE THAT AT ALL!
WELL, WHAT-EVER.
REGARD-LESS, YOU SHOULD SIT BACK DOWN.
SYLVIA DOESN'T HAVE THE FIRST CLUE WHERE TO LOOK.
HUH?

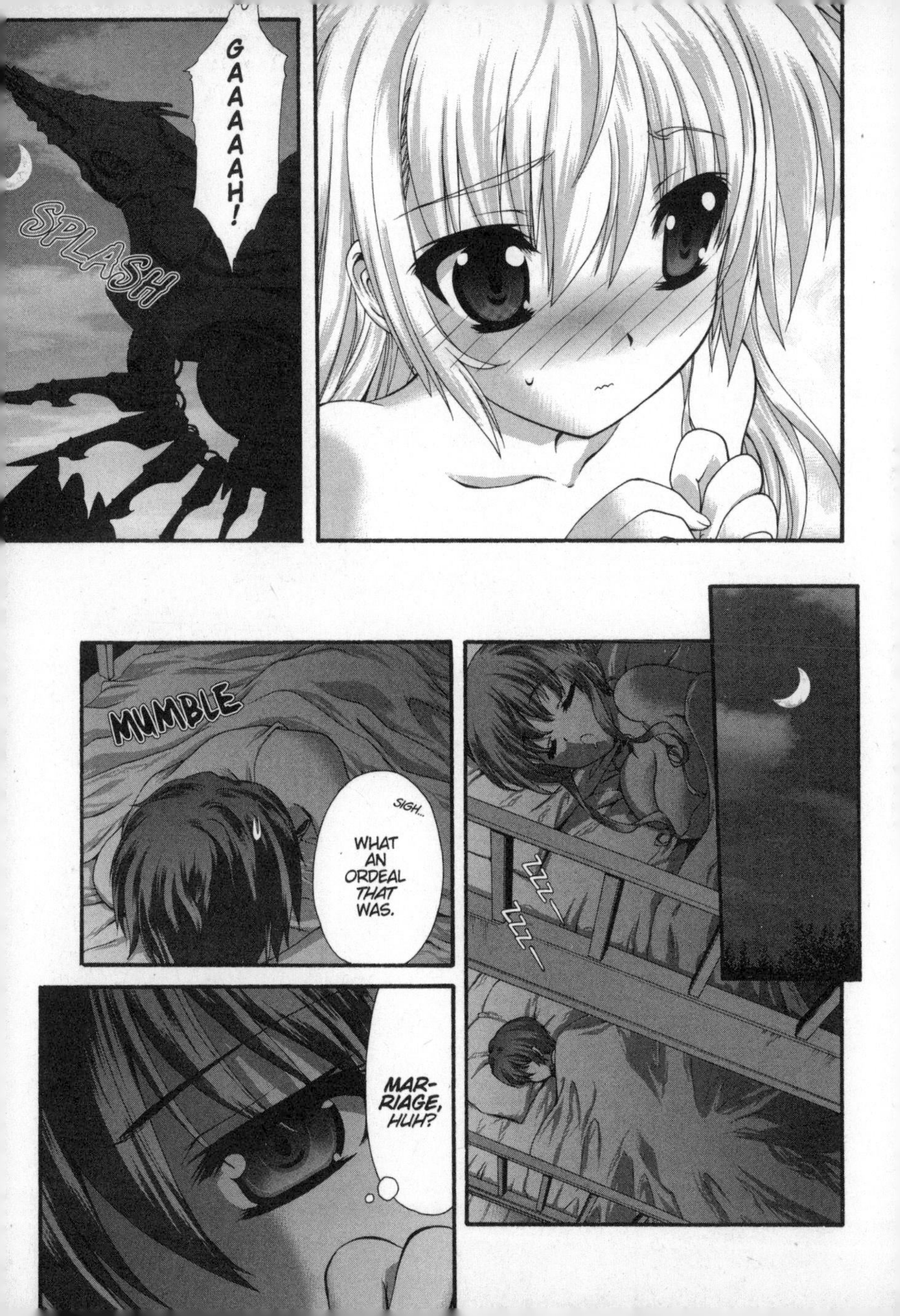
GAAAAAAH!
SPLASH
ZZZ—
ZZZ—
MUMBLE
SIGH... WHAT AN ORDEAL THAT WAS.
MAR-RIAGE, HUH?

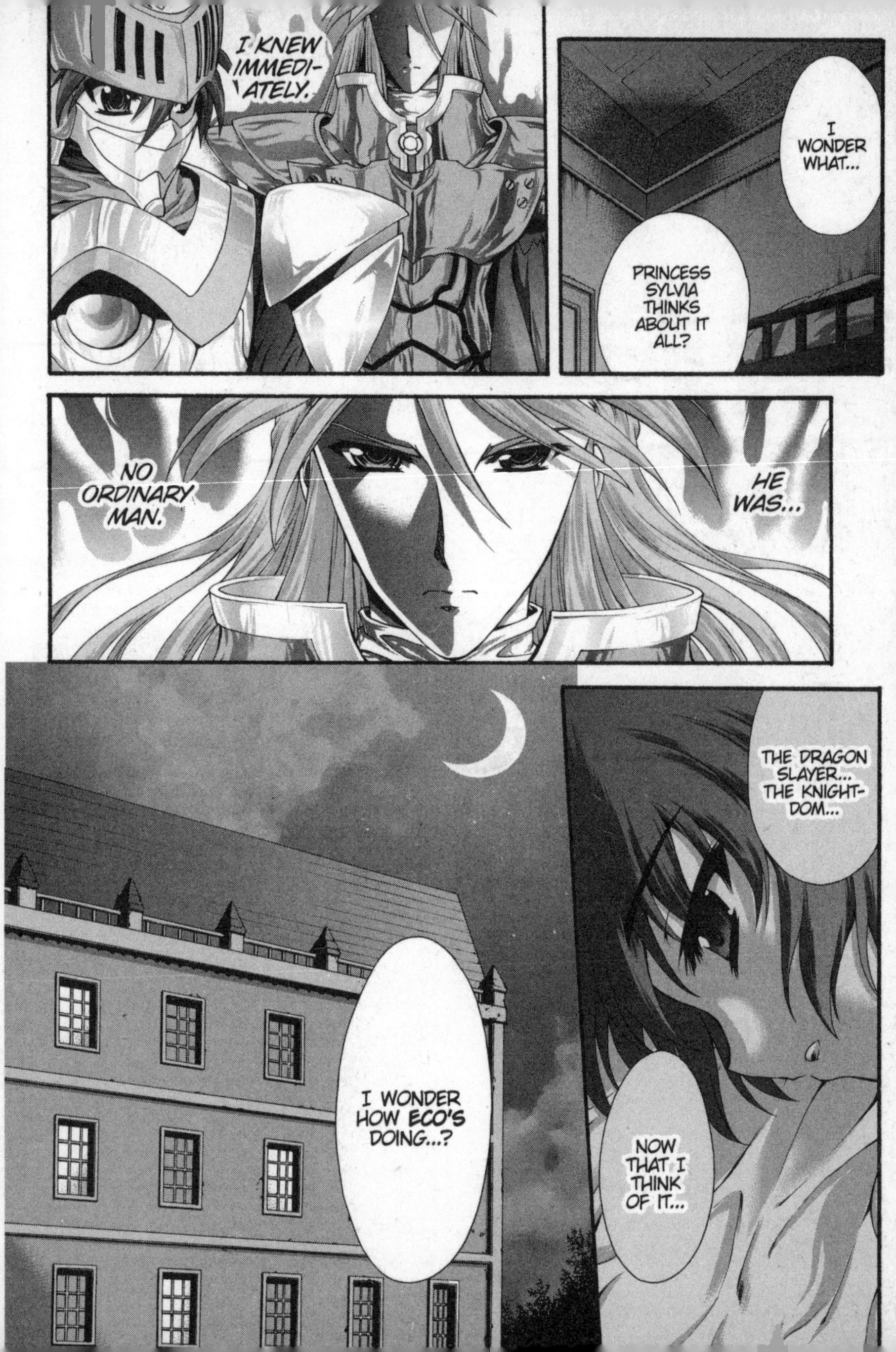
I WONDER WHAT...
PRINCESS SYLVIA THINKS ABOUT IT ALL?
I KNEW IMMEDIATELY.
HE WAS...
NO ORDINARY MAN.
THE DRAGON SLAYER... THE KNIGHT-DOM...
NOW THAT I THINK OF IT...
I WONDER HOW ECO'S DOING...?

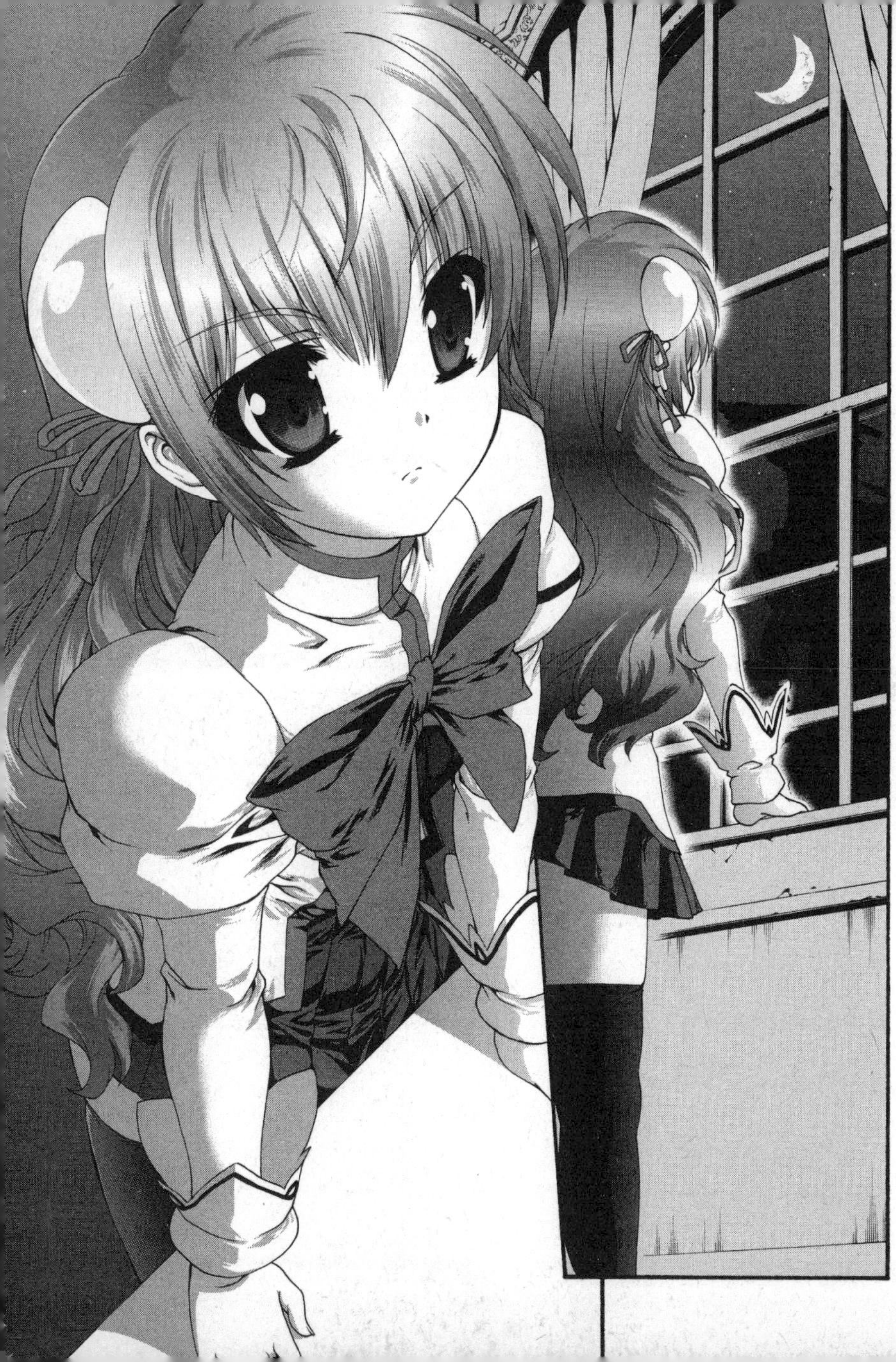

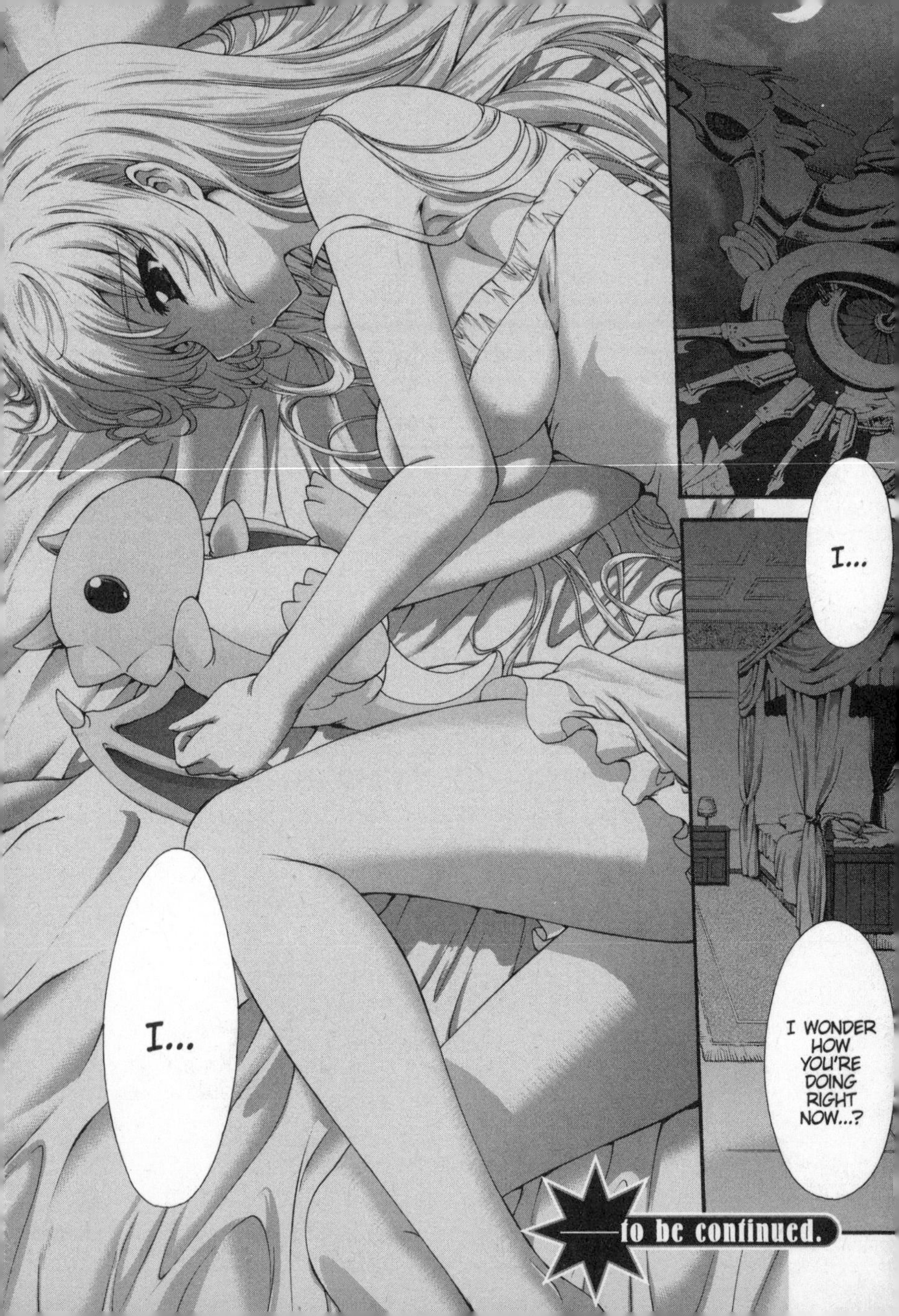
I...
I WONDER HOW YOU'RE DOING RIGHT NOW...?
I...
to be continued.

# AFTERWORD

IT'S ME, RAN!

THANKS SO MUCH FOR PICKING UP VOLUME 2 OF *DRAGONAR ACADEMY*!

IN THIS VOLUME, SYLVIA GETS TO DO ALL SORTS OF DIFFERENT THINGS.

WHEN I DRAW HER, I DO MY BEST TO SHOW OFF HER CHARM AND HOW WONDERFUL SHE IS!

I HOPE YOU'LL ALL WATCH OVER ASH AND THE OTHERS AS THEY DO THEIR BEST TO FACE EVERYTHING COMING THEIR WAY!

AND WITH THAT, I HOPE TO SEE YOU ALL AGAIN

RAN

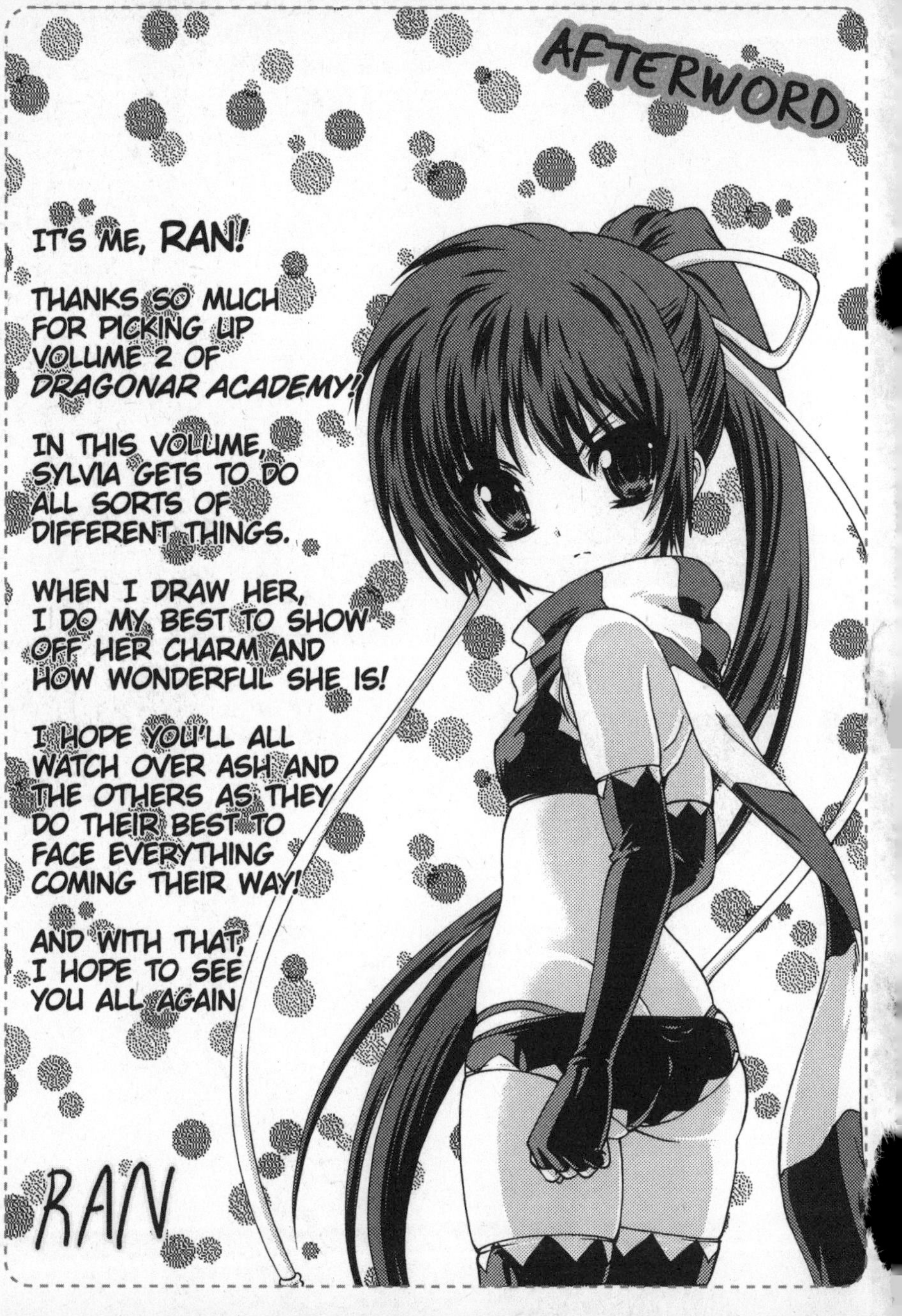

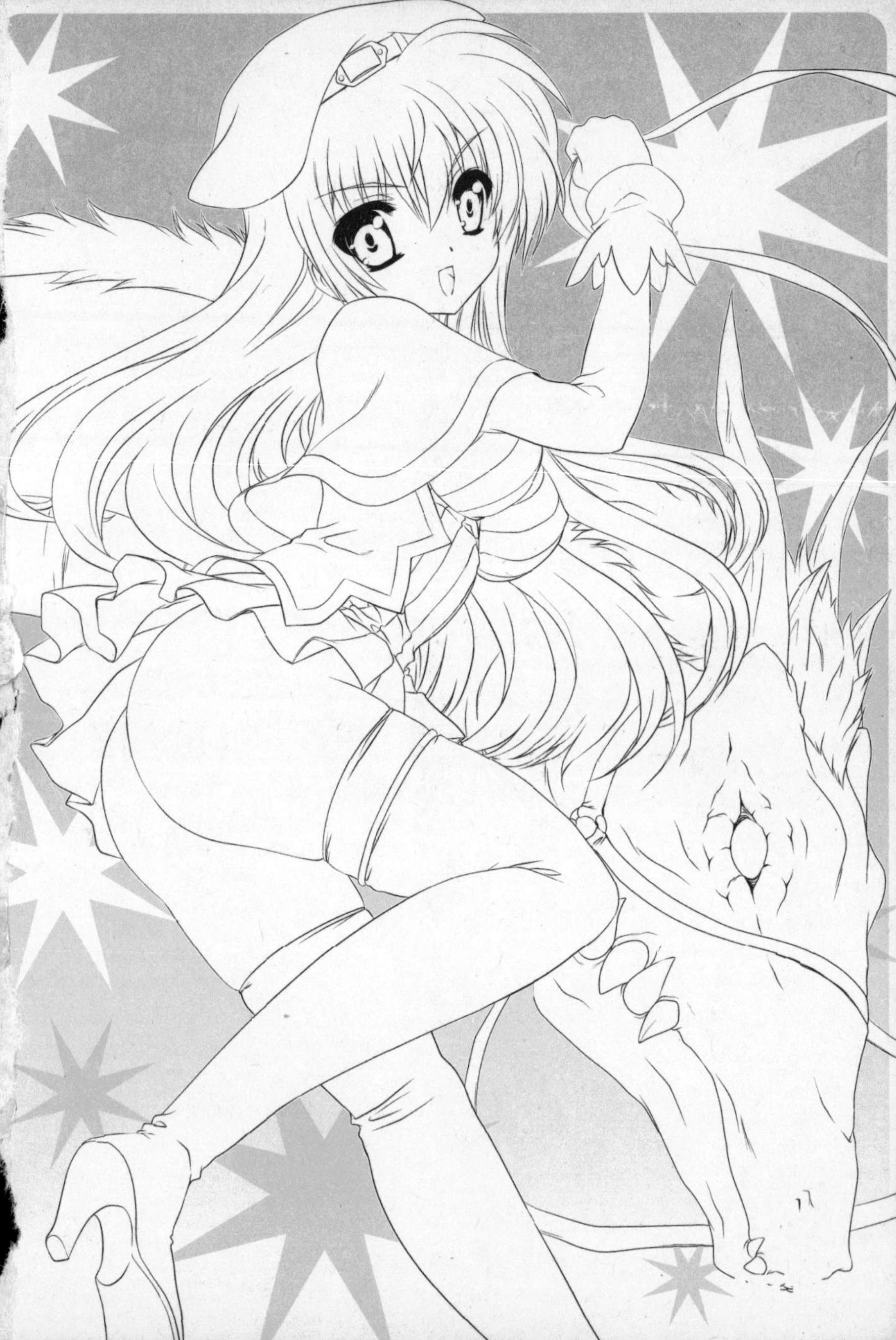